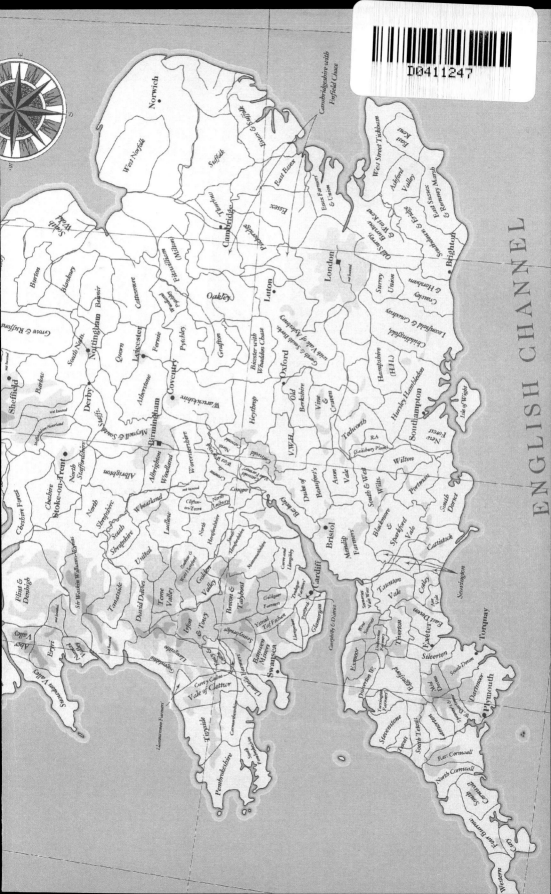

Endangered Species

'MFH Number One' of the twentieth century, 'Master', the 10th Duke of Beaufort, taking his hounds from Badminton House to the first draw after his sixtieth birthday meet.

Endangered Species

Foxhunting – the history, the passion and
the fight for survival

Michael Clayton

To my grandchildren –
and all tomorrow's foxhunters

By the same author:
A Hunting We Will Go
Foxhunting Companion
The Hunter
The Golden Thread
The Chase
Foxhunting in Paradise

Copyright © 2004 Michael Clayton
Photographs copyright © Jim Meads

First published in the UK in 2004
by Swan Hill Press, an imprint of Quiller Publishing Ltd
Reprinted with revisions 2005

British Library Cataloguing-in-Publication Data
A catalogue record for this book
is available from the British Library

ISBN 1 904057 49 7

Typeset by Phoenix Typesetting, Auldgirth, Dumfriesshire
Printed in England by Biddles Ltd., www.biddles.com

Swan Hill Press
An imprint of Quiller Publishing Ltd.
Wykey House, Wykey, Shrewsbury, SY4 1JA
Tel: 01939 261616 Fax: 01939 261606
E-mail: info@quillerbooks.com
Website: www.swanhillbooks.com

CONTENTS

ACKNOWLEDGEMENTS

I express warmest thanks to Alastair Jackson, Director of the Masters of Foxhounds Association, for reading the manuscript, and writing the Foreword, and to John Gardiner, Head of Public Affairs at the Countryside Alliance, for reading the political chapter, and making helpful amendments and advice.

I am particularly grateful to George Pearson, proprietor of the invaluable annual record *Baily's Hunting Directory*, for permission to make various quotations from past issues, and especially for permission to reproduce Baily's excellent map of hunting countries as end papers.

The 10th Duke of Beaufort, Sir Peter Farquhar, Daphne Moore, Sir Newton Ryecroft, Capt Ronnie Wallace, and Ulrica Murray Smith, all deceased, gave me interviews for articles which are invaluable elements in a twentieth century foxhunting history, and with Daphne's permission I have quoted briefly from her excellent *The Book of the Foxhound*, and have referred to the collection of Sir Newton's writings *Rycroft on Hunting*, so well edited by James F. Scharnberg, and Ulrica's *Magic of the Quorn* which I instigated and edited. My thanks also to Lord Donoughue for permission to quote him on the Middle Way issue from his *The Heat of the Kitchen (Politico's)* and to Meriel Buxton for Lord Paget's remarks from her *Ladies of the Chase* (The Sportsman's Press).

Ben Hardaway and Marty and Daphne Wood were especially helpful in providing first hand experience, and much information, on foxhunting in the US, and Dennis Foster, Director of the American MFHA has been most helpful with information on US and Australian hunting.

I am deeply indebted to the greatest hunting photographer of all time, Jim Meads, who accompanied me on most of my hunting correspondent's tours, for generously providing nearly all the photographs in this book; also to *Horse & Hound* for pictures of Countryside Alliances marches and protests and saboteur pictures (pages 63, 65, 264, 269 (lower)),to Mary Tarry for the Scarteen hound blessing picture (page 227), and to Leicestershire County Council's Heritage Services for reproduction of photographs from the Melton Carnegie Museum hunting section (pages 3, 11, 21).

Special thanks are due to the gifted and enduring sporting artist John King, who hunted with me for many years, for permission to use some of his evocative, elegant drawings in this book.

I owe immeasurable thanks to so many Masters, huntsmen, farmers and landowners, and my former management and editorial colleagues at IPC Magazines, now IPCMedia, proprietors of *Horse & Hound*, who made possible my visits to over 200 packs of hounds. Finally, but most of all, heartfelt thanks to my wife Marilyn for her encouragement and support, including production of the index and other elements in *Endangered Species*.

FOREWORD

by Alastair Jackson,
Director of the Masters of Foxhounds Association

oxhunting was endangered for a variety of reasons throughout the twentieth century. In the United Kingdom the sport has suffered from an eroding countryside, too often in areas where it has traditionally been most popular. Its demise was predicted in two world wars, yet it revived rapidly and made many thousands of new recruits.

The political threat sharpened perilously in the 1900s and still looms at the start of the twenty-first century, largely due to the bigoted views of some politicians who do not reflect an encouraging trend of tolerance and understanding among the general public.

None of these dangers overwhelmed foxhunting: it absorbed newcomers and adapted to change. The sport continues to make a unique and fascinating contribution to the quality of life in our countryside, interesting and entertaining people from all parts of the community. For many, foxhunting still has the power to become a life-time's passion.

The story of fuxhunting's survival as a way of life and as a sport, and its appeal to each new generation, is well worth telling. Michael Clayton is uniquely qualified to write this modern history having hunted with over 200 packs as *Horse & Hound*'s hunting correspondent 'Foxford' during his Editorship of nearly twenty-five years when he developed the magazine as a modern publication attracting wide readership. Indeed, I first met Michael when I arrived as a young Joint Master and Huntsman of the South Dorset in 1969 and he was working for the BBC and hunting regularly with the Portman. How well I remember him coming hunting in the South Dorset vale on his brave little roan Ballyn Garry and what fun it is to read in these pages of sport in those days and of the variety of characters who have enriched the world of hunting over the years.

He records the fascinating evolution of the modern foxhound, the horses used to follow hounds, the management of the sport, and the vast social change in the countryside to which it has adapted. The extraordinary political battles fought to save our hound sports, led by the BFSS and nowadays the Countryside Alliance, are told perceptively in detailed, chronological order by a journalist who has worked closely within both organisations for over forty years.

Experienced foxhunters may not all agree with every nuance of the author's opinions on the sport he has loved and followed for a lifetime, but his interpretation of foxhunting should stimulate, entertain and inform everyone who cares about the sport, and provide a valuable link with the wider public.

Above all, Michael Clayton has sought to communicate with warmth and humour the sheer fun of foxhunting, in all its diversity. Some of the greatest characters of the Chase in the past century come alive in these pages. I am glad he has reported foxhunting's flourishing history in Ireland and in North America where he has hunted widely, and where there are so many vital links with the sport in Britain, and he records foxhunting elsewhere in Europe and in Australia.

I share Michael Clayton's optimism about foxhunting's future on this planet, no matter what its enemies may currently be plotting in Britain. Its enormous contribution to the quality of country life shines through the pages of this book which may confidently be regarded as a standard work on the subject.

Introduction

SETTING FOR SURVIVAL

On 18 November, 2004, the Speaker of the House of Commons invoked the rarely used, highly controversial Parliament Act to force on to the Statute Book a Bill to ban hunting with hounds throughout England and Wales only three months hence - from February 18, 2005.

It was an appalling day for hunting people, for the countryside, and for Parliamentary democracy which was mocked in a farrago of confusion and anger in the Commons and Lords.

MPs had voted by a 190 majority for the banning Bill, although it was condemned by its opponents as unworkable and unenforceable. The vote was the most oppressive and shameful hammer blow on a law abiding British minority in modern politics.

MPs had debated hunting on 15 September amid extraordinary drama and turmoil. Up to 20,000 pro-hunting protestors jeered in Parliament Square, and some, including women, were injured in confrontations with controversially tough police wielding batons in riot gear.

Inside Parliament the hunting debate was suddenly interrupted when, for the first time in 350 years, protestors invaded the floor of the House of Commons. They were eight young men, including an MFH and a professional huntsman, keen to demonstrate their passionate defence of their sport and their way of life.

It has been widely acknowledged that Labour's oppressive banning bill had little or nothing to do with animal welfare, but was motivated by old class warfare antagonisms towards stereotypes of hunting people as toffs, and was used by Prime Minister Tony Blair to reconnect with his rebellious anti-hunting back benchers.

Hunting has been part of our countryside since before recorded history. Wrenching away this right, a traditional symbol of our national identity, is a libertarian issue which could make many foxhunters strangers in their own land, transforming them into internal exiles. Many pledged to break the law if necessary after a ban, and much strife and unhappiness was predicted.

Yet my story of foxhunting since 1900 is not an expression of mourning, but a celebration of magnificent survival. Despite mounting political attacks in an increasingly urbanised Britain, foxhunting survived throughout the twentieth century, and I believe that in some recognisable form it can yet live on in the twenty-first.

Our hunting landscapes dotted with coverts, the conservation of foxes, the science of venery, the breeding of superb hounds and horses, sporting literature and art, centuries of fellowship in the hunting field, and above all the true spirit of the Chase, are priceless legacies that no amount of prejudice and spite can cancel out.

The love of the sport itself has always been shared widely through all layers of rural society, significantly outnumbering objections from individuals or small groups. Such objections were very seldom based on moral arguments; the local Hunt could all too easily find itself embroiled in private or family rows over land ownership. Dealing with petty feuds, ensuring that land, stock and fencing were respected, and protecting hunting coverts, grew in the nineteenth century as Mastership responsibilities ensured that the sport was a cement binding together widely disparate parts of the rural community.

Foxhunting has an extraordinary record of survival in the face of massive sociological and environmental changes, restrictions, and latterly an opposition able to afford the most sophisticated forms of mass persuasion.

There are many complex reasons embedded in history and sociology for farmers and landowners to allow others to ride over their land behind hounds, and for the riders' wish to do so. Money was never the sole key to riding on other people's land. It is a mistake to view the sport in isolation: it has grown in prominence over the past 250 years or so, but its roots are embedded in man's addiction to hunting for food, and for sport, long before recorded history.

The ancient British tribes, the invading Romans, and the Saxons all regarded hunting as a natural part of their life-style. The Anglo-Saxon English kings hunted deer, wild boar, hares and foxes enthusiastically right up to the Norman Conquest, and had already established the essential link between the sport and the ownership of property. A man could hunt his own land, but not another's, except by invitation, and the king's hunting rights above all had to be respected. The pleasures and rewards of hunting were well understood throughout the community, and poaching was a risk sport widely practised by those without the rights of ownership or privilege.

Deer were the noble beasts of the chase; foxes were little more than vermin, and hunting them with hounds was considered an inferior sport until the eighteenth century. In Saxon England hunting methods were flexible: frequently deer were hunted by hounds into nets where they were dispatched by man, not by hounds.

William the Conqueror brought ruthless law to the Chase, as to all other aspects of English life after 1066. Blinding was one Norman penalty for poaching the king's deer, and flagrant cases could result in execution. His successors continued the jealous preservation of the royal hunting Forests and sometimes increased the penalties for poaching; castration was added to blinding by King Richard I.

The new laws preserving game caused immense hardship and ill-feeling among the conquered Saxons and remained a running sore in rural life for many generations. Reforms of Forest law were part of the demands in Magna Carta submitted to King John. Hunting was a recreation and a means of filling the pot for the ordinary citizen from the humblest levels of catching rabbits up to the largest beasts of the Chase.

When modern foxhunters protest that a hunting ban would abolish their ancient 'rights' they are on firm historical ground, and politicians should not be surprised by the depths of anger aroused by such threats. Man's ancient links with hunting are so generic and powerful that people with urban backgrounds where hunting was no part of their childhood can become extraordinarily addicted to hunting after brief exposure to the sport as adults. As established religions well know there is no-one more passionate than the recent convert.

Norman discipline produced more defined techniques for hunting with hounds as well as strictly defined hunting grounds known as Forests which could include hill country, heathland and even pastoral land as well as afforested areas. The modern foxhunting term 'Tally ho' derives from the French cry 'Ty a hillaut', the shout signalling the rousing of the deer at the start of a hunt. 'So ho' was a Norman wolf hunter's cry as hounds found, and it gave it name to London's West End's 'saucy square mile' which was a hunting ground for wild animals adjacent to Westminster long before its human quarry were to be found in the sex industry. 'Leu in' is another Norman derived term, used to encourage hounds to draw a covert, and heard today from huntsmen more frequently than the other ancient hunting cries. The importance of territory, of hunting 'rights', and of social obligations, remained part of hunting and are reflected in symbolic as well as in certain tangible aspects of modern foxhunting. A modern Master of Foxhound's most important task is to maintain the assent of landowners and farmers to the use of their land for hunting by the pack and its followers. Only if this is achieved can the Master take up the challenge of providing sport for his followers.

A Hunt's clearly defined territory, its hunting country, is still an essential element in hunting practice, with various rules attached to the boundaries ordained by the Masters of Foxhounds Association, which it will be appropriate to describe in detail later. Kings and queens, the aristocracy, and the squirearchy led the pursuit of hunting through medieval Britain, and its pleasures were shared in varying degrees by the peasantry.

Part of hunting's charm is its blurred edges, its extraordinary lights and shades, and its magnificent inconsistencies. Throughout its history it has been an arena in which England's class boundaries could dissolve more easily. When the ruthless Norman hold on the countryside had dissipated, and local squires took their places among aristocrats of old lineage as Masters of Foxhounds, it was ever more necessary for them to maintain good relationships with their neighbours over whose land they wished to hunt.

Even the largest landowners, such as the Dukes of Beaufort, credited with boosting the eighteenth century switch from staghunting to foxhunting in farmed areas, needed to hunt on many farms outside their own estates of several thousand acres in Gloucestershire. Shrinking medieval forests, and the growth of land enclosure made staghunting less feasible, except on the moorlands.

It is a famous landmark in the sport that the 5th Duke of Beaufort, at the age of eighteen, was returning from a disappointing day's staghunting in 1762 when he put his hounds into Silk Wood, a covert still existing near Tetbury. His hounds went away on the line of a fox, and the run was so exciting and enjoyable that he decided thereafter to make the fox his permanent quarry, thereby forming one of the most successful packs in the world – certainly among the most popular in Britain early in the twenty-first century.

As the most famous Shires hunting correspondent Nimrod (Charles James

Apperley, 1777–1843) pointed out, no matter how devoted to the Chase were the Dukes of Beaufort their country could never be anything but 'provincial'. They hunted honestly and earnestly over their stone walls, and their deep riding vales, and relied for devoted support from the residents to whom the current Duke was a local monarch.

Birth of Modern Foxhunting

The impetus to make foxhunting fashionable, sometimes in the worst of fashions, erupted in the East Midlands. Leicestershire was discovered to be the ideal place for the Chase at its fastest, its most competitive, and at times, its most

Hugo Meynell, first Master and founder of the Quorn (1753–1800). Known as the 'Father of Foxhunting' because he developed the techniques of hunting the fox in open country.

raffish. Hugo Meynell, a Derbyshire squire, moved east to Quorn to take advantage of the huge swathe of deeply rural grassland, stretching from Nottingham down to Market Harborough.

The early nineteenth century development of the art of leaping fly fences at speed, credited largely to the example of a provincial arriviste, William Childe, from Shropshire, vastly increased the value of the springy old turf, and neat fly fences of undulating Leicestershire, and parts of Nottinghamshire and Northamptonshire. Hunts in these counties, provided their country included a portion of Leicestershire, called themselves 'Shires packs' and hunting with them attracted cachet, as well as genuinely providing the most exciting cross-country riding available anywhere in the world – an attraction to such exotic foreign aristocrats as the athletic and flighty Empress of Austria in the 1870s.

To Hugo's eventual despair near the end of his forty-seven years' Mastership (1753–1800), the Quorn increasingly attracted young men whose addiction to speed too often interfered with the abilities of his hounds to hunt a fox. Leicestershire was eminently suitable for fast horses – and during the nineteenth and twentieth centuries proved an equally happy hunting ground for fast ladies.

'The night air of Melton Mowbray was alive with the sighs of adulterous love', said one observer of the hectic winter scene. Like the 'cocktail sport of steeplechasing', as Nimrod acidly dubbed it, Leicestershire attracted risk-takers. Horse dealing, horse breaking, house letting, and top-class tailoring all profited.

Leicestershire's reputation as the 'capital' of foxhunting resulted from its dependence on visitors, many from London, who imported metropolitan tastes and spending power. As well as encouraging faster techniques of hunting the fox in the open, their appetite for thrills accelerated the growth of steeplechasing by matching Thoroughbred horses in races across natural country for big purses, from one village to the next – signposted on the horizon by the county's tall, pointed church spires.

Apperley, an excellent rider, worshipped Leicestershire, and created an audience avid for his riveting accounts of Shires sport he had personally experienced in the saddle. He invented the role of the intrepid hunting correspondent, and sometimes ventured beyond his beloved Leicestershire in his quest for new adventures. Readers in the West End and City would queue for copies of *The Sporting Magazine* with the latest instalments of Nimrod's 'Hunting Tours', from 1820. His tendency to patronise 'provincial' Hunts in comparison with the Shires sometimes infuriated readers, but he built up a loyal following as one of the first sports reporters with a national audience since copies of his magazine eventually percolated to even the most remote country houses.

Apperley was the iconic Shires foxhunter, but shared the dilemma of some of his readers: he simply could not afford foxhunting at the level he aspired to, and when he fell out of favour as a journalist, and his pen could no longer subsidise his sport, he declined into an exiled debtor in France. Long before that Apperley had been cruelly reviled and lampooned by a greater writer on hunting England, Robert Smith Surtees (1803–64).

His reputation depended not on his writings as an entirely different sort of hunting correspondent to Nimrod, but on Surtees' brilliance as one of the nineteenth century's greatest novelists, sometimes compared to Charles Dickens as a creator of comic characters. Not a thrusting rider, but a devoted enthusiast of purist foxhunting, Surtees heartily disliked Leicestershire and its dashing mounted fields, possibly because he was unable to emulate their prowess, although the main fuel for his ire was his profound loathing for the use of the hunting field as a means of social climbing.

Sadly he was unable to appreciate that as well as its fashionable trappings, Leicestershire offered an exotic, unique equestrian challenge that was the real mainspring for its popularity among each new generation of young sportsmen willing to risk their necks in a challenge of skill and nerve across superb riding country.

Whilst Nimrod conveys the thrills of the hunting field, Surtees magically fills in the rich tapestry of sporting England, its eccentricities, discomforts, its smells, its bad weather, and its rascals. Although a satirist who could write with a biting pen, Surtees always pays homage to the gold thread of venery which binds it together.

The influence of both writers on the mythology and legend of foxhunting was profound, all the more effective because of their widely different perspectives. Young men, and increasingly young women too, thrilled to Nimrod's stirring accounts of great runs across old turf and challenging fences. It strengthened their resolve to include at least one season in Leicestershire as an essential experience in their sporting lives.

For a far wider readership throughout the nineteenth century, the lure of hunting as a source of fun and fantasy in England's grey winter landscapes was enhanced by reading Surtees. His great characters, Mr Jorrocks, the sporting Cockney grocer, Mr Soapey Sponge, the foxhunting con-man, and Mr Facey Romford, an amateur huntsman of great ability although a rogue. Surtees vastly entertained the literate classes, and reminded those who lived in cities that there was a colourful world of recreation to be found in the countryside increasingly within easy reach by road or rail.

Nimrod and Surtees were to have many imitators; by the end of the nineteenth century there was a school of hunting correspondents and novelists of varying degrees of literary ability conveying the thrills of foxhunting in sporting magazines and the press. Otho Paget and 'Brooksby' (Capt.Pennell-Elmhirst) were the most effective Leicestershire correspondents in the late nineteenth century. The former was drily perceptive and analytical, whereas 'Brooksby' relied mainly on name-dropping and fervid descriptions of hectic 'quick things' across obstacles he tended to exaggerate in size and frequency. Through the sporting scribes, foxhunting England learned of heroes such as Tom Firr, who rode like a jockey but looked like a judge as the revered huntsman of the Quorn from 1872–99.

Quoting Jorrocks's famous 'lectors' on foxhunting became a popular Victorian party piece. Surtees was to survive as a well read novelist, and would find generations of new readers in the twentieth century whereas Nimrod continued to be read mainly by connoisseurs. Rousing poetry by such as Will Ogilvie ('Give me a horse that ne'er turns his head . . .') contributed immensely to the romance and passion of foxhunting.

Just as influential was the increasing flood of sporting art stimulated by foxhunting in the nineteenth century. The previous century's artists produced paintings to grace stately homes. In Victorian England sporting prints of the Chase could adorn the walls, the curtains, and the dinner plates in middle class villas and in manor houses owned by new landowners spawned by the industrial revolution. George Stubbs (1724–1806) and his eighteenth century contemporaries had given sporting art a glorious beginning, soon to be followed by nineteenth century illustrators of the Chase whose work would become a nationwide cult so powerful it could share the spell of Christmas on our greetings cards. In depicting sport they were recording the countryside with a vividness and intensity which makes their work of increasing interest and value, reflected in recent London exhibitions.

John Leech (1817–64) brilliantly illustrated some of Surtees' novels, adding to the growing popularity of foxhunting, coaching and racing prints. The development of etching, line engraving and lithography in the nineteenth century ensured wider publication. At the turn of the century, foxhunting had long since ceased to be a semi-private recreation, and had become a national sport. One of the more helpful myths about foxhunting which remained alive well into the twentieth century was that Hunts had a right to cross other people's land.

The issue had, in fact, been decided in the courts early in the previous century. In 1809 the Earl of Essex sued for trespass against his brother, the Master of the Old Berkeley Hunt, the Hon and Reverend William Capel. The Earl claimed that the Hunt being warned off, had entered his land, breaking fences. Unfortunately Mr Capel chose to defend the trespass by claiming that it was committed not merely for the purpose of diversion and amusement, but 'as the only way and means of killing and destroying the fox.'

The judge, Lord Ellenborough, did not agree, finding for the plaintiff, and declaring 'these pleasures are to be taken only when there is the consent of those who are likely to be injured by them, but they must be necessarily subservient to the consent of others'. It says much for foxhunting's immense influence throughout the countryside that although Masters became far more careful not to upset landowners after this judgement, it was rural custom which usually prevailed in enabling Hunts to have remarkable access over privately owned land.

In many rural districts in the nineteenth century the quickest way for a landowner to become a social pariah was to deny the local Hunt access to his coverts, and persisting in the 'crime' of vulpicide was likely to achieve the same result. In Victorian and to some extent Edwardian England anti-hunting landowners willing to risk social boycotting were likely to find themselves opposed within their own households by their wives keen to maintain contact with neighbours of similar rank – and younger members of the family who wished to join their friends in the hunting field.

It cannot be claimed that such pressures were the only factor in keeping the countryside open for foxhunting for most of the twentieth century when so many newcomers bought land. It was the creating and maintaining of good relationships with landowners and farmers which produced a miracle of access for large bodies of people on horseback on privately owned land in an age when landowning was not necessarily a family tradition.

This access has stood all sorts of stresses and strains, including attempts by some local authorities to ban hunting on agricultural land which they own, only to be opposed by pro-hunting tenant farmers in this course. Significantly, the Blair government's 2002 attempt at a total ban involved legislation which would prosecute landowners who allowed hounds on their land. Many such landowners joined in the widespread protests against a government ban.

The greatest prize of foxhunting, and the other hound sports, early in the twenty-first century was the co-operation and friendship of the vast majority of landowners and farmers, certainly sufficient to allow the sport to continue and flourish as a nationwide rural activity. Early in the twentieth century it was not surprising, when power had transferred so emphatically to the industrial cities, that many feared hunting in all its forms could not possibly survive long in the new century of mechanical 'progress'.

William Bromley-Davenport forecast more than twenty years earlier in his poem 'Lowesby Hall':

> For I looked into its pages, and I read the book of fate,
> And saw foxhunting abolished by an order of the State;
> Saw the heavens filled with guano, and the clouds of men's command,
> Raining down unsavoury liquids for the benefit of land;
> Saw the airy navies earthwards bear the planetary swell,
> And the long projected railroad made from Halifax to H-ll . . .

Despite all the predictions, foxhunting was to survive and flourish throughout a century of vastly increasing urban domination and devastating global wars. In the twenty-first century it has so far saved its brush from the firm promise of abolition by a Labour government with a massive majority. The hunt is not up yet. How has it survived so many ills – and how long before the hunting horn blows its last 'end of day'?

More than a few twenty-first century Britons are puzzled as to who they really are; what are their national characteristics, and what do they stand for? I suggest that interesting and entertaining clues to these questions are contained in the following story of a rural sport, both blessed and cussed, born out of ancient, unrecorded recesses of our heritage. It captures brave, optimistic recruits from each new generation – and simply refuses to die.

MICHAEL CLAYTON
RUTLAND
September 2004

CHAPTER 1

SCARLET EDWARDIANS

FOXHUNTERS had nothing to fear for the health of their sport in the early years of the twentieth century. Under the deceptively serene surface of the century's first 'golden decade' the struggle for social change was seething at home and abroad. For a while middle-class England was enjoying a period of false security before the devastation of two world wars.

When Edward VII at last succeeded his mother, Queen Victoria, on her death at the beginning of 1901, Britain had a monarch aged fifty-nine who had spent most of life enjoying himself. Country sports were high on his list of pleasures. Edwardian England was rich, and field sports benefited from the surplus incomes made possible by low taxation and cheap and plentiful labour. There were plenty ready to work long hours for little pay to ensure that life ran smoothly in the country house and garden – and in the stable yard. Most of the middle and upper classes were comfortable and many were complacent. There were extravagant displays of wealth during the social season. Huntin', shootin' and fishin' had firm positions in the calendar for the rich, some of them manifestly idle.

Foxhunting inevitably reflected this at the top end, reinforcing the misapprehension that it was entirely linked to wealth and privilege. The Shires and other fashionable packs reflected expensive elitism, but scores of smaller packs throughout Britain continued providing recreation on a far less grand scale, often in beautiful rural settings. In the smaller Hunts mounted sport was within the means of a considerable section of the rural community who were still using horses as a prime means of transport.

There were in addition plenty of farmers and villagers who had never hunted

1

on a horse, but had a strong interest in the fortunes of the local Hunt, regarding the pack as 'our hounds'. Many non-riding farmers walked Hunt puppies every year, rearing them free of charge for entry into the pack, and taking the closest interest in their performance ever afterwards; it was a historic link with the old trencher-fed packs, formed by people taking their own hounds to a meet to join together in a pack hunting that day. The 'meet' referred originally to hounds as well as people.

Plenty of Edwardian country people followed on foot or on bicycle, and there were, and still are, strong links between the foot packs, especially beagles, and foxhunting by the mounted Hunts. Many a lifelong foxhunter first hunted beagles, or followed beagle packs; the influence of the school packs was immense.

Early photographs show huge crowds on foot attending popular meets; other forms of entertainment were scarce, and hunting offered a free spectacle, and opportunities for involvement in such activities as earth stopping, covert maintenance, as well as puppy walking; all rewarded by invitations to Hunt functions and teas, and free tickets for the Hunt's annual steeplechase, its point-to-point.

The best literary evocation of hunting's close involvement in rural life in unfashionable Kent before 1914 is to be found in Siegfried Sassoon's masterpiece *Memoirs of a Foxhunting Man*. He describes the simple, even humdrum, pleasures of provincial hunting from the perspective of a shy young man riding to hounds for the first time. Sassoon records foxhunting as a year-long way of life in which the point-to-point, the summer cricket match and social events are part of a rural idyll.

The popular farming novelist, A.G. Street, said later in the twentieth century during an 'Any Questions' broadcast on BBC radio: 'In the true countryside, hunting is not a contentious issue; it's just part of country life. It goes with the seasons: there is sowing, and mowing and harvesting – and in the winter there's hunting.'

In the Edwardian era, the sensible hunting cob, the ride-and-drive horse which transferred from the shafts to the saddle at the meet, the hack-hunter, and the hardy native pony continued to make hunting possible and accessible in provincial hunts throughout the land. This was foxhunting in far less than the grand manner, but it was the way the sport was enjoyed by the majority.

A charming book called *Hunting in Hard Times* by G. Bowers at the start of the twentieth century (published first by Chapman and Hall; reprinted by Methuen 1986) describes a spinster and her bachelor brother hunting 'in the unfashionable Home Counties' on what Miss Bowers insists was a limited budget.

Living in a rented cottage with barn and stables, she and her brother 'managed' with a groom, and 'our invaluable cook who manages the maids', plus a lad to help in the stables. In the spring the whole establishment decants to the New Forest for more hunting, and there is a plan to go to Exmoor in late summer for the staghunting.

Miss Bowers' own delightful illustrations show a Home Counties hunting field of pasture, fences and patches of wildnerness which flourished as a splendid setting for foxhunting before London engulfed it all with bricks and roads.

Edwardian lady foxhunter about to transfer from her car to hunter, much assisted by chauffeur and grooms (circa 1905).

A few cars, but mostly horse-drawn carriages, attending a meet of the Atherstone at Claybrooke on 21 March 1902.

Edwardian grandeur when the Atherstone met at Newnham Paddox on 17 November 1905. Hounds were all 'old English' type, and the huntsman was George Whitemore.

Badges of Privilege

In the Shires, Thoroughbred hunters, carrying gentlemen opulently attired in top hats, tailor-made cut-away coats and narrow, shiny boots with champagne coloured tops, or ladies in vastly expensive side-saddle habits, appeared regularly in the social and sporting press.

It was still a social asset to be a sporting buck, and obsessions with the cut of a man's riding clothes, and the precise colour of his boot tops helped the arriviste to distance himself from later arrivals in the sporting social scene. Inevitably, in their photographs they were looking down from the saddle at the photographer, the inescapable image of equestrian hauteur, however unintentional, which has always risked antagonising the foot-bound.

If folk memories exist, a far off echo of being ridden down by men on horseback is somewhere in our archives. Try walking about among a throng of hunting people at a meet, talking loudly to each other and quaffing drinks above your head, whilst their horses occasionally wheel about, threatening to knock you over. It was towards the end of the century before the Masters of Foxhounds Association felt it was necessary to advise Masters always to dismount to speak to a farmer or landowner, or anyone else on foot, who wished to make a verbal complaint about the conduct of a day's hunting.

Only the horseman knows that his position on high is far more fragile than it appears to the non-horseman; always fraught with an element of uncertainty, especially in the hunting field. The confident figure at the meet may well have severe qualms about a mount he suspects is inexperienced and unreliable. 'No secret is so close as that between horse and rider,' is an old horseman's saw. A horse is no respecter of rank: Prince Philip, polo player and carriage driver, aptly dubbed the animal the 'great leveller'.

Foxhunting was to pay a heavy price later in the century for its prominent part in the Edwardian display of class privilege. The Shires were to see an even more hectic display, with royalty heavily involved, in the desperate gaiety of the 'twenties. The class warriors found it easy to use foxhunting as a symbol of the elitism they sought to abolish.

Regrettably, the trappings of the Shires disguised the purely sporting element: a large percentage of visiting foxhunters were young men and women, some of limited means, who were keen to take part in a genuine sporting challenge with a significant element of risk. Crossing Leicestershire fast on horseback amid a throng of other riders was still thrilling, and could be dangerous.

In Edwardian England much of the countryside favoured for foxhunting was down to grass; motor vehicle traffic was scarce, and barbed wire was still rare. Where it existed the larger Midland Hunts could afford to have it taken down for the season.

Edwardian Environment

Farming practice still allowed headlands and fallow fields in arable areas; chemical fertilisers and pest killers were not generally in use; ploughing by horse

The famous picture by Basil Nightingale of Tom Firr riding Whitelegs, renowned huntsman of the Quorn for twenty-seven years until 1899. Tom was a great exponent of the 'galloping forward cast'.

was not rigorous, and did not demand the uprooting of hedgerows and enlargement of fields into the arable prairies later to afflict the Midlands and parts of the North.

Even in the increasingly populated Home Counties there were pockets of unspoilt wilderness which eminently suits foxhunting for those who enjoy the venery as much as, or more than, the ride. In 1901 Britain had a population of thirty-seven million, compared with sixty million at the end of the twentieth century.

In Leicestershire the Quorn started the new century recently bereft of two remarkable personalities who had contributed hugely to its fame. Tom Firr retired in February 1899 after twenty-seven years as the Quorn's most famous and revered huntsman. A dedicated professional, who had reached the top job in foxhunting after tough training and much experience, Firr thrilled hundreds of followers with his skill and artistry in hound control. He was adept in producing the 'quick thing', a hunt of perhaps twenty-five minutes at great speed across Leicestershire's old turf and fly fences which he rode with deceptive ease in front of a hard-riding mounted field on blood horses.

Firr perfected the technique of the galloping cast, whereby he would fan his hounds in front of his horse, and canter forward so that the moving pack would hit the line of a fox already holloaed ahead by a whipper-in as it ran from a covert.

They would drop their heads on owning the line, give tongue with a crash of hound music, and accelerate forward in a fast hunt in the open, providing a thrilling ride for the host of eager followers. This technique was anything but a daily occurrence; it owed much to Firr's intimate knowledge of his terrain, and his judgement that scent was good enough to ensure success in a risky manoeuvre.

The cream of the Quorn country, the wolds of 'High Leicestershire' north and south of Melton Mowbray, was exceptionally suited for such an exercise because amid the sea of grass, generations of foxhunting landlords had planted small coverts, often of gorse, known as 'goss' in local parlance. They were usually small in area, but it was important to ensure plenty of 'bottom', a layer of growth which encouraged foxes to settle there.

Sometimes brick-built artificial earths were inserted just below ground level in such coverts to encourage natural fox dwelling, and it was, if necessary, the practice in the spring to move fox cubs, sometimes with a vixen, from threatened sites elsewhere to the artificial earths in these coverts, to ensure they were well stocked. Moving wild animals to safer habitats is not against the law, although in recent years moving foxes at any age has become forbidden by the Masters of Foxhounds Association.

Foxes in hunting coverts were jealously protected by the Hunt from the socially condemned practice of vulpicide during the vital off season in late spring and summer when vixens were rearing their cubs. In the autumn of its first year a cub is fully grown, and the practice of 'cubhunting' or 'cubbing' was used not only to cull colonies of young foxes in coverts as to ensure they knew that the best method of escaping hounds in covert was to run away in the open.

The Hunts employed at that time a more thorough system of 'stopping', or blocking, other earths in the vicinity so that they could not easily get to ground during a hunt until they had run out of the area stopped. Those opposed to foxhunting have argued that the above practices are a total negation of 'hunting the fox in its wild and natural state,' which is the declared aim of the Masters of Foxhound Association's rules.

Leicestershire, and other long hunted terrains on farmland, provide the answer to such criticism. The coverts so carefully planted for sport still dot the Shires landscape, some of them having been allowed to spread to greater than their originally intended acreage. As long as they are used primarily for foxhunting they are classic examples of conservation, since they are ideal forms of habitat for a balanced wild life.

The foxhunter does not wish to decimate rabbits and hares; his precious fox population needs them in the natural food chain. Bird life, butterflies and other insects flourish in the ancient coverts. Much later in the twentieth century the selection of the badger for total preservation by law distorted the balance of wildlife, greatly to the detriment of the badger itself.

The foxhunter is not an exterminator of foxes; far from it, he wants a sustainable population. Fox numbers killed by Hunts vary considerably according to the density of local populations, and dispersing fox colonies has always been regarded as equally useful in reducing the nuisance value to farm stock.

Later in the twentieth century, the practice of game shooting, using reared birds, when practised intensively, in some areas produced imbalances of wild life in coverts. Predators, especially the fox, in intense shooting coverts were eradicated or reduced to a bare minimum to ensure the survival of artificially reared pheasants or partridges placed there solely for shooting. This was by no means the norm for most of the century; otherwise foxhunting would long ago have ceased because its quarry would have been virtually eradicated . Partnership between hunting and shooting continued on a large scale, and has always been highly beneficial to wild life of all kinds through the maintenance of coverts.

Would governments, local or national, have decreed or subsidised the planting of small woodlands on privately owned land solely for wild life conservation purposes throughout the past 250 years?

Without sporting imperatives would landlords and farmers have had the same level of incentives to create beautiful, essentially English, landscapes of pasture dotted with small copses and woodland, to which sporting coverts contribute so much?

Survival of the Fox

Would the fox have been able to remain a significant inhabitant of commercially farmed Britain, or would it not have shared the fate of the wolf, if there had not been a sporting incentive for its preservation at a level acceptable to local farming interests? The survival of 'dustbin' foxes in non-hunting urban or suburban environments has significant animal welfare implications.

Ronnie Wallace, who had claim to be the century's premier huntsman, put earth stopping into perspective: 'Earth stopping is not a dirty trick dreamed up by foxhunters to outwit foxes. It produces what is best in foxhunting.

'Since hounds must kill foxes, how much better that this be done in a clean, fair hunt than by a local mining party.(He refers to groups of men with terriers prepared to trespass to engage in fox and badger digging.) If all foxes were merely chased into holes and then dug out, who among us would call it good sport? Without earth stopping that is the alternative.

'It is no use saying that one could just take off one's hat to the fox, say 'goodnight' and go home, because realities must be faced. Somebody will be tempted to return to the earth and snare or gas him next day. Foxes have a rather better chance of escape above ground than below it.

'That the fox must be controlled is unarguable. Suggestions that foxes might be allowed to let rip to find their own level are palpable nonsense, their food supply being domestic stock, game, and wildlife. If the local pack of hounds kills acceptable numbers of foxes, the scale on which other, less attractive methods are used will be reduced.'

At the start of the twentieth century, hunting a bagged fox, that is a captured live fox put down in a covert from a bag just before hounds drew it, had long been a despised practice by true foxhunters, those who cared deeply that their sport should indeed be 'sporting', governed by rules and a code of practice.

Bagging was depicted as the craven solution to providing a day's hunting by knaves and fools in Surtees' novels early in the nineteenth century. The practice was a prime offence under the code of the Masters of Foxhounds Association from its formation in 1881. The Association would tighten up and modify the rules and practice of its sport, and increase the severity of its self-regulation, by the end of the century.

Hunting Practice

At the start of the century, with literally hundreds of spectators following closely on horseback and on foot, there is ample testimony that Tom Firr was not using bagged foxes to produce his 'quick things' in the centre-stage of the Shires hunting field. Guy Paget, a great authority on Leicestershire, averred: 'Much as Firr liked blood, he was scrupulously fair. No mobbing, or nicking, and above all no bagmen.' (Mobbing referred to crowding round a fox by followers to make it easier to kill during cubhunting; nicking a fox's pad so that the blood droplets made it easier was another despised practice of much earlier times, formally and strictly forbidden once foxhunting became registered by the MFHA.)

Firr hated digging for foxes, much preferring his hounds to catch them in the open above ground at the end of a run. He would only dig when the fox gone to ground was known to be notorious as a killer of poultry or lambs.

There were fixtures in every season when even the greatest of the top-class professionals endured near blank days, or poor hunts, through that most baffling of hunting's obstacles, poor scenting conditions. It is foxhunting's lack of guarantee, its adventure into the unknown, that has helped make it so addictive. That is the basis for the foxhunter's jibe that draghunting in comparison is like 'kissing your sister'.

Remarkable skills were displayed by Firr, and they earned the critical acclaim not only of those who enjoyed risking their necks to ride after his hounds, but plenty of countrymen and instinctive naturalists who watched him closely throughout his famous reign as the most renowned huntsman in the land.

Firr, like many of his followers, ran out of luck in his risky occupation: he suffered a bad fall in 1897, and another the following year, injuring his head, which finished his career. He died at the end of 1902 at the age of sixty-one, having given his life for the sport at which he excelled. Firr had achieved the level of sporting eminence at a national level which would today earn him lengthy TV and radio tributes. Although his career ended just before the new century his record and his style influenced others seeking to hunt the great grass countries of the Midlands.

The other great Quorn character who had left the scene was the 'Yellow Earl', the ebullient, infuriating Lord Lonsdale whose tempestuous five year Mastership of that Hunt concluded in 1898. Hugh, 5th Earl of Lonsdale returned to foxhunting eminence in the twentieth century as Master of the Cottesmore twice. Although he became distinctly unpopular in his first Cottesmore Mastership (1911–13) in his second term of office (1915–21) Lonsdale made a crucial contribution to carry the Hunt through the Great War and its aftermath. He threw himself in war work as well as ensuring the survival of his beloved foxhunting. In answer to criticisms that the maintenance of foxhunting was not essential to

Autocratic, ebullient, and a great foxhunter: Lord Lonsdale, 'the Yellow Earl', Master of the Quorn 1893–98, and of the Cottesmore twice (1911–13 and 1915–21).

the war effort he replied: 'What on earth are officers home from the front going to do with their time if there is no foxhunting for them?'

Despite the efforts of foxhunters still on the home front, the loss in the trenches of the 'flower of a generation', and the profound social changes accelerated by the war, made it seem hardly possible that such a traditional sport as foxhunting could ever revive after the war to its former glory.

Once again the prophets of doom for foxhunting were to be confounded. Its revival after 1918 was on a scale proving emphatically that foxhunting was one of the strands of normal life in the British Isles which more than a few officers and men in the armed forces felt they had been fighting for.

CHAPTER 2

THE FIRST TEST

I N 1910 when George V succeeded to the throne, foxhunting had not been
forced to make obvious changes to adapt to the new century.

Baily's Hunting Directory recorded at the beginning of the century a
remarkable array of Fox Hunts: 168 in England and Wales; twelve in Scotland;
and twenty-five in Ireland. There were thirty-seven packs of Staghounds in
England, and nineteen in Ireland; and 103 packs of Harriers in England and
Wales, and thirty-seven in Ireland. Significantly, *Baily's* recorded only eight
packs of Draghounds in England and one in Ireland.

The Hunts reflected the serenity, and the complacency, of the upper and
middle classes in Edwardian Britain, and were as little prepared as society in
general for the disruption of the world war to come. There were, however, under-
currents of change in the countryside each season. Hunting's ability to cope was
already being tested when leading landowners and Masters felt the bite of new
taxes and agricultural downturns.

The 10th Duke of Beaufort, the leading MFH of the twentieth century, known
to many simply as 'Master', born on 4 April 1900, remarked in his memoirs
published in 1981: 'In so far as an estate like Badminton was concerned, those
early years of the century were still times of plenty. Income tax was ridiculously
low compared with the crippling sums we are called upon to pay nowadays – but
on the very day of my birth it went up from sevenpence to eightpence in the
pound! However ridiculous that sum seems to us now in these days of inflation,
and high taxation, believe me eighty years ago it caused the greatest concern, for

it was felt to be an encroachment on civil liberty that people were called upon to dip into their pockets in such a way.'

Although the Duke of Beaufort's Hunt had begun to take subscriptions, the estate continued throughout the century to make a major contribution to the maintenance of one of the largest hunting establishments in Britain. It was estimated that only about a dozen packs out of some 180 were not collecting subscriptions of some sort by the turn of the century. Yet there was still a significant group of aristocratic families, and wealthy industrialists, providing substantial annual backing for the running of Hunts since the volume of subscriptions collected left large deficits.

The Quorn was the forerunner of the modern subscription pack: throughout most of the nineteenth century the Quorn relied on ad hoc contributions from members of its mounted field who were visitors to Leicestershire for the season's hunting, to supplement the major financial input from the Masters. The Quorn, Cottesmore and Belvoir jointly agreed to levy a visitor's cap of £2 per day from 1893. Otho Paget, *The Field*'s excellent hunting correspondent, was the first 'capper', and reported ruefully that 'extracting those golden coins from the pockets of visitors to the Quorn was one of the most unpleasant tasks that has ever fallen to my lot.'

He recalled 'searching for strange faces' among a mounted field of 300, and reported that his successor as 'capper' pursued a fair lady across country all day, and only managed to corner her in late afternoon when she handed over a coin wrapped in paper. That night he unwrapped it to find it contained only half the correct amount.

The 9th Duke of Beaufort was Master of his family pack, kennelled at Badminton, from 1899–1924, but as the Marquess of Worcester he had already

A mounted field in the Shires in 1908: an increasing number of lady foxhunters, all riding side-saddle in well cut habits and bowlers

11

proved one of the most dedicated foxhunters in the land as a distinguished amateur huntsman since in 1869.

As a twenty-three-years-old subaltern, on 22 February 1871, Lord Worcester achieved one of the most famous foxhunts recorded, the Greatwood Run.

The Beaufort hounds ran twenty-seven miles, with a furthest point of sixteen miles, in three-and-a-half hours, with only one check. The young huntsman swam the Thames near Cricklade on his horse, crossed it again, and ended the hunt on a borrowed cob in the Old Berks country.

Twenty-nine years later, as the 9th Duke, he announced at a meet of his hounds that his wife had that morning given birth to a son. His professional huntsman suggested they all gave three cheers. The Duke replied : 'Certainly not! You might frighten the hounds.' The 9th Duke became very heavy in later life, but continued hunting his hounds until 1914 when he was sixty-seven, and thereafter followed on wheels as a close observer. His devotion to the sport was enhanced by his skills as a hound breeder and a handler of hounds in the hunting field. He was held in high regard throughout the extensive Beaufort country, where his hounds were warmly welcomed well beyond his own estate.

The Beauforts' East Midlands cousins, the Manners family of the Dukes of Rutland, of Belvoir Castle, were devoted to the chase. The 4th Duke of Rutland married Mary Isabella Somerset, daughter of the 4th Duke of Beaufort, and sister of the the 5th Duke of Beaufort, who made the crucial decision to switch from hunting deer to fox.

The Dukes of Rutland continued their passion for hunting throughout the eighteenth and nineteenth centuries, but in the 1890s the agricultural depression forced Lord John Manners, the 7th Duke, to reduce the heavy financial burden on his estate of supporting the four-day-a-week pack of hounds belonging to the family, and operated on a lavish scale for hordes of visitors as well as local followers who paid no subscription or caps.

The aged Duke gave up the Mastership in the 1895–6 season, his family always retaining ownership of these traditionally bred 'old English' hounds, and continuing to kennel them at Belvoir Castle in the buildings erected in 1802 which they still occupy. It was remarked at the time that the Hunt passed 'from the peerage to the beerage': the new Master was Sir Gilbert Greenall, forceful and enterprising head of Britian's largest regional brewery. It was rumoured that Greenall had been turned down as a Master of the Cheshire Hunt in his native north-west because he was 'in trade', although local rivalries were probably more relevant.

The Duke of Rutland had no such snobbish inhibitions, and his Hunt was well rewarded: Gilbert Greenall, created Lord Daresbury in 1927, spent huge sums on the Hunt, and provided top-class management skills and direction throughout his Belvoir Mastership until 1912. He bought the Hunt horses for £18,000, an astronomic figure at that time, built a spacious new stable block for seventy horses, and installed a special railway siding so that hounds could be more easily transported by train to far flung meets.

Aristocratic families who clung to Masterships and ownership of packs of hounds at the start of the century included the Earls of Yarborough at Brocklesby, Lincolnshire; the descendants of the Earls of Berkeley in

Gloucestershire; Earl Fitzwilliam at Peterborough; Lord Leconfield in Sussex; Sir Watkin Williams-Wynn's on the Welsh Borders; the Marquess of Zetland in North Yorkshire and Durham; and the Duke of Buccleuch in Scotland.

There were other aristocratic foxhunting connections, for example the 8th Duke of Northumberland began a Mastership of the Percy in 1921, and was succeeded by the 9th Duke in 1930 until 1940 when the 10th Duke began a Mastership lasting forty-nine years. The 11th Duke was in office until his death in 1995.

Yet at the start of the new century aristocratic ownership and control of Hunts was a minority in the list of MFHs, although aristocratic influence was to be crucial, especially through the 10th Duke of Beaufort's leadership of the MFHA and the first organised defence of the sport against its political enemies.

Foxhunting up to 1914 already owed its survival and its future to injections of money and enthusiasm from the beneficiaries of the industrial revolution who created a new squirarchy. As in the Belvoir country, they often brought valuable management skills as well as money to packs of all sizes.

Mastership of a pack of Foxhounds was beginning to involve some awareness of public relations, and more intensive liaison with farmers and landowners as more tenanted estates began to break up into owner-occupied holdings.

Although litigation was highly unlikely, Masters at the start of the new century

The famously bewhiskered 8th Earl of Harrington, Master of his own pack from 1882–1917 in his car at a meet before mounting to hunt hounds. He hunted the Derbyshire side of the South Notts country, and was loaned part of the Quorn.

knew they did not operate above the law, and could be sued for trespass by a landowner willing to embark on the cost and the local unpopularity provoked by such an action. The most significant difference between foxhunting's heyday in the late nineteenth century, and its Indian Summer in Edwardian England was that young men and women with surplus income had a far wider choice of recreation after the turn of the century. Shooting was a passion for King Edward VII and George V, and therefore became far more popular and fashionable. Racing, rugby, soccer, yachting and rowing all made progress.

The Army remained a strong element in the hunting field throughout Britain. Foxhunting was officially encouraged for the cavalry, and many other regiments believed the element of risk and courage associated with riding to hounds was of benefit to officers. The Army has for generations produced recruits for Mastership and other Hunt offices, especially the role of Hon. Secretary where organisational skills and integrity in handling money are essential.

There were already tangible signs of change in the countryside which worried traditional foxhunters, although they were not seen as terminally threatening. The sport had survived a growth of railways, roads and canals. In the first decade of the new century barbed wire was rare by today's standards, but becoming more frequently encountered in the hunting field.

To the horror of senior hunting people the menace of wire, invented in the USA, had been seen for the first time in Britain in the 1880s. It was darkly suspected that some farmers and landowners used it sometimes as a mute protest when they disliked a Mastership, but it was more likely to be used as a cheaper alternative to timber or hedges which needed maintenance.

Back-wire, set on posts behind hedges to discourage cattle from boring through, was soon recognised as one of the worst threats to the hard-rider. Leaping a hedge only to be brought down abruptly by an 'oxer' wire fence beyond was dangerous for horse or rider .

The solution adopted by many Hunts was to establish 'wire funds' to pay the cost of taking down barbed wire in the most favoured riding areas at the start of a hunting season, and erecting it again at the end of the season, at no expense to farmers and landowners.

Hunters in War

When Britain and Germany went to war on 4 August 1914, many greeted the government's decision with exhilaration, expecting a series of short, victorious battles. There were cheering crowds in the streets, but leading politicians knew 'the lamps were going out all over Europe'.

Patriotic Britons surged to volunteer for the forces, and foxhunting, with its strong military and equestrian connections, was in the van of the immediate war effort. It was believed the war would be fought mainly on horseback; few were able to imagine the implications of modern, mechanised warfare. Ancient Yeomanry regiments expected to be engaged in battle, just as much as the smart cavalry regiments.

The Army Remount Service requisitioned over 15,000 top quality hunters in the opening weeks of the war for service as Cavalry Chargers. Every kind of draught and pack animal was also in demand, and huge amounts of fodder were required from hunting countries for the expanding Army which depended so heavily on horse power.

Hunts were rapidly denuded of subscribers, supporters, and Masters. All lawn meets were cancelled and the wearing of scarlet in the hunting field was discouraged. Horses left in Hunts were kept on a Remount Service register, as part of the strategic reserve. Hunters becoming permanently unsound were struck off the register.

It has been estimated that over 450,000 horses left Britain during the Great War to serve in Europe, the Western Desert and Gallipoli. None returned, except some officers' chargers repatriated at their owner's expense. It was possible to find ex-British Army horses in emaciated condition pulling carts in Cairo's poorest slums for years after the war; some of them had been proud hunters from Britain's hunting fields.

The Sinnington in Yorkshire saw fifty farmers' sons and subscribers join the colours, each supplying his own horse, and the Hunt Stables provided ten mounts. Both Masters, Viscount Helmsley and Mr Sherbrooke went to war, never to return.

In the Puckeridge Hunt in Essex and Hertfordshire one of the Masters and twenty-two horses left the Hunt stables to join the Expeditionary Force, described by the Kaiser as the 'contemptible little Army'.

Despite this the Puckeridge continued to hunt four days a week until 1916, the Masters accepting a very much reduced guarantee. In the last two years of the war, reductions of hounds in the Puckeridge kennel caused the Hunt to operate with a single, mixed pack hunting not more than three days a week, still a remarkable number of fixtures in a war-time countryside.

The Cheshire Hunt committee ordained that subscribers on military service were to retain their membership on payment of half subscription, although this did not apply if their families continued to hunt in their absence. Colonel Hall Walker generously advanced £1,000 to enable the Hunt to carry on, and hounds were out four days a week.

Foxhunting during the Great War was sometimes remarkably good because there were great swathes of grass, and mounted fields were small. Military men on leave were always warmly welcome. One who hunted during the war with the Cheshire was Siegfried Sassoon when stationed near Liverpool. After a day in 1917 his Diary recorded: 'The contrast between Litherland Camp and the Cheshire Saturday country was like the difference between War and Peace, especially when at the end of a good day I jogged a few miles homeward with the cheery huntsman in my best pre-war style.'

Horses and hunting had little relevance for millions when the war developed into a horrendous slogging match, with huge armies facing each other from entrenched lines. There was massive conscription, and it was clear that men would not be coming home for years; women went to work as never before, to fill their places. Food rationing and other shortages afflicted many on the home front.

It was an extraordinary testament to foxhunting's firm place in rural life that

Stanley Barker who later hunted the Pytchley (1931–60), started work at fourteen as second whipper-in at the Sinnington during the Great War. He handed over at the Pytchley to Bert Maiden, left, who hunted these hounds 1960–71.

it survived at all during the Great War. In fact, only a few Hunts closed; the majority continued, and women and older men filled many Masterships, and sometimes hunted hounds, or whipped-in.

Stanley Barker who was to be huntsman of the Pytchley for thirty years from 1931, was put on as second whipper-in to the Sinnington in 1915 at the age of fourteen, an early appointment which would never have occurred in peace-time. At that age he would have been a strapper, or possibly a second-horseman or kennel boy. Up to 1914 there was a long ladder to ascend in hunt service for an aspiring huntsman.

The number of women out hunting had increased in the 1870s and '80s although they seldom formed more than ten per cent of the large mounted fields in the Shires. There was always a small number of bold and skilled women in nineteenth century hunting fields, and as Surtees had remarked: 'When women do ride, they usually ride like the very devil. There is no medium with them. They either "go" to beat the men, or they don't "go" at all.' There was a growing acceptance that foxhunting was not only a respectable recreation for respectable women, but could be fashionable as well. In the Great War women worked in much reduced Hunt establishments to enable the sport to survive.

Traditional sexist attitudes were still strong: the number of women permanently appointed to Masterships remained small. In 1903 there were two lady Masters of Foxhounds; in 1921 there were only seven lady Masters, and there were seven women Hon.Secretaries in Foxhound packs. However, foxhunting reflected the social environment: the first votes for women came in 1918, and universal female suffrage did not arrive until 1928.

The Quorn broke its firm rule that it would not allow its hounds to be hunted by an amateur, and allowed its Master, Capt. Frank Forester, to hunt hounds throughout the Great War. He did so with much success in keeping down foxes, but never received the recognition he deserved. In the 1917–18 season he was without a whipper-in, and his remaining staff were called up. He finished the season single-handed, except for the help of his young daughter. He resigned in February 1918, and was succeed by a professional, Walter Wilson from the Cheshire. By the end of Wilson's first week's full hunting the Armistice had been signed; the Quorn Hunt had only just survived the war.

Feeding horses and hounds became a desperate problem. Poultry was still kept on the free range system, and the war government recognised hunting as a practical aid to agriculture in 'controlling vermin', and therefore resisted calls from the Food Commission to order the destruction of all hounds. The pressure was acute because food shortages for the human population was disastrous, and there was considerable malnutrition among working class city populations.

The policy of the MFHA, agreed by government, was that Hunts should keep their countries 'well cubbed', killing as many foxes as possible. The Duke of Beaufort, President of the MFHA, was concerned that Hunts should not close down because he knew hunting's best hope for survival during the war was a role as a national vermin control organisation, and Hunts that folded would jeopardise the existence of the rest.

The Board of Agriculture had received many complaints about poultry losses to foxes and they were much concerned about losses of food production at a time when food imports were jeopardised by the war at sea. Up to 1914 most Hunts paid claims from farmers for poultry killed by foxes, but during the war many farmers abandoned such claims to help save the sport that was part of their lives

During discussions in Parliament there were a few calls for the compulsory destruction of the entire fox population, but this was discounted, no doubt on practical grounds as much as any other. There was government pressure to reduce the hound population because of concern about feedstuffs. It was decreed that they should not be fed oatmeal, only 'damaged rice and maize' and this was strictly rationed.

The hound population dropped partly through putting hounds down, but mainly by greatly reducing hound breeding. Thanks to the dedication of those running the Hunt establishments few valuable lines of Foxhound breeding were irrevocably lost.

Throughout the war the civilian population believed it was essential to 'keep things going', to give a good time to 'our boys' on leave, and to make it possible to resume life exactly as before when the fighting was over. Britain was to be a 'land fit for heroes.' The appalling losses of the Great War meant that many of the 'boys' never returned to the hunting field.

It has been said Britain lost 'the flower of a generation', and perhaps hunting suffered as much as any other enterprise in losing so many young men who would have been leaders. When peace came, however, there were to be plenty of people who found themselves unexpectedly alive, with a gratuity to spend.

Despite initial shortages of horses and hounds, foxhunting recovered remarkably quickly. It was to see another extraordinary rise in its fortunes, occurring while the 'sea of grass' in the Midlands was still largely in place. The desperate agricultural depression of the between-the-wars years ensured for all the wrong reasons that there was all too much land ill-farmed, or left fallow, which produced a wildness entirely suitable for foxhunting.

There was a short industrial boom after the Great War, but soon trade fell off and unemployment soared to one million in 1920, remaining between 1,500,000 and 2,750,000 million for most of the 1930s. Foxhunting, and other 'luxury' sports, enjoyed renewed popularity at a time when a substantial section of the population existed on the dole, ill-nourished, poorly clad and in sub-standard housing.

Such contrasts, embedded in the memory of many, helped to fuel the political prejudice which contributed throughout the twentieth century to the ambitions of urban based Left-wingers to abolish hunting as a symbol of class and privilege whenever a Labour government was in power. At the end of the century when hunting people bemoaned the loss of jobs which a hunting ban would cause, some Labour MPs keen to abolish hunting would yell across the House at their pro-hunting opponents: 'What did you do for the miners?' They were referring to the closure of mines during the Thatcher years when many jobs were lost. It revealed starkly that they saw a hunting ban principally as a form of class-war revenge.

Hunting in its traditional form, producing recreation for a remarkably wide cross-section of society, revived after 1918 – but the spotlight was on the Bright Young Things who flocked back to the Shires for two decades of fashionable, elitist foxhunting. There was a rather desperate gaiety for the minority able to enjoy the full social season in the 'twenties and 'thirties.

Can anyone begrudge them foxhunting among their pleasures when so many would soon be expected to sacrifice their lives in a second world war?

CHAPTER 3

'TWENTIES AND 'THIRTIES

FOXHUNTING absorbed the most unlikely recruits in the hectic, somewhat unreal atmosphere between the wars. More frequently people who had no immediate family background of hunting began to take up the Chase. Some did so as part of a social climbing exercise, but after the horrors of the Great War many more found the hunting field a solace from growing twentieth century pressures.

The hunting field swiftly reflected the growing emancipation of women; another example of the seemingly hide-bound traditional sport's willingness to absorb social change surprisingly swiftly. Foxhunting's inclusiveness applied because whatever social changes occurred, Hunts had to maintain access to land owned or farmed by numerous people to achieve a season's sport. This continued to involve access to whole networks of people connected in various ways to those who owned or worked on the land.

The impecunious far distant cousin, or even a newly met friend, of a landowner could rely on a welcome to the local Hunt during a visit. There were special rates in many Hunts for horse dealers, vets, and sometimes doctors – although hunting medics were usually full subscribers, but all too often ruefully put up with interruptions to their sport, through tending the more seriously injured,

A meet of the Tiverton Hunt in 1935 is notable for the smartness and conformity of 'correct' Hunt dress.

The country weekend had survived and flourished from Edwardian times, and although some house parties were far more concerned with indoor recreation, there were plenty of young people keen to ride to hounds during their visit.

The farmer's family could usually hunt for no subscription or cap if the land was crossed regularly by the Hunt, but increasingly the growing agricultural depression in the late 'twenties or 'thirties meant that all too many could not even afford to keep a riding horse on the farm. Yet their allegiance to local Hunts, simply as an accepted part of the countryside, remained staunch.

More Ladies in the Chase

The 1920s has been described as the heyday of side-saddle riding, but in the 1930s many women changed to riding astride. There had been major adjustments to side-saddle riding through the introduction of the so-called 'safety release' riding habit skirt.

In late Victorian and Edwardian times improvements in the design of side-saddle pommels made it more possible for women not only to ride to the meet, but to follow hounds across country. Early Victorian ladies riding with voluminous habits were all too likely to be caught up in the side-saddle in a fall, contributing to serious injuries or fatalities, which emphasises just how intrepid they were to take part in the Chase.

Flossie Mather-Jackson, *centre*, riding astride, next to Dorothy Hilton-Green, riding side-saddle, with friends about to go hunting from the yard at 'The Limes', Melton Mowbray, in 1932.

Side-saddle riding was more elegant, and continued to be used by some women throughout the twentieth century, but the emancipated flapper who smoked and wore short skirts, was not so bothered by the issue of modesty. She wanted to ride across country effectively, competing with men, and chose to wear breeches and boots to use the astride saddle.

The late Lord (Reggie) Paget, whose family were embedded in Shires hunting, wrote in 1987: 'A better side-saddle was not the answer to women's need. The very pommels that made the riders' seat secure created the danger. As a horse rears or leaps, the rider is pushed into the pommel.

'She cannot get off. She has no escape as the horse crashes down on her. As I write I can see the two fences where Mrs Mason and ten years later my beautiful sister-in-law Baby Whitaker died because their pommels prevented-them getting clear. If ever I was an MFH again I would send side-saddles home. They are for the meet, not for tearing across country. They are too dangerous. 'Women's advance came when it was discovered that equitation depended on balance not grip and that a girl's balance was as good if not better than a man's. ' (Lord Paget's Introduction to *Ladies of The Chase* by Meriel Buxton, The Sportsman's Press, 1987).

I agree fervently with Lord Paget, having seen several horrible falls in Leicestershire where side-saddle riders' injuries were all the worse because they remained close to the horse when it fell. Yet I will concede that ladies who ride side-saddle well can tackle huge obstacles boldly with remarkable success, and superb style.

The best side-saddle rider I saw with the Quorn in the late twentieth century was Lady Margaret Fortescue who was remarkably brave and skilful, with the verve and elegance her mother had displayed in the pre-war years. Fences of all kinds, drops, ditches and five-bar gates were all taken on calmly and effectively by Lady Margaret riding side-saddle.

Regrettably her appearances in the Shires ceased in the mid-1980s after she suffered numerous fractures in a fall coming fast over a downhill fence above Scalford with the Belvoir. Fortunately, she made a remarkable recovery, but listened at last to the blandishments of her family to give up the Chase, having earlier survived a horrendous fall and leg injury when she was trapped after her horse fell from a field bridge during a day with the Quorn. Her courage in returning to ride fearlessly across Leicestershire after that fall had already earned our admiration.

As recently as November, 2002, to the amazement and admiration of spectators and fellow competitors, the annual Melton Hunt Club Ride was completed in second place by twenty-two-years-old Frances Elson, a petite 5ft 3in graduate from Holwell, near Melton Mowbray who rode her ten-years-old-hunter Bruno side-saddle.

Held in driving rain and deep going in the Cottesmore country, over a particularly formidable course between Owston and Knossington, the 2002 Ride was a severe test, with only nineteen riders finishing out of twenty-nine. It was the

Lady Margaret Fortescue, one of the best side-saddle riders in the Quorn country in post-war years, showing the way across country in a Friday hunt from Cream Gorse in 1977.

first time any rider had completed a Melton Ride course side-saddle since the event started forty-three years earlier. Frances proved that side-saddle riding across severe country was far from extinct in the twenty-first century.

A few ladies can still be seen elegantly taking on the fences in this style in the Shires and elsewhere. The Side-Saddle Association, formed in 1974, has 1,200 members, and has achieved much in retaining the side-saddle skills. The Association encourages its use in dressage, showjumping, and working hunter classes, and hold their own annual show, as well as contributing to others. Women riders in the risk sport of eventing, do not compete side-saddle, even in the dressage phase. I should record that first place in the 2002 Melton Hunt Club Ride was captured by the brilliant cross-country rider, Jo Jewell – who rode astride. Admitting that she qualified also for the 'veteran, over fifties' prize, Jo is the sister of the best rider across country I have ever seen, Michael Farrin, former huntsman of the Quorn for thirty years.

First Car Followers

As well as more ladies riding astride, the 1920s and '30s increasingly saw the arrival of the motor car as a means of transport to the meet, and some of the first

Sir Harold Nutting, right, Joint Master of the Quorn throughout the 1930s, with huntsman George Barker. Sir Harold was famous for insisting on 'correct' hunting etiquette, and his hatred of car followers.

motorised horse boxes conveying hunters. They were greeted by traditionalists with the same horror that barbed wire evoked. Sir Harold Nutting, formidable Master of the Quorn from 1932–40, saw a man in a small Austin trailing behind the field. He barked a question at the driver as to what he was doing. When the man quavered that he was 'following the Hunt' in the car, the Master retorted: 'Well, I should take it home immediately!'

According to Ulrica Murray Smith, later Master of the Quorn for twenty-six years, 'If one of his lady friends rang up to ask where to leave her car, Harold would say firmly, "In your garage I hope", and ring off.' Sir Harold was a Canute endeavouring to turn back the first appearance of a huge tide. Car followers were to become valued supporters of foxhunting in the post-war years, and the motor horse box enabled the sport to survive despite the clogged roads afflicting the countryside later in the century.

Magnet of the Shires

Ulrica Murray Smith summed up hunting in the Shires in the 1930s thus: 'The hunting surpassed my wildest dreams. The Quorn, Belvoir and Cottesmore all met within easy riding distance from Melton; you could hunt six days a week, the horses all going by road. The country was nothing but grass, with glorious fences and timber, enabling the field to spread out and take their own line, jumping anywhere.

'But there was a vast crowd, and it was essential to keep wide awake to get a good start, as manners were not apparent in the first gateway or so. There was a certain knack to getting away, soon learned in the Shires, which I think strangers usually found difficult to cope with at first, as they would find themselves pushed aside.'

Ulrica recalled 'in the hunting field the turnout was absolutely faultless. Gentlemen wore scarlet swallow-tail coats with white leather breeches, which they kept from getting a speck of dirt on by wearing a silk apron until they actually mounted their horses. "Leathers" become lethal if it rains, as they are so slippery when wet, which must be a drawback, but otherwise they are warm and extremely smart.' (In fact, gentlemen had the choice of wearing smartly tailored cord breeches, according to the conditions.)

The inter-war high jinks in the Shires attracted special attention from the society press, and added more gloss to the elitist image of the sport, because royalty was once again to be seen riding to hounds. *The Tatler* carried a weekly 'Leicestershire Letter' which was mostly social rather than sporting gossip.

The Royal Factor

Although shooting was the first choice of King George V, his heir Edward, Prince of Wales was an enthusiastic rider to hounds, and relished the social life of Melton Mowbray as much as the chase. He first hunted in Leicestershire in 1923, taking a suite at Craven Lodge, Melton Mowbray, the hunting box of a Mr

Craven in the previous century, but between the wars a residential club for hunting people, with stabling on the premises, run by Major-General John Vaughan.

It was at Burrough Court, at Burrough-on-the-Hill south of Melton, home of Lord and Lady Furness, that the Prince of Wales first met Mrs Wallis Simpson for whom he was to abdicate the throne as Edward VIII. The Prince was renowned for his other female conquests in Leicestershire; an invitation to dine with him at Craven Lodge was the most fervently desired hunting trophy among the hard-riding ladies of the Shires. One of his most constant loves was Winifred May Dudley Ward, a Nottinghamshire hunting lady, and wife of the MP for Southampton.

Local history records that he was popular with the townspeople with whom he chatted easily and naturally when he walked through the town. Sometimes he danced with the town's girls in the Corn Exchange, and he attended the town's church parades. The royal 'walk about' was not a post-war invention.

Edward was especially popular with the hunting set because, although not the most polished of horsemen, he rode to hounds with zest and courage. There were occasional expressions of public concern about the risks he was taking in the hunting field and in riding in point-to-points.

His brothers, Prince George (Duke of Kent) and Prince Henry (Duke of Gloucester) also stayed at Craven Lodge and hunted, but not so frequently as the Prince of Wales. The much less rackety Duke of York, later King George VI, was an excellent horseman and bequeathed his passion for horses to his daughter, our Queen Elizabeth II, and to two of his grandchildren, Charles, Prince of Wales and the Princess Royal. The future King hunted sometimes from Melton but after his marriage to Lady Elizabeth Bowes-Lyon, they took a hunting box at Naseby Woollies in the Pytchley country for several years in the 1930s, the Duke hunting with the famous Pytchley white-collars over a stiff country that was arguably more formidable than the Melton terrain.

Royalty's presence and preferences set the agenda for the social season, and Melton Mowbray was firmly on the list of places to be in the winter. It was possible to indulge in the social scene without actually riding, but to be thoroughly accepted it was vital to 'go well' in the hunting field. The afficianados hunted at least four days a week, and that had to include a Quorn Monday or Friday, a Belvoir Wednesday or Saturday, or a Cottesmore Tuesday or Saturday. The most ardent foxhunters in Melton Mowbray would venture further south to the Fernie's delectable grass country above Market Harborough on a Thursday.

The Foxhunting 'Industry'

Providing and maintaining hunters, clothes, and catering all helped to boost the Leicestershire rural economy at a time when farming was hard hit by depression. Selling fodder and bedding for horses, rearing and selling hunters, were valuable adjuncts to farming in the Shires hunting country. Hunts would buy cobs and smaller horses for their staff for the early cub-hunting season, and sell them at special auctions in Leicester.

George Gillson, much admired huntsman of the Warwickshire (1935–40 and 1945–56) hunting hounds in 1936, with whipper-in Barry Boyle, *right*, kennel huntsman of the Portman in post-war years.

The annual sales of likely hunters at the beginning and end of each season attracted horsemen from many hunting countries. A horse that had performed well amid the competitive cut and thrust of the Shires hunting fields had a special value. Horse dealing was a major activity in the prime Midlands hunting countries. Many a Hunt servant seeking to become a whipper-in and later a huntsman, began his career riding second horse in the hunting field. The second horsemen were under the leadership of the Master's own second horseman.

They would ride in a body in lanes somewhere behind the mounted field engaged in riding to hounds. If hounds ran into a neighbouring country the second horsemen had to stop on the hunt boundary. The knack was to produce the relatively fresh second horse for the hunting man or woman at just the right juncture of the day, and then take home the first horse.

Second horsemen saw a great deal of hunting; they learned the hunting country intimately, and they improved their own horsemanship. Some of the most committed and wealthy hunting men would even have a third horse ready for a second change in the latter part of the season when the days are longer and visiting dog foxes tend to provide longer hunts.

The second horseman system was to be replaced in postwar years by the 'second horses location', virtually a secondary meet indicated on the hunting fixture card, where horse boxes bring fresh horses and take home the original

26

mounts. One measure of a really good morning hunt was that it was so long that 'we did not get our second horses until mid-afternoon.' It is still part of Shires hunting, and is practised in other large Hunts such as the Beaufort and Heythrop, but far fewer riders nowadays have second horses.

Some visitors to Leicestershire rented large houses and stabling for the entire season, but others used local inns and hotels, and stabling was packed with visiting horses. For example, in the small village of Braunston, in the best of the Cottesmore country, it was usual for over one hundred hunters to be stabled in yards during the season. The clip-clop of hunters exercising was the early morning sound awakening householders throughout the winter in Melton Mowbray, Oakham, Uppingham, and other towns and villages in Leicestershire and Rutland.

Hunting lodges catering especially for the well-off visiting Meltonians were a profitable business between the wars. Among those in Melton Mowbray were Wicklow Lodge, Sysonby Lodge, Stavely Lodge, Hamilton Lodge, Warwick Lodge and Wyndham Lodge. Lords and ladies and more exotic titles, such as the Maharanee of Cooch Behar, were temporarily resident. Some of the Lodges survive forlornly as offices, old people's homes, or flats in the a modern Melton Mowbray where a dog meat factory is probably the largest employer.

There are still strong hunting connections, such as joint meets and a New Year's Day meet in the centre of Melton, and the warm, friendly townspeople remain famous for their pork pies and Stilton cheese. The town's museum has a hunting section well worth seeing, but Melton Mowbray has become another busy Midlands centre for light industry and large used car lots on dreary estates clustered around its perimeters. Driving through it in the rush hour is a nightmare.

In the excitable 'twenties and 'thirties, balls, dinner parties, and other jollifications were held throughout the winter season. Fancy dress dances, and practical joking were especially popular with the hunting set. As in London's West End, the frantic gaiety was perhaps all the more intense because it took place in the shadow of economic depressions and the grim threat of another world war.

In his autobiography, Edward VIII recalled the Meltonians in his day: 'Intermixed with the local landed gentry was a lively sampling of dashing figures: noblemen and their ladies, wealthy people who had discovered the stable door was a quick if expensive short cut into society; a strong injection of Americans from famous East Coast Hunts; ladies whose pursuit of the fox was only a phase of an even more intense pursuit of romance – good riders on bad horses, bad riders on good horses.'

As well as the raffish social set, Leicestershire continued to attract plenty of keen foxhunters who simply wanted to enjoy at least a taste of riding across its fabulous sea of grass behind a top-class pack of hounds. Their presence, and the major involvement of many people resident in Leicestershire and Rutland was largely unnoticed in the social colums, but their involvement in the sport was crucial in maintaining hunting in the Shires when the social whirl had been swept away by another world war.

MFH Number One

The seeds of foxhunting's postwar future were being sown throughout most of England and Wales in the 'twenties and 'thirties.

One of the most significant happenings was the succession of Henry Hugh Arthur FitzRoy Somerset as the 10th Duke of Beaufort in 1924. As Master of the family pack of foxhounds at his ancestral seat, Badminton in Gloucestershire, he was to give leadership to the foxhunting world for most of the twentieth century, not least by setting high standards as a creative hound breeder and a gifted huntsman.

Born in 1900, he was known as 'Master' since the age of eleven when his father gave him a pack of harriers as a birthday present. Jokingly his relatives and friends called the boy 'Master', and it remained a life-long nickname as well as an appropriate title. He began hunting the family's famous pack of foxhounds at least one day a week at the age of twenty, and continued as amateur huntsman for the next forty-seven years, remaining in office as senior Master until his death at eighty-four.

The Duke of Beaufort's subscribers wear handsome blue coats with buff facings; the huntsman and whippers-in wear green coats, not scarlet, because green is the Beaufort family livery. Hunting in the Beaufort country in the 'twenties and 'thirties was an enjoyable recreation, but although there were visitors, this was essentially a locally based Hunt. Nimrod early in the previous century had paid tribute to the standards of hunting in the Beaufort country, but patronisingly described it as 'provincial'.

That term could be worn with pride, for hunting with the Duke of Beaufort was far more sober than the giddy social whirl of Leicestershire. It was enormous fun to hunt over the pastures and walls around Badminton, and the deep riding vales below, but it was essentially a sport conducted seriously according to the standards the Duke had inherited. Most followers were resident and they were expected to take as much interest in the breeding of the hounds in kennel as in their performance in the field.

The Duke of Beaufort's annual puppy show was, and remains, one of the high spots of the hunting year, with much valued invitations going to Masters and professional huntsmen all over Britain. They come to Badminton to inspect and admire the annual entry of young hounds, bred on modern, innovative lines.

Although a great respecter of the traditions he inherited, Master was willing to make controversial changes in hound breeding in the 1930s. The tall, balding Duke might at first appear aloof or shy, but he had great natural charm, was especially popular with the ladies, and he was genuinely liked and respected by everyone in the rural community, from the earth-stopper to the local squires. Although essentially affable, he was perhaps somewhat deficient in a ready sense of humour, but did not resort to sarcasm or irony, and his more artless remarks on and off the hunting fields could be most amusing, if unintentional. As President of the Royal International Horse Show I recall him staring down at long maned, prancing Arab horses, and remarking: 'Very nice, but I'm afraid they wouldn't do my job.'

Leader of the foxhunting world through most of the twentieth century: 'Master',
10th Duke of Beaufort, MFH for sixty years, and huntsman of his family pack for
forty-seven years.

'Master' and his Joint Master, Major Gerald Gundry, head the Beaufort mounted field in 1969.

Major Gerald Gundry, one of foxhunting's most popular personalities, and the Duke of Beaufort's indispensable Joint Master for thirty-four years, used to recount an incident in the hunting field when he reported to 'Master': 'I say, there's a farmer standing in the corner of this field who's really angry with us. Apparently he didn't expect us to-day and he didn't want us in this field. Could you have a word with him?'

The Duke rode over, and chatted for some time to the farmer who touched his cap and said: 'Good morning, Your Grace.' When the Duke rode back to Gerald Gundry he said: 'I can't think what the problem was, Gerald. I had a nice talk with him, and he never complained once.'

The ducal calm, especially in later life, could erupt into a thunder storm of awesome anger, although it quickly reverted to sunshine, with no rancour remaining for the target of the temper. As a recipient once or twice, I remembered to take special care about punctuality and the keeping of appointments, which the Duke regarded with a Victorian sternness.

In the early 1970s, as the recently appointed Editor of *Horse & Hound* I once felt it necessary to telephone the Duke's secretary to postpone an appointment I had to meet the Duke at Badminton to see his hounds. I received a fierce response on the phone from Master himself who was most unhappy that his own engagements diary had been seriously disrupted.

With some trepidation I accepted an alternative invitation to stay at Badminton, the lovely Palladian mansion set in Capability Brown parkland, and to hunt next day. I made sure I kept the date and arrived exactly on time.

It was a freezing November day, and the great house seemed as cold inside as the parkland outside. The Duke himself greeted me at a side door. Before letting me in, he said with a wide smile: 'Listen to the hounds. They're singing in kennel.'

Inside the Duke pointed to several stalactites of ice hanging down in the main hall, and said, as if it was absolutely of no importance : 'We've got a bit of leak in the roof, and there is a fault in the heating just now.'

I nodded a response, not trying to speak through chattering teeth. We walked resoundingly on wooden floors through sparsely lit great rooms, with looming shapes of furniture covered in dust sheets, to a small sitting room where there was a screened area round a modest wood fire. A parrot in a cage occupied the key position right in front of the fire. Mary Beaufort, the Duchess, explained with a sweet smile that in such weather its life was at risk if it did not keep warm.

We sat on yellowing horse hide covered chairs; the Duke remarked that his father had been accustomed to using the hide of some of his favourite hunters for this purpose: 'He enjoyed sitting on them while they were alive, and he wanted to continue sitting on them thereafter.'

The only other guest was the redoubtable Daphne Moore, one of *Horse & Hound's* most senior and long serving correspondents. She was the ideal personality to contribute to the atmosphere of historic foxhunting eccentricity which permeated the evening. I felt the evening could have been devised and the script written by Evelyn Waugh. Once I warmed up a little, edging alongside the parrot cage, I thoroughly enjoyed every minute.

I had inherited Daphne, who died recently in her nineties, as *Horse & Hound's* correspondent on hounds and hound pedigrees. She was the foremost journalistic authority on this subject; her passion for foxhunting in all its manifestations was truly remarkable and only exceeded by her devotion and admiration to Master and all his achievements.

The two editions of her great work *The Book of the Foxhound* (first published by J.A. Allen in 1964) are standard works worthy of the attention of anyone claiming an interest in the sport. Daphne, who never married, had started hunting in the 1930s from her native Tewkesbury, and wrote a weekly 'Round the Kennels' article for *Horse & Hound* in the 1950s. Since 1958 she lived at Pond Cottage, immediately adjacent to Badminton House, which was her concept of residing in paradise since she had the task of keeping all the Duke's hound breeding pedigrees, entering his hounds for the shows, and following the Hunt on a large black ladies' bicycle of ancient vintage.

I was fond of Daphne, but during her journalistic career a core of steel could be detected if my staff dared to cut or alter a word of her copy, and for this I cast no blame, since sub-editors can be infuriating when they change the meaning of a true specialist's expertise which in Daphne's case came to us virtually in tablets of stone which must be delivered to the reader exactly in that form. Daphne in full flood of protest could be quite an overwhelming experience for new members of my staff, and I was inclined to answer her occasional telephone calls of protest personally if possible. Long debates about the cost of mileage and bed and breakfast at far flung shows were another cause for telephone discussions where the Editor's decision making process was urgently required.

Master clearly read every word that she wrote, since one of his endearing characteristics was his joy in winning rosettes in hound shows – and his intense dislike if he should lose; the factor of irritation increased greatly with age. This became a by-word in the foxhunting world, and it added much amusement to a hound show to see a new judge, fresh faced and bowler hatted, being given a sharp dressing down by the Duke after a session when he had not won the doghound or bitch championship.

More often than not the Beaufort's main rival in the postwar years was its neighbouring Hunt, the Heythrop, whose Hunt staff also wore green coats because their country is historically an offshoot of the Beaufort country. I witnessed a hilarious occasion at a West of England Hound show at Honiton when Master was much miffed at not winning either championship. He was about to go home when he was told there was a special class for the Champion of Champions. Setting his jaw, he ordered his huntsman: 'Get Pontiff immediately!'

Pontiff was a former Peterborough champion and was soon awarded the overall title at Honiton. Master was smiling happily when he entered the ring to receive the huge trophy. He blinked when his Joint Master, Gerald Gundry, sardonically handed over a tin of Coca Cola. Gerald explained that the previous year's recipient had not returned the Cup for the current show. 'Who was it?' demanded the Duke. 'I'm afraid it was you, Master,' Gerald replied.

The Duke frowned, and we waited for an explosion, but then he chortled with laughter. The Duke's ability to switch from formality to completely natural relaxation was seen at Honiton where he was known to eat ice-cream and travel on a merry-go-round with children attending the hound show and accompanying agricultural show. Having a childless marriage, he was especially fond of children and had a simple directness which made him popular with them.

At Peterborough Royal Foxhound Show, it was serious business for Master throughout most of his life. His main aim was to win both the doghound and bitch championships, a task sharpened up considerably when the Foxhound breeding genius Captain Ronnie Wallace, became Master and huntsman of the neighbouring Heythrop in 1952.

I once arrived late at Peterborough and foolishly remarked just before lunch to Master that it had been 'a good morning'. He snorted and glared at me. 'You think so, do you?' he roared, and stalked off to lunch.

On another occasion I received a stiff note from the Duke complaining that we had clearly truncated Daphne's report on his annual puppy show. I checked the copy and found that for some reason Daphne had written a shorter review than usual of this hallowed occasion. I was torn between revealing this to her patron, and at the same time clearing myself of a major transgression. In the event I wrote a somewhat grovelling response, shamefully relying on weasel words. I doubt that it satisfied Master but I heard no more, and it did not affect our friendship.

He believed firmly in Jorrocks's dictum 'Tell me a man's foxhunter and I loves 'im.' When he learned that the new Editor from 1973 was an extremely keen foxhunter from the Portman country, Master was especially kind and helpful and remained so until his passing. One of his greatest friends was Sir Peter Farquhar, who was Joint Master of the Portman, had encouraged me and indeed 'blooded' me in the hunting field. Their joint efforts in outcrossing the foxhound was crucial in producing the modern version of the breed.

Retaining his Mastership until the end, Master suffered somewhat in latter years from an old man's occasional lapses of confidence, and had uncharacteristic bouts of indecision. He had continued to ride at the head of the Field until several nasty falls caused him reluctantly to follow hounds by car, but this was near the end of his life. I was surprised once when hunting with his hounds, that after a brief flurry of snow at about 2.30 pm he abruptly ordered his hounds to be taken home because 'conditions were not suitable'.

The late Brian Gupwell was the professional huntsman appointed by the Duke to hunt hounds for seventeen years after Master ceased this role as an amateur in 1967. Brian had to put up with a great deal of back-seat driving from the Duke for many years, and some criticisms from Gerald Gundry who had hunted the Beaufort doghounds for many years. Brian endured this with considerable patience, but it must have been an added stress when hunting hounds in front of large mounted fields. He had been elevated to the Beaufort unusually young after hunting the much smaller Eridge Hunt in the more restricted Sussex, but Master had relied on the recommendation of his friend, the Eridge's veteran Master and hound breeder Bob Field-Marsham.

Gupwell was a superb horseman and especially brilliant at showing hounds to their best advantage in the show ring. In the hunting field he provided sport which entertained huge mounted fields despite the most severe changes in the Hunt's history, much of the terrain changing from grass to arable holding far less scent, and there were major restrictions caused by the passage of the M4 motorway through the country.

Gupwell was highly popular in the Beaufort country, but inevitably in nearly twenty years there were occasions when he and his perfectionist employer were not entirely seeing eye-to-eye. On one such occasion, Master was said to have telephoned a West Country MFH and demanded he send over his huntsman straight away to hunt the Beaufort hounds forthwith.

He was somewhat taken aback when the other Master politely but resolutely refused, and referred to such modern technicalities as contracts of employment.

The Duke calmed down, and Gupwell remained huntsman of the Beaufort, continuing as a loyal kennel huntsman to the next huntsman until honourable retirement to a Badminton cottage for life, the traditional arrangement for all huntsmen in the Duke's service. It would be entirely wrong to depict foxhunting's leader for most of the century as merely a provincial aristocrat with a single-track mind. The 10th Duke was a national figure on a far wider stage than his Badminton homeland.

He was a close friend and confidante of the Royal Family, and served as Master of the Horse for forty-one years, from 1936, being ultimately responsible for the Sovereign's horses and carriages at all ceremonial occasions, which included the coronations of King George VI and the Queen.

The Duke and Duchess took care to encourage and assist the heir, the Duke's cousin, David Robert Somerset. He was a fine rider, and an excellent Field

The 11th Duke of Beaufort, Joint Master since 1974, maintaining the traditions and standards of his famous family pack.

Master, and his role in maintaining the Beaufort Hunt after his succession as 11th Duke in 1984 is one of the major planks in foxhunting's survival.

The 10th Duke's royal and political links were of immense help to the cause of foxhunting in a fast changing world. He filled numerous public offices, and he was well known and liked in all the spheres in which he operated. He was a founder of the British Field Sports Society in 1930, and served as President for fifty years, one of many examples of the continuity he provided for the sport which was his abiding passion. Master became a symbolic totem for the animal rights movement to demonise when they became more extreme in the postwar years. After his death an abortive attempt was made by vandals to dig up his grave in the family plot at Badminton.

The Duke was prepared to explain and defend his sport publicly whenever possible. His memoirs, and a book on hunting, produced with the help of his friend Lady Cottesloe, contain words of wisdom on hunting which should inspire and inform each new generation aspiring to ride to hounds.

Master's most memorable contribution to public life outside hunting was his founding of Badminton Horse Trials in his home park in 1949, and his continued support for the great annual event which has grown to be one of the world's greatest sporting occasions, attracting nearly half a million spectators, and millions of TV viewers. The regular attendance of the Queen and her family every year, and the eventual involvement as a world-class rider of Princess Anne are all part of the Badminton legend which has truly become part of the British way of life.

The great event has benefited foxhunting and many other country activities immensely. After the Sunday afternoon presentations there is no louder cheer from the crowd than that for the parade of the Duke of Beaufort's hounds.

Badminton enabled Britain to reach the heights as an international force in eventing, winning us Olympic and world championship gold medals, and far exceeding our prowess in showjumping or dressage at that level. The stewarding of the course has depended for many years on mounted members of the Hunt and Pony Club, although more sophisticated means of communication are also used nowadays. I am sure the Duke's greatest cause for delight in his relationship with the royal family was an invitation to Prince Charles to hunt for the first time in 1975. Most of the Prince's previous equestrian experience had been in playing polo up to high goal level.

I received a delighted letter from Master informing me that the Prince had thoroughly enjoyed his first day riding to hounds, and the Beaufort pack had produced an outstanding hunt which the heir to the throne had followed all the way with great success. Master provided his own meticulous account of the day which I published with much pleasure as a 'scoop', followed up in various forms by the national press.

The occasion began a passion for foxhunting for the Prince of Wales which has endured . He continues to hunt in the Beaufort country where he lives at Highgrove, but has visited well over fifty Hunts throughout Britain, and especially enjoys hunting nowadays with the Meynell and South Staff Hunt in the Midlands. How delighted Master would have been to see Prince William and Prince Harry riding enthusiastically after the Beaufort hounds nowadays.

The Duke of Beaufort led from the front. In case anyone doubted this, his car bore the number plate MFH1. He was the Number One Master of the twentieth century, and by his inclusive attitude and his steadfastness he played a crucial role in enabling his sport to survive and flourish at high levels of venery after the second world war, and the immense changes to come in the British countryside.

New Hunts Between the Wars

Most British foxhound packs were formed in the eighteenth and nineteenth centuries, many with roots much further back. It was evidence of foxhunting's revival after the Great War that some new Hunts were born. The countryside was still open enough for new boundaries to be drawn in some areas. The greatest brake on the opening of new Hunts was financial rather than shortage of land.

The College Valley Hunt in Northumberland was founded in 1924 by Sir Alfred (Bill) Goodson. He remained as Master and huntsman for forty years, and his skills as a hound breeder have ensured that College Valley blood has been widely used elsewhere.

He formed the College Valley on the Cheviots and nearby hills from country given by the Border, North Northumberland, and Duke of Buccleuch Hunts. It became a Mecca for hound enthusiasts from far and wide, including the 10th Duke of Beaufort who used to call at the College Valley country in late summer on his way south after fishing in Scotland.

It says a great deal about the comparatively rural nature of pre-war country-side in the South-East that a new Hunt was formed in 1935 just north of London. The Enfield Chace was so close to the metropolis that at later stages in its history riders following hounds could sometimes look over a hedge into the top deck of a London red bus, and one stretch of hunting country ran alongside the northern end of the Cockfosters Underground Line.

The Hunt's title derives from hunting country hunted for centuries from Hatfield. Queen Elizabeth I and later James I hunted in this area. Major Smith-Bosanquet hunted fox in the Hertfordshire Hunt country from 1907 on his own account, and the Enfield Chace was formed to hunt that country.

Having originally been hunted by a harrier pack, the Ashford Valley Hunt in Kent was formed in 1922 as a foxhound pack, and survives to this day in an area increasingly under urban pressure.

Stresses and Strains

One of the twentieth century's greatest challenges to agriculture was the increased risk of widespread epidemics in farm stock, aided by motor transport for cattle and sheep, and importation of animals from abroad.

Major Smith-Bosanquet's Hounds, later the Enfield Chace, meeting at Potters Bar, Herts., (c 1930), nowadays adjoining the M25. The Major, Master and huntsman 1907–35 is second left. All his hunt staff rode greys.

Jim Meads, later the renowned hunting photographer, being blooded by Enfield Chace huntsman Ted Cox in 1938. Born out of ancient hunting rites, the controversial practice of smearing a little fox's blood on the face of a young person who for the first time got to the end of a hunt, dwindled in post-war years and has been quietly dropped in the last decade. Although often condemned in anti-hunting propaganda, no harmful effect on young personalities was ever established. If anything, blooding was regarded proudly in rural communities as a mark of growing maturity and confidence.

Foxhunting in some countries from north to south was hit sporadically, and severely in some areas, throughout much of the 1920s by outbreaks of foot and mouth in cattle. Although horses do not contract foot and mouth disease, because it is confined to cloven footed animals, there is a perceived risk of carrying the disease from one farm to the next by the passage of mounted and foot followers across the land.

The terrible consequences for farmers in losing whole herds of cattle and flocks of sheep which have to be destroyed, while farms are placed in quarantine, clearly makes hunting impossible in infected areas, or even nearby.

Since foxhunting is deeply embedded in the countryside, and owes its existence to farmers and landowners, some closely involved in Hunts, the immediate response of Hunts is to close down voluntarily even before regulations are imposed. However, the regulations in the 1920s were far less draconian than today and local stoppages of only a week, imposed by the Ministry of Agriculture, were quite common.

Baily's Hunting Directory 1926–27 lamented: 'Only a year ago we heard of a pack which was delayed and had no cubhunting on account of foot and mouth disease, and when it was able to take the field found that many litters of cubs, which had been previously located had moved their quarters, in some cases doubtless owing to the coverts having been shot through, and this pack had no sport worthy of the name before Christmas and very little afterwards.'

Baily's reported in the 1925–26 season 'a good deal of interruption from the regulations imposed to prevent the spread of foot and mouth disease, and a fair number of packs were at times prevented from hunting, some of them more than once.

'The Belvoir, Quorn, Cottesmore, Fernie and Pytchley all suffered, some of them two or three times, as did the packs in Lincolnshire and South Yorkshire, while once or twice there was a good deal of restricted country in the Duke of Beaufort's Hunt, and in the neighbouring country over which Lord Bathurst presides.

'Further north, where the disease had caused a total stoppage of hunting a year or two before, they were fairly free from the restrictions, and this also applies to the Cheshire and Sir Watkin's Hunts which had lost a whole season previously.

'The arrangements made between the government authorities and the Masters of Foxhounds Association worked out very smoothly, and it is quite certain that this ban on restricted areas was removed as quickly as possible. Foot and mouth disease is by no means at an end; lately there have been outbreaks in Shropshire, Kent and elsewhere, and the outlook is not so bright as it might have been.'

Lord Leconfield, Chairman of the MFHA said at their 1926 annual meeting that he had written to the Minister of Agriculture drawing his attention 'to the very serious position which would arise in my opinion in Leicestershire through a continuation of the stopping of hunting due to foot and mouth disease. I felt that Leicestershire was a county which practically lived on hunting; especially the towns of Melton Mowbray, Market Harborough and Oakham would be most terribly hit.'

The Chairman clearly had no success: he received 'a very courteous letter' from the Minister, but he declined to exclude foxhounds from restrictions considered necessary for suppression of the disease. With hindsight the Minister was right. Nothing would have harmed foxhunting more than a direct connection between the sport and a new outbreak.

Lord Leconfield remarked: 'Let us hope that all these efforts will contribute toward the suppression and stamping out of the disease.'

Some modern opinion is that if governments in the 1920s had imposed the nationwide measures used in the controversial outbreak of 2001, it was likely the outbreak could have been confined to one year. It would have entailed a total ban on stock movements throughout Britain, with some disease-free herds and flocks being slaughtered adjacent to infected areas, and strict sanitary regulations. Probably without modern communications and means of recording farm stock, such a solution in the 1920s was impracticable.

The Fernie in the grazing country of south Leicestershire had its fixtures interrupted severely by foot and mouth outbreaks for three years from 1923–26. Sport was so curtailed in the 1923–24 season that some members of the Hunt earned criticism by organising paper chases on horseback across country, although they rode in unaffected areas.

Fox Mange

Mange is a natural scourge which hits fox populations occasionally, and mysteriously. Hunting with hounds is the best method of finding and monitoring it, and Hunts have played a significant part in helping to quell it.

Foxhunters have sometimes blamed the disease on 'dustbin foxes', those that live by scavenging in and around towns and villages, and have then been dumped in the countryside as a 'solution'. This was allegedly being carried out in major towns and cities by certain freelance pest destruction groups working for local authorities which opposed foxhunting, but were willing to export urban foxes when they became a problem – anything but a humane solution for a fox already stricken with mange, and now forced to compete for food with other foxes in a strange environment.

The disease can leave a fox in abject misery, hairless and reduced to a skeleton. Finding and killing such a fox with hounds is a merciful exercise, and it happens. Huntsmen are well aware that mange is communicable to hounds, although it can be treated successfully in kennel if detected early enough.

Baily's reported with satisfaction in the 1920s that the fox population was plentiful, and had fully recovered from the decimations which had occurred at the beginning of the century through a wide-spread outbreak of mange. Some packs at that time were known to draw blank for as many as five days in succession due to the shortage of foxes.

Claims that hunting assists conservation of the fox are supported by the fact that the sportsman's need for a sustainable population makes it essential for Hunt coverts to be kept entirely free of foxes with mange.

Hounds are the best means of detecting and locating outbreaks, and the hunting practice of maintaining a close season during the summer months when litters are being reared, and maturing, has clearly helped Britain's fox population to recover from periodic outbreaks of mange which could have caused near extinction in some areas.

'Ware Wire Again

Despite foot and mouth and the risk of mange in foxes, it was typical of the comparatively care-free atmosphere of 1920s hunting that *Baily's* considered 'the greatest trouble of the present day is without doubt wire fencing and this, we are sorry to say, increases every year.

'Indeed, in a considerable number of Hunts the wire question has become almost acute, for it is not only followers of hounds, but huntsmen and whippers-in who are held up, and this means that very frequently, especially on days of moderate scent, the huntsman cannot get to his hounds when his presence is absolutely necessary if he is to continue to hunt the fox.

'We need hardly say that in many countries a great deal, if not all the wire, is taken up at the beginning of the season, and put down in the spring, and there are also countries in which the wire is well or fairly well marked, but there are also many districts in which it is not marked at all, or so badly marked as to be of little value.'

Baily's bemoaned 'danger signals' of wire which could scarcely be seen until the rider was all too close to the fence. It advised using signal posts six to eight feet high on farms where all the fences were cut and laid, but where the tops of hedges were uncut, signal poles should be at least fifteen feet high, painted scarlet to show wire in a fence, and plain white to denote where there was a wicket gate or slip rails.

Hunts were advised to form Wire Committees to deal with the problem by making annual summer inspections of all danger signals, organising new ones, and putting in hunting gates where necessary.

This was carried out diligently by many Hunts throughout Britain. You can still find small hunting gateways which were first established early in the twentieth century. They may nowadays be used by ramblers as well as riders, and they form an essential part of the network of paths and rights of way which make the English countryside uniquely accessible.

Access by consent, achieved and carefully maintained by the Hunts, has been one of the sport's major contributions to the countryside. *Baily's* 1926 reported with horror a recent occasion when a pack ran into some country which it had not visited for several seasons.

Hounds were held up by a new wire fence in front of a hedge, a mile long. Then the pack found a way through, but none of the mounted staff and followers could

A growing number of cars are seen at meets in the 1930s. Here the Middleton are meeting at High Catton, Yorkshire, in 1932.

catch up with hounds, 'and they were not found until dusk, and then four or five miles away and still hunting'.

Compared with the restrictions imposed by wire and other barriers later in the century, the between the war years were a paradise, but the increasing use of wire to fence pastures was the first warning that the sport would have to adapt to a countryside much changed from the open terrain which had made possible its Victorian golden age.

With lethally busy roads scything through the countryside in the postwar years, Hunts could not risk hounds running beyond the control of huntsmen until dusk, and it says much for modern standards of hound control, and the management of a day's hunting, that the sport has been able to survive in such an environment.

From the 1920s one of the subjects which continue to appear frequently on Hunt Committee agendas was the cost and supply of split rails to make and repair fencing.

The late Arthur Dalgety, Master of the Southdown from 1929–52, is credited with an invention which radically changed the practice of jumping across country, and was probably instrumental in allowing Britons to avoid learning to jump barbed wire as a matter of course, as the Harrier Hunt followers do habitually in New Zealand. Mr Dalgety produced a triangular wooden construction called the 'tiger trap' which sits in hedge-rows, and can conveniently cover an open ditch if necessary.

It offers an inviting jump approached from either direction and is stock proof, although in the summer it may have a single strand of barbed wire stretched along the top which can easily be removed when hunting recommences.

In the United States the triangular jump is often filled in, and is called a 'coop', offering a similarly inviting jump when placed in a wired up field boundary.

Alternatively, Hunts began to use special sets of rails in fences, and later in the century they were major customers for discarded telegraph poles which make virtually unbreakable material for tiger traps and Hunt rails.

The practice of queuing to jump these obstacles became normal in the hunting field in many provincial countries in the 1930s, and increased markedly after the second world war. It eroded some of the cherished 'hooroosh of the chase' which had first attracted risk taking young riders to the sport.

Fortunately, these special Hunt jumps enabled mounted fields to cross the more wired up pieces of country to gain quicker access to the paradises of pasture, cut and laid fences and jumpable rails which still existed. The crucial factor was, and still is, that such hunting land usually belonged to landowners and farmers who firmly supported hunting.

Such a terrain, with an abundance of natural hedges, is precisely that recommended later in the century by conservationists who condemned the more rigorous farming techniques practised on arable farms which involved rooting out fences, creating huge prairies of plough where crops are produced with the aid of chemical fertilisers and pest controls, where no bird sings and insect life is greatly reduced.

Up to the present day many packs employ full-time or part-time fencing men who put in gates and bridges, as well as fencing to help the Hunt's passage across country, while ensuring that land is stock proof to the farmers' satisfaction.

It is far more thrilling to jump three or four bars of rails, perhaps standing by a ditch, and many Hunts have invested heavily in split rails to maintain such fencing wherever possible. They break far more easily than tiger traps, but they are relatively easy to mend, provided the fence-builder can get access with a load of fresh timber in the latter part of a season when the ground may be water-logged. More than a few fence-builders use quad bikes for such jobs nowadays.

The greatest drawbacks of small tiger-traps and narrow jumping places which cause queuing is that the ground either side can become heavily poached in wet conditions. Horses find that although they are not jumping a large obstacle they have to heave their feet out of one mud bath only to land in another, and nasty accidents can happen because some of the more experienced hunters are inclined to treat jumping tiger traps with too little care.

A fall in which you are jumped on by the next horse in the queue is a real hazard in modern foxhunting – it involves little of the zing of jumping an inviting hedge and ditch at a gallop, but the tiger trap accident when it does occur can be one of the worst.

The art of collecting your horse to ensure that is balanced, and jumping prop-erly off a stride, is just as necessary over the lowly tiger-trap as it is over a five-barred gate. On the occasions when gates are jumped, usually only in prime areas of hunting country, the breaker of a gate has to pay for its replacement.

The greatest boon in Leicestershire and Rutland, and some other counties, is

Eve of war: the Puckeridge meet on an airfield on 11 January, 1939 at the RAF Station near Debden, Essex. The Hunt operated in restricted form throughout the war, aided by local farmers.

the existence of wide grass verges alongside roads and lanes, which enables even large mounted fields to canter long distances on old turf, by-passing the most intensely ploughed areas, before returning to pasture. The verges also enable horses to jump more safely on and off roads.

My definition of a top-class riding country, as a hunting correspondent visiting many different terrains, was a country where it was often possible to leap from a field on to a verge reasonably easily; it is one of the quickest ways of speeding up the field's experience of riding after hounds.

The roots of all these essential adjustments to their hunting countries were made between the wars, and they enabled foxhunting to adapt all the more easily to the greater changes coming in the later post-war years.

'Spending money on the country', in fencing, cut and laying fences, repairing stone walls, and covert maintenance, is an investment in the nature of a rural landscape which is so much admired as one of Britain's greatest assets.

Few of the millions of Britons who only view fields from the roads realise that country sports play the key role alongside agriculture, in determining the shape and content of our landscapes.

CHAPTER 4

SURVIVAL ABOVE ALL . . .

FOXHUNTING'S survival in the Second World War was entirely due to the farmers of Britain.

This was to be a far more grim test for the sport than the Great War. More than a dozen packs ceased to operate. Hounds were reduced to a nucleus, and all suffered severe difficulties in struggling to survive. Hundreds of hounds, carefully bred for centuries, were shot in their prime. Some lines were saved by hounds being sent to the USA or India.

The 1938–39 edition of *Baily's Hunting Directory* listed a total of 228 packs of Foxhounds in the United Kingdom and Ireland, comprising 189 packs in England and Wales; twenty-eight in Ireland, and eleven in Scotland.

Evidence that the sport not only survived the Second World War but made a remarkable recovery immediately afterwards is provided by *Baily's Hunting Directory* foxhunting list in its 1949–50 edition, which showed an increase of ten packs, 238 in total, comprising: 197 in England and Wales; thirty-one in Ireland; and ten in Scotland.

It was said that the fragmentation of some hunting countries into smaller packs just after the war was due to the shortage of petrol and suitable vehicles in austerity Britain to convey horses and hounds, making local hunting more convenient. Some Hunts were divided into north and south countries, or other divisions were made. Yet the increase in Hunts was equally due to more people seeking refreshment and recreation in the countryside after the war.

Up to the war many Hunts bred and maintained large packs, partly because they were likely to be decimated by up to a third or more by outbreaks of

44

distemper. The huge cuts in hound numbers in the war seemed at the time to impose damage to the breed which would take many generations to repair. In fact, increased breeding programmes were put in hand remarkably quickly in the austerity period after the war, a sign of the priorities for many country people seeking a return to normality.

One plank of government policy assisted foxhunting: at last British agriculture was to be fully recognised. After the appalling depression of farming in the 1930s when it was desperately afflicted by cheap imports of food, and good farm land became almost valueless in many areas, the British farmer was promoted high up the list of national priorities. Farm subsidies were started, and War Agricultural Committees formed in each county to step-up food production. Michael Berry, who used to write so well on hunting for *The Times*, recorded in his excellent history of the Puckeridge Hunt that 'not only did the farmers not object to hunting continuing in wartime, they took the trouble to approach the Masters of Hounds in the Puckeridge country, and in numerous other countries, and implored them to keep the packs in existence.

'They promised to help in the all important matter of food – hay for the horses and all kinds of waste products, unfit for human consumption, for the hounds.

'The farmers were indeed the only people who could offer such food, so from that aspect again they held the future of foxhunting in their hands, and they made sure it survived.'

Three generations of Puckeridge Masters: Edward Barclay, *centre* (Master 1896–1948), *left* Major Maurice Barclay (1910–62 MFH) and Captain Charles Barclay (1947–2002)

In the Puckeridge at a meeting on 3 February 1940, the farmers begged the Masters to continue on a reduced scale as long as possible, and promised their practical help including forage. Foxhunting was maintained by men and women too old, or unfit for the services, or otherwise exempt, who kept kennels and small stocks of hounds going virtually in the spare time left from war work in many other capacities, such as Air Raid Wardens or the Home Guard.

Staff suddenly disappeared, and Hunt horses and hounds were subject to restricted rations on coupons ordained by government. As the war progressed hunting was stopped at the end of January, ostensibly to obliterate any possible risk of damage to growing crops.

The feeding of rice and Scotch oats to hounds in kennels ceased. Raw flesh was fed to hounds from fallen stock collected by Hunts from farmers as an essential part of farming practice. The Pytchley's veteran huntsman Stanley Barker recalled that someone in the Hunt had been clever enough to buy a large batch of condemned ship's biscuits, of pre-1914 vintage, which fed the Pytchley hounds for about two seasons.

Later potatoes and brewers' grains were the basis of the hounds' diet. Barker's diaries recorded: 'The experience shattered a few long held beliefs on feeding – the hounds were just as fit.' The Pytchley, one of the great Hunts of England, was reduced officially to two days a week hunting, with the season sharply curtailed at the end of January.

Officially foxhunting continued because it was seen to be part of a pest destruction exercise that the farmers deemed necessary in assisting increased stock farming, especially sheep and poultry production. Free range poultry raising was the norm at that time, and thus stocks were much more prone to fox depredation.

Cub-hunting and the full season were officially to be conducted on the same lines, with as many foxes killed as possible, coverts being held up. Inevitably hounds sometimes hunted foxes in the open, and occasionally good hunts across country took place. The wartime fields often included servicemen and women fortunate enough to be on leave in the United Kingdom. More than a few Hunts quietly achieved quite remarkable sport at times, entertaining small mounted fields.

There was no question of second horses, and many followers wore ratcatcher dress in the small mounted fields, some riding unclipped and unplaited horses, far from hunting fit. As in the First World War the government immediately requisitioned many hunters for war service. The Army sent mounted cavalry regiments abroad to Palestine, the 1st Cavalry Regiment and all the yeomanry regiments. Some 20,000 horses, including black cavalry horses and requisitioned hunters, were sent with the intention of 'maintaining a British influence' in the Middle East. The regiments were training to protect the eastern approaches to the Suez Canal, and the horsed cavalry regiments were also earmarked to move into Turkey should the Germans have attacked through the Balkans or Caucasus.

Ulrica Murray Smith jauntily recalled the 1939–40 season during the phoney war as 'the greatest fun' in the Quorn country. 'The hunting was marvellous with very few people out and sport was as good as ever. The field consisted of some

Ulrica Murray Smith, *centre*, and her husband Tony Murray Smith, heading the Quorn field in 1955.

officers in uniform and a few locals; there was a wonderful pack of hounds and still all that glorious grass. 'Of course we realised how lucky we were to be able to hunt at all, and that we must make the most of it; it might be a long time before we hunted again.'

Ulrica asserts that one Leicestershire hunting lady, married three times, was so upset at the thought of her third husband having to go to the war, that to prevent him going she shot him in the bottom with a twelve bore gun as he was climbing over a fence out shooting. It is fair to say that this lapse of patriotism was not typical of the hunting world where keen foxhunters were often among the first to join up, sometimes for the second time.

Some of the military enjoyed foxhunting abroad, but not for long. After the phoney war period, hunting in Leicestershire ceased entirely until after the war for Ulrica and her husband, Tony Murray Smith.

Tony Murray Smith was posted to Palestine in February, 1940, taking his own charger. Ulrica wangled her way to Palestine, with a few other cavalry wives, and they enjoyed racing Army remount horses on the beaches at Nathanya. Tony and other officers hunted fox and jackel in Palestine with Col. 'Mouse' Townsend and his Ramle Vale Hunt. According to Ulrica, when Tony saw the first convoy coming through from Baghdad to Haifa, peering over the tail board of a lorry were two foxhounds, a draft from the Royal Baghdad Foxhounds to the Ramle Vale.

The tradition of the British Cavalry and other regiments engaging in

Bay de Courcy-Parry, who wrote as 'Dalesman' for *Horse & Hound*, presenting a cup to Eskdale and Ennerdale Master Edmund Porter at Rydal in 1979.

foxhunting whilst on foreign service is a very old one, especially in the Middle East and India. The most illustrious military foxhunter abroad in Europe was the Duke of Wellington who insisted on hunting regularly throughout his battles with the French in the Peninsular wars in Spain and Portugal early in the nineteenth century.

The strains of the hunting horn were to be heard sometimes in battle in the Second World War as they had been on the Western Front in the first war. Monty before the Battle of Alamein wished his senior officers 'Good Hunting!'

Horse & Hound's charismatic hunting correspondent, C.N. ('Bay') de Courcy-Parry, writing as 'Dalesman' rejoined the Army for the second time and became a 'mule walloper', an officer in a mule pack company, serving in India. He encouraged readers to send the magazine on to servicemen abroad. Many were hunting men yearning for the pleasures of the Chase again, and hoping the sport would survive the war.

Dalesman's call was answered, and *Horse & Hound* received a special message from the Middle East for publication : 'General Montgomery wishes to thank all the readers of *Horse & Hound* who have so kindly sent their copies to him for distribution to the soldiers of the 8th Army. They have been greatly appreciated.' The Cavalry in Palestine were soon to be mechanised and saw much action in the Middle East and later in the European campaign.

Ulrica Murray Smith spent much of the rest of the war in India, working for

SOE, but she managed to get some hunting – with the Bombay Jackal Club pack. The Quorn, like other packs, was soon subject to wartime shrinkage, and was maintained by its huntsman George Barker, often on a diet of cabbages and potatoes which he grew behind the kennels and boiled up. In 1939 the Quorn sent out thirty-six and a half couple of young hounds to walk; by 1941 only eight and a half couple were sent out, such was the reduction of hounds kept in kennel. Philip Cantrell-Hubbersty was Acting Master for the Quorn committee during the war

Lord (Toby) Daresbury remained Master of the Belvoir, and dashed from Hyde Park Barracks to Leicestershire to assist huntsman George Tongue in running the kennels and hunting hounds on a limited basis.

The Cottesmore was preserved during the war largely through the efforts of Lady Helena Hilton-Green, daughter of Earl Fitzwilliam and known widely simply as 'Boodley'. She was married to one of the greatest Masters of the Cottesmore, 'Chatty' Hilton-Green, a renowned amateur huntsmen, of whom

John Robson, MFH Old Surrey and Burstow (1974–86), Chairman South of England Hound Show.

more later. Herbert Norman, kennel huntsman, hunted the hounds during the war.

Not untypical of many packs in countries outside the Shires was the Old Surrey and Burstow in the commuter country south of London, from the Surrey Hills down to Haywards Heath in Sussex. On the outbreak of war the horses in kennel were reduced from eighteen to two. The Hunt managed to continue sending out hounds one day a week during the season until the war was over, with Col. Robinson as Master and Jim Owen as his Deputy, and Alfred Petts as the sole member of the Hunt staff, carrying out all duties in kennel and in the field.

'From 1942 hunting was conducted on foot and a good many foxes were accounted for and litters destroyed,' records John Robson in his Hunt history (*A Portrait of Jorrocks's Country*, 2000). The Hunt Report thanked 'those ladies and gentlemen who assisted with the arduous task of controlling the hounds when out hunting on bicycle or foot'.

Fox destruction as a form of pest control to aid agriculture during the war was regarded as so important that some counties paid a bounty for each fox killed. John Robson says East Sussex was still paying a 7s.6d. bounty per fox in 1945. In 1944 the Master declared the last remaining horse in kennels was unfit for work, and they were down to seven couple of hounds.

The season ran from the end of September to the middle of March when the Ministry of Agriculture rations for hounds stopped. The history of the Burton Hunt in Lincolnshire, by Robert Fountain refers to the drastic pruning of the pack after the Hunt Committee decided to carry on at the start of the war. Hunting was confined to one, and occasionally two, days per week in parts of the country within hacking distance of the kennels. The days had to be short to ensure hounds could return to kennels before the blackout.

The followers were mainly women and children. A painting of a Burton wartime meet shows the field down to three Army officers, seven women and six children. The pack comprised ten and a half couple of hounds, instead of the usual size, near twenty couple. The Burton hounds were being fed on potatoes, mangolds, swedes and barley. Ted Parry, the huntsman, managed almost single-handed throughout the war, with some help from his young children.

Money to keep Hunts running became an acute problem. Few people had the time to hunt, nor the ability to keep a horse. Total subscriptions to the Burton for 1940–41 were down to £303, rising by 1945 to £525. Robert Fountain wrote: 'It speaks volumes for their sportsmanship that many continued to subscribe without hunting.' The Burton Hunt Committee noted that coupons were available to allow nine hundredweight of food per month: three hundredweight of meal and six hundredweight of horse feed. If the horse allowances were not used there would be sufficient for the hounds for the year, but the Committee was concerned it did not have the funds to buy the meagre rations.

Donations, and gifts from supportive farmers filled the gaps and enabled the Burton to struggle through the war. At each annual meeting the question of whether to continue was considered, but somehow the Hunt survived.

Similar stories in packs all over Britain indicate the importance which hunting people placed on their sport to make sacrifices throughout the war so that it would be part of a peace-time countryside. They confirm that officials and farmers believed foxhunting played a realistic role in fox control, not only in killing foxes, but in spreading fox populations, alleviating the pressure on stock breeding, especially poultry and sheep rearing.

The recreational aspect of foxhunting was as much valued in the countryside in wartime as other entertainments in the cities. Keeping up morale on the Home Front was a priority for a civilian population suffering bombing and other stress. The importance of foxhunting in wartime was somewhat inappropriately emphasised by the veteran Master Lord Leconfield who continued to hunt his own hounds in Sussex. According to legend, during a day's hunting in 1940 his hounds checked when they encountered some young men playing a game of football. His Lordship was so shocked that he stood in his stirrups and yelled across the pitch: 'Haven't you people got anything better to do in wartime than play *football?* Lord Leconfield's generation would have been astonished at the changes to come.

March of the Plough

No matter how helpful to foxhunting were the wartime farmers their efforts were changing the face of much of rural England, especially in the Midlands, in a manner which threatened the nature of the sport for the future.

The sea of grass which had so entranced the foxhunters attracted to the Shire packs, was receding fast, as pasture gave way to plough. The mechanisation of farming accelerated the process; tractor drawn ploughs could produce arable land farmed up to the hedgerows. Some of the precious hedges, and even some smaller coverts, were rooted out to allow more acreage for food production.

Official surveys in the 1920s and '30s showed that eighty-five per cent of Leicestershire was down to permanent grass. The major trend towards arable farming in the war meant that land still down to grass was reduced to forty-one per cent by 1943. Foxhunters who quietly mourned the agricultural revolution as heralding the end of their sport as they knew it did not have an inkling of the far more sweeping changes in the terrain on the way throughout the rest of the century – nor would they have believed their sport would survive them.

Yorkshire and some other northern counties saw similar change, and south of Leicestershire the great foxhunting counties of Northamptonshire, Buckinghamshire, Oxfordshire, and Gloucestershire were among those hardest hit by the change to arable instead of pastoral farming. Yet when peace came in 1945 much of the environment of rural England was still a paradise for the foxhunter compared with today. Mechanical farming still had a long way to go before many more thousands of hedgerows would be destroyed, and motorways and huge enlargements of cities and suburbs were still to come. The uplands, the moorlands and huge areas of pastoral farming land remained suitable for the sport. The spread of arable farming was a patchwork rather than a blanket, and the bulk of the coverts and hedgerows remained in place at the end of the war. The worst was yet come.

By the 1970s British farming was losing 55,000 acres of land to building, industry and roads each year. There were about eighteen million acres of permanent grass, and seventeen million acres of rough grazing – against thirty-five million acres under crops.

The dire state of pasture lands in the Shires by the start of the 'seventies meant that more than 170,000 acres was under plough, compared with 54,000 acres under plough in 1939. In pre-war years ninety per cent of Northamptonshire was under grass; by 190 about fifty-three per cent was arable. Rutland's former grassy surface had given way to about sixty-five per cent arable farming.

One reason why governments allowed themselves to tolerate loss of farming land was the ever increasing production achieved on the remaining land. More intensive farming methods did not help foxhunting; traditional furrows gave way to circular ploughs, cultivating land right up to the hedgerows, instead of allowing headlands, and break crops, or fields lying fallow, became less common.

It was not until the end of the century that the set-aside system of subsidy was installed, producing large areas of uncultivated land, usually crossable by the Hunts. On the credit side in the postwar years, the immense changes in farming as a revived industry, receiving subsidies, and guaranteed cereal prices, was more prosperous and confident than in the 1930s.

More of those who farmed and derived their income from the land would themselves be able to afford to run, and to enjoy country sports in the postwar years – and this proved a far better recipe for survival than heavy reliance on foxhunting 'carpet-baggers' from London and elsewhere. 'Keeping a horse about the place for fun' became much more commonplace again on many British farms. Foxhunting, and indeed point-to-pointing and steeplechasing, and other horse sorts all benefitted.

The Vital Coalition

Foxhunting's weekly bible, *Horse & Hound*, survived a terrible war. Its Editor and proprietor since the magazine was founded in 1884, Arthur Portman, was killed with his wife when his London home was demolished in an air raid in 1940. The company secretary, Walter Case was whisked off to war service after heroic efforts to keep the magazine alive.

The magazine's offices in the Adelphi were severely damaged by bombing, and its printers completely destroyed in another raid, but the magazine never lost an issue throughout the war, passing into the ownership of Odhams Press.

When he returned from service in the Far East, Case took up the reins as the second Editor, and was astonished by the speed and resilience with which the hunting and equestrian scene revived. He recalled: 'The general shortage of quality horses was fairly evident for some time. In the early years of the war thousands of people, finding it impossible to keep their horses, gave them away or in many cases had them put down.

'With the end of hostilities it was not long before the various sports revived with amazing rapidity.'

The weekly circulation of *Horse & Hound* soared from below 10,000 before the war to an all-time high of some 96,000 in the late 1970s, when hunting and racing were still the predominant sports reflected in the magazine.

Leading horsemen who revived equestrianism immediately after the war nearly all had a military background, and regarded foxhunting as a normal part of their life-style. They figured frequently in and indeed were encouraged to use it as their platform in popularising and expanding horse sports.

As a national weekly, the magazine enabled hunting people to gain information in depth on the growing opposition to their sport, signalled most alarmingly by the first attempt at a Private Member's Bill to ban hunting in 1949.

Chief of the nationally known horsemen was Col. Sir Mike Ansell who had adored his hunting during military service in the 1930s. He was a keen point-to-point rider and developed a special interest in showjumping. Blinded during the retreat to Dunkirk he became a prisoner-of-war and during his incarceration devised plans to revive showjumping at home after the war.

He led the postwar successes of major horse shows, notably the Horse of the Year Show. He and fellow Army officers had no hesitation in making sure that hunting was represented in their shows by parades of hounds, and strong hunter showing sections.

On many an evening in the Cavalry Club Mike would regale me with stories of his pre-war hunting, much of it in the north when he was stationed at Catterick. He was very pleased that the new Editor of *Horse & Hound* hunted at least twice a week, and took the closest interest. A genuine hero, Mike Ansell never complained nor whined about losing his own life in the saddle through blindness, but strived mightily to ensure that the new generation had the chance to enjoy horsemanship at its best in the postwar years, and hunting had a high priority.

The links between racing, the horse shows world and the hunting field formed a coalition where there was a close rapport, and a shared enthusiasm among specialist horsemen just at the time when the political opposition to foxhunting was growing after Labour took power in 1945.

What is Public Relations?

It is significant that two voices best known to the public as spokesmen on TV for horsemanship were Masters of Foxhounds: Dorian Williams was born and bred to foxhunting, and was a Master of the Grafton, and most famously of the Whaddon Chase, and Raymond Brooks-Ward, later to be equally well known on BBC Television as equestrian commentator, was Master of the Enfield Chace.

Dorian Williams was a schoolmaster, and an innovator in running his own adult education centre. In his autobiography *Master of One* (Dent, 1978) he revealed some of the strains felt in the foxhunting world in the 1950s in adapting to a new world where communication with the general public was becoming a necessity for a sport increasingly projected by its opponents. The dilemma for the Masters of Foxhounds Association was whether to put its head above the parapet, or simply strive to keep the subject of hunting off the agenda for the national press, radio and the growing medium of television. In the past it had

Dorian Williams, Master of the Whaddon Chase and BBC TV equestrian
commentetor, with huntsman Albert Buckle who had just given Dorian
his hunting horn, on Dorian's last day in 1980.

worked reasonably well simply to look the other way, and not respond in detail
to occasional charges of 'cruelty for fun'.

In 1958 Dorian Williams entertained the Masters of Foxhounds Committee at
his adult education centre, Pendley, in Hertfordshire, for a seminar, mainly on
hound breeding. At the last session he was invited to speak on public relations.
Dorian felt he was not entirely popular with all his fellow MFHs, some of whom
thought he received, and courted, publicity far too much. They distrusted some
of his radical ideas and his own role as a broadcaster.

As late as the 1950s 'a respected Master of Hounds was hardly expected to
have a job, other than as a landowner and a farmer, or possibly as something in
the City,' wrote Dorian. 'To be part of the media was totally alien, even a little
common. My desire to popularise hunting, my enthusiasm for Supporters'
Clubs, was definitely suspect. I was reported as riskily *avant-garde*.'

In his address Dorian declared that the new skills of public relations were just
as important in foxhunting, as with industry, entertainment and government. He
described the right and wrong ways of dealing with the press, and gave imitations
of a blimpish Master saying such things to local reporters as 'No comment, damn
your eyes.'

Dorian recalled that during his talk 'the faces of my audience seemed to be getting longer and longer. I was received in polite and stony silence. Only Ronnie Wallace, at the end, told me he had agreed with everything that I had said.'

Dorian wrote in his autobiography 'Until recently publicity of any sort has been anethama to the so called upper classes, and to the old county families in particular.

'Other than in the society papers one's name should never appear in print, and one never allowed oneself to be interviewed or quoted. In contrast to the publicity surrounding entertainers and politicians, a certain anonymity as far as the media were concerned was considered essential for the country gentleman.' Wallace's response was significant. He was to be Chairman of the Masters of Foxhounds Association for twenty-two years from 1970, a hugely challenging period for the sport on and off the hunting field.

Virtually every recommendation made by Dorian Williams in 1958 was to become standard procedure for the conduct of foxhunting from the beginning of Wallace's reign, which is an appropriate way of describing his chairmanship. His predecessor for six years as MFHA chairman, Lord Halifax, began to move in the direction necessary for a more sophisticated response to increasing press interest, and political pressure, on hunting with hounds, but all field sports were responding, often too late, rather than being pro-active.

During the 1960s and early 1970s when I was a BBC staff correspondent I found Charles Halifax exceedingly affable and approachable, and well aware of the need to ensure good relationships with the media. He certainly knew how to tread the corridors of power; his father, the first Earl of Halifax had been the controversial Foreign Secretary in the dark years of 1938–40.

The heart of the problem at that time was that the MFHA and the British Field Sports Society were operating without the level of public relations muscle and expertise already needed to cope with the fast growing battalions of the media. Dorian Williams's reception by his fellow Masters in 1958 indicates the closed minds of all too many traditional leaders of the sport in dealing with the new challenges.

Founded in 1881 mainly to adjudicate on Hunt boundaries, the Masters of Foxhounds Association had a constitution which ensured that fresh, radical minds from outside hunting could not become even ex-officio members of the Committee, nor that they would be listened to for long.

Although Wallace was prepared to engage any number of changes to save his sport, he baulked at such radical changes as providing a permanent seat on the MFHA Committee for the Hunt Supporters' Clubs, which by the late 1970s were becoming exceedingly important in fund raising and other forms of support for Hunts all over Britain.

'We can't have the tail wagging the dog,' was Ronnie Wallace's response to the idea of role for a Hunt Supporters' representative, even if it was non-executive.

The twelve-strong MFHA Committee is self-perpetuating in that it elects its own members, and chooses its own chairman. Thus Masters from the general membership are selected from above, not elected by their peers to go on the

Committee. The annual general meeting of the MFHA is a reviewing and approving body, not a radical opinion making forum.

In a sport which tends to attract strong minded individualists, with leadership qualities, there has always been plenty of expression of opinion, but it is usually 'off the record' or put to the leadership discreetly through private channels, rather than being the subject of open dispute at such a gathering as the annual meeting.

One reason for such caution is that up to the 1960s the strong military element in hunting instilled extreme caution in allowing unfettered debate by those under command. Hunting was in the unusual position of having to defend its very existence, and some hunting people learned to their horror that a friendly chat to a reporter did not mean a friendly article appearing in the press; indeed it could result in an alarmingly hostile or misleading article in which the views of the animal rights extremist would figure prominently as well.

'No comment' was safer in the short term, but it was already becoming apparent in the late 1950s that it would not suffice for much longer, as Dorian Williams was endeavouring to point out. The august gentlemen of the MFHA committee at that time could look back on a decade in which they and their fellow Masters had led something of a miracle: the revival of their sport to an extraordinary degree after the major setback of the war, followed by a Socialist government causing far greater problems than had been presented at the end of the previous world war.

Leading the Revival

Hunt committees found keen young men, and a few women, willing to take on Masterships; the system of professional Hunt service revived remarkably well, considering the number of better paid options opening up in expanding postwar industries; Hunt countries were being organised into Wire Fund districts to deal with the barbed wire menace; most important of all, hound breeding was swiftly revived and Hunt kennels were returning to full strength, if not the volume of hounds kept in pre-war years, which was not necessarily a drawback in running a modern Hunt.

Horse breeding was another activity which began to boom; there was a larger stock of horses suitable for the hunting field still over the border in Ireland which had been neutral during the war, and importations of excellent Irish hunters soon began to assist the growth of mounted fields in the early post-war years.

Plenty of good sport was still possible despite the increase in ploughed land, and most important of all the post-war farming industry continued to exercise its historic role as the hosts for Hunts throughout Brtain and in the Irish Republic.

To the surprise of older foxhunters, somehow funds were found during the austerity years to pay for the revival. It was a considerable struggle for some Hunts, and it was another testimony to the priority given to the sport that money was forthcoming.

Hunter-trials, hunt balls, farmers' dances, skittle matches, summer cricket,

School children admire the Cottesmore hounds, with their huntsman Neil Coleman at a meet at Brooke, near Oakham, in the 2003–4 season.

and a host of other activity, much of it generated by the Pony Club in summer, revived on a more hectic scale than ever before, aided by the countryside's comparative prosperity since the 1930s.

Paying for It

The first post-war years were the most difficult, especially for smaller Hunts in far flung locations. One of the most eloquent of immediate post-war Masters, David Brock, author of the excellent handbook *To Hunt the Fox*, wrote about the severe problems of foxhunting finance, no doubt based on his own experiences; he was a Joint Master of the Cumberland Farmers from 1948–52.

He suggested, in an article in the 1947–48 edition of *The Horseman's Year*, various economies which he felt could be made in running a Hunt, compared with the expenses regarded as essential before the war.

Brock asserted that the cost of everything in a Hunt had doubled since 1938, and that 'the private incomes of men suitable for Masterships are but little more than half what they were in 1938.' Post-war taxation by the Labour government was biting unearned incomes.

He suggested in a three-day-a-week provincial Hunt where the Master was hunting hounds helped by two professional whippers-in, wages in 1938 amounted to some £15 per week ; now they had risen 'to at least £32'.

Brock suggested it was time to hunt hounds with only one whipper-in. He was ahead of his time: the practice became common later in the century in many Hunts, except packs in fashionable, or well populated, countries attracting the largest subscriptions. For example Hunts in the South-East of England may suffer from cramped hunting countries, but they are supported by the richest cross-sections of society, benefiting from businesses and professions on London scales.

Brock's experiences were therefore not typical of all Hunts, but they showed just how little money could finance hunting in far flung provincial areas in the late 1940s and '50s, even taking into account the much lower levels of monetary inflation at that time. He was seeking to demonstrate that some £1,400 a year could be saved in a Master's budget, and about £400 on the Committee's own expenses.

The arrival of the amateur whipper-in to augment the staff in the field proved to be the answer for many a Hunt, and is still widely adopted. He suggested that feeding a pack of hounds on oatmeal and cooked flesh could cost £600, and he proposed continuing to feed raw flesh, as had been the case during the war years, greatly reducing the cost, since unlimited flesh from fallen stock could be obtained free, apart from labour in kennel knackering the carcases. He proposed abandoning the tradition of the Masters providing a complete new outfit for their Hunt staff every year, which he said cost £200 a year.

A post-war innovation, described by Brock, was the abandonment of the pre-war practice of paying an annual Poultry Fund, a long-held practice in which owners of poultry claimed sums from the local Hunt for chicken, ducks and other birds allegedly killed by foxes. He estimated this cost an average-three-day-a-week country about £200 pre-war and would now cost about £800.

The hard-pressed Brock wrote: 'We can wipe this sum off the slate atogether, for under existing arrangements with the National Poultry Council, foxes are not preserved and claims are not paid. I applaud this agreement. The pre-war £200 was paid, nominally that foxes might be preserved, but were they? Certainly not by the people who used to rake in most of the £200, and who first obtained compensation for poultry which they may, or may not have lost through foxes, and then went back and indulged in a little vulpicide by way of celebrating a windfall. The proof of the pudding is in the eating, and despite there being no Poultry Fund, there are still plenty of foxes.'

David Brock proposed cutting down on the practice of 'filling the farmers with cakes and ale' at the local Hunt races. He believed the average farmer – who is a businessman of considerable capital – inwardly scoffs at such patronage. 'Pay each farmer the compliment of sending him a free pass for his car for the races, but cut out the choir treat atmosphere, and incidentally save a couple of hundred pounds.'

'Looking After' the Farmers

In reality Hunts operate in widely differing types of hunting country, but in areas where they rely heavily on privately farmed land it has remained the practice throughout post-war hunting to the present day, to give tangible benefit to farmers over whose land hounds hunt, in as many ways as can be afforded.

The 'choir treat atmosphere' disappeared, but free passes for point-to-points, entertainment at farmers' suppers, and lunches and teas at the annual puppy show, have remained part of the accepted costs of running a Hunt.

There are other ways of thanking farmers; the 'mending' of fences broken during a Hunt can be interpreted very liberally in some countries, especially in the Midlands, being an opportunity to provide brand new gates, bridges and timber fencing well beyond the cost of rails actually damaged.

Any largesse provided by Hunts to farmers became less relevant during the post-war years, and there is ample evidence that it has never been a key factor in keeping a whole hunting country open, however influential it may or may not have been in individual cases. I recall a certain Hunt Chairman desperately rushing to the home of a farmer to reason with him and his wife, and bearing a huge box of chocolates, because they had just banned the Hunt over a local squabble just before a major meet.

It did no good at all, and I thoroughly disapproved of such tactics; covering the whole country with a layer of chocolates for every landowner and farmer was beyond our resources if we were to use this form of 'opening the country'.

Allowing farmers and their families to hunt on a reduced subscription, or none, is a long-standing practice in foxhunting, and is far more relevant than other so-called benefits. The non-hunting farmer who allows you to cross his land, although he may grumble from time to time, is a major golden thread in the history of foxhunting. Sometimes it happens that later he has a daughter, or grand-daughter who takes up the Chase, and how wise is the Master who notes this and makes sure that she is greeted warmly in the hunting field, and treated with particular discretion. David Brock's analysis and proposals were ahead of his time, but they were somewhat flawed in that Hunts simply could not, and in many cases would not, take these steps because of strictly local factors.

One of the most potent 'solutions' to financial problems was to appoint very rich men to be Masters of Foxhounds, who could fill all the financial gaps, including backing a younger man as a Joint MFH to hunt the hounds, and run the country. This was well known and exploited as far back as the late eighteenth century, and it continued to be employed right up to the present day. Unfortunately it became less possible later in the post-war years.

The twentieth century was to pose new pressures and problems which were to change the structure and manner in which Hunts were to be managed and funded.

How a Hunt is Run

The constitution of a British Hunt grew out of the feudal past when squires owned packs of hounds and simply invited their friends and relations to join them in the hunting field as guests. Although Hunts registered by the Masters of Foxhounds Association, are expected to conform to its rules there is considerable flexibility. The traditional format for a subscription pack which survived into the twentieth century was that the hounds, the kennels, and any coverts and other land owned by the Hunt, was the property of the Hunt committee.

It is usually 'owned' on behalf of the committee by several trustees appointed by the committee. Exceptions to this are packs of hounds still belonging to private owners, such as the Duke of Beaufort, who usually own the Hunt kennels as well, although the Hunt still takes subscriptions from the mounted field.

The MFHA recommends that Hunt committee members resign after a set period of years, and be replaced by others. Usually the Hunt committee itself selects nominees as new committee members and they are presented to the annual general meeting for confirmation.

Even by 2004 there were still some Hunts who continued to allow committee members to sit indefinitely once first appointed. This often caused poor decision making by elderly people who had given up hunting, and allowed inadequate representation for newcomers and younger people in a hunting country who would represent more accurately those riding to hounds and paying subscriptions.

Hunt Committees elect their own Chairman, and this has become an increasingly crucial role, often providing more continuity in a Hunt than Masterships which tended to become much shorter in duration later in the century. Some Chairmen are forced by the Hunts to resign after three to five years, but many remain in office for far longer in the absence of such a rule.

Hunt rules at the end of the twentieth century continued to vary considerably from the exact format recommended by the MFHA. Most crucial is the relationship between the Hunt Committee and the Mastership.

Making Masterships

The Committee invites Masters to take office from 1 May, the official beginning of the Hunt year, until twelve months later. Ideally Masters should inform Hunt Chairmen at the start of a season if they intend to retire at the end of that season, in order to allow adequate time to find their replacements.

A few Mastership vacancies are advertised, usually in *Horse & Hound*, but most are arranged on behalf of the Committee by the Hunt Chairman. If he is lucky there are people within the hunting country who will form Mastership 'packages', small groups who will work together, and make financial contributions.

The role of the Masters is basically to 'provide sport'; that entails engaging Hunt staff, including a huntsman, although this role may be carried out by one of the Masters as an amateur. He will still need a professional kennel-huntsman to run the kennels, feeding, exercising and keeping clean the lodges and other hound buildings.

By the 1970s Hunts were finding it more difficult to engage Masters who could afford the money – and the time. Some of the best candidates for Mastership could not afford it. Variations on the traditional system of funding Masters were brought in, and quietly encouraged by Ronnie Wallace when he took over as MFHA Chairman.

The old system for a 'full Master' was that he negotiated a 'guarantee' for each season: a sum of money given to him by the Hunt Committee who raised the cash through Hunt subscriptions, donations and other means. If the Master, or Joint Masters, could not pay the full expenses required to hunt the country from the guarantee they had to find the excess sum from their own pockets, although sometimes fervent pleas to the Hunt Chairman could result in a late-season bonus from the Committee if it could find the money.

In the nineteenth and early twentieth century there were certain smaller Hunts where full time so-called amateur huntsmen managed not only to run the Hunt but to live off the guarantee, using the huntsman's staff house at the kennels as free accommodation. Whether the financial pressures upon them always benefited sport is open to question, although such a situation did enable the Chairman and Committee to exert great pressure on a Master because sacking him meant that he lost his home and livelihood. This system of 'open-ended guarantees' was quietly shelved in an increasing number of Hunts from the late 1960s onwards. Contracts drawn up between the Committee and the Masters allowed for stipulated additional sums to be provided by Hunt Committees, provided they were incurred in providing sport.

The system accelerated in the years of monetary inflation of the late 1970s when the cost of running a hunt could hardly be estimated accurately at the beginning of the season. The other alternative, which had been available for many years, was for the Hunt Chairman and Committee to provide virtually all the funding, appointing Acting Masters to manage affairs on their behalf. This was increasingly practised towards the end of the century.

Previously Masters had purchased the horses ridden by the huntsman and whippers-in, and renewed them when necessary. This role too was taken on by Hunt Committees, sometimes forming 'Horse Clubs' whereby members of the Hunt contributed through donations, raffles and auctions to a permanent fund used by buying and replacing horses for the staff.

Yet another alternative became increasingly used: the appointment of the 'shamateur' huntsman. This worked well if a Master and amateur huntsman could be found who had enough management skills as well as hunting ability to carry out the running of the Hunt on and off the hunting field.

Some of the most notable Master/huntsmen and hound breeders of the late twentieth century operated in this way. They were paid an annual salary and managed the Hunt in much the same way as a golf professional, except that they were in the spotlight as the main provider of sport for everyone else in the Hunt. Often such arrangements were achieved through a combination of funding from the Committee and from wealthy Joint Masters who were happy to take on the office, but did not have the time or the full expertise necessary.

When there was in place a perfectly adequate professional huntsman, sometimes Joint Masterships would still pay one of their number to carry out the management role in Kennels on their behalf, and to be their main spokesman in dealing with farmers and landowners. This could pose huge problems because the professional staff well knew they were dealing with virtually another staff member, instead of an independent Master, and farmers and landowners too could be awkward. 'I wants to speak to the organ grinder not the monkey' said one disgruntled farmer when a paid Master called on him to 'clear' the country before hunting.

Ronnie Wallace, throughout his twenty-two years as MFHA Chairman, had a consistent policy of maintaining the authority of Masters as strongly as possible. He was well aware that Masters too dependent on Chairmen and Committees could be pressured into making the wrong decisions. Disputes could arise all the more frequently under arrangements where the power of Committees had swelled.

He saw it as his business to keep in touch with Chairmen as well as Masters, either at meetings of Chairmen in London, or individually. Tactfully he would advise them of the need to draw lines of responsibility which ensured as much freedom of decision as possible for Masters. He would advise Chairmen on the best likely candidates for Masterships, and indeed for professional huntsmen's positions.

It was this practice of influencing such decisions that earned him the nickname of 'God' in the hunting world, and he heartily disliked it. Privately he would occasionally murmur that 'maintaining the quality of Mastership' was the biggest problem for foxhunting. Wallace rightly interpreted a Master's role as far wider than running a Hunt; he, or she, should be a visible personality in the public life of the countryside, attending markets, horse and agricultural shows, and a variety of other rural events not necessarily run by the Hunt.

The Master should be available to attend funerals and weddings, especially of those in the landowning and farming community. All this was possible for someone with a large private income, and plenty of time, but even the sons and daughters of the rich were increasingly required to have careers in business or the professions, and if they had a passion for hunting it had to be fitted into a working life-style.

Wallace understood all this, but clung firmly to the basic system he inherited. A radical approach might have been simply to abandon the traditional Mastership system, with Hunts appointing full-time equivalents of Chief Executives who would have to provide solid evidence of their qualifications for the post before appointment.

Although tempting, such a solution would have meant dispensing with the mystique of Mastership, and in many cases would have robbed Hunts of links through Masters to their relatives and friends who were crucially important as extensive landowners or farmers of land maintained exceptionally suitable for foxhunting.

In 2004 there is still a vast, complicated network of friendships, family relationships and old alliances between many Masters of Foxhounds throughout Britain which is an invaluable cement in keeping intact hunting countries, and the sport as whole, in the fact of opposition ranging from letters in the local press to appalling acts of violence in the hunting field.

The role of MFH began to require considerable reserves of moral courage and resolve, and the ability to organise a day's hunting involved dealing with complex situations created by vicious sabotage designed to attract press publicity for the anti-hunting cause.

An MFH had to know his local police as well as his landowners. The Master was briefed fully by the MFHA, and systems of 'action telephone numbers' were organised to assist Hunts in calling on MFHA and BFSS public affairs officers to deal with the press in the event of incidents which were often at weekends.

Entrance of the 'Sabs'

The choice of direct action by hunting's opponents became starkly apparent in the 1960s, and grew in the following decades, when the Hunt Saboteurs took to the hunting field in greater numbers, although the most active never amounted to more than a hard core of hundreds rather than thousands.

To some extent they found that as Chairman Mao said 'power comes out of the mouth of a gun'. They quickly achieve far more prominence by direct action than acres of print had done for the orthodox protestors. Much later they were to find the press bored with, and sometimes highly disapproving of, disruptive tactics. Sabs ranged from misguided students who merely expressed opposition, but took little action, and anyway did not know how to disrupt a hunt, to a few hardened anarchists who delighted in the hunting field as a place to use varying degrees of violence and hooliganism in pursuit of their aims.

Sabs often turn up in hired mini-buses, often cream coloured and rather battered. Some wear balaclava helmets, and fake military combat dress, because they do not want their identities revealed in photographs. Such dress also makes them appear more intimidating.

The intimidation can be real. Women and children hacking home alone have

Some saboteurs wear combat dress and balaclavas over their heads in the hunting field, partly to be more intimidating, but also to hide their identities in photographs.

been attacked and dragged off horses and ponies to be kicked and pummelled. I have heard saboteurs engage in bouts of appalling swearing at hunting women and children, and have seen balaclava clad louts urinating in front of mounted fields. At worst, I have seen saboteurs carrying staves or whips, using them on hunting people, horses, and hounds. They sprayed hounds with substances such as anti-mate, claimed to destroy hounds' scenting abilities, but causing severe irritation in the hounds' eyes.

Holloaing to distract hounds from the huntsman's bidding, and the use of false hunting horn calls are regularly used. If it succeeds in luring hounds to roads they run the risk of being run over by traffic. Some saboteurs have used amplifiers to play recorded hunting horn calls, or the sound of hounds baying, designed to encourage a pack to deviate from its own line. Experienced huntsmen overcome even these distractions; hounds learn very quickly to distinguish between the 'real thing' and the dangerous imititations.

Sabotaging unattended horse transport at meets or elsewhere by tyre-slashing or worse, has been standard practice for years. There are many other variations in a strategy of varying levels of harassment, intimidation and provocation. It is meant above all to be provocative because a frequently used tactic by saboteurs is to rush to the police to register complaints if a hunting person responds physically. Taking pictures of huntsmen and others raising their whips to defend their hounds and horses has been a favourite ploy, and when published in a tabloid such pictures present the foxhunter as the 'angry squire' stereotype, apparently striking down the protestor on foot. Attacks on hounds and horses are difficult to comprehend from people claiming their motivation is 'animal welfare'.

At its most extreme, harassment has involved threatening telephones to hunting people, attacks on homes and Hunt Kennels, and the abduction of individual hounds. When all this started hunting people believed they lived in a peace loving democracy where the full rigour of the law would automatically be applied to menacing people, often tattooed and ringed through ears and noses, who were aggressively disrupting the peace, engaging in threatening and violent behaviour, trespassing on privately owned land throughout. Non-hunting farmers and their families who allow the Hunt on their land, have been targets of abuse and harassment by saboteurs.

Hunting people were amazed to find that in many cases rural police forces said they did not have the manpower to send detachments in sufficient strength, or quickly enough, to deal with the worst mass attacks by saboteurs. Some county police forces clearly regarded their role as keeping apart two opposing groups, instead of protecting one group engaged in a legal activity from active disruption by another group from outside the area. We were at first surprised and appalled that the policy of county police forces appeared to vary widely in dealing with saboteur attacks.

The level of response appeared to depend heavily on the views of the Chief Constable of each force. Policemen would sometimes sit in their cars on roadsides while saboteurs blew hunting horns from the same road, endeavouring to call hounds which would run a grave risk of causing accidents if they answered the call and came on to the road singly or in small groups.

Learning to blow the hunting horn has long been part of saboteur tactics. It's intended to call hounds away from the huntsman to disrupt hunting, but it seldom works.

Backed by animal rights sources, some saboteurs have been recruited on promises of expenses paid for the day, and they have had legal and public relations help. Police have sometimes been deterred from arrests because saboteurs have engaged in occasionally successful actions against police forces for technical 'wrongful arrest'. Police have sometimes arrived just as the patience of hunting people has exploded into retaliatory action, and have promptly arrested and charged the hunters rather than the saboteurs who provoked them.

Hunts in the South-East near the fringes of London have been among the worst afflicted by extreme saboteur activity, but they have been active in parts of the South-West, the Midlands and the North. Occasionally groups of saboteurs have combined to cause a 'big hit' on a special target.

The most extreme elements in the saboteur movement were hit when links were found with extremist animal rights activists who smashed fur shop windows, and broke into and vandalised vivisection laboratories. Arrests and lengthy jail sentences for a few leaders of the extremists movement proved successful as deterrents, and the acquiring of a criminal record for students was another deterrent since it could seriously affect future employment prospects.

A police case against a Midlands Master of Foxhounds accused of 'riding down' a saboteur who seized his horse's bridle while attacking hounds, was withdrawn when not a single saboteur attended court as a witness. The group involved came from a north of England industrial city, lived in squatter accommodation, and some were already on probation for other offences.

Encouraged and helped by the British Field Sports Society, the achievement of a new law of 'aggravated trespass' in the early 1990s was seen as something of a breakthrough, but it involves official complaint by landowners, which is not always practicable, and it has not been used effectively.

To some extent saboteur activity ceased to attract the same level of press attention because the sabs became a stereotype; their negative and entirely limited campaign of protest was dwarfed by the re-emergence of much larger issues involving violence, such as overseas wars involving British troops. The use of violence by international terrorists has blunted public tolerance for protest by thuggery.

How many sports and recreations would have withstood the levels of violence and harassment dealt out to hunting? It says much for the persistence and courage of hunting people and their leaders that hunt saboteurs were never able to halt, nor seriously damage, the fabric of hunting with hounds as a national sport. In 2004 they remained as pathetic groups sporadically and ineffectually engaged in hit and run activities which Hunts had acquired the experience to frustrate.

Watching a huntsman calmly continuing to hunt a pack which is ignoring rogue horn calls from saboteurs is an impressive sight. Mounted and foot followers nowadays manage nearly always to adopt stoic indifference, or even wry humour, to the presence of the 'antis', refusing to resort to anger and physical response.

Extra precautions are taken to protect horse transport, and the advent of the mobile phone has enabled Hunt secretaries to call police all the quicker when the worst forms of sabotage occur. Hunts know all about the use of video film to record incidents as evidence, and occasional use of their own protective stewards has been another useful form of defence, although there is a risk of raising levels of confrontation.

It is not surprising that the hunting community is still puzzled and bitterly disappointed by the lack of understanding among too many Members of Parliament about the full extent of thuggery and vandalism wrought in our countryside by the worst of the Hunt saboteurs.

In April 1993 a fifteen-years-old youth attending the hunting field among saboteurs engaged in active harassment, died after falling under the wheels of the Cambridgeshire Hunt hound lorry as it was taking hounds home at the end of the day's hunting. The incident caused extreme and damaging distress to the huntsman involved.

It caused some saboteurs to re-think the real issues of engaging in direct action, among them the prominent former Hunt Saboteurs Association member, Miles Cooper. In a lengthy interview on BBC Radio 4 in January, 2004, he said the incident caused 'a great deal of fall-out' in the HSA; there had already been, he said, 'a great deal of internecine dispute bubbling for a year'.

Cooper engaged thereafter in political activity against hunting, rather than direct action, because he said he no longer believed it to be an issue 'where one should physically come to blows'. Then he changed his mind entirely, speaking out frequently in public against a ban on hunting with hounds. He said he had produced a special report, based on his own research, stating that packs of hounds which flushed out foxes to be shot by guns, killed and wounded far more than packs hunting by traditional means.

Cooper stated on Radio 4's programme *The Choice* in January, 2004, that it was totally against his conscience to find his report ignored when the Foster Bill, and the later Labour government Bill, sought to ban hunting with hounds, but left loopholes that would allow gun packs to operate.

He has spoken frequently on public platforms and in the media against a ban on traditional sporting hunting because he believes the alternative would cause high levels of wild animal suffering to spread across the English lowlands.

Disciplinary Dramas

It was not surprising in post-war Britain that candidatures for Masterships became more of a problem because the role of Masters, and indeed of Hunt Committees, became increasingly complex. The Hunt Chairman who could build a 'Mastership package' from within his own country was lucky.

Yet in 2004 the number of active Masters of Foxhounds has increased because there are far more multiple Masterships in order to share the heavier load of responsibilities. Some are not 'born to foxhunting', but they are willing to learn, and the MFHA has increased its flow of information and advice, and holds regular seminars on all aspects of Mastership.

Increasingly during the 1970s and '80s the Hunt Chairman might have to call on Ronnie Wallace, or his redoubtable henchman Anthony Hart, Secretary of the MFHA for twenty-four years, for urgent advice and help when Masters were desperately needed through unforeseen resignations. Nowadays Alastair Jackson, Director the MFHA, gives emergency advice and a regular flow of information to Masters, and the Countryside Alliance's public relations team works in cooperation with the Hunts.

It must be admitted that one enduring tradition of foxhunting is the Great Hunt Row. Such are the passions, and the potencies of local rivalries, feuds and suddenly erupting disputes, that just occasionally some Hunts implode into internal strife. These are so intense they find their way into the national media. I used to think they were extremely damaging to the sport, portraying hunting people as inward looking and willing to fight over the positioning of their deck chairs on the deck of a vessel which could all too easily prove to be a *Titanic* heading for the iceberg of abolition.

I have since come to the conclusion that the British public is perfectly accustomed to reading every day of rows in sports and all other enterprises, and does not think much the worse of hunting if it has occasional internal disputes. Compared with the modern spectator sports, especially soccer, hunting's occasional internal disputes seem like mole hills.

The real damage perceived in the post-war years when the political threat grew, was the occasion when a Hunt was the focus of a major public allegation of rule-breaking and abuse of the fox, one of the most notable examples being the Quorn video case in the 1991–92 season.

It was significant within that famous hunting country because it resulted in a series of internal rows which obtained all too much national publicity. On the credit side outside the Quorn country the affair resulted in a major, and much needed, reform of the MFHA's disciplinary and public relations procedures. Undoubtedly the video itself did considerable harm because, accompanied by slanted propaganda, it presented hunting as a sport which appeared not to merely to catch a fox, but to abuse it before doing so.

One of hunting's immense problems is that the arguments for and against are much easier for the anti lobby when the debate consists of quick sound bites. The pro-hunting arguments need much more time for presentation of hunting in the context of what happens to wildlife in general in the countryside.

A spy or 'mole' for the anti-hunting lobby pretended to be a Quorn hunt supporter taking video films. He took some film of a dig after a fox had been marked to ground during cub-hunting. A terrier man and helpers were shown digging, and then the film showed one fox being shot in a hole by the terrierman, and another found in the same earth was pulled out live and thrown into a hedge alongside the earth; the fox ran alongside the hedge then apparently headlong into the Quorn hounds which had correctly been taken away while the dig was taking place, but were now surging down the hedgerow; they immediately killed the fox running towards them.

To hunting people it looked like a botched attempt at bolting a fox which had run the wrong way towards hounds instead of away from them. The crucial factor was that the fox was seen to be handled and forcibly bolted, instead of running from the earth and given time to get well away before hounds were laid on the line.

The antis used the clip as propaganda that foxhunting was an unacceptably cruel method of dispatching a fox, ignoring the fact that both animals had in fact been killed quickly and cleanly, a fate which cannot ever be guaranteed by alternative means. Clips of the video were made available to the press and national television networks who showed them widely.

The story broke on 27 October but it was not until 14 November that the MFHA held a disciplinary inquiry, the gap allowing the antis time for a great deal more damaging propaganda in the media. After hearing evidence from all concerned the MFHA stated that 'a fox handled in such a way should have been destroyed and not hunted further'. In other words the fox should have been run from the earth on its own volition, having been bolted by terriers, not being physically thrown by the terrierman after a dig.

The MFHA handed out the most severe penalties ever exercised in its 108 years history, expelling the Quorn's two senior Joint Masters from the Association for four years, and two who had only joined the Quorn Mastership that season were expelled until the start of the next season.

Unfortunately the Quorn's four Joint Masters had already fallen on their swords by resigning immediately the matter became public, as a way of demonstrating their acceptance of overall responsibility for the conduct of hunting, even though only one was in charge on the day, and others were not present. The Hunt Chairman also resigned, a noble gesture, but it left no-one officially at the helm when the ship was sinking in a storm. One of the most significant problems was that the Quorn had no written constitution, having failed to carry out the urgings of the MFHA for several seasons that all Hunts must possess one. The difficulty for foxhunting's ruling body in achieving action by all Hunts in matters off the hunting field, lay in its role as an association of Masters, and could only effectively act through them.

The lack of written procedures caused internal confusion to mount horrendously, and the press found no lack of people willing to spout all kinds of gossip about the Quorn, most of it grossly inaccurate, and some of it slanderous.

Capt. Fred Barker, a previous Master of considerable authority, generously stepped in as sole Master to rescue the Hunt, and did so by proclaiming publicly everything was run scrupulously 'by the book' which helped to mend public relations for the sport in general. David Samworth as Hunt Chairman ensured the Quorn achieved its first written constitution in over 250 years.

Barker was rewarded later by further rows and confusions about the creation of another Mastership, of which he was unaware, and this caused another round of national newspaper publicity which was extremely irritating for the MFHA Committee, and to many other other Hunts who were tired of reading about the Quorn's problems in the national press.

There were not many laughs in Leicestershire when I published a cartoon in *Horse & Hound,* originally published in *The Daily Telegraph* in which a fox was receiving advice in the office of a public relations expert who was saying: 'Well so far you are well ahead of the Quorn.'

The MFHA's finding and penalties in the video case were controversial because some alleged the MFHA's rules were not specific enough on the exact procedure in digging and bolting, and they believed the penalties were far too extreme. A temporary suspension and a censure would have been adequate it was felt by some, for transgressing rules which were loosely framed. Unlike the Jockey Club which had long ago formed a separate disciplinary apparatus, the MFHA's chairman Ronnie Wallace chaired the disciplinary committee which considered the Quorn case, thereby attracting far more criticism personally.

His response to the critics, although not widely enough published, was that the MFHA had issued all Masters with detailed specific guidelines to accompany the broad rules, and these not been followed.

It was a time of growing political opposition in the House of Commons and foxhunting's ruling body wished to emphasise that it could, and would, regulate itself firmly, however regrettable it was that this matter had arisen from an undercover coup by 'the other side'.

Making the Rules

Soon after the Quorn case the MFHA took legal advice and made radical changes to its rules. The previous rule stated that 'when a fox is run to ground, the Master must decide what is to be done. If the decision is that the fox be killed, it must be humanely destroyed before being given to the hounds.'

The new rule stated '. . . when a hunted fox is run to ground in a natural earth, there shall be no digging other than for the purpose of humanely destroying the fox,' and further states 'a fox which has been handled must be humanely destroyed immediately and under no circumstances hunted.'

New rules were also promulgated on bolting foxes. The statement that when a fox was run to ground *in a natural earth* there could be no digging meant there could be no terrier work and bolting. However, the new rules allowed that a hunted fox could be bolted if it took refuge in a man-made structure, such as a drain, stickheap, or straw bales. The exception also applies to rocks or other places where digging is impossible.

The exceptions for man-made structures were made because it is much easier and quicker to bolt from places where a terrier can be put in and the fox has easy access without the need for the lengthier process of digging. The new rules also declare that 'the practice of bolting should only be undertaken when hounds have been taken away such a distance that they are out of sight of the place of refuge and are unable to hear any operations at the place of bolting' a fox when bolted 'must be given a fair and sporting chance of escape before hounds are laid on'.

In order to add extra safeguards in the area of digging and bolting foxes, recognised as an Achilles heel of the sport in public relations terms, the MFHA in the 1990s set up a system of licensing its terriermen, binding them to strict rules.

The need for such regulation was emphasised in 2003 when the terrierman of the Cottesmore Hunt was alleged to have moved a litter of fox cubs from one earth to another in a different area of the country. He had been instructed to despatch the litter in the original earth after its presence had been indicated by hounds during a day's hunting because this was believed to be the wish of the stock farmer on that land.

A recent new rule of the MFHA forbids such movements, although moving infant wild animals to sanctuary elsewhere is not forbidden in law. Significantly the terrierman was filmed placing fox cubs in a new earth by a camera installed covertly on behalf of an anti-hunting organisation. It was a camera with a self-operating device activated by movement in front of the lens.

This form of covert surveillance, carried out on private land without the owner's permission, emphasises the degree of outside pressure under which Hunts operate in the twenty-first century. The incident occurred in February but was carefully released to Channel 4 TV news by the anti-hunting organisation for transmission just before a House of Commons debate on an anti-hunting Bill in July. It could hardly be claimed to be an urgent matter of animal welfare, but looked far more like an attempt at a propaganda coup.

The Cottesmore Masters were temporarily suspended; they maintained a united front, explaining publicly that they had not authorised in any way, and had not been informed of their terrierman's action of which they totally disapproved, knowing it to be against MFHA rules. An MFHA inquiry was held within a week, and cleared the Cottesmore Masters of any rule breaking, praising their execution of staff training, records and protocol. The terrierman's licence was, however, withdrawn for three years.

In the 1990s Masters on the MFHA Committee were appointed to supervise specific Hunts in regions of England and Wales. Systems of inspection and checking that Hunts are complying with rules were set up in the late 1990s, all part of moves to emphasise the integrity of foxhunting's systems of effective self-governance.

Self-regulation

The disciplinary system was dramatically upgraded by the establishment of the Independent Supervisory Authority on Hunting in 1999 under the chairmanship of former High Court judge, Sir Ronald Waterhouse, sitting with five commissioners chosen by an independent appointments panel. The idea of an independent authority was first mooted in the 1951 Scott Henderson Report, and the Phelps Review of Hunting with Hounds in 1997.

ISAH supervises and regulates rules and the disciplinary actions of each of eleven hound sports ruling bodies . It has the authority to increase or curtail disciplinary decisions. There could be no doubt that the hound sports made a radical step in shoring up self-regulation at a time when the Blair government was seeking to impose regulation, later changing this to an outright banning Bill.

The MFHA has traditionally relied heavily on its rule number one: 'Foxhunting as a sport is the hunting of the fox in his wild and natural state with a pack of hounds. No pack of which the Master or representative is a member of this Association will be allowed to hunt the fox in any way that is inconsistent with this precept.'

This of course can be interpreted as ruling against any practice during the hunt above ground which smacks of artificiality. The fox must be found naturally in its own environment, and there must be no artificial means of catching it beyond the use of hounds. In the 1990s the MFHA firmed up its guidelines on cubhunting, to be called in future 'autumn hunting'.

The traditional practice of 'holding-up' coverts was for members of the mounted field, and foot followers, to gather round coverts, attempting to discourage foxes running into the open, by shouting at them or tapping whips on boots or saddles.

In future coverts should only be held up on sides where it was necessary to prevent the fox running, such as roads, built-up areas, growing crops or stock. Mounted and foot followers were forbidden to chase the fox to attempt to turn it back. Far more of the autumn hunting was to take place in a less intensive manner, with less chance of 'mobbing' the fox by tightly holding up the entire circumference of small coverts, including fields of kale.

At the same time 'autumn hunting' remains a time when the largest cull of foxes takes place because more of the hunting is in covert. It is still the period when young hounds, born the previous year, are 'entered' into the pack, and receive training from the huntsman, also benefiting greatly from the example of older, trained hounds.

Changing the autumn period's name from the traditional 'cub-hunting' was a sensible public relations exercise because the old term can conjure up a picture of baby fox cubs being killed by hounds, whereas by August and September foxes born in early spring are already physically fully grown, and usually indistinguishable from older foxes.

The MFHA has attempted to widen its influence among Hunt subscribers and supporters by issuing codes of conduct for their behaviour in the hunting field, stressing their responsibilities in looking after the property of their hosts, the farmers and landowners, especially in ensuring that gates are securely closed o keep in stock.

It is axiomatic among registered foxhound packs hunting in farmland that each day the Hunt appoints from its regular mounted followers at least two gate-shutters who wear ratcatcher dress, follow at the back, equipped with strings of binder twine, and ensure that all gates are shut and secured, if necessary tying them up, and that where wire is taken down in gaps it is secured.

Hunt Secretaries

The steadily increasing volume of form-filling, and other bureaucracy in running a Hunt, made the role of the Hunt Secretary still more demanding in post-war years.

The term Hon. Secretary is still more appropriate because by the end of the century the majority were volunteers, taking on this demanding task with only the benefit of administrative expenses. It cannot be claimed that a Secretary's hunting day is more enjoyable than a subscriber's because this vital official has the task of collecting caps, checking gate-shutters are in place, and liaising with Masters and fence builders regarding any fence repairing necessary.

There is a mass of office work, with fixture cards to be assembled and sent out, plus numerous other communications, staff contracts, and bills to be paid in running the Hunt kennels and stables, and maintaining lorries, flesh wagons and sometimes quad bikes.

Often secretaryships are shared between two or more volunteers in different parts of the larger hunt countries. Some of the four-day-a-week packs employ full time, paid Secretaries, but it is still a role requiring dedication and a real love of the sport, for a Secretary's telephone can ring at all times on an increasingly wide range of 'urgent' topics.

Many Hunts administer their countries through small, but powerful finance committees comprising the Hunt Chairman, the Secretary, Treasurer, and at least one Joint Master. Turnovers in larger Hunts were running above £200,000 up to £500,000 per year by 2004. Two-day-a-week packs were running on much less turnovers, and their incomes were much smaller. More than a few could not survive without the fund raising carried out for them by Supporters' Clubs. Insurance of the risks during hunting had to be undertaken for millions of pounds. A modern Hunt has the same complexities and requires the same attention to detail as a successful business, but it has the additional risks and responsibilities of a unique sport operating on other people's land, with an element of determined, sometimes fanatical, opposition to its existence, virtually unknown to any other sporting enterprise in Britain.

The burden can be heavy, and it is one more sign of the sport's continuing importance in the life of the modern countryside that volunteers are still being found readily to take on the tough tasks of Hunt administration.

The Way of All Flesh

Lord King, then head of British Airways when he was Chairman of the Belvoir, said when he invited me to join the Committee: 'It will be interesting, but I warn that you we spend a great deal of time talking about split rails and flesh collections.'

Skinning and cutting fallen stock is a malodorous task, carried out in a Hunt's

Lord King, Master of the Belvoir (1958–72) and famous as the reforming Chairman of British Airways.

73

well named Flesh House. Throughout the post-war years the collection of flesh from farm animals which expire naturally required considerable attention. It was a way of returning the farmers' hospitality, and it benefited the Hunt greatly in feeding hounds.

Flesh collections illustrate the prime factor in farming which escapes the attention or understanding of millions of urban dwellers with anthropomorphic attitudes to animals. A Leicestershire farmer summed it up to me once simply as: 'If you have livestock you will most certainly have dead-stock too.' Countrymen, and that includes all true hunting people, are not callous about death; they are accustomed to it, and accept it as part of the natural order.

Much of the neurosis of some urbanites about death in animals and humans is that they have for too long been divorced from the real implications of rearing and producing the meat and poultry which is nowadays so clinically presented in supermarkets.

Country children learn early that dogs, ponies and farm animals are not immortal, and do not always die 'peacefully'. By 2004 the whole practice of collecting stock and feeding it to hounds was in jeopardy because of the application of new European Commission knackering regulations which Hunts would find too expensive, or impractical, to operate.

Paradoxically at the same time the government's agriculture ministry, operating within Labour's heartily disliked Department of the Environment Food and Rural Affairs (DEFRA), was including Hunt kennels in its list of knackering arrangements available to farmers and horse owners. Some hunting people continue the practice of inviting the professional huntsman to put down old or infirm horses, then donating the carcase to the kennels to feed hounds.

A huntsman, or knackerman, coming to your own stable to put down the horse in its home premises is probably less stressful than sending the animal to an abattoir far from home. Horses, and indeed cattle, have sensitive hearing and scenting abilities and may be well aware on arrival that the sights and sounds of an abattoir indicate the death of other animals nearby.

For many years the collection of fallen stock from farms produced extra income for the huntsman and other staff in the form of 'skin money', the price paid for the hides by leather manufacturers. Other parts of the carcase had some commercial value too.

After the BSE outbreak in cattle in the 1980s and '90s, far from bringing in money, the collection of stock became a heavy expense for Hunts because the renderers who collected the offal and bones began to charge considerable sums for their disposal. Collection of stock, and its disposal could cost over £30,000 per year in a larger kennel.

New BSE regulations required parts of the carcase, brains and spines, to be dyed purple and disposed of, whilst other parts could be used for animal consumption. Some Hunts in the early '90s sought to cut the costs by installing their own oil fired boilers to dispose of the remains of carcases within government regulations. They proved costly to buy and maintain, but did make some savings. Others found a solution in charging farmers nominal fees for collection of fallen stock to help defray the Hunt's burden. This was still regarded as a better option by many stock farmers than using commercial knackers, and some schemes continued on this basis. Hunt Committees were concerned about the cost, but even more concerned about withdrawing a service to the most important people in their hunting countries, their hosts on the land for up to eight months a year.

Some Hunts by 2004 had exercised another option, withdrawing their own stock collection scheme altogether, but arranging its replacement by commercial knackers. This appeared to have no effect on land usage by these Hunts, proving again that rural custom, and a genuine regard for 'our local Hunt' are the real keys to the continuing availability of privately owned farmland for foxhunting. In 2004 many Hunts were still collecting flesh from farmers, but the practice was under threat from new regulations, emanating originally from the EC. They were predicted to impose conditions on knackering and flesh preparation in kennels which would be too expensive for Hunts to undertake. As usual, in matters ordained by the EC and imposed by DEFRA, there were clouds of confusion about the eventual outcome.

Geoff Key cutting and laying a hedge Leicestershire style in the Quorn country. Maintaining fencing and coverts is part of foxhunting's contribution to conservation to the present day.

Raymond Brooks-Ward, Joint Master and huntsman of the Enfield Chace, BBC TV equestrian commentator and public relations officer for the MFHA, hunting hounds just north of London in 1983.

Enfield Chace huntsman (1946–54) Tim Muxworthy with the celebrated romantic novelist Barbara Cartland at a lawn meet at her home near Essendon.

Major Bob Hoare, Joint Master and huntsman Cottesmore (1958–69), organiser of the BFSS Fighting Fund.

Capt. Simon Clarke, in charge of MFHA boundary changing project, seen hunting the Cottesmore in 1970 during his Mastership (1969–76).

Foxhunting is embedded deeply in Welsh rural life. Here, members of the Taf Fechan Hunt at a meet in Ystrad Fellte in 1977.

Two long-time followers of the Brecon hounds, Joe Gwynne, and Dudley Thomas who began hunting in the First World War when his father was huntsman.

The Prince of Wales hunting with the Meynell and South Staffs in their Derbyshire country. The Prince took up foxhunting as an adult and loves it. He hunts in his own specially designed blue hunting coat with scarlet cuffs and collar, and silver buttons bearing his crest.

Anthony Hart, hunting hounds as Albrighton MFH, served as MFHA Secretary for twenty-two years up to 1997.

Many follow foxhounds on wheels instead of on horseback. This line-up of foxhunters on quad bikes are following the VWH Hunt.

Foot and Mouth

There had been a post-war outbreak of Foot and Mouth in cattle in the1967–68 season, and hunting with hounds of all kinds voluntarily ceased immediately, well before movement restrictions were imposed by the Ministry of Agriculture in infected areas. It was exactly the right response for a sport so intertwined with the fortunes of farming.

The outbreak began in Shropshire and spread to Cheshire. Fortunately, although tragic for farmers who lost precious herds, it did not spread to the scale of the national disaster which occurred in 2001.

Again hunting ceased immediately and voluntarily for the remainder of the season when the first cases of Foot and Mouth appeared in February. As new cases appeared in many areas of England during the summer it was clear that a normal resumption of hunting in the autumn was impossible.

The MFHA and the other hunting organisations held lengthy negotiations with DEFRA and agreed on a risk assessment which would eventually permit hunting again, but recognised that it would have to wait longer than any other sport because of its need to cross farmland. After the outbreak subsided in late summer, some Hunts began to operate under special permit and strict precautionary regulations, including the disinfecting of riders' feet before mounting, and for horse transport to operate only locally. Lists of everyone in the mounted field were sent to DEFRA offices. Not one pack had its permit revoked, and a constructive relationship of trust was established with DEFRA's regional officials throughout Britain.

Most packs began carefully and cautiously in a low key manner, usually still wearing ratcatcher dress. Areas of the North and North-West and parts of the West Country were the last to be freed from restrictions because they had seen the most intense outbreaks. During DEFRA's highly controversial mass culling of sheep in the spring some Masters and Hunt staff went to the aid of the veterinary staff who were swamped by the massive task of putting down hill sheep.

A kennel man in the Midlands who did his stint in Cumbria, told me afterwards it had been his worst experience in a lifetime in Hunt service where he was well accustomed to putting down horses and other farm stock as part of the flesh collection service. He said many ewes were aborting as they were being culled, and he was amazed that the major animal welfare organisations did not make the welfare of the sheep a national issue with government.

Anti-hunting MPs might have noted hunting's self-discipline, its identification with the needs of farmers, and its willingness to give practical help. If so they would have been impressed by the farming community's wish to cooperate with the Hunts for the earliest possible resumption of sport where restrictions permitted in the following season.

The following March MPs, including the Prime Minister, voted by 386 to 175 for a ban on hunting with hounds, all part of a bitter struggle which has been a predominant element in souring Labour's relations with the countryside in the first years of the new century, adding to much of the distrust and bitterness in the farming industry over the conduct of the battle against foot and mouth disease, and a general perception in the countryside that Labour is unsympathetic to, and sometimes in opposition, to rural needs.

Virtually a year without hunting could have decimated Britain's packs of hounds through lack of income. MPs who still under-estimate hunting's deep involvement in the lives of many thousands of people, should have noted that the reason Hunts survived was that the majority of subscribers were perfectly prepared to continue to keep their Hunts alive by paying full subscriptions for the 2001–2 season even though their packs provided less than half a season's sport, and in some cases none at all.

The Rabies Threat

One scourge which haunted senior figures in the foxhunting world throughout the twentieth century was rabies in foxes which was rampant in Eastern Europe, and moving west towards the Channel.

The dreaded disease spread in the 1960s through Poland, Czechoslovakia, through Luxembourg and Gemany into France. The principal carrier of the selvatic rabies virus was the fox. In France a programme of spreading bait treated with anti-rabies vaccines was engaged in energetically and had long term success in virtually eliminating the disease's continuing spread westwards.

Hunting people were especially concerned when a case was identified in a dog at Camberley, Surrey, in the autumn of 1969. The dog had been brought into England by an Army officer from Germany, and had undergone lengthy quarantine. It had nevertheless retained the disease, and it was known that the dog had been walked in woods at Camberley. The dog was put down and amid much publicity, government vets descended on Camberley, trapping wildlife and testing them. Fortunately none was found positive, and no further cases arose.

The MFHA well knew that if rabies became endemic in wildlife in the United Kingdom hunting with hounds would probably be suspended indefinitely. The hunting community has always supported the maintenance of strict quarantine regulations for imported dogs, and many viewed the advent of the Channel Tunnel with horror. Fortunately, the threat never materialised in the United Kingdom in the twentieth century, but further relaxations of quarantine on imported dogs could still pose a threat which would alter the way of life for millions of dog owners, and many others involved with animals.

In the United States rabies is endemic in wildlife, especially down the Eastern seaboard; hounds have to be vaccinated, and sometimes Hunt staff too. Each hound wears a blue collar to signify vaccination. Because of the size of the rural hinterland, there appears to be no special concern about rabies in urban populations, but the reaction from our sensationalist media would be very different in our small, cramped island.

Supporters' Clubs

When Dorian Williams was Joint Master of the Grafton (1951–54) he noted that the leader of the car followers, Ernie Griffiths, started an informal club which they called the Car-ites. Dorian tried to persuade the Hunt Committee to recognise the little group officially, but they could not agree to do so, believing it to be too unconventional.

Soon after he became Joint Master of the neighbouring Whaddon Chase (1954–80), Dorian encouraged the formation of a Supporters' Club. He believed one had been started first by the Cleveland in Yorkshire. The Whaddon Chasers was an immediate success, with a membership of 500.

'From the beginning their contribution to the Hunt was magnificent,' Dorian wrote. 'Not only did they raise money but they acted as valuable ambassadors for foxhunting, coming as they did from such a wide background.' Through the club, said Dorian, he had made 'many close, lasting and greatly valued friendships. It is a wonderful feeling for a Master of Hounds to know that he has friends in every village on every farm, at the roadside, wherever hounds go. It is very largely the Supporters' Clubs that provide these friends.'

Ronnie Wallace similarly ensured that the Heythrop was among he first to encourage the formation of a supporters' club. He said in an address to the American Foxhound Club: 'What a Supporters' Club really means is that the hounds are not just the property of the Master or the committee. They become the property of anyone and everyone who wants to be interested.

'The whole basis of hunting in England is to be able to do so with the consent of the community. I believe that instead of hunting being just an exclusive sport for people dressed up in fancy clothes it is far better to make it a sport which all can have a part if they want it.

'Supporters' Clubs are not, however, things you can push. It is no good persuading people to join if they are not interested; they must do their own recruiting at their own pace. Most important of all it has to be their own show. They must organise their own party and ask you, as Master or subscriber, to join them if they wish it. Let it be their performance.' Ronnie asked me to speak to the Heythrop Supporters' Club soon after I had become Editor of *Horse & Hound* in 1973. I made some after-supper jokes and then launched into a passionate plea for unity to combat the growing political threats to the sport. Ronnie remarked afterwards: 'Very spirited speech. You should do more of these.'

Curiously a host of invitations to speak at supporters' suppers came in from all over England soon afterwards. The Wallace network of daily 'phone calls to his favoured contacts throughout his kingdom was at work. By the late 1970s it was reckoned that over seventy per cent of Hunts had Supporters' Clubs, and by the millennium they existed in virtually every foxhunting country. They buy new vehicles for the Hunt, sometimes horses too, and they assist enormously in keeping up the tempo of social events associated with the Hunt.

Most of it is far removed from the stereotyped Hunt Ball with all its connotations of class and privilege, although I have to say that I have attended Hunt Balls in rural Ireland which were punctuated by broken glass and punch-ups in the men's loos.

I have seen a dishevelled gentleman emerging drunkenly in the early hours on to the dance floor where he weaved about with his tail coat ripped from collar to bottom. No-one batted an eyelid at a certain amount of robust enjoyment following the earlier part of the evening which was impeccably sedate.

I recall dancing endless old fashioned waltzes with a delightful lady in her seventies who had more stamina on and off the hunting field than I could muster at little more than half her age. When the fisticuffs began later she merely remarked: 'I'm glad the boys are enjoying themselves.'

Amalgamations

By the end of the 1960s it was abundantly clear that the spread of motorways and urbanisation would continue to swallow up rural Britain.

The MFHA knew that incidents involving hounds running through housing estates, or suburban gardens, were much more likely in hunting countries close to the big population centres. These Hunts were also more likely to attract attention from the growing bands of saboteurs who came out of the towns, mainly at weekends.

The very existence of the MFHA, founded in 1881 with the 8th Duke of Beaufort as its chairman, was dependent on its role in arbitrating the thorny question of Hunt boundaries. In this it had a distinctly patchy record because although Hunt Chairmen and Masters might sometimes be in favour of joining a neighbour there was usually a firm body of opinion within the country against such a move, and it came from groups including influential landowners and farmers.

Local loyalty to 'our hounds' and 'our country' was a huge factor in maintaining foxhunting, but it certainly worked against any form of boundary change. Capt. Simon Clarke, former distinguished hound breeder and amateur huntsman, was appointed after the millennium to tackle the formidable task of assisting future amalgamations.

He forecast in 2002 that whatever the political threats, the number of Foxhunts in Britain was likely to drop from its present 178 packs registered with the MFHA to about 150 in ten years' time. There were in that season eighty-three hare hunting packs, three hunting deer, and twenty minkhound. *Baily's* that season listed eighteen packs of Draghounds and eleven Bloodhound packs.

Simon Clarke believed there were three main reasons justifying amalgamation: lack of country, unsuitable kennels location due to build-up of nearby premises, or financial problems. The Burns Inquiry (see Chapter 10) recommended that all hunts should be 'more selective about the areas in which they hunt' to avoid disturbance, disruption or trespass in residential areas, and suggested reductions in Hunts.

Instead of piecemeal amalgamations the MFHA was endeavouring to hold discussions with groups of neighbouring packs so that boundary solutions would be helpful for more people.

The number of amalgamations at first proved to be a trickle, but led the way to more later in the century. In the 1968–69 season the Vine and the Craven

Farmers' Hunts on the Berkshire-Hampshire borders amalgamated because of pressure from the M4 motorway and growing urbanisation stealing land. These were Hunts of distinction and long standing; the move to amalgamate took much careful consideration before the marriage was decided. The Vine originated in 1790 from the harrier pack of Mr William Chute, whose home, The Vine, near Basingstoke, gave the hunt its name.

The Norfolk and Suffolk Foxhounds disbanded that same season and re-formed as the Dunston Harriers because of a chronic shortage of foxes in the country. The Foxhound pack had been created only four years earlier to replace the Norwich Staghounds, the last pack in mainland Britain to hunt the carted deer. The tradition was maintained within the United Kingdom in Northern Ireland by the County Down Staghounds.

The Vale of Aylesbury's creation in 1970 was much more ambitious, and seen as the way ahead. It was formed by amalgamating the Hertfordshire, Old Berkeley and South Oxfordshire Hunts, packs on the northern and western rim of Greater London, and under huge pressure from motorways and spreading suburbs.

The Hunt has worked well, retaining the distinctive yellow livery for the Hunt staff which the Old Berkeley had espoused. The join-up proved that with horse transport and communications a modern Hunt could straddle areas of build-up to provide sport in pockets of remarkably rural land which the planning authorities had maintained as lungs amid the growing urbanisation of the Home Counties.

Support was forthcoming from an area where there are plenty of people with large surplus incomes, and able to contribute a great deal of know-how in running businesss and professions. In the 2003–4 season the Vale of Aylesbury amalgamated again – this time with the Garth and South Berks which was itself an amalgamation of two packs in 1962, but remained much afflicted by the M4 and new roads around Bracknell in south Buckinghamshire. Hounds remained in the Vale of Aylesbury's kennels to be hunted by their Joint Master and amateur huntsman Alan Hill. The large amalgamated country supports hunting four days a week, alternating Fridays and Saturdays one week a month. Its chairman since 1992 is John Gardiner, one of the most astute minds in the hunting world who is the Political Director of the Countryside Alliance, largely responsible for the brilliant political strategies which caused the 2003 abolition Bills to founder.

As a former subscriber of the Whaddon Chase and its neighbour the Bicester and Warden Hill I shared the angst of subscribers in these splendid countries, once known as the 'Londoners' Leicestershire,' in Buckinghamshire and Oxfordshire.

What fun we had following Dorian Williams as Field Master of the Whaddon, with the great Albert Buckle conjuring consistent sport from such marvellous coverts as Christmas Gorse. I hunted with the Bicester occasionally when it was hunted by one of the boldest riders I have ever seen in the hunting field, Tony Younghusband (1968–73). We pointed afterwards in awe at a wide brook with wire fencing on either side, all of which Tony had cleared entirely in one leap.

Then I was fortunate to hunt in the early part of Capt. Ian Farquhar's brilliant Mastership of the Bicester when he brought in new Welsh outcrosses to transform the pack. Alas, the spread of the new town of Milton Keynes wiped out too much of the Whaddon country for it to remain viable, and the Bicester was suffering somewhat from the new M40 and its off-shoots. They amalgamated in the 1986–87 season, and have formed a remarkably successful and lively Hunt, still all too close to London, providing a great deal of sport over a varied country, with a devoted following.

South of the Thames, the East Sussex and Romney Marsh amalgamated as far back as 1966, and the Chiddingfold, Leconfield and Cowdray forming a major new Hunt in Sussex and Surrey in 1973.

The Southdown and Eridge Hunts amalgamated successfully in 1981, but others much nearer London waited until the next decade. The Old Surrey and Burstow and its neighbour the West Kent joined up in 1999. They were Hunts of long-standing and had provided immense fund for generations of sporting business and professional people in great need of rural recreation after working in central London.

In the 2002–3 season the Badsworth, with a history dating from 1720, amalgamated with its neighbour, the Bramham Moor, founded in 1740, owing to the huge build-up of Yorkshire between Leeds and Sheffield, with growing networks of busy roads. In South Wales the Tredegar Farmers, hunting north of Cardiff, showed another way for a Hunt to retain its identity whilst sharing facilities with a neighbour. The pack became a Hunt Club because much of its country was eroded by motorways and a main railway line.

They kennelled their hounds with the neighbouring Gelligaer Farmers Hunt. The Tredegar country was to be managed by its own Hunt committee, but hunted once a week on alternate Tuesdays and Saturdays by the Gelligaer huntsman. The severe threat to hunting with hounds posed by the Government Bills in 2002 tended to put on hold plans for amalgamations until a more secure future could be perceived by Hunt committees.

Foxhunters and those who follow the other hound sports are among the most ardent of conservationists, and deeply deplore Britain's policy of annually destroying so much of its countryside, but the sport's willingness to amalgamate much loved Hunts, with histories of several hundred years, indicates its determination to see hounds continue hunting that country which can be saved from modern society's obsession with 'progress' in the twenty-first century.

Hunting and Shooting

Although not a matter either sport wished to debate publicly, since the end of the Second World War a constant theme emerges in British foxhunts' problems in providing sport: the need to secure effective relationships with local shoots.

Gamekeepers list foxes as major predators of young birds put down in shooting coverts to mature before each season. The gamekeeper's primary role is to ensure that the shoot for which he is employed has sufficient birds to provide adequate sport. Therefore culling foxes has long been part of many gamekeepers' role in protecting his precious birds.

Traditionally landowners who enjoyed shooting as well as hunting instructed their gamekeepers not to be so harsh on the fox population that the local Hunt would draw the coverts blank. In post-war years rented commercial shoots multiplied, and links with the Hunts grew tenuous in some districts. No-one in such a shoot blushed if a fox could not be found, and increasingly the Hunt was banned from drawing the coverts until the game shooting season was over at the end of January.

On some estates the Hunt was permanently barred, but where hounds were allowed after the end of the shooting season it could become a fruitless exercise because foxes were not to be found. In the early post-war years gamekeepers were relying mainly on snares, and occasional pot-shots with shotguns, to keep down foxes, or else they were destroying litters in earths in the spring.

Later the 'sport' of lamping became increasingly used, and it became easier to extinguish whole populations of foxes on estates.

One of the main preoccupations of the British Field Sports Society and the MFHA was to bring together hunting and shooting interests in joint 'give and take' measures which would benefit both sports. During Ronnie Wallace's chairmanship of the MFHA he secured sponsorship from sporting magazines for hunting/shooting projects designed to show that hounds drawing shooting coverts even a few days before a shoot did not harm their sport; indeed it was claimed to improve shooting by making the birds fly quicker and higher.

There was evidence that this argument was well understood and accepted among more than a few shooters and their gamekeepers, but there was no response in too many shoots. At the end of the twentieth century, and in the early years of the twenty-first, when farming was suffering a new recession, the value to a farming estate of letting the shooting commercially became even more significant. I witnessed blank days, or near blank days, with certain well known packs in the Midlands, when hounds were taken for the first time in February into shooting coverts and spent the rest of the day parading from one draw to the next, all blank.

The gamekeepers were often young men wearing mock combat battle dress, driving Land Rovers and accompanied by friends similarly attired. On the roof would be a mounted spot-light used for night operations, including lamping. They were not a bit abashed that hounds were not finding a fox. One got the impression they would have been horrified if such a phenomenon occurred, and would doubtless have returned to the scene of such a find that very night. Even a visit by the saboteurs could not extinguish a day's hunting in the same way that a hostile shooting estate could achieve.

In vain it was pointed out at high level in the field sports world, and agreed by both shooting and hunting representatives, that shooting was high on the agenda of the animal rights movement, and any success in banning hunting would soon be followed by anti-shooting legislation.

If shooting, a less high profile sport, was left more isolated as a widely practised country sport its impact on foxes and other wildlife and birds would be all the more exposed to opposition from politicians already engaged in supporting animal rights issues.

Some of those who rented shooting, very expensively, would point out that they paid money directly to the benefit of estate owners, or farmers, whereas a Hunt made no direct financial contribution. It was in vain that hunting interests would point out that helping to extinguish hunting's long established place in the countryside would eventually spell curtains for shooting too.

It was in the interests of shooters to help keep hunting alive, if only to remain second in the queue for attack from Parliament. Labour's protestations that it had no plans to abolish shooting could hardly be relied upon when it had already abruptly converted a hunting licensing Bill into a banning Bill. Demonstrations and attempted sabotage of shooting had already occurred on the 'Glorious 12th' of August when grouse shooting commences, and on other shooting days.

Some saboteurs had even been foolish enough to engage in isolated acts of aggression towards anglers, which helped to jolt even the coarse fishing fraternity, said to be five million strong, into fearing that one day it could be on the animal rights agenda for the full treatment meted out to hunting.

Further, the Countryside Alliance pointed out that it was much easier for government to abolish reared game shooting by imposing piecemeal restrictive legislation on gun licences rather than an outright ban on all forms of sporting shooting. Shooting has its own organisation, the British Association for Shooting and Conservation (BASC) which endeavours to maintain high standards for shooting as a country sport rather than as a ruthless exercise mainly for people from outside the countryside who may care very little for local sporting traditions on a broader front.

The inordinate size of the bags sought in some shoots was another cause for concern and criticism, and it was a controversial country topic receiving far more coverage in the media by 2004. BASC has voiced concerns about such problems, and endeavours to achieve reforms, but clearly no single organisation has genuine control of shoots which can operate independently provided they are within the law.

Sex and dress

Tabloid newspapers have always revelled in exposing sexual indiscretions by hunting people who are perceived as colourful risk takers. It was often said in my youth that a mistress was 'something between a Master and a mattress.'

As alpha males in smartly cut red coats and peaked caps, some Masters of Foxhounds have been the hunters, and the hunted, of a few *femme fatale* followers, but this is no more prevalent among foxhunters than any other grouping in today's permissive society.

Despite warnings from public relations advisers against overt class labelling, foxhunters throughout most of the twentieth century defied radical modernisation in their dress, adhering to modified versions of nineteenth century hunting kit, mainly because it was still practical for day-long winter riding, and red shows up best on the winter landscape when you are following a Field Master and hunt staff.

Hunting breeches are cut with much less baggy flares, and white, or champagne top-boots are rare, but some red coats may still be seen in the mounted field, worn after a subscriber has been allowed by the Masters to wear the Hunt button. Subscribers' coats have three front buttons, Masters' four, and hunt staff's five.

Machine washable fabrics often supersede cavalry twill breeches, and some men and women wear styled rubber boots all season instead of the more common leather boots, nowadays worn plain or with tan tops, and more widely available off-the-peg. Foxhunters still wear 'ratcatcher' dress – tweed coats with bowlers or caps – during early morning 'autumn hunting' until the opening meets around 1 November when full fig in red or black is attired.

There has been a major decrease in hunting top hats, highly expensive, and picturesque, but almost useless as head protection. The trend accelerated in the 1982-83 season when a prominent army officer's top hat came off before he fell on the road and was killed in the Grafton country. Serving UK military personnel of all ranks were ordered forthwith to switch from top hats to modern, insulated head gear with chin straps when riding to hounds. This led the MFHA reluctantly to recommend that all male foxhunters could opt to wear caps, with or without chinstraps, instead of top hats.

Further relaxation of dress arrived since the millennium: the MFHA, under chairman Lord (Peter) Daresbury, quietly recommended a switch to black instead of red coats for male mounted followers, but red for MFHs and hunt staff. In 2004 a substantial minority of men subscribers in many Hunts staunchly persisted in wearing red or scarlet (it is incorrect to call coats 'pink' which was the name of a nineteenth century tailor).

Grey caps are, thankfully, far less frequently seen now, but many men, including most huntsmen, wear black caps with rigid peaks, and neither side insulation nor chinstraps. Modern back protectors are seldom seen on adults out hunting. Women continue to wear black or dark blue coats, nearly all abandoning traditional bowlers for caps, many more nowadays worn with chinstraps and insulation.

Fortunately all Pony Club foxhunters put sanity before vanity by obeying their Club's insistence on modern headgear, and some children wear back protectors. Regrettably, far more adults carry cutting whips than traditional hunting whips with bone handles which are so useful in gate-opening. Riding macs are sometimes worn by a few, but still frowned on in the hunting field, although more frequently seen in moorland and hill countries.

CHAPTER 5

HOUND AND HORSE

THE English Foxhound was recognisable as the same breed at the end of the twentieth century, but it had evolved considerably. The most notable difference was that many packs followed a widespread trend towards introducing considerable Welsh hound blood in their traditional lines. This was not achieved without huge controversy, some of it rumbling on throughout the century.

There is no stipulation on the Foxhound's height in the MFHA's stud book, but it is generally not more than twenty-six inches to the top of the shoulder. In the showring no judge makes decisions based on the colour of the hound. No knowledgeable Master breeds hounds to achieve a particular colour, but it is true that so-called 'modern' hounds often tend to be white or lemon and white, and traditional old English hounds are tri-coloured: tan, black and white.

The Foxhound world in the showring regards as a fault a hound with an excessively curly tail, called its stern. This is the only decision based on fashion; all other judging decisions are strictly utilitarian and assessed on conformation which the judge thinks will make it a more effective working animal in the hunting field.

In 1900 most British packs used hounds of so-called 'traditional' breeding, but there had been modifications throughout the previous 150 years to cope with the increased pace of foxhunting. The modern foxhound is derived from an animal which for most of its history was bred to hunt deer. Hunting hounds are broadly divided into those which hunt by scent or by sight. In the British Isles the latter are greyhounds, whippets or lurchers, known as gaze hounds, used mainly to hunt hares, and to catch their fast quarry by a burst of speed.

Foxhounds derive from the hounds using scent to hunt deer, wild boar, wolves and foxes, in approximately that order of priority. The Romans called breeds which hunt by scent 'sagaces', and from these evolved packs of hounds better suited to longer hunts in varied terrain which included woodland and scrub.

The Romans used gaze hounds and scenting hounds during their occupation of Britain. The Saxons were hunters, but they used hounds mainly to drive the quarry into nets, in front of archers. Hunting, like everything else, changed drastically from 1066 when the Normans brought discipline and organisation into hunting.

The deer was the noble beast of the chase, highly valued by English kings, while the fox was just vermin, hunted by some in the seventeenth century, using slow, lop-eared hounds with bell-like voices. The technique was to hunt in the early morning the drag, or scent, of the fox which had returned from his own night's hunting. This line led back to his earth where hounds bayed mightily to mark him to ground, and he was then dug up and thrown to the hounds amid much canine and human rejoicing.

The clearance of the English forests, and enclosure of land in the late eighteenth and early nineteenth centuries, created the 'modern' sport of

Three great Foxhound breeders of the twentieth century, *l. to r.*: Capt. Ronnie Wallace MFH, 'Master' the 10th Duke of Beaufort, and Ben Hardaway MFH (Midland, USA).

foxhunting, still requiring scenting abilities, but much sharper and faster because hounds were followed by men riding far better bred horses who were prepared to leap obstacles at speed in pursuit. When foxhunting became fashionable, so did the Foxhound.

Although originally compiled from 1800, the maintenance and ownership of the Foxhound Kennel Stud Book was undertaken by the Masters of Foxhounds Association from 1886, and had a profound influence on the breed. The careful recording of pedigrees, published in annual volumes of the FKSB, enabled Masters to use line breeding to produce their desired type.

The English Foxhound was derived from the old Norman blood known as the Talbot breed, later known as the Northern hound, and from the Southern hound which prior to the eighteenth century was used mainly to hunt the hare, and was a slower type, with an excellent voice.

Welsh hounds derived from an original Celtic breed, giving them a distinctive rough coat, which is why some people call them 'woollies'. These hounds also contain some French blood, brought to England by monks at Margam Abbey in Glamorganshire, and hunted here until the dissolution of the monasteries.

The French imports had remarkably fine noses and good voices, and came originally from the Monastery of St Hubert in the Ardennes. These qualities can still be found in the Welsh hound – and were the source of a major controversy in twentieth century hound breeding.

The late nineteenth century packs, certainly the more fashionable ones, produced the 'Belvoir type' as the most desirable, and this became the most commonly sought after, although a few individualists refused to follow fashion. The Belvoir kennel was regarded as the height of fashion and achievement, and

Capt. Brian Fanshawe, former Master and huntsman of the Cottesmore (*right*) judges Cottesmore's young hounds at their puppy show in June 2004, with the assistance of his cousin, Capt. Ian Farquhar MFH (Duke of Beaufort's).

its sires were much in demand. This remained popular until well after the Great
War. For reasons which now seem hard to defend, it had become the fashion to
breed Foxhounds of considerable bone and substance. Their coats were in the
handsome 'Belvoir tan' livery, being universally tan, black and white, and a high-
class pack was expected to adhere closely to the same type and colour.

Daphne Moore says the Belvoir type stood 'woodenly on four legs like
bedposts teminating in round club feet; wide barrel ribs pushing forward a
shoulder which was placed perpendicular with the ground.' The Belvoir hound
became known also as the 'Peterborough type' because it was favoured by judges
at Britain's leading Foxhound show. In her *Book of the Foxhound* (J.A. Allen,
1964) Miss Moore says there was a proud boast from a foxhunting pundit in 1914
that 'The modern Foxhound has the forearm of a lion, and shows short solid,
good bone form the knee to the toes.'

Daphne comments: 'Since foxhounds, and not lions, were being bred to hunt
foxes, why anyone should wish to breed an animal with a lion's forearm is difficult to comprehend.' She believes the 'fashionable massive Foxhound' was an
over-reaction to the light framed racy types used in the mid-nineteenth century,
depicted in sporting paintings of the early nineteenth and late eighteenth
centuries after Meynell invented the new sport of hunting the fox in the open at
speed.

'Pure' English Hounds

Although I am an admirer of Daphne Moore and trust her judgement on most
Foxhound matters, I have learned to take some of the condemnation of the 'old
English' with a pinch of salt. Daphne has always been a great disciple of the 10th
Duke of Beaufort, and therefore firmly supported his switch from traditional to
modern hound breeding which included the importation of Welsh blood.

There were conformation deficiencies in the most extreme examples of the
traditional English type, but there were some great virtues in their hunting
abilities. Their close breeding meant they behaved as a proper pack, thinking and
acting similarly. It is still a virtue of the few remaining 'pure' English packs. I put
the word 'pure' in quotes because these hounds do not come from one source
over hundreds of years, but no doubt had other influences from a number of
sources until their breeding was documented in the Foxhound Kennel Stud
Book.

The current examples of 'old English' have voice, good enough nose, and
certainly they have great drive – hunting forward on the line of their fox with
great relish. This was no doubt why they were so much admired over the endless
good scenting hunting grass countries. As I have described later (Chapter 9) I
have enjoyed marvellous days riding behind English packs, especially the Belvoir
and the County Limerick. These hounds were a fine sight in their smart colour,
they ran together 'as if a blanket could cover them', and they hunted with a drive
which made added greatly to the pleasure of the hard-riding set in the mounted
field. If they hunted on over the line, the cynical might say that a fashionable
huntsman would simply lift them and gallop on to the next covert in the hope of

finding another fox, or if he had room, he would cast widely in a loop, hoping to pick up the line of the hunted fox again, both manoeuvres providing still more grass and fences to traverse for the 'cut 'em down' brigade bucketing along behind.

The critics of traditional English hounds said that from 1918 they found many of these hounds too big, not active enough, lacked drive and intelligence and were short of nose and tongue. This was the verdict of Sir Peter Farquhar (1903–86) who was one of the most effective amateur huntsmen and hound breeders of the century, and a keen supporter of using Welsh out-crosses. He used them as a young man in his pre-war Mastership of the Meynell, and he was an innovative breeder after the war when he was Master of the Portman in Dorset.

Since breeding a working species of hound must be a dynamic process, no-one could quarrel with the enterprise of Sir Peter and a group of other Masters and amateur huntsmen who sought to remedy what they considered were the ills of the English hound. This needed a certain amount of moral courage because it was fiercely resisted in the more conservative areas of a sport famous for its appeal to traditionalists.

The dispute over the introduction of Welsh hound blood split families and ended friendships. One of the first signs of battle occurred when Capt. Charlie McNeill, who was Master of the North Cotswold (1901–6) and the Grafton (1907–13), wrote to *The Field* complaining that if the best Belvoir stallion hounds sired as many litters as they were said to have achieved in the stud book, they could not have done much hunting.

There was an angry response from traditionalist hunting men who said it was an impertinence to attack another Master's management of his kennels, and in any case the Belvoir was performing a service to others in allowing so many bitches to be sent to their sires.

The Captain retorted that the Belvoir was a national institution, that hound breeding was of national importance, and therefore he was thoroughly justified in raising the matter. The debate wrangled on for some weeks, but reached no conclusion.

The dreaded innovation of Welsh outcross breeding occurred briefly within the Belvoir Hunt when a great enthusiast, and highly knowledgeable foxhunter, Major Tommy Bouch took over Mastership (1912–24), and worked hard to improve the Belvoir pack. He found a very limited number of lines of 'pure' English hounds, and at one stage introduced some Welsh blood. He was sternly rebuked and refused permission by the pack's owner, the Duke of Rutland. The 10th Duke who succeeded to the title in 1940, recalled the outrage of his family caused by the attempt 'to introduce an element of white Welsh hound into the breeding.'

'This caused great offence and was immediately changed,' said the Duke.

Any Belvoir hounds with Welsh blood were immediately drafted. However, Tommy Bouch ensured through selective policies that the accent on breeding for bone and stature was much reduced, and the pack was becoming more athletic and lighter in build by the time he finished twelve years in office notable for good sport.

Frank Freeman, the Pytchley's renowned huntsman, from 1906–31, achieved superlative sport with English-bred hounds, but they were not big, heavily built animals; he made his name by acquiring and hunting a pack of lightly built English bitches, many of them purchased at the old Rugby hound sale.

The Duke of Rutland continued the traditional English policy at the Belvoir for the rest of the century, declaring: 'I am so anxious to ensure that the breeding policy should follow our distinctive traditional lines of colour and conformation.'

By the end of the century the pendulum had swung so far against packs entirely comprised of 'pure' English blood that only three kennels in England could claim this distinction, the Belvoir, the Brocklesby hounds in North Lincolnshire, owned by the Earls of Yarborough, and the York and Ainsty South.

The most fervent enthusiast for traditional English breeding was Lord (Toby) Daresbury who was Master of the Belvoir for a decade (1937–47), hunting them during the war. Next he achieved a great Mastership of the County Limerick as Master and huntsman (1947–77) when he proved that traditionally bred Belvoir hounds could hunt just as well over the great banks and walls of Ireland as they could over the galloping grass of Leicestershire. He ensured the Limerick remained a highly successful outpost of English breeding.

There are a number of kennels where there are still large elements of English hound breeding, for example Sir Watkin Williams-Wynn's, another family owned pack, with an excellent record of producing top-class sport on the Welsh Borders. In recent years, leading hound breeders have returned more frequently

Famous old English hounds, the Belvoir pack, with their huntsman Jim Webster (1956–83) on his last day in the Belvoir Vale in March 1983.

Belvoir Principal, winning doghound at the Belvoir puppy show in 1980.

The renowned old English Brocklesby pack, arriving at a meet, with Cooper Atkinson as huntsman

to 'pure' English lines to refresh the breeding of the 'modern' Welsh-influenced Foxhound, and there have been some excellent results.

The most obvious example was much admired at the 2003 Peterborough Royal Foxhound Show when the Heythrop won the bitch championship with Poplin '01, a superb product of one of the leading modern kennels, yet sired by a Belvoir stallion hound, Poacher '98.

Roddy Bailey, Master and huntsman of the Morpeth, was so concerned that the importance of the traditional English hound was being overlooked, that he introduced several classes recently at the Great Yorkshire Hound show specifically for these hounds.

The Belvoir's bitch pack admired by supporters after a puppy show at their Belvoir Castle kennels.

The Belvoir and Brocklesby long since ceased to show at Peterborough because judges 'look the other way' when English hounds come into the ring, and there has been no move anywhere else to introduce special classes for them.

Toby Daresbury invariably supported the Irish hound show at Clonmel by entering his Limerick hounds which frequently won the two-couple class because they were always the best matched. Toby hated the modern hound which he considered had a poor under-line, with not enough depth, and because he alleged that Welsh hounds were too inclined to 'beagle' about, doing their own thing; they were 'self-hunting' hounds ideal for the true amateur, he said. To hunt across a really good country in front of a keen field there was nothing to beat the traditional English Foxhound, he believed.

Showing is interesting, but the purpose of hound breeding is to produce performance in the hunting field .

My own view, having hunted with all the existing packs of 'pure' English hounds, especially the Belvoir where I subscribed for some twenty years, is that the breeding pendulum swung much too far away. I am certain the extreme criticisms of the traditional hound at the beginning of the century do not apply today. They have manifest virtues in the hunting field, although significantly old English hounds have been hunted by very few leading Masters and amateur huntsmen, who are influential in overall breeding trends.

Martin Thornton has been the professional huntsman of the Belvoir for twelve seasons, achieving excellent sport in a country which in riding terms has deteriorated somewhat due to greatly increasing plough. His hounds hunt over arable as well as grass with great success, and certainly catch their foxes. Previously he hunted the Bicester with Whaddon Chase 'modern' pack.

'The pure English hound is strong-willed and can take some handling,' Martin told me near the end of the 2003–4 season when I re-visited the Belvoir for a good day's hunting. 'English hounds have tremendous drive, and it takes a brave man to follow them straight when they run hard,' he said. 'I hunted modern hounds with Welsh crosses before I came here. Since I hunted the Belvoir I wouldn't be without pure English hounds to provide good sport.'

Jim Webster, who hunted the Belvoir hounds from 1956–83, a period when I can testify this pack enjoyed some great sport, had a dry sense of humour. Speaking after judging at puppy shows he used to refer to any pack containing Welsh blood as 'them other 'ounds'.

Sir Newton Rycroft, who was to become one of the most experimental users of out-crosses, believed many old English hounds had excellent noses through generations of hunting on plough land. He commented: 'For over 200 years the English Foxhound has been bred, sometimes by stupid and sometimes by intelligent people, and while I am fully prepared to admit that some packs could, and have been, improved by outcrosses, I also believe that to breed a great pack of hounds without these priceless old English strains as a genetic base, would be extremely difficult and undesirable for the future of foxhunting. Where then would be your stamina and constitution?'

I have seen these qualities well illustrated by the performance of the Brocklesby when I hunted with them in their country in north-east Lincolnshire. It is virtually all arable, and requires excellent scenting abilities, and strength from hounds to hunt a fox over such land, especially in the wettest parts of the winter when the land is heavy.

Welsh Influence

To praise the essential virtues of the 'pure' English is not to denigrate the many Welsh-cross packs, although some are far better than others. Undoubtedly the infusion of the Welsh blood achieved much in producing hounds with excellent noses and 'fox sense', the ability to find a fox and retain its line.

On the other hand, the 'independence' of the Welsh hound can be something a problem until it is properly assimilated into an English kennel. Another problem is that absolutely pure Welsh are confined to a limited number of packs hunting in Wales, and it is necessary to be absolutely certain about the pedigree of a hound chosen for an outcross.

English Masters usually breed out the broken coats inherited from Welsh ancestors; this is achieved in a generation or two, although it can recur, and some hounds still have the domed, occipital skulls of the original French hounds imported by the Margam Abbey monks.

Biddable hounds which can be controlled swiftly and effectively when it matters, are a major factor in producing sport, especially in today's more cramped hunting countries. Ensuring the pack obeys the huntsman as required, but has the confidence to find its own fox and cast itself to recover a line when necessary, is one the key achievements of the most successful huntsmen in the field.

Ikey Bell, the American-born Master of the South and West Wilts, the Galway Blazers and the Kilkenny, early in the twentieth century was the principal

A modern example of Welsh hound breeding at its best: the Pembrokeshire's Galchen '96, champion Welsh doghound at the Wales and Border Counties Hound Show 1999.

prophet who preached in favour of Welsh crosses. A talented writer, Ikey produced some of the most interesting and amusing books on his favourite sport. He remarked that those who cried out loudest about Welsh blood put into English kennels were often those who knew least of its ancestry or had no experience of it in the hunting field. 'It was looked upon, in fact, by these gentlemen as a form of heresy,' he said.

Bell began by using outcrosses from the kennel of Sir Edward Curre, Master from 1896–1930 of his family pack of white hounds at Itton, Montgomeryshire, which amalgamated with the Llangibby in 2000.

Ronnie Wallace described Curre as 'perhaps the greatest hound expert of the lot'. Daphne Moore says Sir Edward was so skilful he could have bred a pack a hounds of any colour of the rainbow. That he chose to breed his hounds *white* in an era of Belvoir tan, is the main reason for today's mainly light coloured Foxhounds, tending to be white or lemon and white, asserted Miss Moore.

He took the trouble to study genetics and had a natural gift for selecting hounds. He aimed to produce active hounds, comparatively light of bone. His formula in own words was: 'Cross Berkeley with the best Welsh blood available; breed "out" to the badger-pied strains at Badminton and Milton (the Fitzwilliam kennel), and to Belvoir . . . Pure Welsh blood only exists in two or three kennels, and while these produce very good hounds to hunt their rough countries, they also provide the means of crossing with English strains, and this is invaluable.'

This 'Squire of Itton' on the Welsh Borders produced hounds with marvellous working qualities. Ikey Bell was one of the first to use them, and increasingly other Foxhound breeders were following suit. The rough coats were speedily bred out, and by the 1930s some hounds containing Curre lines were winning at Peterborough.

Glog Nimrod '04, a wire coated, wheaten coloured hound of great athleticism founded at Itton a dynasty which later existed in most kennels in the British Isles, being the most celebrated of the Welsh sires used. Other influential Welsh sires were Llangibby Foreman, Ystrad Topper, and Gelligaer Hamlet 1911.

Newton Rycroft wrote that the 'greatest part of Sir Edward's genius was that he showed you could have all the virtues of the Welsh without any loss whatever of either stamina or constitution.

'Firstly by so wisely filling his kennel with so much of the tough old Berkeley-Fitzhardinge blood, itself full of Bentinck and as stout as steel; and secondly by breeding a pack whose stamina points, such as their backs and loins and sensible feet, were so outstanding . . . of all the good Foxhounds he bred I believe his Danger '15, with better pace points than some of his later sires, was an even greater dog than his famous son Brecon Paragon '23, and that he was indeed one of the greatest Foxhounds ever.'

Among the other most influential Welsh breeders were George, Earl of Coventry, Master of the Carmarthenshire (1926–31) and of the Croome (1932–40) who died at Dunkirk, Lord Davies, Master of the David Davies (1905–44) and Capt. Jack Evans, Master of the Brecon (1922–35).

Carmathen Nimrod '24 inherited a blue mottled coat from his Harrier ancestors and passed on that colour to generations of Foxhounds, including illustrious Beaufort and Heythrop hounds seen in the show-ring today.

Ikey Bell recalled that after using the Curre hounds: 'Many Masters criticised

David Davies Lawyer '03, champion Welsh doghound and overall champion, and Teme Valley Lyric '03, champion Welsh bitch, at the 2004 Wales and Border Counties show. Huntsmen: David Jones of the David Davies, and Roy Savage of the Teme Valley.

me at the time, some actually declaring me to be a "menace to Foxhounds!" Many of these critics in years to come bred to these lines, which certainly much amused me.'

He summed up the virtues of the Welsh thus: 'Their necks and shoulders are generally very good, they hunt low on a weak scent, are remarkably persevering, try hard at a check and continue to try under all circumstances.

'When cast for long distances, they continue to concentrate and do not suddenly get their heads up like many pure-bred hounds I've seen.'

The fears of traditionalists in the foxhunting world were translated into action in 1928. The MFHA closed the Foxhound Kennel Stud Book to hounds not bred, entered and worked in recognised Foxhound kennels. This excluded many Welsh hounds from packs not registered with the MFHA, and applied to some other breeds from non-registered packs, notably some Fell hounds, Harriers, and imports from abroad.

Far-sighted breeders such as the Duke of Beaufort, Sir Peter Farquhar and Major Maurice 'Mo' Barclay, Master of the Puckeridge, urged after the Second World War that the stud book closure was far too restrictive. For example, there were some Harrier packs hunting foxes very effectively. The Cotley's famous pack of white West Country Harriers was registered with the MFHA in 1948, but the stud book remained closed to Harriers.

After much argument, in 1955 it was ruled by the MFHA that it was only necessary to prove that hounds eligible for the stud book had pedigrees going back five generations, later increased to six, to ancestors kept for hunting only the fox, and that they came from established packs of Foxhounds which had been hunting the fox only for at least ten years. These packs were to be entered in a special section at the back of the stud book.

These sensible amendments widened the opportunity for the most astute and imaginative hound breeders to seek dynamic out-crosses which helped greatly to ensure that modern English Foxhounds remained arguably the greatest breed of working pack hounds in the world. The most helpful rule introduced by the MFHA was the refusal to allow registered Foxhounds to be sold within the United Kingdom, either between Hunts, or to individuals.

It had been a long-standing practice up to the 1930s for Foxhounds to be sold at annual sales at Rugby. Masters would literally buy whole packs to start a new Hunt, or sell them at the end of a Mastership. The new rule immediately took the Foxhound out of the commercial dog market which has arguably spoilt so many other breeds of dog in Britain, bred to extremes of fashion to satisfy market force.

In some cases these demands have led to some pedigree dogs carrying genetic faults from one generation to the next. The Foxhound's true role as a working dog is the key to its evolution during the twentieth century to emerge as a superb athlete with great powers of endurance, and a co-operative temperament.

Sir Newton Rycroft produced the most influential Welsh stallion hound of the twentieth century during his Mastership of the New Forest hounds for twenty-two years (1962–84). Known affectionately by many younger Masters as 'the Newt', he was one of the most interesting personalities in foxhunting, an academic, an exceptional naturalist, an immensely knowledgeable hound breeder, and an effective huntsman in the field. He had been founder and Master for twenty-two years of the Dummer Beagles in Gloucestershire before he became an MFH.

Sir Newton was inclined to cause eyes to glaze over when he addressed Hunt Supporters' Clubs on such esoteric aspects of hound breeding as the influence of the French revolution on the conformation of French deer and hare hounds, but his views and comments on hound breeding were full of interest, highly regarded when he addressed seminars and wrote for the sporting press.

His own hound breeding experiments verged on the eccentric at times. During an excellent day's hunting with the New Forest he turned to me and said: 'Now what do you think that hound is that you can hear speaking loudly?'

The answer, which I did not get right, was the bell-like voice of a Bloodhound which was hunting with the pack to enable the use of its great scenting powers. It cannot be said that this controversial addition was notably successful; I believe the Bloodhound soon showed that it could not keep up with English Foxhounds when it really mattered. 'The Newt' said a third-generation cross Bloodhound was a more practical possibility and he had hunted such cross-breds with success.

I noticed one bitch was an unusual pink colour, and Sir Newton advised me he had given her a 'pink dye wash' so that she was easy to see in the hunting field and he could judge her working abilities accurately before he decided to breed from her.

'The Newt' used Harrrier blood with some success, but his greatest triumph was achieved through his Welsh outcrosses when he produced the most influential Welsh cross-bred sire of the post-war years, New Forest Medyg '69, by putting a pure Welsh sire Miller '63 from the small Welsh pack, the Plas Machynlleth, on to a New Forest bitch, Traffic '65 who came from generations of English lines on the top and bottom line. Her sire was Old Berks Playfair '60 and her dam was New Forest Truelove '61.

Sir Newton judged the Plas Machynlleth Hunt's puppy show in the summer of 1963. He became much impressed by the prowess of the Master and huntsman Harry Roberts in breeding hounds of quality, and this led to the link between the New Forest pack and the Plas Machynlleth.

New Forest Medyg had a good conformation, a most attractive head, and a kind, intelligent eye. Above all, he soon proved to be an excellent performer in the hunting field. By the year of his death, 1982, Medyg had been widely used as a stallion hound, and was much admired for his pre-potency. He had descendants in more than forty kennels in his life-time, including the Duke of Beaufort's where Medyg's greatest success was to sire Monmouth '77 who was judged Peterborough champion doghound in 1978.

The dam of Monmouth was Beaufort Crimson '72, and Monmouth became a highly influential sire in the Beaufort kennel, ensuring the continuance of the Medyg line at Badminton. The Duke of Beaufort was so pleased with Medyg that in 1982 he gave a special luncheon at Badminton for MFHs who had used this Welsh outcross, and presented Sir Newton with a bronze of his famous hound. When I mentioned the lunch to Ronnie Wallace he remarked drily: 'Just occasionally there is distinction in not being invited to a party.'

Another highly successful use of Welsh breeding was achieved in the Bicester and Warden Hill kennel by Sir Peter Farquhar's son, Captain Ian Farquhar,

Joint Master and huntsman from 1973–84. He acquired a small Welsh bitch, Fairy '73, from the Vale of Clettwr kennel in North East Carmarthenshire.

Fairy founded an illustrious cross-bred line through her son, Bicester Farmer '76, by Bicester Freshman '73, which still exists in the Bicester kennel, and in the Duke of Beaufort's where Ian Farquhar has been Joint Master and huntsman since 1985. Bicester Farmer was one of the most successful Welsh-cross sires of the post-war years.

Ian was delighted when his unentered Beaufort bitch Fancy was reserve bitch champion at Peterborough in 2003; she has no less than three lines back to Vale of Clettwr Fairy.

At the Beaufort kennel in recent years Ian Farquhar has used David Davies blood with success. The winning bitch at Badminton's puppy show in July 2002 was Bootlace, a granddaughter of the David Davies sire Bouncer '94.

In June 2003 Ian was believed to be the first English Master to judge in the Welsh hound ring at the Wales and Border Counties show at Builth Wells in June. He and his co-judge selected as their doghound champion Biscuit '00, a son of Bouncer. The annual show at Builth Wells is the best known shop window for the pure Welsh hound. The breed's fervent admirers have been somewhat concerned in recent seasons to note that fewer Welsh Hunts contain packs of entirely pure Welsh hounds.

There has been a growing trend for Welsh packs to use outcrosses from Fell packs, and in the 2004 Welsh show at Builth several classes were being introduced for Fell hounds for the first time. Huntsmen have found Fell-Welsh hounds excellent in their work – and it is another sign that performance in the hunting field, not rosettes in the show ring, is the priority in making hound breeding decisions.

The Fell Hound

The Fell hound is a lighter framed, racier version of the standard Foxhound used in lowland packs. The Fell has a more open 'hare' foot which is helpful in traversing the rough terrain and steep hills in its native Lake District in Cumbria, formerly Cumberland and Westmorland. This work requires a good shoulder; a lengthy humerus and long flexible pastern to lessen concussion when running down rocky slopes and jumping walls; and a well let-down hock and a developed second thigh for speed and impulsion uphill.

Although the Fell strain of Foxhound is distinctively different it has had outcrosses of Welsh and standard Foxhound blood over the past 150 years, but remains a wiry, rangy type so well suited to its arduous task. In the main the Fell hound breeds true to type, and therefore can safely be contemplated as an outcross likely to convey Fell qualities.

The six Fell packs hunted on foot are the Blencathra, Coniston, Eskdale and Ennerdale, Melbreak, Lunesdale and Ullswater.

For nose, endurance, and intelligence the Fell hound has much to offer, because it frequently hunts completely unaided by the huntsman for many hours, since the terrain often prevents him from being close to hounds.

Fell hounds in their natural setting: the Blencathra pack at their Threlkeld Kennel in 1976, with *centre to right*: Joint Master Major Phil Davidson, whipper-in Barry Todhunter, and huntsman Johnny Richardson (1949–88).

Champion Fell hound, Eskdale and Ennerdale Trueman, with Edmund Porter MFH.

Continuity has been a major factor in Masterships and huntsmen of the Fell packs. Johnny Richardson, for example, hunted the famous Blencathra hounds for forty years up to 1988 when they were taken over by his protégé, Barry Todhunter.

Foxhunters who view Fell hounds through binoculars, hunting so effectively over the highest peaks in England admire some of the truest hound work to be seen anywhere. Visitors to the Lakes in the spring from other hunting countries

Sir Alfred Goodson,
founder Master and
Huntsman of the College
Valley (1924–79) who
developed the cross-Fell
hound with with much
success

watch the hounds by day and in the evening join the Fell hunters for convivial evenings in Lakeland pubs, singing hunting songs which go back to the most famous Fell huntsman of all, John Peel who hunted much of the Blencathra country.

Could the best of these qualities be blended into lowland packs followed on horseback? The most notable success in achieving this was in the College Valley pack, founded by Sir Alfred Goodson in 1924 on the Northumberland-Scottish borders.

He used sires from the Ullswater, Blencathra, and Coniston packs, crossing them with standard English hounds, and some infusions of West Country Harrier blood from the Cotley. The result was a pack of lean, racy hounds, noted for their speed, their ability to drive hard, and when necessary to cast themselves swiftly over the heather clad hills of the Borders. Martin Letts who succeeded Sir Alfred as Master and huntsman of the College Valley for a notable forty years, 1964–2004, is a leading breeder and judge of hounds, and maintained the Fell element in his pack with skill and sensitivity, continuing this trend after the College Valley amalgamated with its neighbour, the North Northumberland.

One of Sir Alfred's great friends and mentors was Mr Jacob Robson, Master of the Border Hounds who hunt a distinct type of rangy, racy Foxhound with excellent feet. Their sire Border Stormer '19 was described by Sir Alfred as 'the best hound I ever saw run on the hill' and contributed much to the breeding of the College Valley pack. Newton Rycroft paid tribute to the College Valley's 'enormous and beneficial influence, first of all in the North and then all over England and in America.'

Some experienced huntsmen think the drawback with hill hounds is that they can be nervous and unsettled when subjected to the pressures of hunting in a lowland pack under closer control from a huntsman and his staff. Yet they are undoubtedly an excellent outcross if used with expertise. This was proved by Ronnie Wallace who became firm friends with Edmund Porter, Master of the Eskdale and Ennerdale.

Ronnie used to visit the Lakes in spring and much admired the ability of this pack to cast itself and pick up the line of the hunted fox. He used the Eskdale and Ennerdale stallion hound Bendigo with much success in the Heythrop pack, although he was to remark: 'The trouble with the Fell is that, as they get older, they become a bit more cunning.'

Nevertheless he was full of praise for the remarkable hunting abilities of Bendigo and his progeny and his benign influence on the Heythrop, and later the Exmoor packs.

The Fell has contributed to some other remarkable packs, notably the Cotley, Cotswold, Exmoor and Tiverton, and the West Waterford in Ireland where the husband and wife Masters Tom and Elsie Morgan used this blood in creating a superb hunting pack from 1953–89.

Tim Unwin, Master and huntsman of the Cotswold (1971–99) introduced valuable fox-catching Fell blood through the Blencathra hound, Glider '75, whose son Glencoyne '84 became a much valued stallion hound, producing offspring who were excellent in their work.

An interesting source of excellent Foxhounds was the Carlow kennel in Ireland, where hounds were bred by Olive Hall, Master for forty-five years until her death in 1965. She won the Peterborough bitch championship in 1928, with Vera '23, the first Irish pack to gain this honour. Ikey Bell was a firm friend and his famous sire South and West Wilts Godfrey '28 was bred in the Carlow kennel and given to him unentered.

The Cottesmore's renowned Master and amateur huntsman Brian Fanshawe maintained a Carlow line in his various packs since 1963. It was a great boon in the Cottesmore pack where some forty per cent had Carlow blood on the bottom line. 'They are terribly easy to handle, nearly like pet dogs; they need plenty of hunting, but they are biddable and they have "fox sense",' said Fanshawe.

The Carlow became defunct from 1966, but in 1979 the Carlow Farmers' Hunt was formed to hunt the country.

The Green Jackets

The great Foxhound breeding packs in the twentieth century, the Duke of Beaufort's and the Heythrop, were both in Beaufort terrain until the Heythrop became a separate Hunt in 1835. The huntsmen and whippers-in of both packs wear green coats, the livery of the Beaufort family, rather than scarlet.

The reason for their huge successes in hound breeding was not due to geography but personalities who had great continuity in their Masterships: those of the 10th Duke of Beaufort, Master of his family pack from 1924 until his death in 1984, and Capt. Ronnie Wallace, Joint Master and huntsman of the Heythrop for twenty-five seasons (1952–77), and of the Exmoor for another twenty-five (1977–2002).

Master as a hound breeder at Badminton had green fingers, exhibiting skill in selecting the best from existing English lines to produce the sort of Foxhound he liked to hunt: athletic, intelligent, with excellent noses and drive. His best achievement was to match size with sheer quality, and his annual puppy show

Modern English breeding at its best: Heythrop Poplin, champion bitch at Peterborough Royal Foxhound Show 2003. She contains old English Belvoir lines with superb modern breeding from the classic Heythrop kennel.

Bred by a genius of the hound world, Capt. Ronnie Wallace: Exmoor Greatwood '93, champion doghound at the supreme English show, Peterborough, in 1994.

was an event virtually as important as a major hound show. Enthusiasts came to Badminton, and still do so, to admire each new Beaufort entry.

The Duke recalled: 'When I became Master of my own hounds, though I knew they were as stout as ever, I did feel they lacked cry. To remedy this defect, I successfully introduced new blood with Sir Ian Amory's Tiverton Actor, and Mr Isaac Bell's best lines in the South and West Wilts kennel.

'Ikey Bell used Welsh blood and this is an infusion which helped the cry of many other packs, as well as my own.'

Master was using Welsh lines carefully in the 1930s. At the 1935 Peterborough show the Duke of Beaufort's Pelican '35 was one of the winning couples of young doghounds; his dam, Petrel '32, was a bitch from the Brecon kennel, with much Welsh blood mixed with English lines; her tail female line traced back through the old English Brocklesby kennel.

The following year Pelican won the Peterborough doghound championship, and the Welsh-cross enthusiasts were overjoyed with this recognition.

Like his father, the 10th Duke became very interested in winning rosettes in hound shows, although he never lost sight of his goal in breeding for work. He won twenty-four doghound championships and thirteen bitch championships at Peterborough Royal Foxhound Show, and numerous rosettes in other classes at that show and the other leading hound shows.

Among the best doghounds bred by the Duke during the latter part of his Mastership were Distaff '52, Tetrarch '52, Dreamer '53, Woodcock '55, Dragon '56, Godfrey '60, Beadle and Bellman '66, Gaffer and Grocer '68.

Daphne Moore believed 'possibly the most renowned and influential sire ever to be bred at Badminton was the incomparable Palmer '58, who founded a lasting dynasty. His pedigree is filled with the finest blood of the Foxhound Stud Book, and his mating to Woeful '60 (the alliance of two Peterborough champions of the same year) produced four brood bitches and a stallion hound. This family might be said to be the backbone of the kennel today.'

It was of great benefit to the Beaufort Hunt and the sport in general, that Master was succeeded on his death in 1984 by a devoted foxhunting man, his cousin David Somerset. A superb horseman and a leading member of the Beaufort mounted field before he succeeded to the title, the 11th Duke understands perfectly the importance of the pack he had inherited at Badminton, and made the excellent choice of Ian Farquhar to join him in the Mastership, and to hunt and breed the hounds. The annual Badminton show in June exhibiting their new entry remains a high spot in the calendar for Foxhound enthusiasts.

Since 1985, Ian has proved a huge success in maintaining the highest standards at Badminton, and as noted above, he has continued judiciously to use Welsh out-crosses with the best of English lines.

This has been reflected in good sport in front of large mounted fields, and in the continuing flow of championships won by the Beaufort hounds at Peterborough and elsewhere. Badminton continues to be generous with the use of its stallion hounds in other kennels, and its influence remains crucial to the success of English foxhunting.

Ronnie Wallace's pre-eminence as a hound breeder was legendary, and continued throughout his later life until his death in a car crash in February 2002, at the age of eighty-two. His annual duel with the other greencoat pack at Peterborough resumed amazingly quickly after he donned a scarlet coat when he took Mastership of the Exmoor, hunting in a very different West Country moorland country where Wallace soon re-established a major Foxhound breeding kennel, relying heavily on Heythrop lines he had brought with him.

Altogether Wallace achieved an unassailable record of thirty-three championships at Peterborough: eleven doghound and eight bitch championships with the Heythrop; and eight doghound and six bitch championships with the Exmoor. He remained firm in avoiding an outcross from the Welsh, to the disappointment of some other hound breeding afficianados. 'Some will say I am prejudiced against the Welsh hound. Not so,' he said. ' Quite simply, I have seen English kennels where they have had too much Welsh blood, and it has upset the balance of the pack.'

Ronnie recalled being loaned a Welsh doghound named Abraham from the Pantysgallog pack, which he hunted when he was Master of the Cotswold, one morning during cub-hunting.

Abraham distinguished himself by running heel line as soon as the pack ran up to their fox, and when Abraham had run back to where they had found the fox originally he went back again on the line. Very soon the Pantysgallog hound went back to Wales. Ronnie Wallace remarked: 'I wouldn't want to make too much of that incident, but it was an interesting example of a problem you can have with outcrosses.'

In addition to the Fell outcross from the Eskdale and Ennerdale, producing a female line, Wallace used West Country Harrier and American outcrosses, and refreshed his 'modern' Foxhound lines with occasional returns to old English blood at the Brocklesby. His favourite was the Heythrop Brigand '54 male line, exemplified by Craftsman '62, Brigand's son. His next favourite was that of Exmoor Hackler '78 by Heythrop Grossman whose forebear was Sir Peter Farquhar's Portman Wizard '56.

When he arrived at the Heythrop, Wallace used what he believed to be the best male line in the stud book which already existed in the Heythrop Kennel: it descended from Warwickshire '06 in the nineteenth century, then considered the best, and went through Heythrop Carver '36, to Sergeant '46 . Wallace used Sergeant as the sire to breed Heythrop Brigand '54 who became a corner-stone of modern Foxhound breeding.

A notable descendant of Brigand was Exmoor Daresbury '87 who was Peterborough doghound champion in 1990 and has been one of the most widely used stallion hounds.

Ronnie Wallace said the first outcross of any significance he introduced at the Exmoor was the American hound, Old Dominion Gorgeous '68, a bitch given to him by his friend, Bill Brainard, veteran Master of the Old Dominion pack in Virginia. Wallace was delighted with her progeny, especially when a product of this dynasty, Gladness '90 won the Peterborough bitch championship in 1991.

Later Wallace acquired an American doghound, Barber '89, from the Orange County pack of small red and white matching hounds in Virginia, and Drummer '89 from the Live Oak pack bred by his friends, Marty and Daphne Wood, in Florida. Their American-English cross-bred pack includes some of the best Exmoor and Beaufort lines.

At Exmoor Wallace introduced a West Country Harriers line through a doghound, Catlow, from the Taunton Vale Harriers. He pointed out that Harriers had long been valued as fox-catchers because of their ability to turn short.

Martin Scott, former MFH and amateur huntsman of the Tiverton and the VWH – where he has bred the influential sire VWH Guinness – has summed up some of Ronnie Wallace's achievements thus: 'He was a great strategist, using trusted friends to introduce female lines – one from the South Dorset which produced the S line at the Heythrop, and one from the Kilkenny . . . He acquired my father's (Major Bill Scott) female line, brought from Sir Edward Curre in 1931, which is the female line of Heythrop Berry '78, and their recent champion, Chorus 2000.'

Newton Rycroft, who was no ardent disciple of Wallace, said one of the greatest challenges for breeders was producing top-class hounds with accuracy enabling them to turn with their quarry. 'I have always thought that one of the reasons for Captain Wallace's great success with his hounds is that they possess this accuracy in the greatest measure, even in top gear,' said Sir Newton.

Black and Tans

Two unique Foxhound packs, the Scarteen and the Dumfriesshire, are black and tan coloured, but have no direct genetic connection, and have not cross-bred successfully. The Scarteen, which hunt in Counties Tipperary and Limerick, have been hunted by the Ryan family for over 300 years. There are various versions of the hounds' history, but their origins are certainly continental.

Thady Ryan, senior Master who began hunting the family pack when he was twenty-three in 1946, believes they are of the Gascon-Ariegeois breed from South

The Scarteen 'Black and Tan' hounds in full cry.

West France. They are small bloodhound types, some black and tan, others black and white, and blue-mottled. They have excellent hunting qualities and are renowned for their deep resounding cry.

They were also bred and hunted in Catalonia, and Thady Ryan thinks they were imported by his ancestors into Ireland through the island of Valentia, off Kerry, which engaged in regular trade with Spain. Very similar hounds are known to have hunted in the Pyrenees.

There are other unsubstantiated stories that Irishmen who were persecuted Catholics fought as mercenaries in French armies, and brought back hounds from the French-Spanish border. When crossed with the native Irish hounds, which were Talbot, or Northern strains, the black and tans still retained their original characteristics, although having more substance.

They were known as Kerry Beagles because it was a term used for any light-boned hunting animal in that south-west area of Ireland.

Such hounds were hunted in trencher-fed packs by Irish farmers, but the Ryan family provided a continuity which preserved the Scarteen as a pack. They hunted hares and deer for many years, only ceasing to hunt carted deer in 1927, before they switched to full time foxhunting.

The Kerry Beagles continue to produce remarkable sport over their country of grass, banks and deep water-filled ditches. The Ryans believed in recent years they needed an outcross and tried the Black and Tans of the Dumfriesshire Hunt, but this did not work, and therefore the Scarteen have relied on outcrosses from the remaining trencher-fed packs in Kerry which tend to hunt on Sunday afternoons after Mass has been said.

The Scarteen retain their remarkable cry and drive, but they are sensitive and need careful handling, still keen to hunt independent of their huntsman as much as possible.

I have enjoyed sport with them in their native country, but last saw them when they visited the vastly different Cottesmore country in Leicestershire near the end of the 2003–4 season. It was a poor scenting day, and hounds were clearly unsettled, but near the end of the afternoon when it grew colder, the Scarteen began to hunt together more effectively, and I heard their distinctive cry which made the hairs on the back of my neck stand up when I first rode behind them over the Limerick banks.

Dumfriesshire

The Dumfriesshire black and tans were a remarkable example of truly creative hound breeding by Sir John Buchanan-Jardine who took over the Mastership in 1921 at the age of twenty-one, from his father, Sir Robert.

'Jock' Buchanan-Jardine was a gifted breeder of virtually any mammal, taking a close interest in genetics. His achievement was to produce an entirely new breed of Foxhound which continued to breed true to type.

He put traditional English foxhound bitches to a field trial champion

Sir John Buchanan-Jardine creative breeder of his Dumfriesshire pack of black and tan hounds of which he was Master from 1921 to 1969.

Sir Rupert Buchanan-Jardine, MFH (1950–2001) with the Dumfriesshire hounds at Water of Milk, 1975

Bloodhound called Ledburn Boswell, and used a French hound of Gascon breeding called Triomphe. He crossed Triomphe with the sisters of Harlequin, a grandson of Boswell, and used Welsh-cross and English-French staghound crosses to produce his distinctive black and tan type, generally larger than the standard English Foxhound, being up to 28 inches at the shoulder, and with great stamina, scenting abilities and a bell-like voice.

Buchanan-Jardine, author of the classic *Hounds of the World*, intended his new breed to hunt successfully over the steep hills of Dumfriesshire, and they certainly achieved this with much success. His son, Sir Rupert Buchanan-Jardine, succeeded his father and hunted hounds from 1950, but sadly the Hunt became a casualty of the Scottish Parliament's foxhunting ban from 2002.

The distinctive pack was drafted in various directions, and it seemed unlikely that a full pack of these remarkable hounds would survive. Prejudice and ignorance by politicians in the new devolved government smashed a unique breeding achievement, an irreplaceable element in Scotland's sporting heritage.

American Hounds

American hound breeding can be more confusing than English. The diversity of quarries hunted by the Foxhound in the US and Canada, and the vast differences in geography and climate are reflected in the strains of hounds.

There are four distinct strains of Foxhounds in America which are American, English, Cross-bred, and Harrier, all eligible for registration in the MFHA of America Stud Book provided they belong to a recognised Hunt.

Foxhounds in North America may hunt the red or grey fox, the bobcat or increasingly, the coyote which in recent years has migrated from its native West and Middle America, and Canada, to the East Coast states.

Deer are not hunted by packs of hounds in America, but they abound in vast areas and are culled by shooting under licence, with variations in different States.

Americans did not simply take English foxhunting with them when they colonised the North American continent. They took hounds from England, and from Ireland, and they used some in quite different ways to traditional foxhunting in the old country. Many hounds were kept for the popular sport of night hunting, especially suitable in the balmy South. Owners bring together their hounds, or 'dawgs', and let them loose to find a fox on their own, and to join in 'the race' as hounds drive their fox onwards, usually in large circles. Meanwhile the owners sit round a nocturnal fire, drinking locally distilled spirits and wines, listening to their hounds, claiming to recognise their own, and able to assess whose hound caught the fox.

I spent a similar night in Georgia racoon hunting, with hounds running across the floor of a forest on the line of the coon, then baying at the foot of a tree which the coon had swiftly ascended. The plan then was to shine a torch into its branches, and shoot the coon thus illuminated. On this occasion any amount of firing into the trees did not hit a single coon.

No-one minded, the local whisky was strong enough to offset any sporting disappointment. There is a distinct strain of American hound known as the Coon hound, with a domed head, and lean and rangy body, sometimes black and tan, or blue mottled. As well as racoons it hunts the opossum which also climbs trees. Some US Foxhound packs include a Coon hound in the pack because of its excellent nose in woodland and its distinctive voice when it finds the quarry.

Champion American bitch, Orange County Melody with huntsman Adrian Smith at the Virginia hound show, USA, 2003.

From night hunting the Americans developed Foxhound Field Trials. Hounds with numbers painted on their sides are released just before daylight, with judges following on horseback, while owners and other spectators follow in cars and trucks. Several hundred field trials are held annually in the United States and Canada, and participants have their own stud books and specialist magazines. Judges assess the hunting skills of each hound having noted their performance in the field with the aid of their prominent numbers.

Walker and July Hounds

Two leading strains used in Field Trials are the Walker hound and the July hound. The first was bred and created originally in Madison County, Kentucky, by the four Walker brothers born between 1841 and 1852.

The Walker brothers were mainly interested in night hunting, and their hounds were bred for endurance, with no emphasis on biddability.

The July hound was developed in Virginia and Maryland to be used for hunting in early morning conditions from dawn. Ben Hardaway, the much acclaimed Master and creator of his own Midland pack based in Georgia, says in his autobiography (*Never Out-Foxed*, 1997): 'Unless you have personally experienced the thrilling cry and execution of a pack of Julys close on a red fox just as day is breaking, and the sun starts pulling the dew, and scent is breast high, it's hard to describe to you just what a sensation it is. Peter Beckford came the closest: "It's like trying to pen a whisper".'

The July hound descends from a couple of Irish foxhounds, Mountain and Muse, bred by the Duke of Leeds, on his estate in Northern Ireland. Mountain and Muse were taken to America in about 1814 by the Duke's friend, Mr Bolton Jackson, and they were developed in Virginia, Georgia and Kentucky by enthusiastic foxhunters.

At that time the more favoured quarry along the Eastern seaboard was the newly imported red fox from the British Isles, rather than the native grey fox which tends to run short, or in circles. The Irish hounds were ideal for the task. 'The old, long-eared, rat-tailed, coon-hound type that the hunters had used to run grey fox couldn't cope with the speed of the imported red, 'says Ben Hardaway.

Penn-Marydel Hounds

During the mid-eighteenth century there were importations into the Southern states of Virginia, Maryland and the Carolinas, of England's Southern hounds, one of the ancestors of the modern English hound.

These were bred to be hunted in packs and followed on horseback in the English fashion. Their excellent scenting ability, and ability to trail a cold scent over arable land with great persistence made them ideal to follow the twists and turns of the red and grey fox in these Southern states.

Owned by farmers and landowners to hunt in packs these hounds derived from

Penn-MaryDel, the breed special to the United States: champion bitch Rose Tree Needy, shown by eleven-years-old Codie Hayes at the Mid America Show, 2003.

the Southern hound were established in parts of Virginia, Maryland, Delaware and Pennsylvania. With their long ears, high domed skulls and rangy conformation they are a reminder of the hounds the English were hunting before they developed much more substance in Foxhounds later in the nineteenth century.

To ensure the survival of this strain of pack hound, in 1932 they were named the Penn-MaryDel, a combination of the main states in which they were found, and a Penn-MaryDel Association from 1932 maintained a separate stud book. They are shown in a special division of the annual Bryn Mawr hound show in Pennsylvania.

American Foxhounds

The American hound, registered in the US Foxhound Kennel Stud Book since 1930 is a distinct type: a light, racy hound compared with its English cousins. It was evolved with the use of the Field Trial strains, July and Walker, and other individual strains, to produce a tough, tenacious hunting animal which breeds true to an established type.

The American hound is exceptionally low-scenting, having to hold the line in high temperatures once the sun is up, and has a remarkable turn of speed in the open where it needs to out-run its quarry.

It has a slightly high domed head and its coat is a handsome tan and white. Judges insist American hounds must not show notable characteristics of other breeds such as Bloodhounds, Welsh, French and English Foxhounds.

Judge Lt. Col. Dennis Foster, Director of the American MFHA with the
American Foxhound Champions at the Mid America show 2003:
Keswick Orderley and Orbit

Among the best known Hunts adhering to American Foxhound breeding are
the Orange County in Virginia, the Potomac in Maryland, and the Essex in New
Jersey.

English Foxhounds in America

A steady importation of English Foxhounds into America continued throughout
the twentieth century. These have included modern English hounds, Welsh, Fell
and old English types. Some US Masters have chosen to hunt all-English packs,
and achieved excellent results.

The Trans-Atlantic export of English hounds continues today – but in recent
years some English hound breeders have reversed the trend. Ronnie Wallace as
referred to above, used American hounds from the Orange County pack.

A few of Ben Hardaway's cross-bred hounds at the Midland have been
imported into Britain, and have been used successfully. The Cottesmore and the
Cattistock are among packs with Hardaway blood lines which have nicked in
well.

All-English packs prominent in America are the Blue Ridge in Virginia, Mr
Stewart's Cheshire in Pennsylvania, and the Arapahoe in Colorado.

Champion English bitch in a US pack: Iroquois Bonfire, at the
Mid-America Show 2003.

US Cross-Bred Hounds

About half of America's 44,000 registered hounds are of American or English
strains, and the remainder are Cross-Breds which have been the increasingly
popular choice of American Masters.

This is partly because the greater substance, biddability and drive of the Cross-
Bred makes it perhaps the most suitable to hunt, in addition to the fox, the
coyote, the quarry which has increased so dramatically in the late twentieth
century in hunting countries formerly only occupied by red or grey foxes.

The Cross-Bred was produced initially by the first cross between an American
and an English Hound, with subsequent crosses. They are registered as such in
the American Stud Book. A 'pure' American hound, or a 'pure' English must
each have fifteen-sixteenths of the relevant blood from that source.

Harriers are registered in a separate section of the Foxhound stud book
because although they are bred mainly to hunt hares, some in America are often
used to hunt foxes as well.

Cross-Bred hounds are judged in a separate category in America. Among the
best known Cross-Bred packs, renowned for sport and for prizes at hound shows,
are the Midland in Georgia, the Live Oak in Florida, and the Green Spring Valley
in Maryland.

I have hunted in the US with packs of hounds in the main categories, apart
from Harriers, and have much enjoyed sport with all of them. The variety of
American hounds, and the keen interest of hound breeders emphasises that
venery is a dominant shared interest among dedicated US foxhunters, far less

Mid-American Hound Show 2003 –
champion, and grand champion,
Cross-Bred doghound Live Oak Cruiser,
bred by Marty and Daphne Wood. A
superb example of English and American
lines cross-bred.

Champion Cross-Bred doghound
Midland Import, bred by Ben Hardaway,
with huntsman Marc Dradge, at Virginia
Hound Show 2003.

mixed up with the 'quality of the ride' issue so often encountered in English foxhunting.

No hound breeder has been more daring and experimental than Ben Hardaway of Columbus, Georgia. He has used outcrosses from most of the available sources in America, plus hounds from France, England, and Ireland. Ben wrote: 'I have yet to find any individual or any strain of American hounds that could touch the intelligence of the Fell crosses from the College Valley or the West Waterford hounds. Then why not just use the pure English hound for American fox and coyote hunting? The answer to that is : nose and music.

' I have yet to find the English hound individually or by strain that could touch the delicate fox nose or the exciting cry of the American Foxhound. So, I say to obtain the best Foxhound for our present day needs the best course is judiciously crossing the best of these two breeds, or crossing the best of the strains of established Cross-Bred hounds.'

The Master and founder in 1950 of the Midland pack always wanted to hunt a pack of pure-bred July hounds, but he was unable to do so because they were inclined to riot on the line of the Virginia Whitetail deer which abound in his hunting country and carry a compellingly strong scent. A Foxhound which is not steady to deer ruins sport in such conditions.

Hardaway is immensely keen on the virtues of July hounds, their drive, good scenting abilities and voice, but he also uses a small percentage of Penn-MaryDel among the American element in his pack: 'This breed has very good nose and cry and in most cases is easy to make steady to deer.'

During a hunting trip to Ireland in 1952 the Midland Master met Ikey Bell when he was living in retirement in Ireland, and Mr Bell advised Hardaway to see the West Waterford pack where Tom and Elsie Morgan had produced highly effective Fell-cross hounds. Ben Hardaway loved this pack and imported some of its lines, later making firm friends with Martin Letts at the College Valley.

Hardaway strongly advises all American Masters only to use English hounds from packs regularly in deer country, and steady to deer. On the whole he favours the modern English Foxhound for crossing most successfully with American packs.

Marty Wood III and his wife Daphne founded in 1974 their own Live Oak pack in north Florida, near Tallahassee, hunting on their thousands of acres of pine plantations where quail shooting is a long established sport. They became firm friends with Ronnie Wallace and used his Exmoor lines, as well as blood from the Beaufort and other kennels producing the most successful modern Foxhound breeding. Crossed judiciously with American hounds the Live Oak pack has a unity and grace, plus excellent working abilities in the demanding setting of thick woodland, which make it one of the finest in modern US foxhunting.

French Hounds

Foxhunting is not the major hound sport of France, although it has its roots in hunting antiquity. It suffered as a hound sport greatly in the post-war years because of the presence of rabies in French foxes, but this scourge was almost extinguished in France towards the end of the twentieth century, and there was growth in foxhunting with hounds.

I have never hunted in France, and I rely on two main sources for information on the French breeds: Sir John Buchanan-Jardine's excellent *Hounds of the World* (Grayling Books 1979), and *Hounds of France* by George Johnson and Maria Ericson (Saiga Publishing, 1997) which lists twenty-eight breeds. I would refer foxhunters to both these sources if they wish to learn about the extraordinary variety of French hounds in detail.

In 2001 I attended France's annual Game Fair, in the beautiful grounds of the chateau at Chambord in the Loire Valley, and I was greatly impressed and fascinated by what was almost certainly the largest and most diverse gathering of hounds in the world – 6,783 hounds representing many of France's forty breeds from 183 of France's 440 Hunts.

The pride and interest of French hunting people in their hounds was abundantly clear. Many Hunts are small, and privately owned, and I found several run by teenagers. It is in stag, boar and roe deer hunting that France's panoply of the Chase is seen, with liberal use of French horns, and hunt staff and followers in colourful livery.

By the millennium up to one hundred French packs were hunting foxes, many Chasse-a-Tir, the method of hunting when hounds are used to drive game to waiting guns, but latterly there has been some increase in foxhunting with hounds only. Staghunting remains France's premier sport, and the boar, the hare, the rabbit and the badger were being hunted by packs, many of them small, privately owned packs in remote rural areas.

Hounds used in foxhunting (La Venerie du Renard) are mainly cross-breds, using drafts of hounds used in the other forms of venery, with importations of English Foxhound blood in at least every fifth generation.

Since foxhunting only is the focus of this book, I do not propose to engage in detailed descriptions of all French hound breeds, but the crucial importance of French hound breeding as an influence on Foxhound development in Norman and medieval England has been referred to above. The great medieval forests of France ensured that staghunting remained a premier hound sport far longer than in England; there are about forty French staghound packs still operating.

In the twentieth century it is fair to say that English influence on French hound breeding has been the greater, although there have been usages of French hounds by experimental hound breeders such as Sir John Buchanan-Jardine and Sir Newton Rycroft, as described earlier.

The three English staghound packs surviving in the West Country use large Foxhounds, not French staghounds.

The French Revolution in the late eighteenth century caused the closure and dispersal of many packs of hounds belonging to the aristocracy, but the new citizens of republican France soon proved they too enjoyed the chase as a recreation and essential part of rural life, so that Hunts were re-established and hound lines restored, although two World Wars fought on French soil, and German occupation, were further massive disruptions.

There are three main groups of hounds in France:

- Chiens d'Ordre, mainly large hounds used for hunting in packs to hunt and account for their quarry.
- Briquets, generally smaller in size, from about fifteen to twenty-three inches, often kept by local sportsmen, and hunted singly or in groups of a couple or so to flush game out of coverts for shooters.
- Bassets, well known in England too, and used in France in small groups to put up game for the gun, or in smallish packs where they hunt with excellent scenting ability, much persistence, and lots of hound music. There are at least four types of Basset in France, and some have been imported into England.

Hound breeding in France has seen far less of the English practice of sending bitches long distances to sires in other packs, so that local types have often became in-bred, and the system of puppy walking has not been established in the same way. There has been some commercial breeding of hunting hounds by farmers and others, so that Masters could purchase ready-made drafts of hounds to form a pack. This may work adequately but it is not comparable with selective breeding over generations within a pack.

In Grande Venerie the larger breeds are used to hunt deer and wild boar; the fox is classed with the hare and the rabbit as Petite Venerie, and involves crossbreds of the large, medium or small hounds.

Emphasising that French hounds used for Foxhounds are cross-breds from various sources, the following breeds are among those which may be used:

The Poitevan: from Poitevin in Western France, developed from strains of staghound, but having several infusions of English Foxhound blood. They are tall hounds, up to 0.72m. with long, flat heads, long thin necks, flat and sloping shoulders and deep chests; often

French hounds: the Blanc et Noirs pack of the Pic'Ardie Valois Hunt in full cry in the snow-clad Foret de Compiegne.

The Pic'Ardie Valois huntsmen, adorned with French horns, returning home after hunting their Blanc at Noir hounds in Compiegne.

tricolour with black saddle, sometimes orange and white or badger-pied.

Anglo-Francais: there are three breeds of Anglo French:

Anglo-Francais Tricolore, Anglo-Francais Blanc et Noir, and *Anglo-Francais Blanc et Orange.* The Tricolore is the most numerous of the large hound breeds in France today, according to Johnson and Ericson, and they are principally descendants of the tri-colour Poitevins and the English Foxhound. The Francais Blancs et Noirs are exceptionally impressive looking hounds; huge hounds, well set up and massively boned, with a magnificent voice. I was not surprised to learn that this formidable breed is especially used for the arduous task of boar hunting.

The *Billy* is another hound used in Grande Venerie, and there are five other breeds of large hounds mainly used for hare hunting, and wild boar with the use of guns: *Grand Bleu des Gascogne, Gascon-Saintongeois, Griffon Nivernais, Grand Griffon-Vendeen* and *Grand Fauve de Bretagne.* The Gascon-Saintongeois, used in the creation of the Dumfriesshire black and tan Foxhound, is mainly black and white, and has good hunting qualities.

The medium-sized hounds, some of whom are used as pure or cross-bred packs to hunt foxes, include the following:

Aregoeis, Porcelaines, Brunos du Jura, Petis Bleus de Gascogne, Petits Gascon-Saintongeois, Briquet Grioffon-Vendeen, Anglo Francais Petite and *Moyenne Taille,* and *Beagle-Harriers. The Beagle Harrier* is a popular breed hunt roe-deer, wild boar and fox, usually 'a-tir'.

English Foxhound Shows

Peterborough

By the end of the twentieth century four main annual Foxhound shows survived in England. Peterborough Royal Foxhound Show, held in mid-July on the East of England Showground, remained pre-eminent, having been founded in 1877, and retains reminders of formality and past elegance. The gentlemen wear suits, bowler hats and some carry rolled umbrellas. Ladies wear best summer dresses, some with hats which would not be out of place at Royal Ascot.

Judging takes place in a covered ring where members and guests of the Show Society watch from tiered seats. There is a President's box, and a section for bowler-hatted professional Hunt staff. Results are shown on a hand-operated indicator board above the hound entrance. There are large tents adjoining for restaurants and bars. Luncheon is a social occasion for Foxhunters from all over Britain and abroad, with visitors from the US frequent.

Doghounds are judged in the morning, and bitches in the afternoon. There are two judges for each section, and the Committee usually arranges for a highly experienced judge to be accompanied by one who is younger, and less experienced.

There are a few classes for packs which have not shown, nor won, at Peterborough in recent years, but the open classes predominate, and competition is exceedingly keen.

Judges are judged as much as the hounds, by the surrounding cognoscenti, and there can be much wry head shaking in the bar afterwards if the judging is deemed inconsistent or faulty.

Not everyone in foxhunting believes the influence of hound shows is beneficial. It has certainly helped to place heavy influence on the leading showing packs, the Duke of Beaufort's, Heythrop, and latterly the Exmoor, and has made some other smaller packs almost satellites for their breeding.

It is possible that Peterborough and other leading hound shows encourage too much uniformity in hound conformation, but there are many packs who never show and yet achieve consistently good sport .

The shows are remarkable opportunities to see beautiful Foxhounds. The two-couple classes fill the ring with movement, and among the hounds are the scarlet and green coats of the attendant Hunt staffs. Above all, the Foxhound is shown as a working animal; each hound is accompanied by a huntsman and whipper-in who holds it on a lead, but it is not restricted to a lead throughout its judging; the most important phase of the judging comes when hounds are released and run across the ring after pieces of biscuit thrown by their huntsmen. The judges are looking for the best movers, and the hound's paces, its key requirement as a true working animal, is the crucial issue which decides the final top placings.

Winning a Peterborough championship is a great accolade, and for many MFHs it sets the seal on the desirability of breeding from a doghound or bitch – provided they are also reported to be 'good in their work'. The accompanying East of England agricultural show recently put its date back to June but the Foxhound show resolutely retained its date in mid-July and is well enough attended to fill most seats.

South of England Show
The first Foxhound show of the summer season, taking place early in June within the South of England agricultural show at Ardingly, Sussex. Judging is in a smallish outdoor ring, and packs from the south and south-east predominate. It is easily accessible to people attending the agricultural show, and an excellent shop-window for the Foxhound and hunting.

Wales and Border Counties
Held at Builth Wells, Powys, in late June, this show is a real delight for the hound lover. Although it takes place in the Royal Welsh showground it is a stand-alone occasion, with an informal but highly focussed atmosphere.

English and Welsh Foxhounds are judged simultaneously in adjoining outdoor rings, and Beagles in a third ring. The Duke of Beaufort's and Heythrop often show their hounds here before they clash again at Peterborough.

The 'woollies' in the Welsh ring are not shown off the lead; the style of judging is different, with the judges sometimes touching the hounds and looking into their mouth, which I have not seen English Foxhound judges indulge in.

In 2004 several classes for Fell hounds were introduced in the Welsh ring because some Welsh packs were increasingly crossing their hounds with the Fell.

Great Yorkshire

Organised in conjunction with the Great Yorkshire agricultural show, in early July, the week before Peterborough, this is an excellent Foxhound show, and a splendid opportunity to see the northern packs.

Special categories for pure English hounds have been included in recent years because some northern packs have more of this blood than packs in the south. The Beaufort and Heythrop sometimes make raids on the championships at this show which are keenly fought over. There is a highly convivial Yorkshire atmosphere in the restaurants and bars.

West of England

Held at Honiton, Devon, early in August this is a great gathering of hunting people and hounds just before autumn staghunting and foxhunting start on Exmoor.

Now held on a new showground in conjunction with Honiton's annual agricultural show, just west of Honiton, the hound show has outdoor rings where Foxhounds, Harriers, Staghounds, Beagles and Bassets are judged.

It is often a hot day, and there is a relaxed, informal atmosphere, popular with hunting people on holiday in the West Country, often going on to watch the early moorland hunting starting at the weekend.

Lowther and Rydal

Taking place on later dates in August, these are shows where Fell and other breeds can be seen in glorious settings.

At the Rydal Hound Show, near Grasmere, there are sheep dog trials, and hound trails over the surrounding hills as an extra entertainment to the judging in the rings below.

Lowther Hound Show is held in conjunction with the highly popular annual country sports fair in Cumbria.

Foxhound Conformation

The judges in an English Foxhound show are looking for the following key points of conformation:

Height: Not more than 26 inches to the point of the shoulder.

Colour: Neither the colour of the hound's coat nor its eyes is of any importance and is not considered.

Stern: The hound's stern, its tail, should ideally be straight, although a slightly curved stern is sometimes overlooked if the rest of the conformation is good.

Head: The hound's mouth must not be under-shot, or over-shot which means that neither its lower or upper jaw should protrude noticeably. Some like a dog-hound to have a wider jowled, noticeably masculine head, but this is a personal preference.

Neck: A longer neck is preferable to a short one.

Shoulders: A key area of conformation. They should slope back into the body rather than be noticeably upright. A good length of humerus bone is highly desirable. Looking down from above the shoulder blades should not appear to be set widely apart. A certain amount of breast bone should be visible in front when looking at a hound in profile, but it should not be 'bosomy'.

Elbows: Elbows that stick out are bad; even worse is a 'tied in' elbow, restricting the hound's movement and its speed across country. A long elbow 'slash' is desirable, giving the foreleg plenty of room for extension in a long stride which covers the ground. Young hounds are sometimes more 'out at the elbow' but this fault rectifies with maturity, and allowance made for this.

Foreleg: Should be strong and reasonably straight. The knee should not 'knuckle over'; it is preferable if it is slightly back. As in a horse, the pastern is better if it slopes back, rather than be straight in line with the knee. It should be a shock absorber, helping durability.

Foot: A fault the judge looks for is a 'toe down'; one toe-nail is seen to be much lower than the others, a sign of a foot fault likely to cause lameness, and a fault which can be communicated in breeding. The hound's feet should neither be too fleshy, nor too tight.

Chest: Neither a wide 'bosom', nor so narrow that both legs seem 'to be coming out of the same hole'. The chest should be proportionate with the rest of the hound's conformation.

Back: Either a straight back, or a slightly arched back known as a 'wheel back' are acceptable. The backbone should not stick up in a knobbly fashion, but be set between two lines of muscle. A weak, narrow back, with a pronounced dip below the spine to the ribs is known as a 'roach back' which is a fault.

Body: Some spring in the ribs is essential, but depth through the heart is vital to provide room for the hound's 'engine'. Under-line of the body can 'run up' towards the hind legs, but accentuation of this means the hound is too narrow gutted.

Loins: Should be broad and strong, with tops of quarters, the pin bones, set well apart. Plenty of muscle on buttocks and second thighs. Should not have a 'chopped off' appearance at the back.

Hind legs: Should tend towards straightness, neither cow-hocked nor sickle-hocked as in bad horse conformation. Hocks should be set low and not way back behind the hound's body.

Horses for Hunting

Foxhounds are followed by horses, ponies and cobs of all types, sizes and colours. Riding to hounds is the largest equestrian sport in Britain, making a huge contribution to the rural economy of some areas.

The horse industry has repeatedly urged government not to ban hunting because of the disastrous impact it would have on the horse population, removing at a stroke a working role for thousands of horses.

As Chairman of the British Horse Industry Confederation, the body representing the industry to government, I presented a detailed case to the Burns Committee of Inquiry into Hunting. It was played down lamentably in the

Always a risk sport: Mrs Rosemary Taylor in trouble, hunting with the Heythrop.

No stopping to open a gate in the cream of the Shires: Graham Vere Nicoll shows the way across country, hunting with the Belvoir.

West Country hedges grow well: Mrs Sarah Cobden, Joint Master of the Seavington clears one confidently in 1981.

Wood or metal, fencing comes in varied forms: Tony Ellis hunting with the Warwickshire in 1983.

Mr Joss Hanbury, one of the most consummate Field Masters across Leicestershire, hunting with the Cottesmore as Joint Master (1981–90). Now in second term as Quorn MFH.

Side-saddle riding is still to be seen in the modern hunting field: Anne Earl following the Bedale hounds in Yorkshire.

Alan Lillingstone shows the way to cross Irish bank and ditch country, hunting with the Co. Limerick in January 1977.

Burns report, which referred to jobs and incomes lost but did not deal specifi-cally with the horse welfare problem. Burns did, however, admit there would be serious problems in the horse industry, which I will refer to below.

We reported to Burns that Britain's mounted Foxhound Hunts use about 62,000 horses, ponies and cobs each season, according to an independent economic survey by Produce Studies for the Countryside Alliance in 1998.

Adding another eighteen mounted packs engaged in Hare or Staghunting brings the number up to 65,700 horses in use. The number of foals and young horses awaiting a career in the hunting field, plus those in other sports who may be drafted into hunting has not been quantified, but the demands of hunting on the horse population are the largest of any other single activity except non-sporting leisure riding.

When we made our submission to Burns in 1999 the racing industry employed about 40,000 horses of which about 13,000 were in training; there were 7,800 horses registered in eventing; 17,900 in showjumping; 6,400 in dressage; and lesser numbers in such specialist sports as endurance riding, and competition driving.

There is said to be a total equine population in the UK of between 600,000 and 1,000,000, but clearly the highest levels of expenditure are on those horses and ponies in work. Apart from horses specifically intended for the hunting field a number are switched to this use after they fail to reach the highest standards in the competition sports. Retired racehorses, and some ex-eventers, often make excellent hunters.

As one more sign of bigotry, the anti-hunters in the House of Commons, who claim to be animal lovers, have never expressed the slightest interest in the major welfare problems they would cause among horses if they achieved a hunting ban. Blandly, and ignorantly, anti-hunting MPs on both sides of the House have arro-gantly advised hunting people to take up Drag-hunting, the hunting of a line of artificially laid scent, which they claim would absorb all the horses currently used in traditional hunting.

This is complete nonsense, as only a cursory study of the situation would reveal. In 2000 there were thirty Drag and Bloodhound packs in the UK, compared with 197 mounted packs hunting live quarry, proving that far more people preferred the latter. Drag packs do not have the same level of access to private farmland because they make no contribution to fox control, nor do they need to maintain coverts.

A drag hunt is a half-day sport, and cannot be followed by anywhere near the number of horses which can follow a pack of Foxhounds all day. The Masters of Draghounds Association has stated that in the event of a ban, drag-hunting could not provide hunting anywhere near the scale of hunting currently available in Britain.

The Burns report referred to jobs and incomes lost, but did not deal specifi-cally with the horse welfare problem. In our BHIC submission we pointed out to Burns that the Produce Studies report showed that:

Total annual expenditure on Foxhunting in the UK was over £243 million. Equine costs were by far the largest element, as follows:

- Annual expenditure by 178 Fox Hunts on horses kept for staff at Hunt stables – £2.5 million.
- By Hunt followers on keep of their own horses: at livery, £22.6m.; at home, £130m.
- Capital expenditure on vehicles, trailers, stabling etc., £39m.

We pointed out that removing about £150m. worth of business a year from the equestrian supply industry by banning hunting would result in closures of small and medium businesses.

Suddenly robbing 65,700 horses and ponies of their working role would be far more than an economic disaster. Hunts throughout the twentieth century remained the local focus for hunter-trials, team 'chases, sponsored rides, and point-to-pointing.

The British Horseracing Board told the Burns committee that a ban on hunting would reduce the number of point-to-point venues and the volume of sport by at least a quarter immediately. It would lead in the long-term to more course closures, and a reduction in standards. A decline in the number of owners would hit racing under Rules, with a consequent loss of runners.

The British Horse Society stands aside from the ethics of hunting but it opposes a ban because it would harm horses. The Society pointed out that many would be put down and there was a risk of others being neglected. Most hunting people cherish their horses dearly and would not abandon or neglect them, but the risk would increase for the many horses and ponies which had failed to shine in competition sports and could no longer find an alternative niche in the hunting field.

Anyone who has visited the lowest levels of horse auction will know the fate of some old horses and ponies which have dropped to the bottom of the ladder: a life of drudgery or worse in cheap hiring yards, constant changing ownerships for a few pounds, and finally slaughter in the meat market. It can happen to illustrious racehorses, competition horses or hunters if they are not given retirement homes by loving owners.

Partnership of a Lifetime

For those of us who have been lucky enough to ride to hounds for most of our lives, the hunter is a wonderful part of our heritage. A good, sound hunter is under-priced in 2004; it is possible to buy one for £5,000 or less, cheaper than the price of a larger brand of motor-cycle. Many lighter men and women, and teenagers, ride horses costing considerably less.

We put our lives on the hunter's back, and we expect it to turn out twice a week, or perhaps three times a fortnight, throughout a long season. The animal has to be tractable in temperament, load in and out of lorries in all weathers, keep its feet on slippery roads and rutted verges, and tolerate road traffic.

In the hunting field the modern hunter has to be sensible enough to queue to jump a Hunt jump in single file, taking its turn in the depths of winter to bucket out of deep, muddy going over a telegraph pole, only to land in another

Thrills of the chase in one of the most formidable fenced countries: Rob Cursham MFH jumps over faller Michael Batten during a day with the Blackmore Vale in February, 1980.

Comte Richard de Pelet, Chairman of the Blackmore and Sparkford Vale, over a typical obstacle in their vale country.

quagmire. It must alternatively be bold enough to jump upright timber or a hedge and ditch without a lead, and it must gallop over going ranging from good to appallingly bad during any day.

At the end of the season in still chilly April the hunter often has its rugs taken off, and is turned out to change its entire diet to grass before being brought in again in August or September for a month's road walking to get fit for another hunting season. The good-class hunter who keeps up this regime for many seasons is a remarkably tough, resilient horse.

The horse shares my risks in the hunting field; if he makes a disastrous mistake he is likely to be severely, or even fatally, hurt too, and usually bears the brunt of the less serious biffs and bangs. I count my partnerships with hunting horses among the greatest privileges of my life.

They shared my love of hunting, and they certainly understood the conduct of the chase a great deal more intimately than many of the human followers of hounds. Such a paragon has not suddenly arrived in our midst. The hunter which carries a middleweight or heavyweight adult in the British winter has been evolved from centuries of selective breeding, with the natural 'survival of the fittest' selection which attends a genuine working animal, by any standards one of man's best friends.

My best hunters stand patient and resigned while I chat and drink at a meet, but they note hounds moving off immediately, and frisk away even if I am not ready. A good hunter pricks his ears and stands rigid with excitement when he hears hounds give tongue; then he plunges off in pursuit. He learns the terrain and the obstacles in the country where he hunts regularly, and will of his own accord chose the best going as he crashes along a deep-riding boggy track.

Teaching the young hunter these skills, inviting it to share your fun in the hunting field, is one of the greatest pleasures of riding to hounds. I have always relished the zing of riding hard on an experienced horse in the wake of hounds, but I have equally had hours of quiet joy when a shy, diffident four-year-old suddenly raises his game and jumps a ditch or a fence with a new confidence because he is beginning to understand the challenges of the sport which is to be his working life.

One of the greatest joys is to breed a horse from a mare you have hunted, to break it in, school it and enter it to the hunting field, therafter sharing a partnership for the rest of its working life.

I have been fortunate in experiencing this through breeding nine foals from my hunter mare, Josephine, an Irish hunter I bought as a five-year-old. Wearing a flannel suit, and bare headed, I rode her in a field in County Limerick one August, and bought her for £1,100. I was to hunt her for nearly a decade in over forty hunting countries, easily one of the most brilliant hunters I have ever ridden, and then she bore nine foals before her retirement and death at the age of twenty-six. I am still riding her seventh offspring, Ranksborough, a 17.2 hands bay gelding by John O'Gaunt, who was by a Thoroughbred out of a part-bred Irish Draught mare.

Josephine was by a Thoroughbred sprint racehorse in Ireland, Chi Chi Costenango, out of a part-bred mare, and she was a full sister of one of the most successful showjumping horses of the post-war years, Graham Fletcher's

Buttevant Boy. Deep through the heart, with powerful quarters, exceedingly agile, and with a great turn of speed when necessary, Josephine had the great qualities of the best mares in performance: boldness combined with a strong sense of self-preservation.

She made the transition remarkably quickly from County Limerick's stone wall country to the old turf, fly fences and timber of Leicestershire. In her first day with the Quorn she made a major error in jumping a high set of rails with a ditch in front. She suddenly stopped, as a novice will, when she saw the ditch, but still jumped, heading I thought for a certain crashing fall. But she used her Irish 'fifth leg', and her intelligence, to bank off the top rail, using her hind legs to spring off and land lightly on the landing side. She was highly intelligent and never made that error again, responding to my legs to go on boldly to jump a ditch and obstacle in one bound. In ten seasons she gave me only two falls, both when being brought down by other horses out of control at a fence.

The formula for breeding a top-class hunter was well established at the beginning of the twentieth century: it had to be a Thoroughbred, or one crossed with another native of the British Isles, preferably an Irish Draught Horse, or a Cleveland Bay, or perhaps a heavy draught horse, such as a Shire or Suffolk Punch. Middle and light-weights might have crosses with pony blood, preferably a Connemara or a Welsh pony mare. Many a good hunter would be of completely indeterminate and mysterious breeding. The famous reply by an Irish dealer to a prospective buyer when asked the name of the horse's sire, was: 'And who would ye *like* him to be by, Sor?'

To hunt the most demanding galloping and jumping countries a horse without too much mystery in its breeding has always been desirable. Thoroughbreds are excellent, but increasingly in the twentieth century lighter strains were bred for racing and too many of these may perform well in the hunting field but lacked the substance to withstand the mud, the thorns and the bruises. They take far longer to recover from long days of 'rugby on a horse' which is a closer description of hunting, in contrast to occasional appearances on a manicured racecourse.

Without doubt the finest foundation stock for superb hunters, and indeed many competition cross-country horses, is the Irish Draught. From 1900 until late in the twentieth century the export of such cross-breds has been a major part of Irish agriculture where horse breeding has long been an adjunct to stock farming.

Although its name implies the horse is used in harness, the Irish Draught is a much lighter, more agile horse than horses which were used on the land in England. Ancient tribal Irish cavalry was lightly armed and relied on speed and manoeuvrability in tackling invaders. Irish farmers used such horses to produce animals with more substance, but they retained a marvellous versatility, ploughing and drawing a cart as well as providing an excellent mount for the farmer or squire.

After farm mechanisation the breed was nearly lost, but the Irish government in the 1960s set up a government Horse Board, and with subsidies and other encouragements the Irish Draught was saved. Its huge value as a foundation stock enabled Ireland to continue its hunter breeding, and to branch out into the more profitable areas of breeding top-class showjumpers and eventers. English and continental dealers attend the famous Irish equestrian shop window, the Dublin Horse Show every August, but they also tour the country to their favoured sources to buy direct from breeders and producers.

Generations of breeding businesses continued throughout most of the century in the English hunting fields, depending heavily on Irish imports of young horses. It is essential to buy them young for huntng; they have to learn the different challenge of the English hunting field as soon as possible: it is perilous to bank off an English hedge!

An Irish Draught Horse Society was also formed in the UK and has helped to maintain the foundation breed for cross-breeding here. The major influence on hunter breeding inside England was the Hunter's Improvement Society, formed in 1885 partly to alleviate fears that the British cavalry was woefully short of good home-bred horses.

A Royal Commission on Horse Breeding in 1908, the last one, gave grave warnings of a lack of cavalry mounts in the run-up to the Great War. It found there were 2,087,000 horses in the United Kingdom, of which 150,000 were for cavalry use.

The HIS operated a system of premiums, or subsidies, for the stallion fees of horses which its judges carefully selected and graded, being shown in an annual stallion show at Newmarket. By the 1970s the HIS was distributing about £50,000 annually in premiums, largely funded by an annual grant from racing via the Horserace Betting Levy Board. This was justified by the number of HIS bred Thoroughbreds running in point-to-points and National Hunt racing. The scheme helped enormously in keeping Britain ahead in producing the best cross-country horses in the world. This was reflected in the prowess of our international eventing teams who won Olympic gold medals on home-bred and Irish imported horses.

At the 2004 Games in Athens the British team was a favourite to win medals in eventing. Disastously, Britain did not even qualify a showjumping team to compete at Athens, and our dressage team was an outsider for medals. These inadequacies reflect the long term failure of British horse breeding to compete with the leading continental nations in producing specific 'sport horse' types for showjumping and dressage.

By the end of the century British showjumping and dressage international teams were having to buy continental bred horses to compete on level terms with world-class teams. In contrast, continental riders were buying British and Irish horses to compete in international horse trials.

Germany, Holland, Belgium, France and latterly Sweden, have all succeeded in crossing Thoroughbreds with native cold-bold breeds such as the Hanoverian, Westfalian and Holstein, to produce tractable, powerful horses which excel in the exactitudes of showjumping and dressage.

It is highly relevant to our foxhunting heritage because it is highly likely that our history and culture of galloping and jumping across country after hounds has tended to produce superb riders in eventing, but far less in the other international riding disciplines.

Showjumping, having lost most of its UK television coverage, was languishing on the home front by the millennium, but many more recruits were entering dressage, although at top level the Britons could not prevail against the Germans and Dutch.

The intensive use of selective breeding for the other non-cross-country sports, where mares as well as stallions were strictly graded, was a trick the HIS never learned adequately. Its fortunes were much linked to the decorous ritual of the summer hunter show classes where, to the mystification of the outsider, rapt horsey audiences watch horses somewhat ponderously paraded, then ridden by judges before being stripped of saddles for conformation inspection. It is all accompanied by much doffing of hats, and bows from the saddle, like a nineteenth century meet transformed to summer-time.

Let me not be derisive, because I thoroughly enjoy old fashioned hunter classes, especially at the Dublin show. The ladies' side-saddle classes are still a joy to watch, and the need for good horsemanship in riding a four-year-old, largely of TB breeding, is great fun to observe. Thank heavens the traditional type of young TB cross-Irish Draught hunter is nowhere near as Germanically obedient as the Warmblood who seems to inherit the notion that 'we have ways of making you do this . . .'

I suspect that more than half the attraction of the Warmblood is the ease with which it can be broken in and schooled by somewhat less experienced riders who 'do their own horse' at home. Rather like continental and Japanese car manufacturers, the continental horse breeding industry produced a product the consumer really wanted – and look what happened to Britain's car industry.

The growing attraction of 'working hunter classes' where hunters have to jump as well as parade in the ring, has seen the Warmblood influence pervading the hallowed sanctums of the British show hunter world in increasing numbers.

I am one of the traditionalists who would not knowingly hunt across natural country on a Warmblood, but I concede that the increased element of Thoroughbred breeding in Warmblood crosses has increased their quality levels. It saddens, and amuses me, that the continentals have found a way of selling back to the British Warmblood horses who have only been improved by lavish infusions of the great British invention, the Thoroughbred horse which we produced from Arab blood in the eighteenth and nineteenth centuries for racing and hunting.

At their worst I find Warmbloods too stuffy in the shoulder, with upright pasterns, and rather bad feet which do not wear well. This stable door cannot be closed because Warmbloods have galloped through it to huge popularity in the UK.

Many British breeders use Warmblood crosses successfully, having found it a far more profitable market. One sign of abandonment of the old foundation stocks is that Britain's old breed of Yorkshire horse, the Cleveland Bay is so out of favour for driving or riding, that it finished the century on the Rare Breeds list!

It is equally significant that in the 1990s, without making much of a fanfare, the Hunter's Improvement Society quietly folded its traditional tent and re-formed itself under the new title, Sport Horse GB. Sadly the change came too late, and continental horses continue to invade the British market in the twenty-first century.

132

It is all the more vital that the hunting field continues to nurture children and teenagers as riders on the best of our nine native breeds of ponies who are superb conveyances for the young across country, especially with TB crosses for the larger types. I learned to ride and hunt during the Second World War on New Forest ponies, sensible, tough and intelligent who kept their feet in all circumstances.

Thankfully one special member of the hunting field, the cob, remains highly popular. They are still excellent workers, and they are tremendously popular in the show ring. Breeding a really outstanding one is something of a freak achievement, but crosses between Suffolk Punch or Welsh cob mares with quality riding horse sires may well result in the desired type of substanial, short-legged, active, and tractable riding types, well up to weight, and with an element of quality.

I had a blue roan Irish-bred cob, called Ballyn Garry, of a middle-weight, active stamp, which carried me brilliantly for ten seasons at least in Dorset and in the Home Counties. His breeding was unknown, but for toughness, sagacity and jumping heights he was superb; his only shortcoming was his limited galloping scope for the Shires, although nowadays I suspect he would keep up well in the more cramped modern Leicestershire hunting country, littered with artificial timber jumps, and he would certainly do well in the fashionable Hunts of Gloucestershire.

I bought a characterful red roan cob at the Dublin horse show three years ago, and was amused to learn that its career had started pulling carts containing seaweed on the beaches of Donegal. Although it had its good points I decided I was not quite ready for such a 'steady' mount yet, and sold it on for riding club and showing work in the North.

Hunting in Rutland and Leicestershire I am frequently overtaken at a fence in the school holidays by tiny children on Welsh or Connemara-cross ponies who hurtle past and jump huge places with immense confidence and skill. Many graduate to eventing or point-to-point riding with amazing assurance and ease. They learn the essential partnership with their mounts as infants, and that essential quality in riding, nerve, is inherited through the hunting field.

The banning of foxhunting would be a huge cultural as well as material disaster for branches of horse-riding where the British are still among the very best in the world.

CHAPTER 6

THE ENDANGERED FOX

*'And yet, it aren't that I loves the fox less, but I loves the
'ound more.'*

JORROCKS'S famous remark in one of his great 'untin' lectors', in R.S.
Surtees' great sporting novel *Handley Cross*, still sums up the attitude of most
foxhunting people.

Do I love foxes? Of course I do.

I know my answer would be derided by the anti-hunting zealots, but they seem
uninterested in the realities of a fox's battle for survival. In the modern countryside where farmers and landowners still regard foxes as agricultural pests, and
where gamekeepers are under increasing pressure to ensure that commercial
shoots have a large supply of reared birds, which foxes are inclined to eat, I am
certain that the best solution to the fox's future is the influence of a sporting cull
through the continuance of organised hunting with hounds.

As a life-long foxhunter I have seen more foxes in their natural environment
than most people. I have observed them at all times of the year, especially of
course when they are being hunted. I know that the odds are weighted in favour
of the fox in a hunt, and that the chase is not one long exhausting sprint.

In a longer hunt there will be pauses, we call them checks, when hounds
temporarily lose the line of scent and will have to recover it, greatly to the fox's
advantage. If it is a very short fast hunt the fox is likely to be caught above ground

Near the end of a hunt, the Woodland Pytchley are about to catch their fox. When hunted by hounds the fox is either killed instantaneously or escapes unscathed, which cannot be guaranteed in alternative forms of culling.

and killed immediately. Unlike any other form of cull I know the hunted fox will escape completely unscathed or be killed outright.

In the hunting field I see a beautiful wild mammal, conducting himself with an amazing confidence and *sang froid*, I have seen a fox in woodland where hounds are hunting, pause to engage in catching a small rabbit which ran across his path.

He is a hunter too and he seems to know a lot about scenting conditions. He has a scent gland under his tail, we call it his brush, and its these droplets of scent which hounds pick up. It is believed that nature protects vixens carrying cubs, or having recently given birth, by ensuring that her scent gland is not working at that time. Certainly she appears to carry far less scent.

In contrast, a large, senior dog-fox appears to carry most scent – and this could be nature's way of ensuring that older animals are culled, assuming there was a natural top predator above the fox, such as a wolf, still existing in the British countryside.

Venery, which has elements of an art and a science, says that when the air temperature is lower than that of the ground the scent tends to hang in the air longer before evaporating. Hounds pick up the scent just above ground level more easily in these conditions. That is what we call a 'good scenting day', perhaps with a 'breast-high' scent; that is the hound's breast level.

On such a day the fox tends to bustle about a great deal more when he is roused in covert by the pack of hounds drawing to find him. The adult fox will on such days break covert and run in the open far more swiftly and purposefully. He, or she, knows the terrain well, and has a very good idea of the route they will take which will include various kinds of sanctuaries, or scent baffling obstacles such as roads or streams.

When the air temperature is markedly higher than ground level, the tenuous scent of the fox rises above it and quickly evaporates. That is a 'bad scenting day', and it is truly remarkable how Charles James will tend to lounge about in such

A hunted fox running through a farmyard in the North Herefordshire country, in much less hurried mode. Hounds hunt by scent and foxes run well ahead of the pack, and have time for checks, in most hunts.

conditions. In the East Midlands a blue haze above the land often denotes a bad scenting day.

A 'good scenting day' tends to occur when snow is in the wind, so the air is rapidly chilling as the day wears on. Hounds pick up the scent well and give tongue all the more loudly. Conversely when a white frost is coming out of the ground scent is usually poor until another frost sets in later on a winter's afternoon.

The combination of temperature and evaporation factors is the main reason why autumn hunting takes place soon after dawn when the air is cooler. It also explains why, later in the season, the late afternoon hunt on a colder temperature is likely to be the best of the day.

In the southern states of the USA they tend to hunt early in the day at most times of the season to benefit from lower temperatures, but I have seen hunts in which hounds could pick up and maintain scent for long periods in temperatures above 80°F. This could be because there was virtually no difference between the ground and air temperatures, and evaporation of scent droplets was not far above ground level, and therefore remained immediately available to the hound's nose provided they were not too far behind their quarry.

Romantically called Charles James, or more commonly Charlie, after the tempestuous eighteenth century Whig politician Charles James Fox (1749–1806) the wild fox (*vulpes vulpes*) is a remarkable example of 'managed wildlife' in the twentieth century, provided it lives in a well run hunting country.

How Many Foxes

No-one knows the size of Britain's fox population. The Burns report said it is thought to be some 217,000 just before the annual breeding season starting in March, but admits this figure has 'low reliability'.

Naturalists think the fox population almost trebles by the early summer, which means that in the twelve months up to the following March about 400,000 foxes die each year. I find this figure hard to believe because some estimates published only fifteen to twenty years ago were saying that some 50,000 foxes were destroyed each year.

Without reliable data, because shoots and freelance terrier work do not contribute to national lists, it is safe to assume that several hundred thousand foxes die each year, but there is still a remarkable amount of mystery about foxes, and that is no bad thing if the species is to survive in our increasingly urbanised island.

Foxhunting with hounds, through the MFHA, nowadays keeps a national tally of foxes killed by the current 185 registered Hunts, and although not all Hunts send returns, it indicates an annual cull by foxhunting with hounds of around 15,000 to 16,000. There are a few non-registered Hunts, mainly gun packs operating in Wales, and some harrier packs catch foxes.

It is clear that foxhunting with hounds accounts for only a very small proportion of those killed annually. To select for abolition just one form of culling, which has a strong case for being the most humane, would be a disastrous government intervention.

Apart from its own cull, the Hunts contribute enormously to fox conservation by their own close season, and by the pressure they tend to exert on others not to perform culling at extermination levels. A sustainable cull for sporting purposes, without commercial pressures, is the best for all forms of wildlife, as seen in Africa.

Fox cubs in summer; by autumn they will be adults, hunting on their own account.

Dr David Macdonald, the Oxford zoologist who specialises in studies of the fox, has said that 'foxes have such resilience that populations can withstand about seventy-five per cent mortality without further decimating.'

Foxes mate from late December to February. Gestation is about fifty-two days and cubs are born mainly in March and April, in litters of three to seven. They soon venture from the breeding burrow with their mother and quickly learn hunting skills. Foxes are known to live in pairs, with both assisting in parenting, although they may also live in groups of up to five adults, comprising one adult male and several vixens. Usually one or two vixens in each group breeds.

Can the fox be truly monogamous? The question was famously asked at a Foxhunting Seminar presided over by the four-times married Capt. Ronnie Wallace. He referred slightly pompously to Sir Newton Rycroft for an answer, who heaved his shoulders in his inimitable high pitched chuckle, and then said: 'I think it is fair to say the fox is considerably more monogamous than a great many Masters of Foxhounds.'

The rural fox likes to live snug and dry underground and returns to his earth after a night's hunting; in the mountains he will live among rocks; in the lowlands he can be found in scrub or woodland, in unused mines, or even in sea cliffs.

Vixens give birth and rear their young underground in earths where the terrain makes this possible, but in summer the adult will usually live above ground continuously, choosing thick undergrowth, cornfields, hedge banks or ricks and strawyards.

The English fox, when fully grown at twenty-five weeks, may be up to twenty-two inches in height and fifteen pounds in weight. Foxes in the Fells or in the Scottish Highlands are generally bigger, weighing perhaps twenty pounds.

There are other hazards for the fox than hunting. In the early 1960s many in Eastern England were found to have died painful deaths through eating pigeons and other birds poisoned by toxic seed dressings. Foxes increasingly living in towns and suburbs are far more liable to catch mange. It has been alleged that some pest destruction agencies have caught urban foxes alive in cage traps and dumped them in rural areas where they spread mange, and succumb to early deaths in a strange environment.

Waves of mange among foxes in the West Country, spreading to the Midlands and north have been noted in recent years. Hounds are the best means of monitoring and catching enfeebled foxes and despatching them immediately, a vital contribution to the conservation of a healthy species.

Studies of foxes living in towns show that most have evidence of past injuries received in road accidents. Their native cunning does not prevent them from becoming frozen in the glare of a vehicle's headlights. Any journey along England's roads in the early mornings sees a great many wild mammal carcases, including hundreds of foxes. They often suffer slow, grievous deaths after impact from vehicles.

What do foxes eat? Are they really a pest? A fox is remarkably omnivorous, but it likes hunting and killing smaller mammals and birds. The Burns Report said farmers and landowners gave as reasons for killing foxes, their fear it would transmit disease, its predation on livestock and game, and some saw it as a preventative measure.

The reasons vary in the regions, so that the Welsh farmer cites fox predation on lambs, and the East Anglian farmer refers more to the loss of game; if not controlled foxes may kill large numbers of pheasants and partridges during their breeding period.

The shooting fraternity is often urged by the foxhunters to be less draconian in culling foxes. It has been pointed out to shooters that the ultimate aim of the animal rights lobby is to ban shooting as well as hunting. The pressure of culling by gamekeepers would be best removed by a ban on reared game shooting, say the more extreme members of the anti-hunting lobby.

The need for the utmost co-operation between shooting and hunting in uniting to preserve both sports was emphasised in the spring of 2004. The government was suggesting further curbs on shooting in a consultation paper: limits on the number of guns owned, tighter restrictions on shotgun licences, and a new minimum age for shooting, denying thousands of youngsters the opportunity to learn to shoot under adult supervision.

Burns asserts that the loss of pre-weaning lambs to foxes in a mid-Wales survey was less than one per cent, but how much larger would that figure be if there was no cull of foxes?

Burns admits that although large scale poultry rearing is nowadays intensive and in secure buildings, there is a growth in small scale fee range poultry rearing, and fox predation there is potentially catastrophic because foxes indulge in surplus killings. Pig breeders using outdoor units in some areas cite foxes as the cause of over a quarter of pre-weaning deaths of piglets.

Because of his 'pest' status, Charlie will remain an outlaw in the British countryside. The argument still rages as to how he should meet his end – to the sound of horn and the cry of hounds in his own environment, which gives him a sporting chance, or solely to unmonitored freelance killings which too often continue right through the fox's breeding season?

The fox will surely not receive the 'protected' status so erroneously and disastrously granted the badger by previous government decree. This has resulted in an uncontrolled over-population of badgers, sometimes short of food and sanctuary, causing increasing agricultural problems, notably the badger's tendency to spread tuberculosis to cattle, and to erode banks with its earths.

As a result in 2004 government was expected to allow farmers a programme aimed at gassing many thousands of badgers in Britain, causing major welfare concerns. Gassing can result in particularly slow and painful deaths underground according to veterinary opinion. Anti-hunting MPs do not complain about 'final solutions' for wildlife culling provided by men in white coats.

There are some signs of illegal culling of badgers which police are totally unable to control. Unmonitored digging of badgers or foxes can be carried out by rough gangs using terriers for the cruel sport of 'badger baiting', a night time activity exceedingly difficult to prevent. It is one reason why MFHA registered Hunts only used licenced terrier men, and refuse help from freelance terrier enthusiasts. 'When a fox is run to ground, digging is allowed only at the request of the landowner, farming or shooting tenant . . . If the decision is that the fox be killed, it must be humanely destroyed,' says MFHA rule 12 as referred to in Chapter 4.

When a hunted fox is run to ground in a natural earth there shall be no digging other than for the purpose of humanely destroying the fox, under the rules. Only the bolting of a 'fresh fox' is permitted, and this must only be done if it has taken refuge in any manmade structure, such as drains, stick-heaps, straw bales, banks and the like, or rocks and places where digging is impossible.

Ruling out the digging element in bolting a fox ensures that the fox avoids the trauma of a long dig before being hunted. Only one terrier may be used. The fox usually goes away swiftly in these circumstances; the pack of hounds is first taken out of sight and hearing, and the rules say 'the fox when bolted must be given a fair chance of escape before hounds are laid on.'

Humane Cull

In veterinary findings approved by four hundred members of the Royal College of Veterinary Surgeons, a submission was made by two distinguished veterinarians to the Burns Committee which emphatically supported hunting with hounds as the most humane and conservationist form of control.

Dr Lewis Thomas, and Professor W.R. 'Twink' Allen, stated that up to eighty-five per cent of foxes evade capture by hounds in longer hunts. They assert that the chase, the element in foxhunting so often condemned by its opponents, brings into play the fox's *natural* 'fight and flight responses', and it 'cannot be considered to be a period of unnatural stress to the fox'. Many of its evasion tactics are carried out at a leisurely pace after the initial flight.

'As with autumn hunting, the short final phase of the (successful) hunt, usually less than two minutes, will involve stress but this, in physiological terms, will be no more than that experienced by the extended athlete or racehorse.

'The animal is not hunted to the point of exhaustion rather to the point when still running hard it is overhauled by the fitter and more durable hounds and again often because the fox makes a tactical mistake. The kill occurs as a swift, almost instantaneous, procedure made possible by the considerable power weight advantage the hound has over the fox. The powerful exercise-induced analgesic actions of centrally released endorphins and enkephalins, generated during the hunt, will mitigate or eliminate any pain.'

Thomas and Allen point out that neither wild nor domestic animals appear to have any premonition of death. They cite post mortem evidence that where foxes are killed by hounds most causes of death was diagnosed as 'cervical dislocation and fracture', and the remainder from 'massive trauma to the thorax and abdomen.' Damage to the carcass by hounds, including disembowelment, will have occurred after death.

The RCVS vets say shooting foxes is 'intrinsically unsafe and inevitably produces a percentage of animals that are wounded'. A Welsh gun pack survey found up to twenty per cent of foxes wounded, not killed, and another source estimated that of 135,000 foxes shot annually as many as forty per cent are wounded.

The practice of 'lamping', to which I have referred in Chapter 4, is unmonitored and impossible to quantify. Groups of men go out at night with four wheel drive vehicles fitted with strong spot lights. They use squeakers and other noises, sometimes played on tape, to mimic fox calls, intended to attract foxes.

Foxes caught in the beam of light are shot with rifles. Although this is meant to be a pragmatic form of 'fox control' it has become something of an unofficial sport, much enjoyed by 'assistants' of certain gamekeepers, farmers and others. In some areas the practice is known to take place during the breeding season. The RCVS vets point out that, since as many as forty per cent shot by rifle and shotgun are wounded, 'most of these are left to suffer, and many of those wounded and incapacitated in the spring will be pregnant or lactating vixens.'

Thomas and Allen say that not only are many areas of the country impractical or unsafe for lamping and the rifle shooting of foxes, but 'there exists the well known phenomenon of "lamp shy" foxes that requires many man hours per fox killed – at best, two to five hours, and increasing as the pool (of foxes) decreases.'

The vets say free running snares, the only type which are legal for catching foxes, may be acceptable but they need careful siting and frequent inspection to ensure captured foxes are unharmed, and there is a real danger of snaring other similar sized animals. I have seen during some hunting days crippled foxes trailing broken snares, with appalling leg and body injuries, their agony only ended when they are swiftly caught by hounds.

Leg hold trapping is illegal in the UK and causes protracted suffering. Poisoning or gassing are illegal and, as mentioned above, causes too long suffering. Cage traps produce considerable psychological stress for foxes who react strongly against restraint in an unnatural environment, including transport to a new location.

These vets recommend hunting because it is 'selective and seasonal . . . whereby the weak, the diseased and the injured are detected and killed . . . No other method of culling performs this function and, were hunting to be banned, the welfare implications for all hunted species would be profound.

' An uncertain but unacceptably large number of animals would be condemned to a lingering death through disease, injury, malnutrition or illegal poisoning . . . In all respects hunting not only controls the fox population but both by selectivity and breeding maintains the health and vigour of the species.

'In all respects, for all four quarry species, hunting is therefore consistently more humane than any of the other culling methods.'

CHAPTER 7

SOME HUNTSMEN

T HERE is no league table for huntsmen. They are remembered only by reputations gained among those who hunted with them, and recounted to others.

It is always irritating when anyone who 'goes hunting' is erroneously described as a 'huntsman'. There is only one such in each hunting field. He alone is responsible for the control of hounds; he gets the praise – or the blame – for the hunting that transpires.

In selecting some of the leading huntsmen of the twentieth century I cannot avoid being subjective in praising some of those with whom I hunted, although I am indebted to all huntsmen whose hounds I have been fortunate to follow. I include mention of some of the giants early in the century who earned exceptional reputations.

This is bound to be an incomplete survey and will do injustice to many excellent huntsmen. The following will give just a flavour of the dedicated, skilled, in some cases inspired, huntsmen who made foxhunting possible throughout the century at such high standards.

Huntsmen who stayed with one pack for at least a score of years tended to earn higher reputations. Excellent huntsmen who changed packs frequently had less chance of becoming famous in the hunting world, and it must be admitted that the spotlight of publicity on Shires hunting helped to project its successful men into hunting legend and history.

Arthur Thatcher, huntsman of the Fernie from 1907–23. He was famous for being 'roasted alive' by Lord Lonsdale, the Yellow Earl, who was his Master when Thatcher hunted the Cottesmore (1900–7).

Lonsdale wrote an inexcusably arrogant, but highly amusing, letter to Thatcher in 1904. It was a 3,000 word critique of what he considered Thatcher's hunting errors, and is a classic dissertation on hunting hounds, whether you believe it to be fair, or not.

The Yellow Earl accused Thatcher of 'constantly changing foxes, taking hounds on to yet another holloa . . . not identifying your line, whereas you ought to be able to see whether your hounds take up a fresh scent or not, and you ought to have stopped your hounds three times on 12 December and gone back and identified your line, when you could have killed your fox.' He accused Thatcher of being 'the headless huntsman'.

The letter was meant to be entirely confidential, but it became public many years later. Thatcher at the Cottesmore, and later at the Fernie, was hailed by nearly everyone in Leicestershire as a huge success. He certainly caught foxes in addition to providing supremely entertaining hunts.

He was often compared to Tom Firr of the Quorn, although some thought Thatcher provided more fun. Thatcher was a 'showman huntsman', but he must have deserved his high reputation for consistent sport. He hunted hounds with great dash and verve, even if he was not a purist. He was a well known 'poacher' of foxes from neighbouring countries, not literally, but through darting his hounds over the border to draw their coverts – anything to 'keep the tambourine a rolling'.

Frank Freeman hunted the Pytchley from 1906–31, and achieved a widespread reputation as a truly great huntsman. The Master who appointed him, Lord Annaly (in office 1902–14) was hailed as the 'greatest Master in the land', and Freeman 'a genius of the first water' in Guy Paget's superb history of the Pytchley Hunt.

After a tough apprenticeship for seventeen years in countries ranging from Kent to Kildare, Freeman's success at the Pytchley was instantaneous, says Paget, but says he started 'with a perfect pack of hounds and a good scent'. Freeman had a 'one track mind', concentrating entirely on hunting and catching his fox. He lived with his hounds and for them, never taking a holiday for years.

He had a pale face, walked with a decided limp, and was later crippled by falls, due to his bravery across a big country in being with his hounds. He liked racy, active fox-killing hounds, and Paget declared 'the infinite charm of hunting with him was that he had so very few bad days.'

Quickness of decision, the ability to 'think like a hound or a fox', were among Freeman's qualities, and they mark other exceptional huntsmen. They cast their hounds unerringly and recapture the line swiftly after the pack has checked long enough to need help. A combination of field craft and instinctive knowledge of the quarry's line of flight which contribute to the highest forms of venery. Frank used to visit his brother Will Freeman when he hunted the Eridge in Sussex. While they talked an avid listener was a nine-years-old Ronnie Wallace.

Stanley Barker huntsman of the Pytchley 1931–60, earned a great reputation for maintaining remarkably consistent sport during a period when the Pytchley country saw great change from a mainly pastoral to an arable country. He exhib-

George Barker, redoubtable huntsman of the Quorn for thirty years (1929–59) who kept the hunt going during the war.

ited strength of character, as well as hunting skills, and served as a Magistrate in later life.

George Barker huntsman of the Quorn from 1929–59, was an outgoing personality, and a very good huntsman, if not perhaps a 'great' one. He was born and bred in the Quorn country, and had a flair for public relations, cementing a bond with the farmers and landowners with whom he was usually very popular. The excellent Quorn history by Colin Ellis says: 'George Barker could convince anybody of anything. To convince the Quorn farmers he came as a benefactor had been his role for years.' Like his namesake at the Pytchley, George Barker kept the Quorn going during the war, and ensured the revival of peace-time Shires hunting at a remarkably high level. He died in 1975 aged seventy-eight.

George Tongue hunted the Belvoir for twenty-eight years (1928–56); a tough man who earned a reputation as a highly effective, disciplined huntsman whose whippers-in spoke of him not merely with respect, but with awe. In the Great War he had been awarded the DCM for gallantry under heavy fire at Ypres. He hunted the pure English hounds in traditional style, expecting them to obey his voice and horn swiftly, maintaining the pack with immense attention to detail, and producing consistent sport across a formidable country in front of very large,

George Tongue, huntsman of the Belvoir (1928–56), a strict disciplinarian and highly effective in the hunting field.

hard-riding fields. It was said he could summon his pack, and gallop them back through the mounted field without hounds being at all daunted by the huge throng of horses before Tongue made a backward cast after a fox which had been headed. The heavy mental and physical demands of hunting a pack in a demanding four days a week, plus directing work in the Kennels and the country, are too little recognised.

Professional huntsmen have a somewhat lonely performer's role, the only person in the hunting field in charge of hounds, and need to be robust to withstand unfair criticism as well as overweening praise. During the good times they need moral strength to bear up to constant offers of hospitality, and the fair sex can be all too attracted to a successful huntsman. Every professional needs a 'good wife', supportive at all times, and able to assist in running the kennels effectively through maintaining good relationships with the wives and families of Hunt staff subordinate to the huntsman.

Major C.C. 'Chatty' Hilton-Green was Master and huntsman of the Cottesmore from 1931–46. Ronnie Wallace greatly admired him, and to some extent modelled his technique on Hilton-Green's.

He said 'Chatty' had the art of hunting his hounds correctly to catch the fox and at the same time 'keep several hundred horsemen at bay'.

He kept up the tempo of the chase with great success, making decisions swiftly and yet not lifting his hounds unnecessarily. Sir Henry Tate, later a Cottesmore Master, said 'Chatty' was one of the two best huntsmen he ever saw in that country. Hilton-Green was not one of the greatest horsemen, but good enough to stay in front near hounds when it mattered.

He served in the Royals during the Second World War, and had a tough time: he was on board a ship torpedoed on the way to North Africa. He was among those rescued from the sea by a destroyer, and as he was pulled up on deck the sailor holding the rope, said; 'I thought it was about time you had your second horse, sir.' The sailor had been on the Cottesmore Hunt staff before the war.

After he retired from the Cottesmore, Hilton-Green hunted the Berkeley, the Ballymacad, the Craven and the Tivyside before giving up hunting in 1962, spending his last years in Badminton village fighting ill health. His second wife, 'Boodley' Hilton-Green, went to Ireland and eventually married Lord Daresbury, Master of the Limerick.

'Master', 10th Duke of Beaufort I have extolled his Mastership of sixty years (1924–84), but his prowess as a huntsman for forty-seven years was alone remarkable enough to establish a great reputation.

He was an example of a huntsman who created the pack he hunted, breeding them brilliantly to his own requirements. He knew every inch of the country, much of which he owned, and he entertained very large fields with a certainty and flair which were natural gifts.

The Duke was exceptionally clever at ensuring hounds stayed on the line of a fox, and that every hunt had a beginning, a middle, and an end. He was very critical of what he called 'mystery tours'. Hunting with Master at the height of his powers, was a pleasure and a privilege, an opportunity to see venery at a high level by one who was so much at home in the environment he had inherited and loved so much.

Unfortunately because he remained in office until the end of his long life, later generations of Beaufort followers knew him mainly as an elderly gentleman who fussed over the shoulder of his professional huntsman, Brian Gupwell.

Charles Sturman was professional huntsman of the Heythrop from 1901–22. His reputation was very high, according to Robin Rhoderick-Jones, author Ronnie Wallace's biography. Sturman 'was a quick thinker with marvellous powers of observation and an unusually retentive memory.

'He lived for his hounds and never left the kennels except to hunt . . . His use of the horn, although sparing, was an art form; his hounds had unbounded confidence in him and were as one in the field.'

George Gillson at the Warwickshire (1935–40), **Percy Durno** at the Heythrop (1937–52), **Bert Peaker** at the Fernie (1928–48), and the amazingly resilient **Joe Wright** at the Cheshire (1920–36) were among huntsmen shining at the top of their profession between the wars.

There were a number of leading amateurs between the wars, some already mentioned as hound breeders, who had great influence on the future of foxhunting in setting a style where modern, active hounds were given as much freedom as possible to hunt the fox, whilst always remaining subject to the huntsman's control.

Prominent among them were **Sir Peter Farquhar** (Meynell 1931–34, and Whaddon Chase 1934–38) who earned a great reputation, confirmed after the war in his Portman Mastership (1947–59), **Sir Alfred (Bill) Goodson** (College Valley 1924–79), Major **Maurice 'Mo' Barclay** (Puckeridge 1910–62), **Major Bob Field-Marsham** (Bicester with Warden Hill 1936–42), and **Percival Williams** at the Four Burrow in Cornwall (1922–64).

Dermot Kelly was an exciting talent at the Meynell from 1962, continuing with the amalgamated Meynell and South Staffs until 1975. He was not a man to upset in the hunting field, and he communicated great drive to his hounds across a daunting country. Dermot is a thoughtful, articulate hunting man and bred some splendid hounds, using New Forest Medyg and other new outcrosses to improve his pack.

Some of his lines were used by **Johnny O'Shea** who became professional huntsman of the Cheshire for twenty-five years from 1966–91, and undoubtedly one of the finest ever to hunt that superb grass country. He has an Irishman's easy going temperament and exhibited a great talent for horsemanship, and handling hounds naturally and effectively in front of keen riding mounted fields.

I put a red star in my diary for every day I was fortunate to ride to hounds hunted by Johnny O'Shea, and I was delighted when he came to the *Horse & Hound* Ball and won the hunting horn competition.

In the Cheshire's neighbouring Sir Watkin Williams-Wynn country on the Welsh borders I rated as one of the finest professionals I ever saw, **Bill Lander,** who had been kennel huntsman for Ronnie Wallace from 1964–72, and hunted the Wynnstay with tremendous verve, and high skill from 1972–83.

At the Heythrop he was once asked if he enjoyed hunting hounds when Wallace was ill. 'I don't know,' said Lander. 'I've been here for years and the bugger hasn't coughed yet.' At the Wynnstay he was succeeded by a line of good

Dermot Kelly, Master and huntsman of the Meynell (1962–70) and Meynell and South Staffs (1970–75), still one of the best preserved grass hunting countries in Britain.

amateur huntsmen, from 1983 **Neil Ewart,** followed by Gerald Gundry's son **Robin Gundry** from 1991 to 1998, with **William Wakeham** until 2004.

Percival Williams was succeeded at the Four Burrow by his son, **John Williams,** for twenty-two years (1955–77), producing good sport over the Cornish banks, pastures and moorland.

Bill Goodson's successor as huntsman at the College Valley **Martin Letts** joined the Mastership in 1964 after hunting the Bolebroke Beagles in his native Kent. He has a natural aptitude for hunting hounds effectively in a moorland country where they may well surge far ahead.

In 1982 the College Valley amalgamated with the North Northumberland to form an excellent country twenty by twenty-five miles up to the Scottish Border, farmland as well as the forestry and hill country. Maintaining the valuable Fell element in the pack, and judiciously using modern English lines, Martin kept his pack on top form for forty seasons, until handing over to **Ian McKie** who came up from the Bicester country to take the Mastership in 2003.

Soon after the war, there was an influx of talent into amateur and professional huntsmen's positions, ensuring the revival of the sport. **Major Bill Scott** at the West Waterford (1947–49), the Portman (1949–52), and the Old Berks (1957–65) and **Maurice Kingscote** at the Meynell (1937–52) were among those prominent in early post-war years when the tide of mechanised arable farming had still not overwhelmed traditional pastures, and the hunting field was nearly recognisable in pre-war form.

Col. Guy Jackson lost both legs in the war, but taught himself to ride again using a special saddle, and was triumphant as Master and huntsman of the Exmoor for fourteen years from 1946–60. His daughter, **Charmian Green,** hunted hounds in America, and since 1990 has been a Joint Master of the Warwickshire with much distinction as a hound breeder and judge.

Major Gerald Gundry, often affectionately known as 'Gundogs', was Joint Master of the Duke of Beaufort from 1951–85, and huntsman mainly of the doghound pack from 1951–74. Gerald had a deep knowledge and understanding of foxhunting, inheriting much from his family being descended from the famous Parson Milne MFH in the Cattistock country. He shared Master's passion for hound breeding, and was a successful huntsman in his own right, giving most of his life to the best interests of one of the greatest Hunts at a golden period in its history. He was a splendid raconteur, one of the best after-dinner speakers in the hunting world.

His recounting of conversations between himself and Master was an extremely funny impersonation of a double-talk act, with Master as the straight-man. On one occasion Gerald was announced as retiring from the Mastership, but at the presentation ceremony Master announced with great relief that Gerald was not going after all, although they had collected a testimonial present for him and he might as well have it now; cheers echoed all round.

Capt. Ronnie Wallace at the Heythrop (1952–77) and the Exmoor (1977–2002) was the most formative influence on my hunting life, as he was for so many others, notably a whole school of young men who became amateur huntsmen, emulating his style of hunting hounds and his theories on hound breeding.

Wallace has rightly been paid many tributes by other huntsmen, but as a mere observer for many years I found that no hunting day with him was inconsequential. Even from the most unpromising meets he would conjure sport, by finding foxes and pursuing them relentlessly, sometimes into the most surprising venues. Since his death, Wallace has been acknowledged as the major figure in foxhunting in the twentieth century, after Master, 10th Duke of Beaufort.

As a huntsman Ronnie Wallace provided endless 'good' days, and certainly exhibited almost supernatural qualities of divining the routes taken by foxes, and the needs of his hounds in pursuing them.

He did not like his whippers-in to ride anywhere near him, but to keep out on the wings of the hunt as observers of foxes, ready to help and advise the huntsman only if absolutely necessary, using whistles instead of holloas to indicate foxes had gone away from coverts. It was often pointed out that Wallace was not an outstanding horseman, but his ability to keep up a regular pace all day in any terrain was remarkable, and he would always appear at the end of a hunt when his precious hounds caught their fox or marked to ground.

If I had any reservation about hunting with Ronnie Wallace, it was that there was not quite enough jollity about the proceeding, although he was certainly enjoying himself underneath the stern mien. Especially in latter years, it was 'a bit like hunting in church' someone said. We had come to follow and admire, not

Ronnie Wallace in his final season as Joint Master and huntsman of the Heythrop for twenty-five years (1952–77).

to join in and have a laugh. More frivolous members of the field did frolic about with some laughter taking place, and perhaps dodging the frown of the Master and huntsman added to their fun.

I remember one occasion with the Heythrop which perhaps summed it up: I was in a large mounted field, many of us chatting cheerfully while hounds checked some way ahead. Unusually, Wallace was out of touch with them momentarily, and was listening hard. He turned to the field, which included a Duke and several other notables, and said in a steely voice: 'Shut up, you bunch of half-wits.'

We all did so immediately; there was a chasm of silence, then Wallace heard his hounds; and the hunt resumed. He had nearly as much control over us as did over his hounds. Yet after a day's hunting Wallace could sometimes laugh and joke over dinner about the foibles of the day, and he very much wanted his field to enjoy themselves.

He could perform amazing feats of hound control, such as casting them far away across valleys on Exmoor to pick the line of a distant fox. In the Heythrop country on rare occasions he was said to approach a covert with hounds hunting slowly on the line of a fox well ahead, pick up his pack and gallop past the covert instantly to hit the line of another fox running hard from covert, thus adding sudden impetus to a hunt.

I was never aware of this; changing foxes in that way is not generally desirable and requires extreme hound control. I am sure he could have done it easily if he felt it necessary. Like all great artists, Wallace's apparent invincibility on-stage was based on a huge amount of time and thought on organisational detail off-stage.

I have hunted with virtually all the younger huntsmen in the 'school of Ronnie Wallace'. They all produced good sport, and added immensely to the overall quality of foxhunting. All had been thoroughly indoctrinated with the essential links between breeding and performance.

They include **Martin Scott,** a brilliant hound breeder who hunted the Tiverton (1969–77) and the VWH (1977–83), **Stephen Lambert** who was Master and huntsman of the Warwickshire (1975–81) and Heythrop (1981–88), **Alastair Jackson,** nowadays Director of the MFHA, who was a great success when he hunted the South Dorset (1969–80), Grafton (1982–84) and Cattistock (1984–89), **Edward Lycett Green,** York and Ainsty South (1977–78), Ludlow

Stephen Lambert, Joint Master of the Heythrop (1981–88), hunting hounds at Upper Slaughter, Glos. Previously he was Joint Master and huntsman of the Warwickshire from 1975.

(1980–82), Portman (1982–94), and Golden Valley(1997–2000), and **Nigel Peel** at the Chiddingfold, Leconfield and Cowdray (1977–88) and since then he has hunted with distinction the North Cotswold, sharing the Mastership with his wife Sophia, sister of Stephen Lambert.

Stewart P. Tory, senior Master and huntsman of the Portman (1959–69) impressed me greatly in my earlier years in the hunting field, as a dedicated fox-catcher, and his persistence in hunting the fox produced long hunts across lovely grass country for his mounted field, although Stewart himself jumped as few fences as possible. It illustrated perfectly that venery and 'riding just for fun' can go together, the but the former is the priority.

Jack Champion, huntsman of the Old Surrey and Burstow for thirty-eight seasons (1947–85) was a 'fun huntsman' who I thoroughly appreciated and liked. He was a fine horseman and showed it was possible to produce highly enter-taining sport in an increasingly cramped hunting country just outside London.

If I had the choice of recapturing the thrill of a twenty-five to forty minutes burst across the cream of Leicestershire with the huntsman of my choice, I would unhesitatingly seek to ride behind hounds hunted by **Michael Farrin,** huntsman of the Quorn for thirty years (1968–98). Born and brought up as a farmer's son

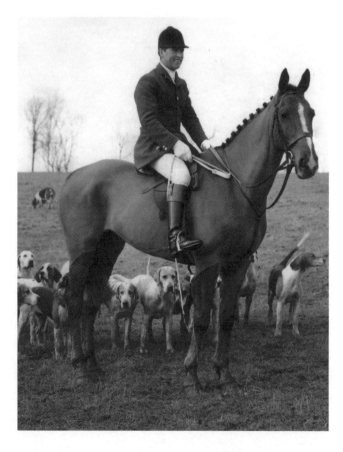

Huntsman Michael Farrin with his Quorn bitches at the meet at Lowesby.

in the Atherstone country, he became a second horseman in their Kennels at the age of sixteen. He whipped-in to Capt. Brian Parry at the North Cotswold, before joining the Quorn as whipper-in to Jack Littleworth.

At the early age of twenty-five Michael succeeded as huntsman of this major Shires pack when Jack retired through ill health. Ulrica Murray Smith and her Joint Masters already admired the qualities which were to make Michael a great Leicestershire huntsman: a flair for hunting the fox at speed, coolness and quickness of decision, superb horsemanship.

Quiet, modest and even shy at times, Michael was an impeccable professional. In the hunting field he would meet all sorts of setbacks and provocations without a word, merely speeding on with his hounds to continue a hunt, or start a new one.

He was a superb sight in front of the field: beautifully balanced on his horses, always presenting them just right at every obstacle, and flitting across the country with deceptive ease. He believed firmly in trying to get away on the first fox leaving covert to keep up the tempo of the day.

Michael was always conscious that Leicestershire's fame rested largely on the 'quick thing', the brilliant dash across country after a fox. The quarry would either be caught above ground, or if it went to ground, it would be left and hounds swiftly taken on to draw again. The urgency and drive of a day with Michael Farrin was a keynote of the sport.

There were longer hunts too: in 1975 his hounds ran seventeen miles in a wonderful hunt across grass and fences, in one hour forty minutes. At one stage when hounds made a big circle Michael overlapped some Quorn followers still riding the first circuit.

He said to me: 'When they check I love to see hounds cast themselves and do it all, but there are times when I have to step in and say to them "Come on. The fox has gone this way . . ." With our mounted fields, huntsmen have always been under a special sort of pressure.'

Since his retirement to take up a career with the Jockey Club staff, Michael Farrin continues to hunt occasional days with the Cottesmore. One morning the Cottesmore huntsman was having medical treatment and Michael hunted hounds again. It was one of the greatest pleasures of my hunting life suddenly to see the clock turned back – Michael, as trim as ever in the saddle, soaring over the turf and fences, with the Cottesmore hounds hunting in full cry ahead.

I turned to a young lady visitor near me in the mounted field, and said: 'Isn't Michael Farrin marvellous!' She beamed agreement, but asked: 'Who exactly *is* Michael Farrin?' I stifled a bitter retort, and merely felt sorry for her; those who hunted with Farrin over the best of Leicestershire have special memories no-one can replace in to-day's environment.

Hunting the Fernie hounds when I first came to Leicestershire was **Bruce Durno,** son of Percy Durno, and one of the nicest and most able huntsmen I ever saw. Unflappable, quiet with his hounds, Bruce slipped across country with no fuss, and his hounds trusted him immensely. He produced some superb sport for thirty years (1966–97), including one of the greatest runs of my thirty years as a hunting correspondent. (Chapter 9).

At the Belvoir during most of the years I subscribed was the wonderful **Jim**

A huntsman renowned for his quiet, effective style, Bruce Durno who hunted the Fernie for thirty-one years (1966–97).

Webster, possessor of a dry sense of humour, apparently imperturbable, with a rock-like constitution and strong nerve which enabled him to continue hunting hounds at least four days a week in this highly demanding country, with an especially hard-riding field for twenty-seven years (1956–83).

I had many happy days following Jim's pure English hounds of which he was rightly so proud, and defended him against some unfair criticism for being 'slow' towards the end of his career. Jim once told me with an engaging smile he did not expect much scent in September because it would be too dry; the leaf would be falling in October which would spoil things; it would be too frosty for much sport in November and December; and after Christmas he expected the ground would be too wet; then the season would be over.

In truth, his hounds were exceedingly fast and in excellent form throughout his term, and this was proved when he handed them over to **Robin Jackson** (1983–92) who was able to produce excellent sport straight away.

Since 1992 the Belvoir has been hunted at a high standard by one of the most effective of contemporary huntsmen, **Martin Thornton.** He adapted swiftly to the different technique of hunting the volatile pure English hound and in my experience these have not hunted better throughout the postwar years despite the loss of much of their grass country to arable farming.

When I hunted with the Cottesmore in 1969 hounds were being hunted by the other man Sir Henry Tate thought the best he had seen, **Capt. Simon Clarke.** I had already observed Simon Clarke's skills when he was hunting the South Dorset (1962–69).

A step-son of Gerald Gundry, Simon was brought up in the Beaufort country to imbibe foxhunting lore at its most correct. He hunted hounds with great intelligence and a natural talent, always following best practice in not lifting nor hurrying hounds unnecessarily. Allied with his great abilities as a hound breeder, Simon's qualities produced a notable run of good sport at the Cottesmore, with lengthy hunts and many foxes caught above ground.

Many thought it a great pity that this was not to be a much longer Shires Mastership, but Simon moved on after seven years to the Duke of Buccleuch's in Scotland, and to the South and West Wilts (1979–90). He finished his Mastership and huntsman's career at the New Forest (1992–96). Simon hunted hounds impeccably, despite latterly being afflicted by weight problems, and he has contributed hugely to modern hunting as a hound breeder, judge, and administrator in the former BFSS Campaign for Hunting, and later at the MFHA.

The Cottesmore was fortunate when **Capt. Brian Fanshawe** one of the greatest post-war amateur huntsmen, took the Mastership in 1981. His father and mother, Major and Mrs Dick Fanshawe, both hunted the South Oxfordshire hounds, and he is a nephew of Sir Peter Farquhar.

Brian had hunted the Warwickshire, the Galway Blazers and the North Cotswold with much distinction, bringing this great experience as well as hunting talent to the Cottesmore, a country which well suited him. He was fortunate to have the staunch support of his wife, Libby, a great foxhunting lady.

Brian followed Ronnie Wallace's precept that organisation was the key to good sport. The Cottesmore country, its kennels and stables were managed single-handed by Brian with firm, expert leadership. He injected new and worth-while lines into the pack, using French and later American outcrosses with success. Farmers and landowners thoroughly appreciated Brian's care for their interests at all times.

In the hunting field the sport was extraordinarily exciting every day. Keeping out of trouble added tremendously to the followers' thrills. 'Get involved!' he would bellow at groups of flustered followers standing at covert-sides on cub-hunting mornings. Expletives were hurled at all and sundry if things went wrong, but fortunately the roar usually made it impossible to interpret the words precisely, which was just as well. Brian especially hated my chinstrap, and roared at me for not taking off my hat to indicate the line of a fox I was holloaing. It was all good fun.

I comforted a young lady follower weeping copiously out cub-hunting one morning, having been chided for being 'in the wrong place'. She cheered up when I told her: 'Never mind, you can tell your grandchildren you headed Fanshawe's fox and survived.'

Brian would apologise afterwards, if he could remember who might possibly have been offended. We locals considered it simply part of the territory during a great Mastership.

Off a horse he was mildness itself, and led a devoted hard core of helpers and followers who knew they would never see better hunting in their lives. Hounds knew it too; although their huntsman was not the quietest, they did not lift their heads but worked mightily to run hard and catch their fox – because they well understood this was the burning ambition of their Master.

After a tremendous hunt across the cream of the country after a fox found well outside it one Saturday afternoon, which only a few of us experienced, I warmly thanked Brian who merely replied: 'It wasn' t that good – we didn't catch the fox.'

He has a tremendous sense of humour, and enjoyed it when Urky Newton asked him which were his forthcoming 'good' fixtures and which his 'bad' ones so that she could advise Melton Hunt Club visitors. 'I'm afraid I can't promise any bad ones,' he advised her.

As a former winning amateur race rider Fanshawe was excellent across country, giving his Field Masters a daunting task in keeping up with him. He especially enjoyed a long hunt into the territory of a neighbouring country, and the Cottesmore hounds got to know the Quorn Friday country very well.

At the age of fifty-five Brian gave up hunting completely. 'It's all or nothing' he said. The Cottesmore mourned their loss, and had a major task in filling all the roles he had carried out. Since then Fanshawe has worked unceasingly for foxhunting through the Countryside Alliance, and the Council of Hunting Associations. He is still seeking an outright victory in hunting's political battle; nothing less has ever suited him.

One of the most popular and effective of modern huntsmen, Sidney Bailey, huntsman of the VWH since 1966.

Peter Jones,
huntsman of the
Pytchley since 1971,
a remarkable
example of resilience
and talent in a highly
popular Hunt.

One of Brian's finest legacies to the Cottesmore was the young whipper-in he trained so thoroughly, **Neil Coleman** who came up from Gloucestershire with the Master and whipped-in from 1982 until taking over as huntsman in 1992. Neil is a real hound man, with high standards in kennels, and never more effective than when he is hunting hounds in the thickest and most difficult country among the Cottesmore's varied terrain.

He understands the pack and its breeding intimately, and has great fox sense, especially useful on poor scenting days. Neil is now the longest serving huntsman in the Shires and in twenty-two years service has had to cope with massive changes in the country: busier roads, sprawling villages, major increase in shoots, and setbacks such as the foot and mouth stoppage, plus occasional visits from Hunt saboteurs using harassment, intimidation or secret surveillance cameras.

It is easy to under-estimate these problems which afflict most foxhunting countries, and make the task of a modern huntsman far more difficult than some of the 'greats' of the past would ever have envisaged.

Other long-serving huntsmen in current service I especially admire are **Peter Jones,** amazingly resilient huntsman of the Pytchley since 1971, **Jim Lang** who has hunted the Burton since 1967, **Sidney Bailey,** huntsman of the VWH since 1966, and **Anthony Adams** who whipped in to Ronnie Wallace, and hunted the Exmoor, Warwickshire (1982–88), and the Heythrop since 1988.

Tony Wright had the daunting task of hunting the Exmoor following Ronnie Wallace, since 1982, and Wallace has paid him tribute as a first-class huntsman.

All the above have loyal and devoted admirers and followers in their own countries, and have entertained generations of hunting people, including many visitors. Their staunchness in the face of change, and unfair political threat to their jobs and way of life are an example to many others in modern Britain.

'We've got simply the best huntsman in England,' said VWH Joint Master Norman Thomas in looking back over **Sidney Bailey**'s long career. 'He really is a hero to so many of us in our country, and the farmers and landowners think the world of him. The years don't seem to make any difference to him. No day is too long; it's quite a job sometimes to persuade him to blow for home. That spirit of enthusiasm is marvellous in a huntsman; it makes for good sport and a good atmosphere in the Hunt.'

In 2004 the leading amateur huntsman in the British Isles is undoubtedly **Capt. Ian Farquhar**, Joint Master and huntsman of the Duke of Beaufort's since 1985, and previously in the same role with much success at the Bicester (1973–84).

Ian has tremendous skills as a huntsman, an apparently relaxed manner, but able to switch into top gear immediately. Martin Scott who hunts with the

Capt. Ian Farquhar hunting the Bicester and Warden Hill hounds when he was Joint Master and huntsman (1973–84), before taking office with the Duke of Beaufort's.

Beaufort since giving up his own career as MFH, says of Ian Farquhar: 'He is a very good horseman and a brilliant hound man. I have always liked his quiet way of hunting hounds. He appears never to be in a hurry; he will pause and light up a cigarette sometimes when hounds check, and give them every chance to sort out the line on their own.

'Nothing appears to worry him, and this confidence communicates to his hounds. But he can put on the pressure when appropriate. As a top-class huntsman he knows exactly when to let hounds solve a problem themselves and when he is able to pick them up and cast them.'

There is a great spirit in the Beaufort country and it is largely due to Ian's leadership. The Hunt sent forty-five packed coaches and many car-loads to the Countryside March in London.

Ian's senior Joint Master and owner of the pack, David, the 11th Duke of Beaufort says: 'Ian has been a huge success hunting our hounds. I was determined he was the one to appoint when the opportunity arose, and I have never regretted that decision.

'He is a very attractive, charming person which is a great help in being a Master of Foxhounds who has to get on with everyone. But, above all, he has a natural gift for the art of venery, just as his father possessed. Ian is undoubtedly the best amateur huntsman in the land.'

Albert Buckle is a neat, spry figure, and one of the most truly professional huntsmen I ever encountered. After hunting the North Cotswold for four years, Albert began his great partnership (1954–80) at the Whaddon Chase with Dorian Williams as Joint Master; it was one of the success stories of post-war hunting. Albert was an excellent horseman, and a sympathetic but firm hound man.

'He ensured the Whaddon Chase retained its nickname as the "Londoners' Leicestershire", attracting large, enthusiastic mounted fields.' Dorian Williams wrote: 'Albert proved not only to be remarkably talented, but over the years has proved himself to be an exceptional ambassador for foxhunting, and a very great friend.'

After twenty-six years hunting the Whaddon Chase hounds, Albert continued for three years as kennel huntsman assisting his successor David Barker. In retirement Albert has remained fit and active into his eighties, and is to be seen every year as a ring steward at Peterborough Royal Foxhound Show.

David Barker quickly formed a devoted following at the Meynell and South Staffs as huntsman from 1986–98. In his youth an Olympic level show-jumping rider, then a major producer of show hunters, David learned much from Albert Buckle at the Whaddon Chase, and succeeded him as huntsman until that hunt amalgamated with the Bicester.

At the Meynell, David's phenomenal skills as a horseman enabled him to realise the full potential of the country in south Derbyshire and north Staffordshire which remains one of the best riding countries in the United Kingdom. David displayed excellent hound control, and produced consistent sport.

One of his great admirers is the Prince of Wales who hunted regularly with the Meynell through most of David's term of office, and benefited greatly from

David's help in finding and schooling the most suitable horses for the considerable challenge of following the Meynell hounds.

Hunting's strong threads of family continuity were demonstrated when David was succeeded by the **Hon. Johnny Greenall**, a grandson of Lord (Toby) Daresbury of the Belvoir and Limerick. Johnny's eldest brother, the present Lord Daresbury, formerly Peter Greenall, performs great services for the sport as Chairman of the MFHA, and Joint Master of Sir Watkin Williams-Wynn's since 1991.

I have so many happy memories of hunting in Ireland, and I am forever in the debt of **Hugh Robards** who hunted the Co. Limerick so brilliantly (1971–94) and has now made a new life in the US as Joint Master and huntsman of the Rolling Rock Hunt in Pennsylvania.

I greatly admired the tremendous skills and enthusiasm of **Michael Higgens** hunting the Tipperary (1971–93). I was fortunate to hunt with **Thady Ryan** at the Scarteen a few times. He seemed very relaxed, but I saw him put on the pressure to stay in front when the Kerry Beagles screamed over a narrow banked stretch of country, and I was vastly impressed. His talent was to know just when to help his highly volatile Kerry Beagles, and when to leave them alone.

Thady's Mastership from 1946 has been one long demonstration of the power of personality. He has the charm and the authority to ensure that any time in his company is a pleasure for anyone with the remotest interest in horses, hounds and the countryside. Nowadays living in New Zealand where his wife was born, Thady handed over the horn to his son Christopher who has continued the family tradition since 1986.

In America I place unreservedly at the top of my list of huntsmen I followed, **Ben Hardaway** at the Midland (see Chapter 8) and I rate **Marty Wood** at the Live Oak as one of the most gifted woodland huntsman I have ever seen. He displays a remarkable ability to hunt by sound for long periods during the day, accurately divining what is happening to hounds and the quarry. I have seen more than a few otherwise top-class huntsmen who are far less effective in dense woodland than in open country.

CHAPTER 8

FOXHUNTING IN THE US, CANADA AND AUSTRALIA

BITING winds and lashing rain . . . hounds screaming ahead on the line of a big, rangy coyote . . . grass, fences and limestone walls, just like the Cotswolds . . . the lush heat of the Deep South . . . hounds speaking among the cotton fields, pine plantations and swamp lands of Alabama and Georgia.

I have so many happy memories of hunting with Foxhound packs in North

America. Although I have yet to hunt on the West coast, I have been fortunate to hunt in Canada, and in widely varying country down the Eastern seaboard to Virginia and the South.

There are just over 170 registered packs of Foxhounds in thirty-five States from Florida to California, and from Vermont in the far north-east to Washington State in the Pacific north-west. About 20,000 people ride to hounds regularly out of a total population of more than 250 million – a minority interest indeed, but avidly supported by loyal Hunt members, and exceedingly well administered by the Masters of Foxhounds Association of America.

Although the terrain is so diverse, the visitor finds a common thread: the friendliness and hospitality of American and Canadian foxhunters. They are intensely proud of their hounds, and some are closely interested in hound breeding and venery. As in Britain, there is an element who go out solely for the pleasure of the ride. Without the traditional English hedge, the American foxhunter is faced with reasonably modest 'fence panels' which may be rails or 'coops', triangular shaped panels of boards laid over wire. Just occasionally, however, you will meet 'line fences', high wooden rails built to keep in stock, and they may be a formidable challenge.

There are marked differences in the way Hunts are structured in North America, and I think some British Hunts, in an eroding environment of smaller hunting countries, might benefit in the twenty-first century from adopting some of the US methods. Americans and Canadians run their Hunts as friendly clubs. Often a number of subscribers keep their horses in the stables at the Hunt

Master and huntsman Terry Paine with the Santa Fe pack of Cross-Bred hounds, hunting coyote in 60,000 acres of rolling county in California.

Joint Master and huntsman Alexis Macaulay with the Misty Morning Hunt pack established in 1995 at Gainesville, Florida, hunting in 80°F temperature.

Kennels, their livery payments also covering the cost of keeping the horses used by the professional Hunt staff. At the Hunt Kennels there is often a clubhouse, or sometimes more elaborate club facilities, and it can be a social centre as well as somewhere to house the hounds and horses.

All this helps to foster a sense of belonging by US subscribers. They are usually smaller in number, and by English standards sometimes pay surprisingly small subscriptions.

Some US Hunts are private packs, mainly subsidised by wealthy Masters. Ben Hardaway, Master of the Midland, used to say he charged his subscribers twenty-five dollars a season – 'and they only get twenty-five dollars worth of say!'

Since hunting with Ben was a non-stop entertainment on and off the hunting field his mounted field and other supporters were the most subsidised, and thoroughly appreciative, Hunt members I have encountered anywhere.

In contrast, especially in parts of the English Midlands, too often subscribers to the larger four day a week packs in the UK have been regarded as 'customers' who pay a certain grade of subscription to hunt on a particular day, and have little or no contribution to the policy and running of the Hunt. There are smaller UK packs with a club philosophy, but adhering to the British structure. The model constitutions recommended by the British MFHA nowadays, with Committee members serving fixed terms of office, are aimed at preventing self-elected oligarchies.

Americans and Canadians tend to give their professional huntsmen the status of golf professionals, rather than the old 'Hunt servant' relationship with the Masters. In Canada there are no private packs. All are subscription packs, and are governed by boards of directors who appoint the Masters and do not operate the guarantee system.

Killing the fox above ground in North America is the exception compared to the UK, but the close scenting American packs end many hunts by marking to ground in zero or high temperatures. I have seen foxes dug out and killed with a gun in the South, but in many other areas it is left in the earth.

The terrain in many US and Canadian countries does not lend itself to earth stopping which is virtually unknown; there is a plethora of ground hog holes in many hunting areas which could not be stopped, and offer innumerable opportunities for escape. The native American grey fox has a habit of escaping by climbing trees; he is a wily quarry and because he tends to run in small circles, and has many evasive tricks, he forces hounds to hunt slowly, patiently and with great persistence. You will see excellent hound work in hunting the grey fox. He does not compete with the coyote or red fox for food, and can co-exist with both.

The red fox, originally imported from Europe in the eighteenth century, runs somewhat straighter and faster, and can provide long points in those areas of North America where urbanisation, roads and fenced farming are scarce. There is evidence that the red fox has been 'seen off' by large influxes of the coyote from the West to the East Coast, although by 2004 the trend was reversing a little, and more foxes were being found by hounds in areas where coyotes appeared to have taken over.

In the late twentieth century the coyote dramatically attacked red foxes and destroyed their populations in southern states on the Eastern seaboard. This is a difficult animal to catch with hounds, and alters the nature of hunting fundamentally.

The coyote will burst out of covert like a runaway express train, head across country at amazing speed, will cleverly pass hounds on to another coyote, and the hunt may continue at a sudden burst of increased speed on the fresh quarry. There is little chance for the huntsman to cast hounds, nor to employ other, more subtle, forms of venery.

The hunt is all about keeping up with the fast, strong, and extremely clever wolf running in front. He does not go to ground nor climb trees, although he may dive under a barn; he is sometimes caught by hounds when he runs into an obstacle he cannot leap, such as high, close-mesh fencing, and a pack of Foxhounds will kill him immediately, just as they do the much smaller fox.

The number of coyotes caught by one pack in a season may be no more than a dozen, and often less. Some foxhunters relish the new dash of the coyote hunt; others sigh for the traditional fox hunt.

However many of the quarry hounds kill, the monitoring of wildlife by hounds is an invaluable aid to wildlife management. The Fox Hunts were an important means of gauging the dramatic influx of coyotes to the eastern seaboard States.

The coyote (*Canis latrans*) originated in the hot desert lands of the west or the much colder rural areas of Canada. It may be about four feet long, including a bushy tail a foot long. In the East the coyote has been recorded at forty-five to sixty pounds in weight, compared with its western cousins of the deserts which are usually up to twenty-five pounds. In the west the coyote usually has yellowish fur but in the east it may be black, red or even brown.

They inter-breed in the eastern states with domestic and feral dogs, producing bigger hybrids of great stature. Because of their ability to kill young farm stock, and they may be carriers of rabies, they are firmly regarded as rural pests, and control by hounds and the gun is approved. They are tenacious and extremely clever quarry, and very difficult to catch with hounds.

A major difference from the UK is that rabies is endemic in much of North American wildlife, and the fox is a main carrier. American and Canadian hound packs, like domestic dogs, are vaccinated regularly against rabies, and wear distinctive blue collars as proof. Huntsmen and whippers-in are also vaccinated. Due to North America's vast terrain, and the huge gap between urban and country living, the rabies threat is not perceived as a problem in hunting a live quarry with hounds.

It says much for the excellent management of North American Hunts that no problems arise, and it may indicate that in Britain the threat of rabies is sometimes over emphasised. It has long been feared among the British hunting community that a rabies outbreak in the UK would halt hunting with hounds permanently.

Experience in North America, and in France, shows that programme of feeding foxes with oral vaccine in bait, often dropped from the air, has been remarkably successful in clearing the disease. Unfortunately, in North America rabies tends to recur, and it has been especially severe in Ontario, at times making foxes scarce. The scourge has long been especially prevalent in that territory. Some Canadian packs have hunted the jack-rabbit, slightly bigger than a hare, with success.

The lynx or bobcat is another quarry of American Foxhound packs, especially in the South and Southern Mid-West. In Tennesee and Kentucky it is possible for packs to hunt the coyote, red fox, grey fox and bobcat on the same day. The bobcat slows down the pack, brings them to their noses, and involves a great deal of patient hound work in a smallish area.

On the whole, foxhunting with hounds in North America is scarcely noticed by millions of citizens. They use the term 'hunting' for the sport of shooting, and they do not see packs of hounds meeting regularly in the centre of small towns and hamlets as they do in the British Isles. There is a growing attack on hound sports by well funded US animal rights extremists, but the threat of abolition is far less apparent than in the UK. I suspect the American citizen's personal freedom written in the constitutional Bill of Rights has more than a little do with this. Americans, for example, are allowed to 'bear arms' under their constitution, and this is one of the main supports for their powerful gun lobby.

One of the striking differences which can somewhat bemuse an English visitor is American readiness to use technical assistance. Perhaps the most unusual is a whipper-in or huntsman using a pistol firing 'rat shot' at their own pack of hounds to stop them running riot on the wrong quarry, usually American white tailed deer which abound so profusely in some hunting countries. The shot only stings the hounds, but some Masters say it can be highly effective.

The rat shot, I am assured, causes no injury and does not hurt any more than the use of a hunting lash, but it can be effective because the whole pack takes note of it at the same time, whereas chastisement with a hunting whip has to be more selective. I emphasise that the use of a whip on hounds to ensure their obedience in the hunting field is neither approved, nor effective, by huntsmen in the US and the UK. The whip would only be used in extreme cases of riot, not as a regular means of control. Hounds have to be biddable to the voice and the horn.

Two-way radio transmitters seem widely used in the US hunting field. They are employed by whippers-in and others in thick woodland to warn the huntsman that hounds are approaching perils such as busy highways, but I have heard some huntsmen and their whippers-in advising each other by radio on the whereabouts of the quarry or hounds. I do not say this is general practice, nor do I quarrel with it in America where the wildness of the terrain, with vast areas of woodland in some countries, is totally different from much British foxhunting.

Another American practice in certain countries is to attach miniature aerial wires to the hound collars. Lost hounds may be tracked on a scanner, saving hours of searching by mounted or car borne whippers-in, I was assured. Hounds also wear blue collars to denote they have been vaccinated against rabies.

Members of the mounted field may use another piece of equipment seldom seen in an English hunting field – sun-glasses! American packs often meet much earlier than ours during the season proper, largely because of climate and temperature difference. In the South it is quite common to meet soon after dawn, with 'end of day' at noon.

Americans are good at convivial Hunt 'brunches' before, after, or even during, a day's hunting. Foxhunters will drive for days and nights in their huge trucks and long trailers to visit Hunts hundreds of miles away. They are received with warm welcome, and hospitality flows. It is a frontier tradition which is very attractive.

There is an informality far different from the strict conformism of old-style English meets. I can still smell the smoke of a large log fire blazing at dawn in an Alabama woodland clearing, as groups of genial and friendly Foxhunters stood around, sipping hot coffee, before the 'dawgs' were sent out to find a fox.

They have been foxhunting in the US and Canada as long as the sport achieved more prominence in eighteenth century England, and it is an aspect of North American rural life very precious to the comparative few who know and enjoy it. During a day's hunting in Virginia a member of the Hunt asked where in England I lived. 'Leicestershire', I replied. 'Oh really? And is there any hunting there?' came the reply.

Foxford in US and Canada

I met Ben Hardaway, Master of his own Midland pack of hounds, in September, 1978, at the World Three-Day-Event Championships at Lexington, Kentucky.

Within minutes Ben asked: 'Why don't you come down and see my hounds working?'

Ben Hardaway MFH with hounds in his Midland Hunt kennels at Columbus, Georgia, USA.

I gulped and asked: 'Which flight?'

'You take my flight,' was the answer, and sure enough we flew to Columbus, Georgia, in Ben's private jet plane

I was accompanied by Jim Meads who was photographing the horse trials for *Horse & Hound*, but whose priority is the hunting field. He learned to photograph hunting from his father in the Enfield Chace country north of London, and has become the world's foremost specialist photographer of venery. He has accompanied me on a couple of hundred Hunt visits; a highly knowledgeable hunting man, and a good friend.

Our visit to the Midland country started a close association with North American hunting for Jim which has continued for the rest of his career. Nowadays, in his seventies, he visits the American packs regularly, and is highly popular with Hunt followers who greatly admire his stamina in running on foot with hounds for many miles to take his pictures.

At Columbus airfield Ben Hardaway transferred us to a car waiting for him by the runway, and headed for the perimeter fence where he paused to press a button on the dashboard. 'Got my own personalised exit,' he grinned. A section of the perimeter fence slid back, and we were completing a pilgrimage to the eccentric, amusing, exciting world of foxhunting Hardaway-style.

A few foxhunters had already made their way down to Columbus from Britain, and had returned agog, amazed, and in some cases converted to Ben's passionate belief in his way of out-crossing hounds with daring and insight.

Benjamin Hardaway III, inheritor and developer of a major family construction company, founded his Midland Hunt in 1950 to hunt red and grey foxes in his native Georgia and over the border in Alabama.

'Columbus, Georgia, is the hottest place in America today' said the local radio announcer on my first visit. It seemed quixotic to expect successful foxhunting in such heat.

We enjoyed an evening of generous Southern hospitality from Ben and his wife Sarah, who epitomises for me the definition of an elegant Southern lady. We rose at 5 a.m. in temperatures already in the eighties. I was amazed to see Ben hunting a pack of some thirty-six and a half couple of hounds, about twice as many as a huntsman would use at home.

Ben's whippers-in were Jefferson 'Tot' Goodwin, an imperturbable black man who had his own pack of hounds on the side, and a recent recruit, Ronald Schwartz. Ben kept his whippers-in on the wings of the hunting field, similar to the style of Ronnie Wallace. There was no 'dog walloping'; hounds were biddable to their huntsman's voice and horn, used sparingly until Ben holloaed them on to a fox with huge enthusiasm.

The Midland pack largely comprised hounds with about five-eights Fell blood, a quarter July blood, and one-eighth Penn-MaryDel lines. We rode out from Ben's Kennels where the hounds were in lodges elevated above the ground to reduce the risk of disease, and to increase coolness. We were in thickly wooded country, interspersed with grass paddocks, riding along sandy tacks, and occasionally jumping wooden coops.

The woods were full of the white-tailed deer carrying a strong, near-irresistible scent. Ben had tried many 'solutions' to prevent riot in the early years building up his pack. They weren't 'deer proof' he admitted, but they weren't 'deer crazy' either. He joked that he had once tried putting hounds, one at a time, into a fifty-five gallon steel barrel containing a deer skin. If the hound took any interest in the deer skin it was given a quick shock with an electric cow prodder.

When asked later if his hounds would go near deer after that, Ben replied: 'Yep, they'll still go near deer – but they won't go anywhere near a fifty-five gallon steel barrel.'

He asserted the best solution was to breed biddable strains of hounds, and train them exceptionally carefully in the field when they were being entered. When I first visited him he told me he was using a herd of goats as a training exercise, making the hounds go among the goats without showing the slightest interest. I saw no signs of rioting on deer during my visits to the Midland pack.

On our first morning hounds hunted prettily in the open on the line of a fox, but although there had been a heavy dew in temperatures into the nineties there was little or no scent in covert, and we did not make it a long morning. Ben maintained a fixture card in his season proper but he could pull out hounds from his extensive pack to entertain himself and a few friends whenever he felt like it. Next day we drove south into Alabama, and a different time zone causing Ben's meet card to show different times for the same meet.

This was Red Indian country in pioneer days, and I could imagine Cherokees galloping from the rolling wooded hills down to the many lakes dotting this area south of Phoenix City. We enjoyed a fast, exciting hunt after a red fox; hounds running hard with a great cry.They marked their fox to ground accurately with great enthusiasm, and I was much impressed by their hunting qualities.

Next day we moved to Fitzpatrick, Alabama, where Ben keeps a separate kennel and stables, some seventy miles from his home base. There is rolling grassland, and small coverts in this country, an opportunity to hunt in the open.

We started at dawn in eighty degrees, and hounds were soon screaming on the line of a red fox. They maintained a remarkably good line in the open despite the heat, and achieved a farthest point of over four miles, the fox eventually being given best after a lengthy check at a soya bean field.

Celebrating the day's hunting at Fitzpatrick with Ben's ice cold vintage champagne gave the visit another special flavour. I had been brilliantly mounted on Ben's Thoroughbred hunters, and had hugely enjoyed the ride as well as the hound work. There are special hazards in the Deep South: Jim Meads running across the Fitzpatrick terrain was urged to wear snake boots because of the risk of a bite, but he disdained their use 'in case they slow me down'.

It was an introduction to US Foxhunting and the American South which I thoroughly appreciated, and my own high opinion of Ben's prowess as a hound breeder and huntsman have been frequently endorsed by far more knowledgeable and illustrious foxhunters from England and elsewhere.

Apart from sheer skill, the great huntsman should have a willingness to share the sport of the day which communicates to everyone in the hunting field with him, from his staff to the rider at the back of the field. Ben Hardaway has that gift, plus an acute sense of humour, and it has made hunting with him a special treat in the life-time of any Foxhunter lucky enough to follow his wonderful hounds.

On the way home, Jim and I stayed in New York, and made a visit to the Millbrook Hunt in Dutchess (*sic*) County, New York State. At the meet was one of my film star favourites, an ageing James Cagney, and we hunted mainly on his land. Sadly I never had a chance to discuss foxhunting with Cagney. Hounds were hunted by a lady professional huntsman, Betsy Park, with one lady whipper-in, Joint Master Mrs Richard A. Kimball, and two men.

The Millbrook hounds were an old Virginia strain, with a deep rich voice. We hunted mainly in woodland country dotted with lakes, galloping up and down hills, and jumping timber and small walls. Hounds certainly did not catch a fox, and whether they marked one to ground I could not tell. It was great fun, and a reminder that you could easily escape metropolitan New York for a day's hunting in beautiful country.

Five US Packs in Eight Days

Twelve years later, in January 1991, Jim Meads and I made a hectic hunting tour of five packs in the Eastern States. I had a daunting invitation to speak at the annual meeting of the Masters of Foxhounds of America in New York. This is a great gathering of hunting people and their wives; as well as the business meetings, they hold a splendid dinner, and on another night a superb Hunt Ball. On these occasions I saw the more formal side of American foxhunting: a 'scarlet and silver' dress code was *de rigeur*, and my wife Marilyn and I were impressed by the uniform vista at the Ball of every gentleman in evening Hunt dress, accompanied by ladies in silvery dresses.

The pulsating US big band music was terrific, encouraging me to forget I was fighting influenza at the time; I did not miss a dance and finished the evening half a stone lighter.

We had arrived the day the Gulf War broke out, but despite all the big news breaking at that time, the American Foxhunters listened sympathetically and supportively to my account of the UK's political hunting troubles; they generously laughed at my jokes, and nearly every Master present sincerely invited me to hunt with him – which I calculated would absorb the next few years in travelling thousands of miles.

My hectic tour was organised by the indefatigable Master of the Myopia Hunt, near Boston, Russell B. Clark, an excellent horseman whom I had met during his frequent hunting trips to Leicestershire. He accompanied my wife and me, and Jim Meads, throughout our tour and assisted with horses.

Ben Hardaway's enthusiasm burned as brightly as ever when I re-visited his Midland Hunt, but the influx of the coyote had grown immensely in the past decade. Ben had been hunting them seriously most of that time. He said hunting a coyote could be 'as big a thrill as you've ever had running anything with your clothes on.' But he admitted there was a down-side: the hugely increased risk of hounds running into trouble on expressways and into housing projects. We followed his hounds from a meet at the Kennels, and after a hectic hunt in dense

Mr Stewart's Cheshire Foxhounds going home at the end of the day to their kennels at Unionville.

Joint Master Duck Martin leading the Green Spring Valley field in Maryland.

coverts, and along creeks, hounds killed their quarry. To everyone's surprise, especially the Master, they had killed a large, fully grown dog otter, their first ever.

We enjoyed further hunting of grey and red foxes, but inconclusively to the Master's regret. Ben, more than most US Masters, places great emphasis on catching the quarry.

Two days later, hunting from Fitzpatrick, I followed hounds in my first coyote hunt. Riding a delightful Thoroughbred mare from the Hardaway string I was well enough mounted to keep well up with hounds, much closer than I would be permitted in Leicestershire. Hounds screamed to the strong scent of the coyote, and flew ahead, virtually without check.

They ran hard in this fashion for some four miles of breathless, hectic galloping, through woodland, scrub bushes that tore gashes in our arms, and semi-dry swamp land. Eventually they checked in a quail shooting plantation where Ben deemed it un-neighbourly to draw further at length, and gave the coyote best. We had started our tour in Russell Clark's Myopia country, but deep snow and below zero temperatures in Massachusetts stopped hunting.

Much further south, in Pennsylvania, very sharp frosts frustrated our intended hunting with Mr Stewart's Cheshire Foxhounds. I met their Master for forty-five years Mrs John B. Hannum, admired her all-English pack, and enjoyed a frosty hack over beautiful rolling grassland, criss-crossed with jumpable timber. Despite the frost we jumped a few rails, and I could hardly have had a better lead, than from the Master's son-in-law, the great event rider Bruce Davidson who was Field Master for the Cheshire.

Huntsman Melvin Poe with Virginia's Orange County pack of American hounds of 'red ringed-neck hounds of Madison, Virginia' type.

The frosts relented in Maryland and we hunted with the Elkridge Harford pack, near Baltimore. Their American-English cross-bred hounds were well hunted by another female huntsman, Marylee Atkinson, with male and female whippers-in. Senior Joint Master Ellie Schapiro is an outgoing, bubbling personality. She brought me an experienced Thoroughbred to ride, and hounds hunted foxes enthusiastically up and down wooded glades on Mrs Jack Westerlund's beautiful estate.

After hunting we enjoyed a magnificent Hunt tea in the Hunt's own club house. The day appeared on the meet card as: 'The *Horse & Hound* Hunt – in honour of the Editor, Michael Clayton. Formal attire requested, tea following at the Club'. No hunting correspondent, nor any other visitor, would get such a billing when hunting with a British pack.

Next we visited the Green Spring Valley, one of the most renowned packs in Maryland. The famous challenge of the Maryland Hunt Cup timber race takes place on the Worthington Farms Estate owned by the Hunt's senior Joint Master, J.W.Y. ('Duck') Martin.

I had met his Joint Master Frank Bonsall during his visits to hunt in Leicestershire, and he kindly provided me with a horse which had done some timber racing. He was a marvellous jumper, onward bound, and gave me great confidence over the timber rails encountered constantly in crossing from one grass paddock to another.

I liked the Green Spring Valley's cross-bred hounds. They hunted persistently, showed every sign of low scenting ability, ran together well as a pack, and had a good cry. They were biddable for their huntsman for the past decade, Andrew Barclay. I did not note a conclusive end to any hunt, but I saw them on a day when scent was atrocious because the frost was coming out of the ground. The going was firm and slippery, and I blessed my sure-footed horse.

We based ourselves at the Red Fox Inn, dating from 1728, in Middleburg, Virginia, to taste hunting in the State where some of America's oldest and best known Hunts operate, attracting wealthy businessmen and professional people from Washington and New York.

I was particularly looking forward to my day with the Orange County Hunt, founded in 1900, and packed a black hunting coat because the Hunt has a curious rule that only the Hunt staff and one Master may wear red. It was thought originally to be too ostentatious for wealthy Yankees to come down and hunt in a multitude of red coats over this Southern State, scene of so many major battles in the Civil War. It was the last season before retirement for the Orange County's seventy-years-old huntsman, Melvin Poe, who had been carrying the horn with the pack for thirty years. Until recent years Melvin Poe had carried a curved cow horn instead of the more conventional metal hunting horn. He brewed his own liquour, known as Fox Wine which he sold. I took a swig at Melvin's

Jackie Onassis
hunting with the
Piedmont hounds in
Virginia.

invitation after hunting and found it tasted mild, but conveyed quite a kick.

The mounted field was exceedingly affable, and hunted on the basis that hunting is for fun. I had to sign a waiver to decline suing the English immigrant horseman for any injury I received riding the Thoroughbred hunter he hired me. Litigation is another popular sport in the US, I was reminded jocularly by my hosts.

Described as 'red ring-necked hounds of Madison, Virginia,' type, the pack looked orange and white in colour. These long eared all-American hounds, with domed heads, spoke with a distinctive melodious voice when speaking to the line of their red fox. They hunted with much persistence and although I understand they seldom caught the quarry above ground they certainly marked to ground convincingly.

I was especially warned to beware of the ground-hog holes proliferating in the lovely old turf; they had caused bad falls, causing broken necks and fatalities. The shout of ''Ware hole!' reverberated through the hunting day. We met at noon after another frost, and hounds hunted continuously, with the field jumping small rails and coops. I achieved my first fall in America when my horse slipped up on a carpet of fallen leaves. I was unhurt, but my hosts were far more solicitous than fellow foxhunters are after an innocuous fall in the UK.

The Piedmont Hunt was established in 1840 at the northern end of the Piedmont Valley, about sixty miles from Washington. Mrs Archibald Carey Randolph had been Master since 1954, and although this elderly lady did not attend the meet during my visit, she sent for me to ride, Patrick, a big handsome chestnut gelding, one of the nicest hunters I had ridden for many a day. Jackie Onassis used to hunt in this illustrious country, and we hunted near her former Virginia home when she was married to President John F. Kennedy.

Hounds met at Atoka, near Middleburg, on the estate of Senator John Warner, former husband of film star Elizabeth Taylor. For much of the day we hunted on the beautiful estate of Paul Mellon, sporting Anglophile and collector of sporting art.

I was not surprised all these celebrities chose to live in the Piedmont country, a beautiful terrain of old turf, small woodlands, stone walls, rails and those ubiquitous coops. Randy Waterman, a lean, devoted hunting man, was Joint Master and huntsman, and was providing excellent sport. Although officially described as American the pack had an increasing element of cross-bred under Randy's Mastership. He is a disciple of Ben Hardaway and introduced lines into the Piedmont from the Midland pack with success. Nowadays Randy hunts the Mooreland pack in north Alabama.

It was another difficult scenting day after frost, but the Piedmont hounds marked a brace to ground after two interesting hunts, and as the afternoon wore on the pace increased, and they finished the day with a cracking forty minutes hunt which I much enjoyed. The hunting and the ride were nearer the style of English Midlands hunting, with plenty of opportunities to see hounds working in front of the field in open country as we rode over grass and fences.

The Goddess of the Chase chooses to bestow her favours at random, and the most exciting hunt I experienced during this trip was with the Middleburg Hunt established in 1906, and hunting a country of only ten by fifteen miles three times a week. The huntsman was Albert Poe, a leaner younger brother of the Orange County's Melvin Poe. Albert was also something of a veteran, and had his own quiet style of hunting hounds.

The day started badly when we were held up by some transport difficulties, and arrived five minutes late for the meet at noon. Hounds had not only moved off, but had found already and were hunting hard. I was riding a brilliant English hunter kindly loaned by Russell Clark, and I was lucky because we were in for a good hunt.

It was a country of hills, woods and creeks, with timber rails and coops to be jumped, often at awkward angles with little take-off space. Mrs Gary Gardner, an English-born foxhunter was leading the field as Master, and giving a good lead too. When I galloped up to her I asked if she minded my riding close, and she gasped: 'Providing you don't jump on me, sir!'

We jumped some upstanding line fences as well as the much smaller Hunt jumps. Hounds marked their first fox to ground. They drew again and suddenly took off with a great cry, running hard down a strong and icy wind. From woodland we were suddenly in splendid open grassland, heading over a series of rails which needed jumping properly.

Hounds ran hard, achieved a four mile point, and checked at the foot of a mountain – Mount Gilead. The fox appeared to have gone mountaineering, and it was decided to give him best, a decision with which I did not quarrel, being in no mood to ask my horse to test my poor head for heights.

I admired this pack of lean, rangy American hounds. When I asked Albert about their breeding, he merely said with a smile: 'They're a strain I been experimentin' with for some years. Sure hunt don't they?' They sure did.

Canadian Adventure

An invitation which aroused my curiosity came in 1993: would I like to join the one hundred and fiftieth anniversary celebrations of foxhunting in Ontario? I replied instantly in the affirmative, and set off with *Horse & Hound's* full-time photographer, Trevor Meeks, who takes excellent and imaginative colour pictures of the Chase. Jim Meads was loyally sticking to a commitment to take pictures at a hunting wedding.

The trip involved a week of hunting with four Ontario packs, speaking at dinners and other functions, and culminating in a joint Hunt Ball in Toronto.

So severe is the Canadian winter that foxhunting is an autumn and spring sport, usually August to December, and from April to May. Some Canadians go down to hunt in the US Southern States later in the season. My visit was in mid-October, and already Canada's winter was sending early warnings. Drenching rain of a dreadful intensity attended the meet of the Eglinton and Caledon Hunt which I attended first, near Erin, in the rolling terrain of woodlands and open mixed farmland around Toronto. Courageously I took off the plastic riding mac I wore at the meet to brave the rain in a red coat with Belvoir buttons. The temperature had plunged by ten degrees to just above zero. Most of the field were wrapped in yards of waxed raincoats. Englishman Steve Clifton had arrived only sixteen months previously to hunt hounds in Canada, having been in Hunt service with the Isle of Wight and three other packs.

The enthusiasm of the Eglinton and Caledon's senior Master, Gus Schickendanz was immense, and unquenched by the rain. He rode a fifteen-years-old Trakehner stallion as Field Master in front of a mounted field of one hundred. I was mounted on an excellent Irish hunter imported from Willie Leahy of County Galway; it was a type of horse I adore in any country.

Hounds drew in the desperate rain for a while, then suddenly the sun shot fitfully, the temperature rose a little, and then sleet and snow blew into our faces.

There was a great chorus of hound music, and the pack screamed away. I gritted my teeth as the Canadian snow blew into my face, and Patrick strode after the Field Master to soar over a timber fence I could scarcely see. Thank heavens for a horse with a good front I thought as we lurched down the far side. My red coat was drenched through to the skin; I did not care any more.

Hounds had found a coyote and he was running hard into the wind, which few foxes would have done in those conditions. The run reminded me at first of some Irish hunts, and then became somewhat more like Leicestershire. We scrambled over stone walls, negotiated rails, galloped in open country over deepish going, traversed maize fields, and then faced up to some ugly looking line fences guarded by all too much barbed wire.

The Trakehner challenged my prejudices against continental horse breeding by jumping the line fences beautifully. Thank heavens Patrick flew the flag equally well for Ireland, but there were some nasty rasps and rattles as some horses came down behind us in the wire.

Hounds screamed on through some woodland, giving us a rough ride downhill in pursuit. The snow was even more blinding. There were some more riderless horses. This was tremendous fun, more like the Belvoir on a busy Saturday in the Vale.

Patrick and I were thoroughly enjoying ourselves. Steve Clifton was well up with his hounds, and suddenly I heard his voice; then his horn sounding the thrilling notes of a kill. Hounds had caught their quarry by a dirt road on the edge of a field of a maize. It was a formidable coyote weighing about forty pounds. The English bred pack had killed the coyote instantly, but they did not break it up, immediately leaving it.

They had scored a four mile point, running hard without a check, a splendid performance.

I was with the much depleted field when hounds found another coyote nearby, but this animal was immensely cunning, dodging about in fields of maize, at one point splitting the pack, and he was far away by the time the pack was reunited.

We had enjoyed a superb day, and how I enjoyed re-living it with the Canadian foxhunters in their clubhouse afterwards where a massive 'breakfast' was awaiting.

It was a rousing start to a week of riding to hounds, travelling, dining, wining and dancing. Canadians offered a warmth of hospitality which rivalled the welcome in the US Hunts. Dr Jack McDonald, Joint Master of the London Hunt, and his family and friends made us feel much at home in their country on Canada's Thanksgiving Day.

The London Hunt, Ontario: Mrs Elizabeth Klinger MFH, huntsman Derrick Mobey, Dr John McDonald MFH, and whipper-in Peter Andersen.

We met in their elegant Hunt clubhouse for a lavish buffet lunch before a meet at the civilised hour of 2.30 p.m. A drag line had been laid to get hounds alongside a golf course, and a riverside track to open country. There they hunted a quarry, I was not sure what, with great voice and enthusiasm through fields of maize in pursuit. During the week I followed hounds hunting foxes, hares and racoons, and more coyotes.

Bill Bermingham, Master for thirty years, welcomed us to the Hamilton Hunt where the huntsman was Paul Luckhurst, son of Stan Luckhurst with whom I had hunted often in the West Kent country. Scent was terrible, but we had an enjoyable day, mainly hunting foxes in woodland.

My last day was with the Toronto and North York pack, hunted by another Englishman, John Harrison from Ullswater, with his wife, Annie, looking after the Hunt horses.

Again the hounds were English bred with lines from the Oakley and Pytchley. Senior Joint Master was Walter Pady, chief executive of Toronto's Royal Winter Fair which I visited later to judge the Hunt team competitions. Bewigged flunkeys served stirrup cups to produce a theatrical air at the meet near King City, north of Toronto, where the hosts were Mr and Mrs Seymour Epstein – he a TV mogul and she a judge. We hunted for nearly five hours in unrelenting heavy rain, jumping timber fences frequently. Foxes were in short supply because, I was told, there had been a severe rabies epidemic sweeping the area recently.

Hounds marked a fox to ground and hunted a brace and a half of coyotes, providing some fast runs, but not catching any of them – which did not surprise me in those conditions.

I rode a sprightly black horse of Russian breeding which carried me well all day, until it put in a very late stop at a timber obstacle – and Pomponious soared into the air from his sopping wet saddle to land heavily on the top of his head. After a swift X-ray at a local hospital I was released to dance the night away at the Hunt Ball at the Royal York Hotel, Toronto, before flying next day to Heathrow. The life of a hunting correspondent demands reasonably good stamina – but it is well worth it when you can hunt amid the warmth of a Canadian welcome.

Foxhunting Contest Alabama Style

An invitation I could not resist arrived from Ben Hardaway – to act as a judge in a large-scale Foxhound working competition he was organising in Alabama in January, 1996. Seven American Cross-Bred Hunts, including Hardaway's pack, brought hounds to take part in a field trial. They hunted for three days in the Midland country at Fitzpatrick, and on the fourth there was a conformation judging phase.

I could not see how judging the prowess of hounds from different Hunts mixed up in one huge pack could be meaningful. I found to my astonishment each

First lady President of the American MFHA, Daphne Flowers Wood MFH, joint Master with her husband Marty of the Live Oak Hunt, Florida. She is riding her favourite hunter 'Derby'.

American Cross-Bred hounds at the Midland Hunt field trial in Alabama, 1996, when Randy Waterman hunted a joint pack of over fifty couple in a competition won by the Midland and Belle Meade.

Randy Waterman MFH

hound had a large number painted on its sides. There were no less than eighteen judges, four mounted – of whom I was one – restricted to zones, and there were others following in four wheel drive vehicles, including Brian Fanshawe, ex-Master and huntsman of the Cottesmore. Jim Meads was running about constantly, spoilt for choice of unusual hunting shots.

At the end of every day the judges attended a session chaired by the chief judge, the formidable Mr Ed Bacon in black cowboy hat who proved to have wit and wisdom. He had two assistants who were expert in scoring trials, usually Walkers or July, in night trials. Ed has a spread of 1,000 acres in Georgia where they hold such contests.

These are real hound men, dedicated to breeding and selecting hounds which hunt and catch their quarry. Ed, a highly experienced Foxhound Field Trials judge, handled the debrief brilliantly, unerringly honing in on the priorities. I was surprised and impressed to find that there was remarkable consistency from the judges in selecting numbered hounds which excelled in three phases of the hunt: drawing for the quarry; hunting in the pack after a find; and speed and drive in the pursuit. It added up to a worthwhile decision on which individual hound, and which group of hounds from specific packs, were performing best.

We mounted judges spouted our observations into hand-held dictaphones, not always easy when riding through fierce thorns in swamp land. I was accompanied by Daphne Flowers Wood, Joint Master of the Live Oak in Florida, and Bay Cockburn, English born Joint Master and huntsman of the Loudon West in Virginia.

Randy Waterman from the Piedmont hunted the pack of over fifty couple strong, with huntsmen from each of the seven packs acting as whippers-in. I was deeply impressed by Randy's calmness and skill in such a task in front of a highly knowledgeable, and critical, audience. Randy carried no CB radio, casting his hounds and hunting them without radio advice and sightings, which I much applauded.

Ben Hardaway was following on wheels, able to communicate on CB radio his views and queries forcibly to his mounted huntsman Mark Dixon. As hounds drew I could hear constant bellows of 'Are they hunting, Mark?' which seemed to be coming from the huntsman's radio.

Hounds moved off at 7 a.m. each day, a chilly dawn start on frosty going. I was exceedingly well mounted on Hardaway Thoroughbreds, and enormously enjoyed the ride and the view of hounds, one of the great hunting experiences of a lifetime. On the first morning the host of hounds hunted a grey fox inconclusively, which shows the fox can survive a hundred to one chance easily. Then they found a coyote and surged away with a resounding, clamorous cry, from sixty hounds of varying breeding. It certainly made the hairs stand upon on the back of your neck.

I found myself galloping hard through swamps, creeks and woodlands, feeling much less safe than if I was facing fly fences on grass at home. There were ample chances here of being swept off by branches, or falling in holes and creeks.

There was a check in woodland, and while we waited on a ride, a coyote trotted out of the brush, passed within a few feet of my horse. In the absence of hounds, his amber eyes stared at me inscrutably, with no sign of fear, before trotting off calmly. We suspected he was the first hunted quarry and had adroitly passed hounds on to another. Inevitably the huge pack split somewhat but were swiftly reunited; the day ended inconclusively, but it had been an exciting hunt.

After the first day the judges eliminated six and a half couple of hounds which some judges claimed to have seen hunting the ubiquitous deer. On the second day hounds hunted coyote again in another gruelling run in which the quarry escaped. On the third day we saw some pretty hound work when the pack worked up to some coyotes and Randy did well to get them all way in the open in front of us, with a thrilling cry.

The 'clever critters' ahead had their own solutions, and hounds were split, hunting several coyotes in different directions. Someone remarked that the CB airways sounded like 'the invasion of Panama' as hounds were collected. After the final phase of conformation judging, the bitch Midland Secret was awarded the individual hound prize, with Belle Mead Longo second, and Midland Lavish second.

First place as a group of hounds from one pack went to the Belle Meade Hunt, with the Midland second, and the Millbrook and Full Cry third and fourth.

The Belle Meade are another popular Southern pack, based in McDuffie County, Georgia, and their excellent cross-bred hounds were hunted by 'Epp' Wilson, Joint Master and founder of the pack in 1967. Randy Waterman paid warm tribute to Ben Hardaway, and his Joint Master and son-in-law, the ever-amusing wise-cracker Mason Lampton who was chief organiser.

Ben had 'changed the direction of foxhunting in the United States in this century,' said Randy. Certainly the hunting qualities of the cross-breds which he has espoused were abundantly clear. I rather felt the hunting and evasion qualities of the coyotes deserved some credit too.

Although English packs sometimes hold joint meets, the concept of joining hounds from various packs into one, and hunting them in a competitive way is alien to the culture of foxhunting in the UK. It was tried by Frank Houghton Brown in the Middleton country in Yorkshire recently, but although it was fun it did not have the same significance as in America where the sport of Foxhound Trials is so well developed.

In February 2001, as the foot and mouth scourge hit Britain, by chance I was in America again, hunting with Marty and Daphne Wood's Live Oak pack in the Panhandle of sub-tropical northern Florida, an area of pine plantations, lakes and sandy tracks, where rattlesnakes and alligators abound, and there is exotic bird-life.

Marty told me: 'In 1983 I had thirty-two couple of hounds in kennels, in 1988 I had forty-two couple. The influx of the coyote means we require a bigger pack and more hunt horses. It takes more money, faster horses, younger whips and more country to hunt coyote.' He and Daphne have won awards for conservation projects on their 6,000 acres of pine-land plantation where they run a top-class quail shoot.

They have judiciously crossed some of the best English lines with American hounds to produce a highly effective pack in these conditions. Scenting ability is vital because hounds must often hunt in high temperatures.

The meet was 7 a.m. and by noon the heat was so intense Marty's staff, summoned by radio, arrived with a pick-up truck loaded with a water tank. The panting hounds were given a drink and some took a bath. One hound was seen staggering through loss of blood sugar due to over-heating, and Marty's staff swirled a honey bag on to the back of its tongue, producing a quick revival.

I enjoyed several fast hunts on coyotes with the Live Oak, but the most enjoyable was a delightful piece of hound work which ended with hounds catching an American grey fox. Marty kindly had the mask and brush preserved, and presented them to me as a memento of a great hunting trip. It stares at me every morning in the downstairs cloak-room.

By 2004 Daphne Wood had followed Marty as a highly effective President of the MFHA of America, and she invited me to repeat my visit to speak at their annual conference in New York in January. We showed video clips of

Leicestershire hunting which were very well received. More than a few US Masters had hunted with us in the past.

The generosity of American hunting people in sending thousands of dollars to help fund the fight to save hunting in the UK is a tangible sign of our alliance.

I was highly impressed by the efficiency of the Association's stewardship of American Foxhunting. They operate an educational foundation, and keep abreast of game and conservation laws in widely differing States throughout the US and Canada.

During my visit they were concerned about a possible threat to hunting from animal rights activists urging a referendum on the subject in California. It would cost millions of dollars to fight. The MFHA of America has formed constructive links with other sporting groups to fight the cause of field sports.

The Trans-Atlantic Foxhunting links are stronger than ever. If Britain should ever make the tragic mistake of tearing apart its rural communities I am sure the sport will continue to survive and flourish in the United States where individual freedom is so much valued, and where there are sporting traditions firmly preserved since early settlers arrived to found their brave new world.

Venerie Francais

The post-war spread of rabies across the European continent, probably originating in Poland and other eastern countries, made foxhunting with hounds illegal in some areas, or highly restricted in others.

Yet the French have tackled the problem so successfully that by the end of the twentieth century it was no longer required to vaccinate their hounds against rabies. They have greatly assisted the British by halting the spread of rabies towards the Channel ports. Stag and boar hunting remain the premier sports, but foxhunting has increased since about 1980, and there about one hundred packs.

Much of the foxhunting is followed on foot, and in many cases foxes are roused by hounds only to be shot by waiting guns, as practised by some Welsh, and nowadays all Scottish packs. There have been some recent increases in riding to Foxhounds in France.

Pierre Bocquillon, writing in *Baily's Hunting Companion* in 2001, stated 'The preferred method of foxhunting is now to hunt with hounds and leave the guns in their rack. The hounds are a mixed type, made up with drafts from stag, boar and roe hounds, crossed with hare hounds. They are, nevertheless, quick and need to have the same skills . . . Foxhunting is now seen as a very effective, ecological method of controlling foxes, the carriers of rabies, and hunted foxes may be dug out and killed.'

'Our programme of fox vaccination against rabies through spreading doped bait has worked remarkably,' I was told by Pierre de Boisguilbert, general secretary of the Society de Venerie, when I visited the annual French game fair in June 2001, at Chambord.

France's venery has not escaped some urban criticism, and French country people have marched in Paris to demonstrate successfully for their sport against animal rights threats. The subject appears to be off the French agenda nowadays, but hunting people in France are warmly supportive of the British fight against abolition. The French formed their own field sports political party the Chasse, Peche, Nature et Tradition, known as the CPNT which was seeking to get several deputies elected to represent their views at government level.

I have not hunted in France, but friends who have followed French foxhound packs on horse and on foot greatly enjoy its emphasis on venery, and its informality compared with stag and boar hunting. Some English foxhunters have moved permanently to France and continue to enjoy their sport.

French countryside, comprising large forests, pastoral areas and seldom enclosed arable farmland, usually lacks natural hedges, although there are timber fences in some areas. It must be a pleasure just to ride in a countryside often beautiful, spacious, and unspoilt. There are strong links with English hunting through hound breeding. Nearly all French packs have traces of English blood.

English visitors, whether hunting deer or fox, have reported they found it hard to adapt to the French use of trotting horses in the hunting field. These animals are obtained cheaply from the popular sport of harness trotting races in France, but they are not the most comfortable ride all day in pursuit of hounds if you are used to riding a normal gaited horse at a canter!

Strictly Continental

Foxhunting in a limited way takes place in Italy and Portugal, following long traditions, with earlier English connections. In northern and eastern Europe endemic rabies in wildlife made foxhunting with hounds undesirable. Hitler banned it in the 1930s in Germany, a Fascist precedent often pointed out to British anti-hunting Socialist politicians. There is draghunting in Germany, Holland, Belgium and I believe Scandinavia.

In Italy four Hunts are currently shown in *Baily's*, of which the oldest and most prestigious is the Roman Foxhounds (Societa Romana Della Caccia Alla Volpe).

The Hunt was founded in1836 by an Englishman, the sixth Earl Chesterfield who came to Rome for health reasons, and with excitement saw a fox on the Appian Way. He started foxhunting on the Campagna Romana, and it has survived as a sporting club with social cachet, and a history of support from the Roman aristocracy and others.

Visiting diplomatic and business communities have also supported it. Hunt members ride quality horses, tackling a variety of obstacles in a country where red foxes have abounded although there is a great deal of culling by other means. The quality of the country has deteriorated considerably in recent years and the pack only hunts on Saturdays, with occasional bye-days.

The other three Italian Hunts listed are even nearer to riding clubs, hunting drag lines and only occasionally picking up the line of a fox.

Portugal has a celebrated foxhunt, the Equipagem de Santo Huberto, based at Santo Etevao. Its country is about forty-five minutes from Lisbon, through coniferous forests across the River Tagus. This Hunt was founded in 1950, but foxhunting in Portugal is said to derive from the Peninsular War when the Duke of Wellington and his officers formed their own hunt to enjoy sport between battles. There were several foxhunting clubs still hunting prior to the Second World War.

There have been strong aristocratic connections: the Hunt was founded by the Marques de Graciosa and HRH the Countess of Barcelona, wife of the Spanish Pretender, who continued thereafter as Honorary Master.

The Hunt has used imported English hounds, has employed a series of English huntsmen, and hunts in a leisurely, somewhat aristocratic manner. I have read reports of hunting ceasing while the riders return for lunch at the lavish club-house which is run as an equitation centre.

Down Under

One of my unrealised ambitions is to hunt in Australia. If there is ever a second edition of this book I hope I shall be able to include a first-hand Australian experience of the Chase Down Under. Those friends of mine who have ridden to hounds there are warmly enthusiastic.

The Aussies are great company; there are no qualms in the countryside about fox control; and they ride tough Thoroughbred-cross horses, sometimes of New Zealand breeding, galloping over vast areas of grass, or scrub-land, taking on timber fences, which can be formidable, or jumping bare barbed wire as they do in New Zealand. Both countries produce some of the world's best cross-country records with remarkable Olympic records in eventing.

I understand the most likely form of riot in hounds to be encountered in some areas may be due to the intervention of kangaroos which carry a strong scent, and hounds are strictly discouraged from taking on this quarry which may be six feet in height and likely to defend itself!

The fox was imported into Australia for hunting, mainly by Army garrisons in the early settler years, and like most animals introduced there it has flourished all too well. Hunts are registered as a recognised form of control operating under codes of conduct. Such a solution would be so welcome in the United Kingdom if only there was the same level of tolerance among UK politicians of hunting as a sport as well as a humane means of culling.

Most foxhunting in Australia is based in the state of Victoria where there were thirteen packs of hounds registered with the Hunt Clubs Association at the turn of the century, with another ten packs in New South Wales, South Australia and Western Australia. The Australian foxhunting season runs from May to September, with June to August as the best months.

The Hunts have used good English Foxhound blood to improve their packs greatly in recent years, and in Victoria they hold a principal hound show annually at Sherwood in the Oaklands Hunt country.

The sheer size of the hunting countries impresses English visitors. There are huge parcels of grassland available, and it is possible to hunt on grass all day, jumping timber panels or wire when necessary.

Australian red foxes are wild and strong, and are much more inclined to climb trees than their English brethren. John Crosbie-Goold, who I met when he visited the Cottesmore, has been the dedicated and highly effective Master and huntsman of the Ellerslie Camperdown Hunt, based at his home in Victoria, 120 miles west of Melbourne, since he re-established the pack in 1979. They meet four days a week in a country of 120,000 acres of pastoral land, with coverts ranging from large ravines with native grasses and tussocks, to creeks and river flats.

Describing Australian hunting in *Baily's Hunting Companion*, Crosbie-Goold wrote that mounted fields average from twenty to thirty mid-week, and up to sixty on Saturdays: 'The going is generally very good, but when it rains it really comes down. In some countries this can be dangerous.'

Joint meets for hunting weekends are very popular and Australians will travel hundreds of miles to attend them.

Dennis Foster, Director of the US MFHA, has hunted with the Ellerslie Camperdown, and reported 'Every day was fantastic. Each fixture was more beautiful than the last. After each hunt, which lasted three and half to five hours, we would take care of tired horses, and tailgate in the horse van with food and drink. Local landowners would join us and always seemed to relish hearing about the day's sport. The land has huge sheep ranches, and beef and dairy cattle. Foxes are not popular with the locals. Ranchers expect the Hunt to cull foxes, and dig them out if necessary.'

Foster says the best aspect of Australian hunting is the opportunity to view hounds hunting their fox for long periods ahead of the horse in extremely open country.

After his visit to the Ellerslie Camperdown, Foster said he and his companion, Randy Waterman, agreed they had never seen a better pack of hounds and standard of foxhunting: 'We're convinced, if you want to find a foxhunter's heaven, it's Down Under.'

I cannot include a section on foxhunting in New Zealand because the settlers in that country did not import foxes, but there is a great deal of harrier hunting, which I briefly experienced and heartily enjoyed in the Pakuranga country south of Auckland. History relates that some angry sheep farmers drowned foxes in Christchurch harbour which some hunting people tried to import into the country.

This beautiful 'land of the long white cloud', with a population less than four million, has twenty-nine packs of harriers with about 4,400 Hunt members.

I thoroughly recommend the travelling foxhunter to sample the harrier hunting if he should be lucky enough to visit New Zealand. I have three pony riding infant grand-daughters in New Zealand who may aspire to be riders to hounds, and will one day I hope, experience foxhunting with me in the old country.

CHAPTER 9

FOXHUNTING WITH FOXFORD

ITOOK the decision to become a hunting correspondent in 1970. At best my colleagues in BBC TV News thought it was bizarre; at worst they were convinced I was crazy.

The Editor of *The Field*, Wilson Stephens asked me if I would like to take on the role as a freelance while continuing my career as a staff TV and radio correspondent for the BBC, which had included a decade of war reporting, and extreme turbulence on the home front, including some of the worst eruptions in Northern Ireland.

At the start of the 1970–71 hunting season Stephens published, no doubt with tongue in cheek, that *The Field's* hunting correspondent was unable to start reporting the sport yet because he was still trapped in a hotel under heavy gunfire in Amman during the Jordanian civil war. In those days the hunting issue was still considered of such minor importance that Editors in the BBC News Division were tolerant of my hunting aberration, and it was reported as a curiosity in the staff magazine when I published my first hunting book, *A Hunting We Will Go*, in 1967.

I had been a news and current affairs journalist since leaving Bournemouth Grammar School at seventeen at a time when the prospect of two years' National Service made going to university far less realistic for anyone needing to start a salary-earning career, and I was certainly in that category.

Brought up on the borders of Dorset and Hampshire, with the Portman to the west, and the New Forest to the east, I was fortunate in having easy access to

Lt. Col. Sir Peter Farquhar, one of the most innovative twentieth century hound breeders. His most celebrated Mastership was that of the Portman (1947–59). His son, Capt Ian Farquhar is Joint Master and huntsman of the Duke of Beaufort's.

riding since I was seven. In war-time and the early post-war years ponies bred on the New Forest were worth only a few pounds, and all too many were being slaughtered for meat in France.

As I recounted earlier, my enthusiasm for foxhunting was much encouraged by Sir Peter Farquhar when he was Master of the Portman (1947–59), and I was a somewhat reluctant member of the Portman Pony Club. I resigned after only a couple of years because I felt there were 'too many girls in it'; a decision I would have regretted a few years later.

Most of us lacked trailers and horse boxes in those days, and we hacked many miles on our unclipped, grass-fed ponies to Pony Club rallies, to gymkhanas, horse shows – and sometimes to meets. This meant I followed the Portman as often on a bicycle as on a pony.

The Portman's formidable vale country west of Blandford was far too stiffly fenced for a child to tackle, but I much enjoyed attempting to follow hounds on a pony in the hill and woodland country around Wimborne on the eastern side of the country. Traffic was very light, and there were many acres of rideable moorland around Bournemouth, now mostly covered in suburban bungalows.

Hunting had skipped a generation in my family, but I had a great-uncle, Hollis Clayton, who hunted enthusiastically with the East Essex, where he farmed, continuing a family tradition for some generations. They were strictly conforming Quakers, and I was told my great-great grandfather wore very sober hunting clothes, and did not attend meets because drink was consumed there, but once hounds found and started a hunt he joined in, and was suddenly transformed into a passionately keen rider to hounds.

If there is such a thing as a hunting gene this was probably where I inherited it, although I have never objected to wearing a red coat and drinking at the meet. My mother's side of the family were not Quakers, but there were countrymen among them.

I was too poor to enjoy more than a little hunting on hirelings during my late teens. I was fortunate to be a trainee reporter under an old fashioned apprenticeship at the *New Milton Advertiser and Lymington Times* where the fiercely independent owner-editor Charles Curry ruled sternly, but with a kind heart.

I kept up my riding during National Service in Germany with the RAF, and fitted in some sporadic hunting during a hectic passage via the *Portsmouth Evening News* office in Chichester to the giddy pressures of a staff reporter's life on the *London Evening News*. I was only twenty-two-years-old and struggled to cope with the tempo of the world's largest circulation evening paper, publishing eight to ten editions a day.

After marriage, a year's sabbatical working for the *New Zealand Herald* in Auckland, and rejoining Fleet Street, this time as a reporter on the *Evening Standard*, I felt much in need of the solace and exercise of the hunting field.

How could I hunt from an office in Fleet Street and a home in suburban Blackheath? The answer was provided by the *Evening Standard's* Brighton correspondent, Sydney Curtis, who lived in rural bliss near Haywards Heath and hunted intermittently on his own horses with the Old Surrey and Burstow.

Sid invited me to join him, and I was soon a passionately keen follower of the Old Surrey on several unsuitable horses, until I was lucky enough to hire Ballyn Garry, a blue roan, Irish bred hunter from Stangrave Hall riding stable at Godstone. To my surprise I found I could drive from Blackheath to the hunting field in about an hour, often following the part of the route taken by Mr Jorrocks from his home in the City of London to 'unt in the Surrey 'ills.

My great-uncle Hollis Clayton, a keen foxhunter with the East Essex, died at this time, and remembered me in his will. He had always encouraged my ambitions to hunt regularly, and as a child I was hugely grateful when he sent me a hunting bowler to wear.

With his bequest I purchased Ballyn Garry for £350.

The blue roan gelding had terrified various lady hirers by his exuberance in joining hounds and jumping any obstacle, but I was desperately fond of him even though at 16.1 he was on the small side for a 6ft 2in rider. The bold Garry was a superb schoolmaster, and I had at least ten years' hunting on him. No horse ever taught me more, and I never had more fun on any of the larger and better bred animals I was lucky enough to own or borrow.

Senior Joint Master of the Old Surrey and Burstow was Sir Ralph Clarke, looking the epitome of a country gentleman, and a former Tory MP. Foxhunting was his passion, and he had returned from a parliamentary trip to Russia, remarking that 'Russia could be marvellous for hunting; I never saw any barbed wire between Moscow and the Urals.'

At my first meets with the Old Surrey I noted that Sir Ralph dismounted and

Jack Champion, popular huntsman of the Old Surrey and Burstow for thirty-eight years (1947–85), provided remarkable sport in an increasingly cramped country just south of London.

welcomed visitors personally. He chatted courteously with me, noted that I worked for the *Evening Standard*, and said no more.

In the Old Surrey country I met some of the finest foxhunters I have encountered anywhere in my wanderings to hunt with more than two hundred packs since. I owed them much for their genuine friendship, their humour, and their tolerance of an impecunious journalist who paid his £30 annual subscription in two £15 instalments. Some have remained warm friends ever since, especially two later Joint Masters, John Robson and Diana Barnato-Walker, pioneer woman pilot who distinguished herself in wartime delivering planes for the RAF in hazardous flights.

I was impressed by, and grew particularly fond of the Old Surrey's huntsman: Jack Champion had the background, the name, the appearance and the performance of what I considered at that time essential in the ideal professional huntsman. Above all he displayed immense enthusiasm, and was determined to make sure we all shared the fun he was having.

Later, like a theatre critic, I formed layers of judgements on all sorts of subtle qualities in huntsmen, but Jack was an excellent man for a foxhunter in his twenties to follow across a terrain which was surprisingly inviting, considering that the northern boundary of the country was only fifteen miles from Charing Cross.

Amid the growing pressures of urbanisation, there were large areas of conserved land, often covered by old turf, the fields divided by excellent cut and laid hedges patched with timber. The M25 and motorways to the South Coast, plus the huge build-up caused by Gatwick airport, were still unknown obstructions to foxhunting in the 1960s.

'Tally ho!' Jack would cry in his booming voice as he hurtled over a hedge off the road, galloping his hounds across a field to throw them on the line of his quarry. He used the horn frequently, kept us all in touch with his voice as well, and a superb horseman he made the most of the opportunities provided for leppin'.

On one occasion we were convulsed with laughter when Jack had a rare but spectacular fall, and answered Diana Barnato-Walker's anxious enquiries, with: 'Quite all right. Just got me bum wet, madam.'

One or two purists would sigh at Jack's high decibel methods, and his priority in ensuring that we all enjoyed a 'quick thing', rather than always concentrating on a long, slow painstaking hunt. Within the limitations of hunting in an environment closing up around us every season, with more vehicles and roads leading to swelling towns and villages, I felt Jack was a huge success .

My blue roan soared over all the Old Surrey obstacles with great zest, and I foolishly thought riding to hounds was rather more simple than it proved later on worse horses over larger obstacles.

Occasionally I varied my riding fun with an afternoon following the ebullient Philip Kindersley and the Mid-Surrey Farmers' Drag Hunt, but although I greatly enjoyed such jaunts I had no doubt that a far less predictable run behind Jack Champion and his foxhounds was immeasurably superior. I observed him hunting the more enclosed and wooded country to the south in East Sussex far less frenetically than on the grass around Lingfield on the Surrey side, and I began to enjoy again the pleasures of venery I had nurtured as a boy on a pony in Dorset.

Jack, descendant of generations of professional huntsmen, remained a good friend during his remarkable thirty-eight years hunting the Old Surrey hounds, still carrying the horn at seventy. When he died aged eighty-nine in 2003 he was mourned by many who felt he had immensely enhanced the lives of generations of foxhunters – and no better tribute can be paid to any huntsman. I wrote obituaries of him published in *The Times* and *The Daily Telegraph.*

A career move to become News Editor of *Southern Television*, based in Southampton, enabled me to take Ballyn Garry to Dorset to resume hunting with the Portman, this time in the vale country west of Blandford. Susie Woodhouse, wife of John Woodhouse, then the Hunt Secretary, and a marvellous Field Master, assured me on the phone that I would find the Portman vale 'very sporting'. She was not exaggerating; the size of the hedges, set on banks, in the dairy country north and south of Sturminster Newton was a revelation of the challenges which riding to hounds could offer.

It was only due to the devoted, expert care of Sue Mitchell at Fiddleford, near Sturminster Newton, who took in Garry at livery, that the little horse was fit and strong enough to raise his game to jump the big Portman fences. He gave me very few falls, but like all good horses, when they occurred they were memorable: he once buried me in a huge hedge, and we tottered back to a displeased Sue Mitchell who was much concerned about Garry's ills, but said I thoroughly deserved my own painful shoulder for having continued in the hunt when my horse was tiring.

The veteran huntsman was the senior Joint Master, Stewart Tory who seemed not to have changed at all since I saw his tall, silver haired figure riding to hounds during my boyhood. He could be autocratic, but if you were sincerely keen on foxhunting you became a friend.

Stewart, one of the south-west's leading stock farmers, was helped by his elder son, Percy as Joint Master and an excellent amateur whipper-in, with the veteran Barry Boyle as kennel huntsman and first whip; he had formed a famous partnership in Warwickshire with George Gillson, one of the most effective huntsmen of his generation.

I quickly realised I was in heaven: it was the life I had hankered for during years of slogging away in news rooms, and on many a draughty pavement, in reporting's follies and tragedies. My relish for the 'bad news business' was already on the wane.

Stewart's younger son Michael later became a Joint Master, and Stewart amazed us by rejoining the Mastership at the age of seventy-two to assist Edward Lycett Green as Master and huntsman in the 1980s. I formed warm friendships with John Woodhouse, and his brother Dick, a superb amateur race-rider. They were marvellous Field Masters: John, always genial, and exuberantly ready to have a go at anything; Dick, a more stylish rider, and superb over the Portman's biggest country.

Their eldest brother Edward, head of the family brewery Hall and Woodhouse, served as an urbane Hunt Chairman. All three brothers died far too young, but

John Woodhouse, Joint Master of the Portman (1969–78), previously Hon. Secretary, a bold Field Master who gave a great lead across the daunting vale hedges.

Susie Woodhouse has since served as an excellent Hunt Chairman, and Edward's daughter Joanna Mains, joined the Mastership in 2002.

When I subscribed it was a 'Happy Family hunt', with the occasional stresses of family life, but it was a marvellous introduction to hunting as an adult in a deeply rural country among remarkable characters who became good friends.

In all weathers, by night or day, I gladly drove over one hundred miles each way from my home near Maidenhead to hunt with my Portman friends. John and Dick were to form the Mastership after Stewart Tory retired. He had been a devoted fox catcher, and some of my most instructive hunts were on the hills above the Okeford Vale in the spring, with only a few of us out, watching Stewart patiently hunt a fox among the woodland dells, until his hounds had caught it, or marked to ground.

Working pressures increased for me in my next role as a BBC TV and radio staff news reporter, based in London, but frequently working abroad. I was increasingly sent all over Britain and Europe, and then covered war in Vietnam, Cambodia, the Middle East, India and Pakistan.

Dashing down to the Portman country became increasingly difficult, and I accepted an invitation from the BBC's leading equestrian TV commentator Dorian Williams, to subscribe to the Whaddon Chase, hunting in the northern end of Buckinghamshire. I had a brilliant new hunter, an impetuous Irish bred gelding, Foxford, sold to me by Billy Oliver, who ran a dealing and livery yard at Wendover in the Chilterns.

'Mind, he's a young man's horse,' Billy told me, and of course I had to buy Foxford after that; he cost £800, and swallowed a BBC bonus for reporting in Amman under fire, the best reward I could imagine. Although headstrong, and inclined to miss out a fence on very rare occasions, he was capable of keeping me near the front in most hunts over any country. I adored him and seized the chance to try him in Leicestershire when Billy rented another yard at Old Dalby in the Quorn Monday country in 1972.

'This is what we have been rehearsing for,' I said to myself exultantly while Foxford galloped as if on springs over the Leicestershire old turf, taking each fence with an exciting bound; sometimes too exciting when he stuck his head out after pulling like a runaway train. We were hardly off grass in the 'seventies, and there was always another fence to be jumped.

I categorised them as my impetuous mount took on each one with zest. There were cut and laid fences with ditches in front, or away; there was plenty of timber, and sometimes that too had a ditch in front; there were a few open ditches, and brooks; sometimes we galloped over Leicestershire's famous ridge and furrow: turf covered undulations across fields which are the remnants of the ancient method of growing crops on ridges, with the water draining into the undulations.

Ridge and furrow is usually to be found near villages or ancient settlement sites. It is best to ride it at an acute angle, so that your horse drops his leading leg easily into each furrow, rather than taking it head-on when it can strain your horse's back. Michael Farrin was hunting hounds with verve, and riding the country with a balanced, impeccable style.

It was his first season, and already he was gaining a great reputation. As well as enjoying the hounds I always had enormous pleasure in observing Michael's consistent display of superb cross-country riding. A German magazine once asked me to nominate the two best cross-country riders in the world: I chose the New Zealand event rider Mark Todd – and Michael Farrin.

In Leicestershire we were on top of the ground, compared with the much heavier going in Buckinghamshire, and even heavier in the vales of Dorset which were frequently water-logged by early February, causing hounds to move to the hills. It was an easier drive to Leicestershire from London and the South-East, using the M1.

There were two major problems: Leicestershire charged expensive subscriptions and caps, and one horse was not enough. The Shires Hunts changed horses during a day's hunting, and to survive a full day at the galloping pace of the 1960s and 1970s you certainly needed another horse if you were to experience the afternoon hunts, often the best of the day when colder air improved scent.

In 1972 I hunted three days with the Quorn, and reported one of them for *The Field*. Ulrica Murray Smith's Joint Master, Capt. David Keith, was a superb Field Master, combining charm and politeness with firmness.

During my first day when we were lining up at least fifty abreast to take a fence, Foxford to my shame, lunged away and carted me over the fence on my own. David Keith told the field to wait, and jumped the fence, cantered up to me, and with a smile invited me to jump back.

It was a horrendously more difficult fence jumped the other way, and I had to take it under the gaze of the assembled Quornites. Foxford never refused, and somehow managed to heave himself over a huge ditch – towards, climbing up over the hedge to scramble to the other side.

In some Hunts I could imagine a certain amount of tut-tutting. The Meltonians thought it was a huge joke, and a few readily confessed to far worse sins which had escaped the Master's attention. They were a jolly crowd, some of them superb riders, beautifully mounted, and extremely smartly turned out.

There was always someone interesting to talk to when hounds were drawing, although I noticed that we often cantered from one covert to the next to draw, and sometimes had to clear fences to get there.

The trick was always to keep a vigilant eye, and ear, on hounds as soon as they entered a covert, edging your horse forward nearer the Field Master, or parallel to him, after Farrin had blown gone away, and the Field Master suddenly accelerated from a stand-still to a smart canter or a gallop into a fence.

Getting a good start is more than half the knack in Leicestershire, and in the 1970s it was still possible to jump many fences on a broad front, approaching as straight as you could, but giving your horse the best possible chance to clear each obstacle in a balanced style, as fast as possible.

'Keep straight!' was shouted sometimes because the rider who cravenly ducked out from a big place could easily run down someone alongside, causing a multiple fall. In a fast run down to the Vale of Belvoir from the Harby Hills I once galloped into an enclosure where about ten riderless Belvoir horses were dashing about in front of me. I was riding my excellent, hard-pulling hunter named Soloman, and we barged past the riderless mounts to jump a hedge in the wake of hounds. Just as we were committed to take-off, one of the unmounted horses dashed down the hedgerow in front of us.

Two superb Belvoir Field Masters: John Blakeway, *second left* (1983–91), and his Joint Master John Parry.

Soloman leaped over the loose horse's quarters, and cleared the hedge as well, but did not have the impetus to clear the ditch on the landing side. We collapsed into the ditch, only to have two more riderless horses follow us over and land along-side in the ditch. Somehow I extricated myself from the three horses, and was astonished and relieved to find I was relatively unhurt; just a cracked rib and bruising.

Although somewhat exaggerated, there was an element of truth in the verdict of the Leicestershire foxhunting veteran, Lord (Marcus) Kimball, who dubbed Belvoir Saturdays at that time 'rugby on a horse'.

John Blakeway, Joint Master, and a superb Field Master in front of the hard riding Belvoir fields said to me: 'The bravest people in the hunting field are you lot who ride two thirds up the field. You aren't quite in front, so you don't get first cut at the fences, you're very vulnerable if other horses stop and run-out in front of you, and there's an awful lot of people hard on your heels to jump on you if you fall.'

As a 'two-thirds man' I fervently agreed, but I learned far more about surviving such hazards, while keeping my horse full of impulsion, after I made the decision to hunt regularly in Leicestershire. In the 1970s in the Quorn field one still heard the shout occasionally 'Spread out!'. It was the Field Master urging us to attack a fence on a broader front, and we could do so confident that there would not be a back fence of barbed wire on the landing side.

Robin McClaren, who was one of the boldest and most cheery of Shires hunting men, cleared a fence in pursuit of the Belvoir hounds only to find himself landing on the canal tow path near Hose. His horse tried valiantly to jump the canal in the next stride, but inevitably landed in the water.

They swam and floundered to escape drenched, but unhurt. Robin did not approve of my recent change to a peaked cap with chinstrap, and proudly told me afterwards: 'My top hat stayed on throughout the whole thing.'

On another occasion he remonstrated mildly when I had gone back to collect my second horse while hounds were still hunting. 'Good heavens, you missed five of the best fences of the day,' he pointed out.

Riding after hounds is not supposed to be totally competitive, but getting to the most practicable place in a fence ahead of others is advisable in the Shires. In the 1972–3 season I noted two men who both galloped fast to jump the same inviting stretch of hedge; they collided dramatically in mid-air and their horses both fell heavily on landing.

I was impressed when neither rider said a word, but re-mounted immediately their horses got to their feet, and galloped off hard in pursuit of hounds. I reflected on the recriminations I might have heard from some foxhunters less accustomed to riding in a large crowd.

Far more men wore scarlet coats in the 1970s, often in the dashing cut-away style, with tailor-made cream waistcoats, and white tops to their boots. I had a stylish black cut-away coat made in Ireland by a renowned local tailor, Mr Fraser, at a village named Hospital in County Limerick. It seemed ideal for a hunting correspondent, very easy to clean and pack. The secret was to wear a thick, well tailored cavalry twill hunting waistcoat underneath which made the cut-away far more weather proof in front.

There were some extremely pretty girls, in well fitting breeches and dark blue coats, as well as elegant older ladies of the Chase who usually rode exceptionally well. I recognised more than a few prominent personalities from the showjumping, eventing and racing scene. Douglas Bunn, the founder-owner of the Hickstead showjumping complex in Sussex, used to fly up to Leicestershire in his helicopter, putting up cheerfully with some ribbing when fog delayed his arrival sometimes. He generously loaned me one of his horses to provide me with a second horse in the afternoon on several occasions.

I was impressed when the Olympic gold medal event rider Richard Meade turned up one day to 'try a horse' which might make an eventer. We had a storming twenty minutes in the Monday country, with Farrin as usual making it look so deceptively easy in front. I recall Meade being in front alongside the Field Master, Capt. Fred Barker, all the way. I was unseated when someone cannoned into me over an especially crowded piece of timber, but for once did not lose my horse, and was able to stay somewhere in the action – but far behind the great event rider who was jumping fences at a gallop on a strange horse with his usual cool skill.

When our steaming horses were pulled up, Richard dismounted from his, patted it on the neck, glanced at its heaving sides, staring eyes and sweat-streaked coat, and said laconically: 'No good, I'm afraid. It doesn't get the trip.'

For one season I kept my hunter mare, Josephine, in the Thorpe Satchville yard of the late George Rich and his wife Barbara, dealers in high-class hunters. Douglas Bunn kept his horse there, and so did the great Flat trainer Major Dick Hern. He so enjoyed his foxhunting, and on occasions when I was invited to stay overnight after hunting by the generous George and Barbara, Dick would fill his pipe and puff away, talking happily about hunting, with hardly a word about racing where he excelled.

He was to break his back in a hunting fall in the Quorn Friday country, but carried on training to achieve some of his greatest triumphs despite being a wheel-chair bound paraplegic. The price of his fall caused me to reflect on the real dangers we were risking, since Dick was one of the finest horsemen in the hunting field. Despite his personal tragedy in the hunting field, Dick retained fond enthu-siasm for the sport, and the racing scribes were amazed at Goodwood one day when the great trainer in his wheelchair chose to talk to me about foxhunting at some length in the paddock just before a race in which he had an important runner.

I shall always treasure memories of late afternoon hunts, under the big skies of Leicestershire, with a hint of frost in the air, when Michael Farrin's bitch pack would scream over the grass and fences in the best hunts of the day, enjoyed by a smaller field of those who had good second horses to ride.

Pomponious Launched

I had butterflies in the stomach as I heard myself say 'yes' when I was asked over lunch in the Reform Club by Walter Case in late 1972, if I would like to be his successor the following year as Editor of *Horse & Hound*. It was an eccentric career change for a BBC Television reporter mainly covering wars, but I had already seen more than my fill of a tragic waste of life.

I loved life, and I wanted to celebrate it in the best setting I knew: the hunting field. If hunting was Jorrocks's vision of the ' image of war and twenty-five per cent of the danger' it was far more attractive than the modern reality of bombing and maiming thousands of civilians.

It was the best career decision I ever made, achieving over a quarter of a century in a lifestyle I thoroughly enjoyed, not least because I swiftly appointed myself my own Hunting Correspondent, writing a weekly column on my visits to many Hunts, using my horse's name Foxford as my *nom de plume*. I toyed with using the name Pomponious Ego, employed by Surtees in his cruel parody of his rival Nimrod.

Foxford was to be succeeded by the Irish bred mare Josephine I hunted for a decade before breeding nine foals, one of whom, Ranksborough, I still hunt today in Leicestershire, our combined ages amounting to eighty-three.

Not all hunting people approved of my column; some thought there was 'far too much Leicestershire' in it, although I visited packs throughout Britain and Ireland, later venturing to hunt in North America. Foxhunters were not always amused when I pointed out that newspapers gave far more space to Arsenal than minor Third Division clubs. Martin Letts, renowned for his acerbic humour as Master of the non-jumping, hill and moorland College Valley, struck back by dubbing my column 'Poxford's Jumping Diary' in an article I had commissioned, and published, in *Horse & Hound.*

Judging by readers' letters and the flood of invitations to visit Hunts, the column was being well read, and apparently enjoyed. It brought a new dimension to the magazine, but tapped old sources for its inspiration. I recalled that Nimrod and Surtees had at times been sporting Editors, able to choose their sporting tours, and to allocate space accordingly for their own reports.

It seemed the last chance for such a phenomenon in the English sporting press. *Horse & Hound* was founded in 1884, but it had never employed its own staff hunting correspondent, relying instead on a host of outside contributors.

In over twenty-five years the company bought me two horses, and I spent a great deal of my own earnings in buying other horses, and keeping them, but expenses from the magazine in maintenance and transport for one hunter enabled me to extend my hunting horizons far wider than any private hunting man could have managed in modern Britain.

At one stage we hired a horse box in *Horse & Hound* green and white livery, which indicated my presence at Hunts, and in the summer it doubled-up as the conveyance for the magazine's trade stand at horse shows. My publisher in those days, Francis King, son of Lord (Cecil) King of *Daily Mirror* fame, was fond of the saying 'horses for courses' and was perfectly prepared to invest in forms of promotion which suited the quirky and entirely original character of a magazine which had flourished for a century, and had only three Editors in that time.

The only surviving titles in the sporting press still featuring named hunting correspondents were *The Field* and *Country Life*, but neither of these gentlemen was Editor as well. When I became an IPC director I had much pleasure in assisting the purchase of the *The Field* from the Harmsworth empire to join *Horse & Hound* and *Country Life* in an immensely strong rural publishing portfolio, with myself as Editor-in-Chief of all three titles, plus *The Shooting Times* which we had also bought. I tried, but had little or no influence on the ardent shooting journalists, all of whom appeared to regard foxes simply as unwanted vermin threatening game birds.

As a young sporting photographer, Jim Meads, used to accompany my predecessor as *The Field's* hunting correspondent, whose articles bore the resounding by-line Sir Andrew Horsbrugh-Porter, Bt. The baronet, an excellent horseman with impeccable military/sporting credentials, could be crusty, but I liked him immensely when I knew him better, and I was delighted when after retiring from the hunting field he accepted an invitation to write as *Horse & Hound's* main correspondent on polo, another subject on which he was highly authoritative.

His authoritative pen was able to deliver occasional stern strictures to the polo set which they richly deserved. Jim Meads was a marvellous companion, a source of support and information, and I applaud his skills as a photographer, and his amazing stamina and dedication.

My role as Editor and self-appointed hunting correspondent was not an undiluted paradise because I had to fit in my hunting with the demands of a successful equestrian weekly title covering many other specialist interests. I did my best to reassure the proprietors, IPC Magazines, the largest periodical publishers in Europe, that I was well aware that they ran the magazine to make money. Having experienced the full rigours of Fleet Street I had no illusions about the 'romance of journalism' from a publisher's point of view.

As my first Chief Executive at IPC said: 'I don't care if you never come into the office if the magazine comes out on time, and at top quality – but somehow I think you'll only be able to achieve that by being on the spot.'

I had an excellent staff, with Hugh Condry, and later Arnold Garvey, operating as loyal and highly efficient Deputy Editors. But I had been brought up to believe that 'hands on' editorship worked best, and I made sure that the contents of virtually every issue were ultimately my fault. It surprised me when I retired to learn from Arnold Garvey's farewell speech that my office nickname was Ghengis Khan; I had only fired one man in twenty-five years, and most of the staff stayed with me for years.

Fortunately *Horse & Hound* made handsome profits, and still does so under its first woman Editor, Lucy Higginson, who keeps tradition alive through being an exceedingly keen foxhunter. The board of directors was never anything but warmly supportive, and eventually invited me to join them.

The increased emphasise on hunting I placed in *Horse & Hound* in the 1970s and '80s was a major factor in achieving a record circulation of some 96,000, although using a more newsy format, with greatly increased illustrations, worked wonders on all the horse sports, especially the increasingly popular Horse Trials where Britain won Olympic medals.

The circulation dipped a little early in the 1990s, due to fragmentation of the equestrian market by competing new specialist titles, but it has remained the world's largest weekly equestrian sale, and thanks to Lucy Higginson, and her all-female staff, has continued to be abundantly successful for the new owners, IPC Media, part of the vast empire of AOL Time Warner of America. By 2004 Lucy and her team had begun to turn up the circulation in a tough market.

Some of my readers appeared to believe the magazine was published in a thatched cottage where the Editor personally took all the 'phone calls. Deeply rural visitors to our offices were somewhat shaken to be whisked up by lift to the twentieth floor of a bleak office tower block on the south bank of the Thames in an unlovely part of Southwark.

From this unlikely setting I would assume my role as hunting correspondent and, as often as possible, drive my staff car from the basement car park to head as quickly as possible to another planet – a hunting field near or far in the British Isles. Often it meant halting in a lay-by to change from city suit to full fig in scarlet coat. Tying a hunting tie in front of a car rear-mirror is a special art, especially when you drop the pin between the front seats.

The following selected memories of my travels to a few of the 217 Hunts I visited as Foxford, give a subjective flavour of the wonderfully varied hunting terrains which our small, crowded islands still provided in the century of greatest change. I will not state which was the 'greatest run' or 'my favourite hunt', but as a somewhat frivolous foxhunter, who likes the ride as much as the hounds, I admit that I have been especially near heaven when hunting in Leicestershire and Rutland, Derbyshire, the Welsh Borders, Cheshire, and my native Dorset.

All the hunting countries I have visited have special values, and I have had marvellous days on moorland, in deepest woodland, hill-tops, and even on the ploughs. In my busiest season I rode nearly forty horses, and visited twenty-two Hunts. The purist may think that I dwell too much on the ride, but it is impossible to ride fast to hounds if the pack is not working well in front, and good hounds are the absolute priority in producing sport. My attendance at all the main hound shows for many years as a reporter may be taken as evidence that my interest in hunting is not limited to horses.

Unlike any other sporting writer, a hunting correspondent must get on to the field of play to observe properly, and must partake of the thrills and risks – perhaps even more acutely because he is probably riding a borrowed horse in a terrain he or she does not know.

It has been a privilege to ride so many horses I did not own, over land belonging to others, and I am immeasurably in the debt of the Hunts, and most of all their farmers and landowners who were my hosts.

The sheer diversity of the hunting countries of the British Isles make the greatest cross-country riding experience in the world, and I wish more Britons appreciated this jewel in our heritage. The Prince of Wales was later derided by the antis when he said in his address at the centenary dinner of the MFHA in 1981 that 'I have met more ordinary blokes through hunting than anywhere else'.

I agree that the hunting field opens the door to meeting the widest possible cross-section of country people. The most successful huntsman, and the more perceptive of his followers, well know that the success of the day depends heavily on the chap in a cloth cap and dungarees who is passionate about his hunting, and has stopped earths during the night, or has ensured that electric stock wire is switched off where it matters, with the farmer's consent. It is a symptom of our still class-ridden society that it is worth making such points.

Two of Ronnie Wallace's most reliable supporters in the Heythrop country were the foreman of a sewage farm, which tended to attract foxes to its perimeters, and the head fireman in a local fire station which had adjoining rough land where foxes resided. They were part of a whole network of support and enthusiasm in a complex system of checks and balances without which foxhunting as we know it could not take place,

South-West and South

I have indicated something of the **Portman's** pleasures in North Dorset. How I loved runs in the country north and south of Sturminster Newton. I sampled many times the thrills of the vale country to the west by following its neighbouring pack, the **Blackmore and Sparkford Vale (BV)**, arguably possessing one of the most challenging and deep-riding stretches of country in Britain.

I first visited the BV in the 'seventies when Ken Anyan was hunting hounds, and the Comte de Pelet was senior Master. His Joint Master Bridget Holmes à Court was not quite sure when I first asked if I could visit from the Portman.

'It's a wet season,' she said. 'Please park your lorry in a secluded spot so that our farmers can't see we are allowing a visitor here.' We had a romping day over

199

some big fences and Miss Holmes à Court positively blushed when I thanked her most warmly afterwards.

In many visits I especially recall with much pleasure a marvellous Boxing Day hunt in 1975 from a meet at Sparkford where the former Sparkford Vale Harriers hunted before amalgamation with the BV four years earlier. Tony Austin, later to hunt the **Cattistock** with distinction, was in his first season as Blackmore Vale Joint Master and huntsman, with John Creed whipping-in.

The excellent Field Master was Trevor Winslade, who served as BV Joint Master later with his wife Patricia for fifteen years (1977–92). Giving a lead over the BV hedges, guarded by fearsome ditches, often with big drops, was a formidable challenge which Trevor met boldly with much skill, and with a helpful dash of humour. When acting as Field Master of the **Taunton Vale**, Trevor used to wear the initials F.M. on his arm.

He once admonished the sporting farmer and dealer Dick Brake for passing him in the hunting field. Trevor pointed to his armband and asked: 'What do you think this means?'

Dick said with a grin: 'F . . . ing Menace!'

Trevor used to tell the story afterwards with great relish and Dick eventually became a Taunton Vale Joint Master and Field Master, a most effective poacher turned gamekeeper with whom I had some superb hunting, much pleasing the field when my horse Toby endeavoured to jump a huge bank in one bound, falling heavily into a deep ditch on the landing side.

During the '75 Boxing Day in the Sparkford Vale we had splendid hunt after Tony Austin put hounds into Annis Hills. Bill Brake, cousin of Dick, holloaed away a fox he had seen stealing quietly from Cogberry Spinney. Tony had hounds on the line with commendable speed, and hounds ran towards Babcary Bushes, and made various large circles over a lovely country of grass and bushy hedges which it paid to attack boldly. I was riding Foxford for whom the hunt was acting like champagne.

Trevor Winslade kept us well up to hounds, although not interfering, an example to some of today's Field Masters who fail to keep the mounted field close enough to hounds during a run, reducing the real thrill of riding in a hunt where most of the riders can clearly see hounds running and working. This is defeated when the field is kept at least a field or two away throughout the run.

Hounds eventually ran below Slates lane, through Steeple Covert, marking to ground below Pepper Hill. They had run at least twelve miles, with a point of about four miles, all on grass with the fences coming up sweetly to be jumped on a broad front most of the way. Boxing Day can be mainly a traditional day for parading hounds, and not much else. The BV and Sparkford Vale certainly made it the most memorable Boxing Day in my diaries.

In such conditions the BV can offer a ride after hounds as good, and exciting, as the best to be found anywhere. You need a top-class hunter, and a bold rider, to stay among the front rank. Fortunately the challenge has always been met by such foxhunters, with Joint Master Mike Felton and his colleagues currently providing just such a lead for the present generation of Blackmore Vale followers, with hounds hunted superbly by Chris Bowld since 1986.

Friends assured me there was 'no jumping west of the Taunton Vale', but I can dispute this. There is plenty of jumping over banks and some walls in Cornwall, and I have had some alarming experiences in Devon.

I suffered a shock when I visited the **Spooners and West Dartmoor** during cub-hunting in October 1975. I had expected a relatively 'safe' passage across Dartmoor because I would be following long experienced locals who would guide me past the fearsome bogs, and through the awkward rocks.

I did not expect to employ any jumping skills, but certain problems became apparent before the day started. The late Major Michael Howard was the genial and imperturbable Master and huntsman, a small, tough man with a large red nose. He mounted me on a narrow, lightweight Thoroughbred grey mare. I swung into the saddle in his yard, and she promptly reared up vertically, and threw me off backwards, but fortunately I landed on my feet before subsiding, and no great harm was done.

I had touched her mouth slightly, which she did not like, Michael assured me with a grin. I re-mounted with reins in loops, and the mare consented to carry me up on to the moors on one of the wettest days I can ever recall in the hunting field. Hounds hunted below the grim bulk of Dartmoor Prison, towering above us, and then drew Prince Hall where Conan Doyle stayed when he dreamed up the plot of *The Hound of the Baskervilles*, which did not surprise me a bit.

We had a stirring gallop over the heathers after hounds found at Dunnabridge, running above the West Dart River to mark to ground at Huccaby Bridge. To my surprise the field began jumping rugged stone walls during the run. The grey

Alastair Jackson, now Director of the MFHA, was Joint Master and huntsman of the South Dorset 1969–80. Seen here during a day in the Vale, with very muddy hounds.

mare stood in very close to each one and then bucked over with amazing impulsion; I was wet to the skin by then, and shot out of the saddle to land with a thump in front of her.

It happened twice, and I only survived thereafter by clinging desperately to the mare's mane. Three falls in one day was a record I never exceeded, and at least it taught me that hunting west of Taunton in the 'non-jumping countries' could involve some of the most hazardous leaping in the British Isles.

Dartmoor mists come down like theatre curtains, and Mike Howard admitted he went home sometimes without hounds. 'If they run hard down wind and the fog sets in it is sometimes very difficult to get in touch with the pack, but they always find their own way home eventually,' he told me.

Everyone who attended the final vale meet of the **South Dorset** in the 1979–80 season will recall it as a truly special occasion. This happy Hunt, supported by a truly sporting local community, was saying farewell to Alastair Jackson, Joint Master and consummate huntsman, and his bubbly wife Tessa. It was their eleventh season before moving on to a long stewardship of the Cattistock pack, and Alastair's key role as Director of the MFHA.

Tact, good management and a gift for hound breeding, marked Alastair's Masterships, always supported fully by Tessa who proved to be a highly successful MFH in her own right at the Cattistock.

Nine Hunts were represented in a field of 130, joyously setting out to jump everything remotely possible after the meet at Buckland Newton Manor where the hosts were Capt. and Mrs Sandy Maxwell-Hyslop, just about as fervent foxhunters as you could ever find.

The South Dorset has a smallish part of the wonderful vale country stretching north up through the Blackmore Vale and Portman countries from Dorset into Somerset at Wincanton. I wrote: 'Viewing some familiar cut-away coats, I reflected that some of us had turned up not only to praise Alastair – but to bury his followers in deep Dorset ditches if the chance arose.'

The highly competitive field were soon engaged in aquatic variations on foxhunting after Alastair put hounds into the delightful Button and Bows covert, and they ran with a great cry all round Holwell, Pulham, Kings Stag, and almost to Deadmoor in the BV country.

Plenty of huge hedges with drops kept everyone busy if they wished to stay near hounds. Thick Dorset mud daubed the coats of those who had 'bought a piece of land'. There was a splendid forty-five minutes' hunt from Brickyards covert back in the South Dorset country, and a final stirring run followed after drawing Warry's Plantation, a covert shared with the BV.

Suddenly as we jumped into a field near Round Chimneys Farm I saw another pack of hounds entering the same field at the far end. It was the Blackmore Vale hounds being hunted by their Joint Master Tony Austin. Later I heard that one lady member of the South Dorset field had mistakenly joined the BV field and ridden with them for some time before realising she was in different company.

In gathering dusk the BV and South Dorset packs merged for a while, and then their huntsmen blew for home, hacking along together and comparing notes on a day of memorable sport.

Among the most interesting foxhunting experiences in the West Country is to hunt with the **Cotley Harriers** on the borders of Devon, Somerset and Dorset. Their West Country Harriers hunt the fox over downland above the delightful valley going down to Cotley, near Axminster. They belong to the Eames family who have been represented in the Mastership since 1797. They were recognised by the MFHA as late as 1948.

The lovely white Cotley hounds hunt with a great cry, I was impressed by their accuracy when I first visited them in 1982 when they met at Wambrook. The best hunt of the day was from a covert with the memorable name Hell Bottom, and hounds certainly went away, a white smear on the grass, as if they were escaping from hell.

South-East

As I have already indicated, I thoroughly enjoyed subscribing to the **Old Surrey and Burstow**, and I found my visits to all the South-East packs south of London great fun. The hunting field in this lively area was never short of forceful personalities, and attractive lady foxhunters. Whatever was lacking in spacious hunting country was compensated by the cheerful dedication of the foxhunters, the high standards of their hounds, and good pockets of riding country amid the twentieth century horrors perpetrated on this area.

On a 1967 visit to the **Eridge** country in East Sussex when John Cooke was huntsman, I experienced a thrilling and totally unexpected run. John suddenly

Eridge huntsman John Cooke, with whom Foxford enjoyed a superb hunt in 1967. Left is senior Joint Master Major Bob Field-Marsham, one of the best judges of hounds in the twentieth century.

jumped over an uninviting obstacle off the road after his hounds, and a few of us followed. It was only later I realised with a qualm that the Field Master was not one of them. Most of the mounted field remained with him on the road-side.

Hounds were screaming ahead, and there was no time for anything but sitting down and riding hard. We jumped gates, timber and thick hedges, some full of wire. John Cooke went in front brilliantly.

It dawned on me that I was in the company of a select group of superb riders: the elegant Lady (Joan) Shawcross, wife of Sir Hartley Shawcross, Guy Peate, and the irrepressible Nigel Budd who was exceptionally clever at jumping barbed wire. (Joan and Guy died far too young, Joan in a tragic accident whilst out riding on exercise.)

They gave me a tremendous lead across a country I did not know, and my stocky blue roan hunter Ballyn Garry was the ideal horse for this terrain of small enclosures and woodland. Hounds achieved a five-mile point at hurtling speed; as exciting a 'quick thing' as I recall anywhere, all on grass. It was tremendous fun, and we warmly congratulated 'Cookie' on his prowess as huntsman.

The Joint Master who had invited me, Sir Harry d'Avigdor Goldsmid MP, chortled to me afterwards at a party at the House of Commons: 'I heard you had a great day. It's perhaps just as well I couldn't be there; I would have had to stop you because you crossed a bit of land forbidden to the Hunt – but you went so fast hardly anyone noticed.'

Among many excellent days in the South-East was one with the Crawley and Horsham in March, 1987 when hounds were hunted by Cliff Standing who I had already admired at the Zetland. The crushing presence of new towns and motorways on the **Crawley and Horsham** has still failed to prevent this popular hunt from providing an immense amount of fun. Thanks to the influence of the late Molly Gregson, Master from 1939–41, they have a superbly bred pack of hounds, still winners on the flags at leading shows. When I visited the Masters were Leslie Weller, Mark Burrell, Peter Whitley and Michael Richardson who was to serve as Chairman of the MFHA.

We had a most enjoyable day only fifty miles south of London, after meeting at Thakeham Place, near Storrington. Lots of organisation and fence building enabled us to cross some pleasant grass country, despite the busy main roads and railway lines not far over the horizons. At the end of the afternoon hounds caught their second fox above ground at Hydehurst, not far from the A24, after a good hunt of seventy minutes in which hounds ran up to ten miles.

I have hunted many days in the South-East and always enjoyed the sport in extraordinarily varied settings: hunting on cliffs overlooking the English Channel with the **East Sussex and Romney Marsh**, on wonderful downland above Brighton with the the **Southdown and Eridge**, and over some stiff hedges in grassland with the **Chiddingfold, Leconfield and Cowdray.**

Motorways scythe through Kent, and the redolence of horticulture, fruit and hop growing hardly indicate a county ideal for foxhunting. Yet the hunting traditions are immensely strong, and I have had remarkably good sport with the old **West Kent**, the **East Kent**, and the former **Tickham** country where I recall Master and huntsman John Funnell galloping past hop poles to jump barbed wire blithely in the corner of the field.

In Essex and Hertfordshire I found some of the staunchest foxhunters, especially with the **Puckeridge** and its neighbour **the Thurlow.** The Barclay family in the former, and Edmund Vestey and his family in the latter have produced sport, and a great sporting atmosphere which have entertained and captivated generations of foxhunters.

Central England

An abiding memory for all of us privileged to be there, was Ronnie Wallace's last official day in his final season at the **Heythrop**, after twenty-five golden years. Foxhunting 'special occasions' seldom work; scent is poor, foxes run disappointingly. Typically, Ronnie's last day Wednesday and Saturday meets provided excellent sport in terms of hound work, and tremendous riding for those endeavouring to follow – and there were hundreds of us.

I wrote: 'Especially vivid in my memory is Ronnie Wallace's swift reversal of an unfortunate check at the end of the splendid last Wednesday afternoon hunt when hounds ran into Little Rissington Village. An incorrect piece of 'information' sent him to the far end of the village.

He decided it was completely wrong with one deft cast, and I heard him saying apologetically to hounds 'Poor old girls, poor old girls, I'm so sorry . . .' As he hastened back through the village and speedily cast hounds on the field below the church, where they instantly screamed away, scudding down across the grass to kill their fox on the edge of the Dikler brook.

On the Saturday hounds met at Rockcliffe, and within minutes found in the plantation and thereafter ran for three hours fifty minutes, catching a fox at Slaughter Big Copse, and in typical Wallace fashion he had them running almost immediately on a fresh fox.

They swooped over the grassy hills and down into the vale below the Slaughter villages, eventually running hard up the Dikler to circle Quarwood Hill, catching their fox in the open at Bluebell Copse.

There were presentations in the hunting field, and a grand party attended by the Duke of Beaufort, with fine speeches and entertainment, but those of us who had ridden behind the great huntsman in the field that final day remember best his superlative skills while wearing the Heythrop huntsman's green coat for the last time when he showed how to hunt hounds immaculately whilst entertaining large hard-riding mounted fields.

Perhaps 'last days' raise false expectations in the hunting field because no matter how skilful the huntsman, nothing is ever guaranteed on a hunting day.

No matter what the sport we experienced, everyone attending the last **Whaddon Chase** meet of senior Joint Master Dorian Williams and his huntsman Albert Buckle, regarded it as one of the most important in the hunting calendar.

Held at the end of the 1979–80 season, both had been in office for twenty-six seasons, and earned huge support and popularity. Dorian, who battled gamely against severe health problems throughout his life, had suffered fractured ribs and other injuries in a fall down some stairs three days earlier.

He made a brave appearance in hunting kit on his horse at the meet where he made a farewell address, but sadly could not lead the field as he had done so effectively in the Whaddon and Grafton countries.

With his marvellous hound control, decisiveness and all the other attributes of a top-class huntsman – especially his prowess on the horn and his effective horsemanship – Albert could have hunted any country with success. The Whaddon was fortunate that he chose to remain there for a quarter of a century.

Hounds met at Stewkley with Joint Master Peter Stoddart at the head, having been in office since 1969. Alas, Peter had an unlucky fall which caused him to hand over the Field Mastership to Neil Wyatt whose father, 'Puggy'Wyatt had been Dorian's Joint Master and Hunt Secretary.

High spot of the day was the draw at the Whaddon's famous covert, High Havens, which never failed – and sure enough a fox went away for a sharp hunt, followed by a final run from Christmas Gorse up to the Quainton Hills and into the neighbouring Bicester country.

It was the end of a hunting era. David Barker proved himself a superb huntsman in succeeding Albert, but time was running out for the Whaddon Chase country as a separate entity: the new town of Milton Keynes was already consuming acres of middle England.

A brilliant rider, and one of the hardest Field Masters to follow, Col. Neil Foster, *centre*, on his retirement as Joint Master of the Grafton (1950–77). *Left*: Joint Masters Capt. and Mrs Dick Hawkins; *right*, Mrs Ward, Mrs Foster, Joint Master Rodney Ward, and Hunt Chairman Major John Charlton.

The **Grafton** country long held the reputation of being among the most formidable to cross in the Midlands, with very large hedges guarded by wide ditches. The change from grass to plough in the post-war years made the country less rideable in swathes of its country, but it remained a challenge.

I reported hunting with the Grafton first in November, 1975 when the senior Joint Master and Field Master was the late Col. Neil Foster, a small, spry man with a clipped military moustache. I would rate him among the finest cross-country riders of his generation; he appeared to have virtually no nerves, and he rode somewhat jealously, which meant that he did not like anyone close to him – adding another challenge for the field endeavouring to follow him.

In the hunting field his frosty mien was a reason for not getting too close, but the warm, sunny temperament of his wife, the delightful Rose Foster more than made up for Neil's coolness. I think he was simply rather shy, and the longer I knew him the more I liked him. We had a most amusing trip to the Dublin show with Rose and Neil who was one of the leading hunter judges.

After the meet at Sulgrave Neil nonchalantly jumped a couple of iron gates, apparently on the way to the first draw which most of the field emulated. Fortunately I was mounted by the dealer and showman Tub Ivens on a top-class grey hunter which passed this early test in confidence-giving style.

The huntsman, Tom Normington, was an above average horseman, and I soon realised I was in for an eventful day if I was to keep anywhere near the Grafton hounds.

We achieved no great point that day, but Normington and his hounds ensured we were exceedingly busy until darkness fell. The Colonel fully lived up to the advance publicity I had received. He visited Ronnie Wallace in his last season and I relished seeing Neil Foster cross the Heythrop's large enclosures, and modest, inviting obstacles, like a knife through butter. Local followers were aghast when Neil dared to range alongside Capt. Ronnie Wallace while he was hunting hounds.

'Country doesn't get any bigger, what?'Neil remarked cryptically to Ronnie, and then galloped on to jump a large gate in his stride, before the famous huntsman could open it.

In December 1976 I hunted with the **Berkeley,** in its country by the Severn where the man-made ditches known as 'rheens' or 'rhines' are a special obstacle: wide, with deep sides, and devilish difficult to escape from once a horse has fallen in. I stayed at Berkeley Castle, home of the Master and hereditary owner of the pack, Major John Berkeley, descendant of the Earls of Berkeley. The Hunt staff still wear coats in the Berkeley family yellow livery instead of red.

It was not a good scenting day, but the ride was eventful, with several horses sploshing into rheens, and one or two people were carried off the hunting field. I could see why a really good hunt in this country was a renowned challenge. The Berkeley's huntsman Tim Langley handled hounds excellently and made even the most desperate jumping look so easy. When several riders fell into one especially terrifying rheen I decided suddenly to catch their horses when they emerged, and by the time I had finished this, hounds ran back across the dreaded chasm, and I never had to jump it. Like a war correspondent, a hunting scribe had to learn how to survive.

One of the most extraordinary hunting days I ever enjoyed was with the **Bicester and Warden Hill** before its amalgamation with the Whaddon Chase.

It was not achieved in their home country, but during their visit to the Cottesmore on 1 December 1983. The Bicester's Joint Master and huntsman, Capt. Ian Farquhar was visiting his cousin, Capt. Brian Fanshawe the Cottesmore's MFH and huntsman. Hounds met at Braunston, in the cream of the Cottesmore's Tuesday country, near Oakham, capital of Rutland, England's smallest county.

Within a few minutes of leaving the meet, the pack found in a covert at Brooke, and virtually never stopped hunting all day. Those who did not get into the hunt straight away never caught up, and I was fortunate to be riding my mad but exciting hunter, Becher the Creature. He was a lean chestnut gelding who could be brilliant, but sometimes the excitements of the Chase blew his brains out.

The pack swung over the Braunston-Oakham road on to the so-called 'Cottesmore playground' of delectable grass and fences in the heart of the Tuesday country, passing Wilson's, Orton Park, down to Ladywood, soaring onwards to Windmill farm and across the pastures and fences to Cheseldyne.

Those of us still in the hunt had no time to take a pull because hounds were running uphill to the ancient Prior's Coppice covert above Braunston. We were thankful to give our panting horses short respite during a brief check there, but soon the pack was giving tongue joyously again as they ran to Brooke Priory, and up to Gunthorpe. Shooting was in progress here, and Ian Farquhar stopped hounds.

They had been running for eighty-two minutes, covering some twelve miles miles. We had jumped and galloped up and downhill with barely a pause throughout the hunt. If we had done more we would have regarded it as an excellent achievement but a superb afternoon sport's was to follow.

I was fortunate to dismount safely from the sweating, pulling Becher to mount as second horse my Irish-bred mare, Josephine – the most reliable of jumpers. The pack was put into Owston Wood coverts. We waited outside the large covert with much tension, since there were soon great crashes of hound music coming from inside the woods. We were clearly in for another fast hunt, and no-one wanted to get left the wrong side of the covert which is all too possible at Owston.

The Bicester pack, bred by Ian on new lines with Welsh outcrosses, did a marvellous job in pursuing their fox through Big Owston wood amazingly quickly, and emerged running fast for Knossington Spinney, then going on over the fields and fences past Somerby to the higher, lighter land on the Burrough Hill ridge.

They streaked ahead, a classic hunting print come to life in the late afternoon light, and marked their fox to ground exuberantly at Sellars Hill. They had run for seventy minutes, covering some nine miles, with a point of nearly five.

I was one of those perspiring followers who dismounted to slacken my horse's girths, but hastily had to tighten them immediately and leap into the saddle, because hounds suddenly spoke again and roared away on another fox they had just found nearby.

This time they ran along the Burrough Hills, giving a marvellous view over the Quorn Friday country to the west, crossing the Punchbowl and then heading back towards Somerby where their fox was given best in fading light just short of the village. What a visit!

Ian's father, Sir Peter, telephoned me several days later and asked almost shyly: 'Tell me, Michael, was it really as good as they say?'

I assured him sincerely no praise was high enough for his son's pack. There could have been no better way of repaying the Master who had fired my own enthusiasm as a foxhunter.

The Cottesmore paid a return visit to the Bicester country the following Monday, running hard all day, crossing the Grafton border, and catching a brace of foxes. Honour was preserved, but in the Cottesmore country some of us are still talking about that visit from the Bicester.

East Midlands

The **Quorn** country throughout most of the twentieth century continued to epitomise the delights of the Shires: excellent going on old turf, neat and usually inviting fly fences and timbers, small, well maintained coverts, beautifully sited

The author, with his present wife Marilyn, hunting with the Quorn.

One of the most successful Quorn Masterships: James Teacher (1975–83), Ulrica Murray Smith (1959–85) and Capt. Fred Barker (1972–85 and 1991–94).

by our forefathers to provide hunts in delectable country. I was lucky to enjoy it during the brilliant Mastership of Capt. Fred Barker, James Teacher and Ulrica Murray Smith, and later during that of Jim Bealby and Joss Hanbury, still one of the most brilliant horsemen across country as an imperturbable Field Master.

The undulating terrain offers plentiful views of hounds working in front of the field during a hunt. In the vales of the southern counties the abundant hedges often make it difficult to keep sight of hounds if they are more than one field ahead.

The major increases in plough in the Quorn country have still failed to invade some choice areas of country which contain its best qualities for hunting.

It pleased many of us that the final seasons of Michael Farrin's thirty years as Quorn huntsman included especially fine sport. Inevitably in such a long career there were less good seasons, and undoubtedly sport was somewhat blighted by the dramatic events of the video scandal in the 1991–92 season.

The Prince of Wales, who thoroughly enjoyed the Quorn, rode to hounds after Michael Farrin's last Monday meet in March, 1998. Hounds found in the famous Curate's covert, swooped after their fox over Bob Chaplin's farm, the Connors family's Muxlow Hill, then across the border into the Belvoir country, through their covert Sherbrooke's, and on to Slybourgh Hill and Long Clawson.

It was a wonderful tour of a beautiful swathe of pastoral England where the cry of Quorn hounds has resounded for over 250 years. Those who think of Leicestershire as flat are astonished by the work a Shires hunter must do in galloping and jumping up and down hill in pursuit of hounds. At Muxlow Hill there are drops which can catch the unwary, but the principal feature of the Quorn country is that it pays to tackle it boldly.

'Always jump the blackest place in the hedge,' Michael Farrin said. His last official day as huntsman was the following Friday meet at Sanham Farm, Great Dalby, where our host was George Coombes, aged eighty-three, who had ridden after the Quorn hounds for fifty-three years, and was probably the last man to ride regularly every week with the Quorn, Cottesmore and Belvoir.

'The forge is still all right, but the fire is a bit low,' is how George described his health. He was under-estimating his stamina because in 2004 he entertained the Quorn hounds to his ninetieth birthday meet, and he was still following hounds by car.

Anyone who doubts that a long service huntsman is a key member of a rural community should have seen the huge crowd, and the genuine expressions of regret at Michael's last day. Foxhunters are not noted for sentimentality, but more than a few of us were not ashamed of lumps in the throat, and a few wiped away tears, as Michael and the bitch pack left his last meet.

The huntsman himself preserved the impeccable, dignified demeanour he had always presented in the hunting field, similar to that which characterised the great Tom Firr. His last day comprised seven hours of hunting in which every farmer and landowner made hounds welcome throughout the Friday country, south of Melton Mowbray.

The Prince of Wales hunting with the Quorn, with Michael Farrin, Quorn huntsman for thirty years (1968–98), a classic Shires huntsman, and a superb horseman.

In the afternoon we had a taste of classic Quorn country, following hounds over the lovely old turf and fences on the Lowesby estate, beautifully conserved by its owner, the master builder David Wilson.

There were two good omens during the day. The hunt crossed the grass and fences on farms at Thorpe Satchville which belong to Leicestershire County Council whose Labour members' attempts at banning hounds had been thwarted, first by the Council's own tenant farmers who wished to welcome the Hunt, and later when the Council lost a legal battle to enforce their attempted ban.

Secondly, a small, forlorn group of hunt saboteurs vainly tried to wreck Farrin's last day. They were politely but firmly obstructed by the foot and car followers, and had absolutely no impact on the sport. Eventually they stood by the road, tooting foolishly on a horn, while the Quorn hounds ignored them, sweeping past with their huntsman to conclude one of the most glorious hunting careers in the history of the Shires.

Since then I have much enjoyed days with the Quorn, including this 2003–4 season when the excellent new professional, Peter Collins, ensured continuity with splendid sport over the famous pastures.

Of all the many days of tremendous fun I have enjoyed in Leicestershire with the **Belvoir**, none stays in my mind more than the hunting which followed the Melton Hunt Club Ride in that country in March, 1975.

The Ride over four-and-a-half miles of High Leicestershire, above the famous Belvoir Vale, around Holwell and Scalford. The route included the Melton Brook which, contrary to acute forebodings, caused no great problem.

I hunted round the flagged natural course on Foxford towards the rear, and

A meet of the Belvoir at Garthorpe during the Mastership of Lord King, *right*, (1958–72), with huntsman Jim Webster, *centre*, and whipper-in Ron Stouph, *left*.

212

apart from a heavy collision with one of many riderless horses, I suffered no upset. I had been unable to walk the course the previous day, having been confined to the *Horse & Hound* office, and Douglas Bunn rightly pointed out that this was unfair to the team of which I was a member.

Douglas himself had an interesting fall when his horse collided with a post on landing. It was to be among the incidents recorded in an exciting film *Wednesday Country* directed by BBC outside broadcasts wizard Alan Mouncer. We were delighted when it appeared on a national cinema circuit, mainly because the script which I wrote and voiced, contained a great deal of pro-hunting material.

Yet it was not the Ride but the hunting afterwards I recall most vividly. Jim Webster, the Belvoir's huntsman for twenty-seven years (1956–83), and his old English hounds produced a day when we saw them at their best.

As a member of the field, I was particularly fond of dear Jim who has a lovely dry wit, and at puppy shows when he judges in his speech he would refer to his beloved Belvoir hounds and then describe other packs simply as 'them other 'ounds.' One day I was riding an ex-showjumper which deposited me in a deep ditch. Jim looked down sorrowfully at me from his horse and said: 'Sir, they needs a younger man on top when they does things like that.'

The traditional black, tan and white pack can swing in unison superbly, with a great cry, exhibiting the tremendous drive which is one of their greatest virtues, making riding after them one of the most memorable thrills in the hunting field.

Drawing Melton Spinney first, hounds simply ran hard all day, describing great loops over country which at that time was virtually all down to grass, and beautifully fenced. We jumped most of the Melton Hunt line fence again, and after two hours hounds had run more than fifteen miles. Only twenty-two out of a mounted field of about 150 were still in touch, and I confess I was not one of them, although I was by then riding a third horse of the day, having hired a mount called Basil Brush to augment my own.

I reported: 'After we lost touch I had partaken of liquid refreshment in Scalford and was wending my way outside the village when I heard hounds speaking beautifully.

'Riding towards them I caught sight of a brown shape along the hedgerow. Some car followers arrived and holloaed. The Belvoir hounds spoke again and ran on strongly, with only their huntsman and a very small mounted field following. With the evening sun a big red ball in a hazy evening sky, the Hunt was a stirring sight as it surged across the Leicestershire grass and right glad I was to join them again until Webster blew for home.'

The Russian Roulette of hunt visiting produced for me one of the best post-war day's hunting with the **Fernie** in their superb grass country in the hills about Market Harborough, in February 1977.

I summed it up thus: 'From the first draw until home was blown at 4.40 p.m. life was a matter of seemingly endless galloping and jumping, following a superb pack of hounds working brilliantly throughout. From the first draw we had a good sixty minutes hunt. Then after changing horses there followed a wonderful two hours ten minutes run, with a six-mile point, and some sixteen miles as they ran. Only about half a dozen of us in the mounted field finished the day which had started with some 150 riders at the meet.'

I was lucky enough to be among the finishers in the last run, nearly out of breath, plastered in mud and with a great rent in a knee of my breeches.

Bruce Durno, huntsman of the Fernie for thirty-one years (1966–97), always hunted hounds with great skill, but on this occasion they were aided by a superb scent which became obvious at the first draw after the meet at Foxton Grange.

The great hunt in the afternoon began from John Ball covert, with hounds running a great loop over the grass and fences by Furnivals and Saddington, nearly to Fleckney and back through John Ball. The strong travelling dog fox ran straight through, and crossed the Mowsley road, over the Laughton Brook, to Bunker's Hill.

Then the line continued along the hills, by Laughton village, Gumley covert and Lubenham Lodge, this time crossing the canal. Hounds put on the pressure, hunting better than ever, but their fox just escaped with his brush into badger holes below the A6 at Gallows Hill.

My second horse was barely sixteen hands, normally ridden by the whipper-in Mike King. We jumped a perilously narrow piece of high fencing next to a locked gate near the end of the run, to keep in the hunt, having soared over dozens of fences all afternoon with great agility and speed.

I have had many good days with the Fernie since, but this one is etched in my memory as a quintessential Leicestershire run.

Undoubtedly one of the best preserved hunting countries in the twenty-first century is the **Meynell and South Staffs**. It has a wealth of grass, well fenced with fly fences and timber, and a varied country of vale, wolds and the stone-walled Derbyshire hills above Ashbourne.

The country is inviting, but it requires a bold horse and rider of ability to cross it successfully. A local hazard are the 'scoops', rounded hollows in front or behind many fences. Instead of being clear-cut ditches, with a discernible edge, they have rounded edges and can tempt a horse to run down into them when taking off. This can cause the horse to refuse or breast the fence, risking a serious fall.

One of the finest exponents of riding these special hazards is the Meynell's Joint Master and Field Master, Phil Arthers. David Barker proved a remarkable huntsman, and as a former international showjumper he is a superlative rider across a big country.

I have enjoyed many days in this country, and one of the best days occurred in December 1980 when hounds met at the Hoar Arms, by the Sudbury to Ashbourne road. Joint Masters were David Meynell, a descendant of the Hunt's founder, and Douglas Hinckley; hounds were hunted by Graham Roberts. Douglas Hinckley was Field Master and suffered a nasty fall on the flat, but bravely remounted to continue the hunt. Two years later Hinckley died after a fall head first when his horse stopped at a big Meynell drop-fence, and the horse fell on to him. Capt. Mark Phillips, former husband of Princess Anne, was in the mounted field on Columbus, the Queen's famous grey three-day-event horse.

The best and final hunt in a brilliant day was a run of nearly twelve miles, with a furthest point of nearly five miles, over some of the choicest grass country in the world. With temperatures falling all day there was an excellent scent, and when hounds were put into Bentley Carr they surged away with a great cry.

They ran over the pastures towards Alkmonton, over the Cubley road and crossed the Bentley brook. They crossed the Alkmonton-Yeaveley road after swinging left, and sped on towards Booth Hay, the delectable stretch of grass and fences, including holly bushes, the oldest component of the English hedge. Your horse must jump it cleanly, or he risks bouncing off and falling.

Hounds ran on over the Longford Estate, past Longford Carr, through the Sweet Isle covert, crossing the brook below Wormsley. They ran on to Shirley Park, and lost their fox on the Osmaston estate. The run lasted one hour forty-five minutes, and lived up to the description in J.L. Randall's history of the country which stated 'you are always in the air, and if a man does not like jumping he had better not come to Derbyshire . . . to enjoy yourself with the Meynell hounds you must have a horse which can twist, turn, and stop, and ask to jump at the shortest notice, and in Derbyshire especially must be willing to face water.'

Thanks partly to sound breeding by Dermot Kelly, Master and huntsman from 1962–75, the Meynell and SS have long had a lovely pack of modern hounds. This was maintained under David Barker who focussed on producing a high-class bitch pack, drafting the doghound puppies.

Since 1998 the Hon.Johnny Greenall, grandson of the great Belvoir and Limerick Master, Lord (Toby) Daresbury, has succeeded David Barker in hunting these hounds. Among the most ardent foxhunters to be seen often in the mounted field is the Prince of Wales – and no foxhunter could argue with his choice in following the hounds of the Meynell and South Staffs across their fabulous area of marvellously preserved pastoral England.

I could include in this survey many superb days with the **Cottesmore** when hunted by Capt. Simon Clarke, the professional Peter Wright, or Capt. Brian Fanshawe. The two amateur huntsmen both made major contributions to the Cottesmore's breeding, and Fanshawe created a legend in his final Mastership here.

However, lest it should be thought that 'good hunts' ceased by the end of the twentieth century, I will recall here a truly excellent hunt achieved by the Cottesmore hounds in the current 2003–4 season, generally a moderate one for scenting conditions, mainly due to the abnormally dry spell before Christmas. Neil Coleman, trained by Capt. Fanshawe, has been his successor as huntsman since 1992.

We met in February, 2004, at Hilltop Farm, home of devoted foxhunters William and Jane Cross, between Oakham and Braunston. Hounds found immediately in William's new covert, in the next field beyond the meet. They ran over the fine grass and fences above Braunston, passing Wilson's Gorse, going down to the key covert of Ladywood.

They accelerated from the banks of the River Gwash, a narrow brook here, and ran on smartly to Little Owston woods, then diverting past Big Owston.

This was a splendid ride at a pace where we could see hounds working, and there were occasional views of the hunted fox, clearly a large, strong travelling dog fox who had been found whilst making a visit to vixens outside his normal territory. It is the return to their home territory of such foxes which tends to provide the longer hunts early in the new year.

Near Owston village we groaned as the fox ran into Owston Big Wood where the boggy surface is traditionally paved 'with lost horseshoes and the curses of foxhunters'.

However, hounds pursued their fox out of the wood again after only a few minutes, and headed smartly past Whatborough Hill where we crossed the only ploughed fields of the run.

They ran on to the grass and fences of Tim Hercock's farm below Halstead, and then ran down the old railway line past Red Lodge. Visitors in the field were asking me 'where are we?' as hounds headed resolutely to the Quorn border.

Hounds hunted their fox into the John O'Gaunt covert by the Melton Mowbray-Billesdon road. The line was not so strong, but they crossed the road into the Quorn country, and hunted on more slowly across the pastures at Lowesby Grange towards Lowesby village. Scent petered out with Lowesby Hall in sight, and because we were 'abroad' Neil did not cast on, but picked up hounds and returned to the Cottesmore country.

This was a fine hunt with a point of over nine miles, and a run of about fifteen – statistics worthy of hunts in the 'golden ages' of foxhunting.

Wales and Border Counties

If I were a younger man with foxhunting as a ruling passion I would seriously consider in the twenty-first century buying or renting a house with stabling and paddocks in Mid or North Wales. Houses, land and horses still tend to be cheaper in Wales than most areas of the UK, and I have found that foxhunting is a highly effective key in joining the Welsh rural community.

Welsh hounds are superb, their country is still mainly down to grass, although it has a great deal of barbed wire fencing, and there is a multitude of foxes. Welsh farmers are major sheep producers and value the activities of their local Hunts in culling and dispersing foxes as an indispensable local service, and a sport which most of them regard as part of their way of life. Woe betide any government which endeavours to ban foxhunting in Wales! There would be mass public disobedience, backed by direct action, on a scale which will dismay and amaze foolish anti-hunting politicians.

I tasted the joys of hunting in the lovely Welsh Borders country when I visited the **Golden Valley** country in November 1977. Vivian Bishop had been Master and huntsman since 1945 when he founded the pack from scratch in the beautiful country rising from the Wye Valley into the Welsh Border Hills; he died in office fifty-six years later in 2001, truly one of the great Masterships of the twentieth century.

Vivian, a quiet courteous man, was a natural horseman, huntsman and hound breeder. His Welsh-cross pack worked beautifully for him over the old turf and moorland clothing lovely hills and vales. We met at the Ryhdspence Inn, near Hay-on-Wye, where that great producer of hunters and point-to-pointers Bill Bryan kindly provided me with an excellent six-years-old hunter mare with a useful gallop and jump in her. The Bryan family had sixteen horses out with the Golden Valley that day.

The best hunt was from Rhosgoch Bog, a real bog where man dare not walk, and a horse could not venture, stretching for some miles on Major de Winton's land. A good strong fox went away, and I was much impressed by the way hounds went away swifly together with a great cry.

They ran over Newchurch Hill, through Vyalt Wood and over Bryngwyn Hill, just losing this fox near Harabour Farm after an excellent run with a four and half mile point. We seemed to have been galloping on springs, and saw hounds working in front of us all the way.

One of the finest hunting countries in the United Kingdom, still remarkably unspoilt, is that of **Sir Watkin Williams-Wynn's** in the old Denbigh and Flint counties, now Clwyd and in Shropshire and Cheshire.

The Williams-Wynn baronets hunted the fox with their own hounds in the eighteenth century, and formed various packs in the nineteenth, the present family pack being started in 1843.

Owen Watkin Williams-Wynn had been in office since 1957 when I visited the pack in March, 1981. Bill Lander had been hunting them since 1972 with great success, and with his dry humour, and his great abilities in the field, I rate him as one of the huntsman with whom I have most enjoyed sport.

It is a splendid hunting country, mostly down to grass, with favourably sited coverts, and an excellent pack of hounds in which there is a strong element of traditional English breeding. I recorded: 'They hunt with drive, and a good cry,

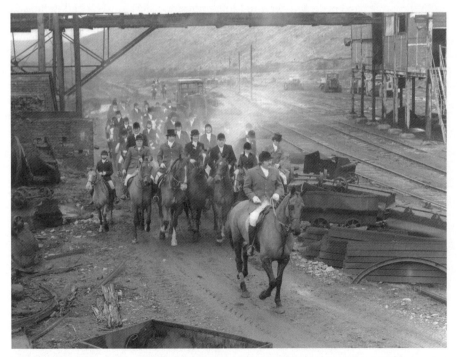

The Banwen Miners' Hunt riding through a working colliery. Formed in 1962 in Glamorgan, hounds were first kept in a colliery lamp room.

and make a fine sight between a horse's ears as you endeavour to follow over the Wynnstay grass and fences which include plenty of fine hedges with broad ditches; honest obstacles, but do not forget to kick on a bit.'

Richard Matson, who was to follow his parents into the Mastership, provided me with an excellent grey hunter for which I was profoundly grateful.

Well within Welsh borders I have had fascinating sport, once hunting with the **Banwen Miners** in West Glamorgan. Its name derived from the lamp-room of the local colliery in Banwen which became the kennels when the Hunt was founded in 1962 with strong support from miners, although the membership has since become far more widespread.

We were not slow in the British Field Sports Society to extol the Banwen Miners as an example of a Hunt with non-elitist origins, but the support of mining and hill farming communities is part of hunting's history throughout Wales, binding it firmly to the Welsh rural culture.

The variety of Welsh hunting is fabulous, and in January, 1977, I particularly relished my visit to **Vale of Clettwr** pack in the village of Llanfihangel-ar-Arth, lying in the green hills above Carmarthen. As referred to in more detail in Chapter 5, Capt. Ian Farquhar at the Bicester kennel benefited enormously from a Welsh outcross he obtained from the Clettwr kennel.

I was much impressed by these Welsh hounds' ability to self-hunt, that is to cast themselves unaided across hills and valleys when their huntsman is unable to reach them.

Trefor Jones had been Master and huntsman since 1961, and he had increased Welsh lines in a cross-bred pack to ensure the kennel was pure Welsh. He told me they needed careful handling; they tended to be somewhat shy and would give up hunting altogether if there was too much whip cracking or shouting.

We rode on old turf over the hills, with the River Tivy glinting below, much enjoying watching hounds hunt their foxes with great verve and a lovely voice. They produced an enormous amount of sport throughout a season, and very economically too. I was amused to hear one Clettwr hunting farmer say 'the subscription is £25 for a season here, but there are threats that it's going up next season!'

The North

They work hard and they play hard in Yorkshire. I discovered the latter in full measure in my first visit to the **Bedale** and **West of Yore** Hunts who share the same kennels at Northallerton, North Yorkshire.

It is a very sensible, business-like arrangement, and I cannot think why more Hunts have not adopted it elsewhere. How lucky I was to experience some of the fun engendered by two of the jolliest and most sporting Masters I have ever encountered, Malcolm Sherwin and Michael Abrahams. They shared the Mastership of the two packs, with Malcolm hunting the Bedale, and Michael the West of Yore pack. George Cooke, a genial character, served both Hunts as kennel-huntsman and first whipper-in.

Superbly mounted on Dai Jones, a half-brother to Harvey Smith's

Michael Abrahams,
Joint Master and
huntsman of the
West of Yore from
1971–83, succeeded
by his wife Amanda
as Joint Master.

showjumper Evan Jones, I had a great day with the Bedale. The Friday country is mildly undulating, crossed by steep-sided waterways known as 'stells'. Hounds found their first fox in one of these, and was lost after being headed.

Then they found in the Fell Gill covert and we had a fine hunt despite a high wind. They ran past Pepper Arden towards East Cowton, on to Stripe House and Forty Acres, and finally they killed their fox in the water at the Arden stell. Hounds had run thirteen-and-a-half miles, including a four mile point, in one hour forty-five minutes.

After an energetic evening cavorting at the Thirsk Friday Farmers dinner-dance, next day we braved even stronger, gale force winds to hunt with the West of Yore from Grantley. They have a lovely country of small grass enclosures, often fenced by hedges patched with timber, the green giving way above to the brown sweep of the North York moors.

Michael Abrahams, who had not been hunting hounds long, had the satisfaction of producing a tremendous day with the West of Yore pack. They started with a rousing hunt from West Hill Edge right up to Skelding Moor where forgivably they lost their fox in a shrieking wind-swept landscape. I reported: 'Michael Abrahams resolutely took his hounds back to the thick conifer woods at Laverton, and they drew so well that in twenty minutes I saw a splendid fox breaking covert, with Mr Abrahams putting the pack on most effectively to hunt the quary running down wind to the lower country.

'And what an entertaining hunt ensued. It was frequently a case of "hark to Romper" as this large doghound, drafted from the Tynedale country, put the pack right when they feathered in the old pastures past Laverton, and then hunted short of Kirkby Malzeard lefthanded and right to Biggin, where this fox had to be given best after a hunt of some seventy minutes.'

I recall finishing the day with a fairly spectacular fall over a hedge, having cleared a great many varied obstacles, but no damage was done and I had to dash to a train to return to London for an essential evening commitment. I learned to ensure there could be nothing else 'essential' on hunting days.

Since then I have always had tremendous fun with the Yorkshire packs, matched by hectic social events in the evening. I recall one occasion when a Supporters' Club dinner-dance lasted well into the night; I was up early next morning to meet some farmers, followed by non-stop hunting on two horses until darkness.

This was followed by an interesting party in a steaming indoor swimming pool, only partially lit and accompanied by piped music. Somehow I drove south to collapse into bed in Hampstead in the early hours of the next day.

Although I had many good days with him later, the **Zetland's** huntsman Cliff Standing was grounded with a broken foot when I hunted first in that excellent sporting county on the North Yorkshire-Durham border in December 1974. I love the generally light going, the plethora of timber and inviting hedges amid mixed farming, and the sporting spirit of the Zetland.

Colin MacAndrew, later Lord MacAndrew, had hunted the Zetland for seventeen years as amateur huntsman, and in this emergency he elected to step in as first-whipper. This must have been daunting for the twenty-one-years-old first whipper-in Colin Hicks in his first season in this country, who had to carry the horn. Bill Snowdon and his son John were Joint Masters, with Willie Barker from the Bedale. It was not a day dominated by one impressive hunt, but there was tremendous fun in constant shorter hunts after the meet at Forcett Hall, just north-west of Scotch Corner.

With the **Sinnington** in 1978 I saw the values of Welsh-cross hounds when Willie Poole, later to emerge as an entertaining and popular writer for *Horse & Hound* and *The Daily Telegraph*, was hunting the Sinnington.

They met at Gillamoor on the edge of the North Yorkshire moors, and I experienced the finest hunting of that season when they concluded an excellent day with a run of ten miles, including a four mile point, ending with a kill in the open; and all in ninety minutes.

They ran from Stauphs hillside covert by a circuitous route to Pennyholme at Fadmoor, home of the senior Joint Master since 1950, Lady Feversham. They cast themselves over the Hodgebeck stream, and afer a big circle went on at top pace to catch their fox in the open at Swinacle Ridge. Huntsman and hounds

Johnny O'Shea, huntsman of the Cheshire (1966–91), consistently provided excellent sport in a great grass country.

were silhouetted against the evening light as my horse struggled below to cross the last few yards of boggy moorland.

In February 1979 I experienced a superb day over one of the greatest grass countries, the **Cheshire**. I recorded it as one of my most enjoyable for three seasons. The Prince of Wales was guest of honour at the meet, at Cholmondeley Castle, and he thoroughly relished superlative sport, although he had to endure a heavy fall.

One of my favourite huntsmen, the ebullient Johnny O'Shea, originally from County Wexford, was hunting the Cheshire; a natural handler of hounds and horseman. I was mounted on a slim hireling named Basher, bearing the scars of bar-firing on his legs, and at the meet I fervently wished I had brought my own best hunter, the remarkable Connell I had imported recently from Ireland.

I need not have worried; Basher never put a foot wrong during a hectic day. We were led by the Master, Mr Joe Heler, an outspoken Cheshire farming personality. Hounds soon found in the Castle park and ran with a great cry; it was clearly an excellent scenting day. We spent the rest of the day galloping and jumping inviting hedges and timber off glorious old turf, in hot pursuit of the Cheshire hounds.

On a falling temperature scent improved still further in the afternoon, and I had to stop poor Basher, who had done too much, early in a last sizzling hunt over Windmill Bank, round Batgh Wood and on over High Ash to Spinslow Lower Hall.

Prince Charles was one of a very small mounted field left; he had survived a crashing fall during the day, but no harm was done. Afterwards he hacked back to the Castle with the Crown Equerry Sir John Miller. They and their horses looked somewhat tired, but supremely happy.

Among my happiest memories of northern packs are my visits to the **Tynedale's** superb grass and wall country, beyond Newcastle. I first rode to hounds there when George Fairbairn was such an excellent Master (1959–75), and later a successful National Hunt trainer.

He mounted me superbly on a Thoroughbred, and we swooped about the grass hills, taking on formidable walls with hounds running hard just in front.

It is a country which has attracted good riders, and excellent hound breeders. The Tynedale hounds have won notable rosettes at Harrogate and Peterborough; much dedicated work was put into their breeding by Rosemary Stobart during her twelve years of Mastership up to 1998.

The Fells

I cannot pretend that I hunted often with the Fell packs in Lake District, but I had enough days to appreciate the major virtues of Fell hounds, and the joys of watching them hunting over the steep slopes of their native setting. The truth is that I have never been a dedicated foot hunter, which I acknowledge as a fault, but I have certainly enjoyed days observing hounds work beautifully in the Fells. My dear friend, Bay de Courcy Parry, 'Dalesman' of *Horse & Hound*, and one of the most naturally gifted writers, invited me to his Lakeland home a number of times. In April 1977 I stayed with him to watch the **Ullswater** pack after they met at Hartsop Hall, south beyond the head of the glorious Ullswater

The Ullswater hounds meeting at Hartsop Hall, in 1977 when Dennis Barrow was hunting hounds, and the Hon. Anthony Lowther was Master (1958–80)

lake, near the foot of the Kirkstone Pass. Dennis Barrow was hunting hounds, and in his red coat, drab breeches and walking boots he traversed the stone-littered hills with the nonchalance of someone striding across a bowling green. Jim Meads skipped up the mountainside with his usual impressive footwork, to take some memorable pictures. Cravenly I stayed at the bottom, entranced by Dalesman's wonderful conversation.

I was thankful that when I made a move to go up the Fell, the route was blotted out by driving rain and then snow. I bravely raked the slopes with my field glasses, and later spent a marvellous evening in the White Lion at Patterdale with Dalesman and a gathering of Fell hunting people.

My fellow members of the Radio 4 *Any Questions* panel were somewhat mystified when I received tumultuous cheers as soon as I was introduced during a programme recorded in the Lake District, but when the subject of hunting came up later it was made utterly clear to them that I had vast local support.

Since various riding accidents have made me even less able to climb Fells I dare say future excursions to see these packs will be confined to viewing from the valleys, but I sincerely recommend a visit to any real foxhunter, especially in the spring. It is worth seeing hounds working beautifully, and untrammelled by the presence of a mounted following.

Scotland

In those happier years before self-government enabled the Scottish Parliament to bring in its iniquitous, bungling Bill to ban foxhunting with hounds, I visited Scotland numerous times to report the Chase. I admire the fortitude of Scottish packs in continuing to hunt hounds by exploiting a loophole in the law which allows gun-packs, but I do not wish to see it.

The depths of tradition vandalised by the new Scottish Labour MSPs is emphasised by the long traditions of the Fife, Britain's most northerly mounted pack. In 1986 I attended the **Fife's** celebration of its two hundredth anniversary. The senior Master, John Gilmour, was upholding long family connections with the Hunt. It was the home country of the nineteenth century sporting novelist and poet George John Whyte-Melville who in his poem 'The Good Grey Mare' coined the phrase 'But I freely admit that the best of my fun – I owe it to horse and hound', in 1884 inspiring the title of the weekly magazine I was later fortunate to edit.

A Scottish pack founded in 1884 was the **Jed Forest** which hunts the Borders country between Jedburgh and Hawick. In November 1984 I attended their centenary celebrations, and for once a special occasion was accompanied by outstanding hunting. Hounds met at Townhead of Cavers, near Hawick, a house derived from the stable block of Cavers, home of the Jed's first Master, Capt. Edward Palmer Douglas.

The huntsman, Derek Cheetham, put hounds into Kirkton Moss covert, and very soon it was time to cram down your hat and ride as fast as possible. The Master, Walter Jeffrey, was acting as whipper-in, and we had a great lead from the former amateur 'chase jockey Charles Scott as Field Master.

Seldom have I enjoyed a longer hunt in more beautiful scenery. Fortunately we were on old turf providing good going because hounds flew o'er hill and dale with little check, and riders and horses were working hard, some 'with bellows to mend' on a sunny morning. We had to jump occasional wooden rails or walls armed with barbed wire.

There was a check at Adderstonlee, but then hounds surged on to Ormston, left to Upper Tofts, then into East Middle and Whitriggs where they marked to ground enthusiastically in some hill-side earths.

The Jed Forest pack, containing Fell blood as well as modern lines from the Duke of Beaufort's, certainly proved its worth and there could have been no better way of celebrating the centenary. They had run fourteen miles, including a four mile point, in one hour fifty-six minutes. I was riding a six-years-old grey mare, Susan, who kept me well in the hunt throughout, and I needed no persuading that the Borders is a great area for hunting in a beautiful wild setting.

I have enjoyed marvellous days on moorland and pasture with the neighbouring illustrious Hunt, the **Duke of Buccleuch's**. The 9th Duke, 'Johnny' Buccleuch, was a paraplegic victim in a hunting fall as a young man, but has kept faith with the family Hunt he inherited through good times and bad, culminating in the Scottish hunting ban.

I much admire the sportsmanship and resolve of Joint Master and huntsman Trevor Adams, an Englishman who, since 1989, has hunted hounds and loyally stayed with the Hunt, helping to fight the political battle in Scotland. Trevor was formerly a professional Hunt servant, and the brother of Anthony Adams, the much respected huntsman of the Heythrop who was trained by Ronnie Wallace.

Ireland

There is a special magic about foxhunting in Ireland. Riding after hounds offers a different challenge to the visitor: walls, banks and ditches, and sometimes endless walls, the going varies from soft to boggy.

But it is the attitude of the Irish to their sport which makes any foxhunting visit memorable. Compared with the English, the Irish seem to be 'two whiskies ahead', their buoyant enthusiasm, their carefree attitude to the hazards of the chase, and their willingness to discuss the day in the local pub – before the meet, and sometimes long after home has been blown.

One of the most exciting hunts I experienced in Ireland came soon after I started my Foxford column at *Horse & Hound*, in February 1974.

I visited Ireland in a dire spring when the countryside was drowning after weeks of incessant heavy rain. Stock farmers were suffering from water-logged land where they could not turn out cattle, and there was a steep rise in prices of cattle feed. There was but a small field of the **Tipperary** when we met at Moyglass, near Killenaule – and it never stopped raining and blowing all day. In Ireland cheerfulness keeps breaking out, and there was plenty of buoyant optimism from the Master and huntsman, Michael Higgens who had just taken over from the much revered Evan Williams, Master of the Tipps for nineteen years; a great

Joint Master and huntsman of the Tipperary for eighteen years, Michael Higgens (1973–91), and *right* his long-time kennel huntsman Micky Flanagan.

breeder of horses and hounds, and a leading amateur jockey who won the Cheltenham Gold Cup twice. Follow that!

The new Master, red haired and spry, looked like an Irishman, but was from England and experienced much of his early hunting in the Puckeridge arable country with Capt. Charlie Barclay hunting hounds. Higgens has always 'done his own thing', has foxhunted all his life, and has an engaging sense of humour. He gave no sign of being even slightly over-awed by his predecessor.

Michael's partner, the beautiful Yvonne McClintock, saved my day by generously making available her five-years-old hunter gelding Callan, who proved wise and capable well beyond his years. This was a godsend because the day proved exceptionally demanding for an English visitor unused to the towering banks and chasm-like ditches of Tipperary.

My diary recorded: 'The first obstacle was almost a baptism: a lurching drop down more than eight feet into mud up to the horse's knees. Callan managed it reassuringly, just staggering slightly on landing which nearly decanted me. I learned later I had survived the Black Hole.'

Hounds hunted hard all day. We had several shorter runs during the morning, in which I was swept out of the saddle by a low tree branch, but landing in oozing mud could not make me any more drenched to the skin.

Then hounds found at Powers Wood, and I enjoyed one of the hunts of my life, not a marathon, but a ten mile run with a four-mile point. Distance and time have no relation, however, to the quality of this almost dream-like experience: 'We rode on over the glorious grass, with hounds speaking in front, surging on over the banks, occasionally checking very briefly, but always feathering beautifully to recapture the line before running on again. I lost all sense of time and direction. It encapsulated the rapture of hunting for me. The horse under the saddle was not a beast of burden, a mere form of transport. He was my partner, thoroughly enjoying the ride, and determined to be in the hunt to the end.'

Higgens had kindly invited me to ride just behind him, and no doubt this view from the ultimate 'front seat' made the hunt all the more memorable.

I followed on to one hedge-covered bank when to my alarm Higgens suddenly stopped. I peered down in horror into a looming, unjumpable abyss on the far side, with a jumble of wire on its lip. My pilot simply turned his horse and walked along the top of the bank to a T junction with another bank, and then leapt into space.

We stumbled after him, like a drunken tight-rope walker, and emulated the leap, descending through a curtain of bushes into a glutinous sea of mud. How Callan kept his feet was a miracle.

Hounds ran to Ann's Gift, on to the Prospect Stud, across Coolmoyne Road, and on to the grassy knoll at Tullamaine Moat, near to the Tipperary kennels at Fethard. We set about jumping some formidable stone walls for a change, and finding some earths closed our fox was jinking back on his line. It was nearly dusk under lowering clouds and Higgens blew for home. The pleasures of that day are impossible to convey fully but I derived them in indivisible measure from horse and hound.

I first had a taste of that great wall country, the County Galway, better known as the **Galway Blazers**, in January 1977 when Lord Hemphill was senior Joint Master, and Lady Hemphill was Field Master, with Joint Master Edmund Crotty from County Waterfod hunting hounds.

They met at the Hemphills' home, Tulira Castle, and it was a goodish scenting day. I revelled in the light-riding pastures, criss-crossed by seemingly endless stone walls. You can jump a hundred or more in day, and not one must be taken for granted.

My day was enlivened when an American visitor thanked me fulsomely for 'giving such a good lead to the second flight'. I was mounted on a superb wall jumper from the Hemphill stable, and had no excuse to be other than fluent over the country. This was just as well when I blithely jumped a wall into a lane, only to find there was a fifteen foot drop on the landing side.

As a good Irish hunter should, my horse 'found a leg' and somehow bounced half way down off the sheer bank to land safely on his feet in the lane. Only one of the 'second flight' followed me, and he was not so lucky. We spent some time scraping him off the ground, but nothing was broken.

On a later visit to the Blazers I rode a superb five-year-old hired to me by the famous dealer Willie Leahy. Barbara Rich had arranged that I could 'try' the horse for her to buy for a client. Another visiting Englishman had a terrible day, constantly falling. He said to me bitterly as we hacked home: ' I was going to ride a much better horse – but I hear they gave it to some bloody hunting correspondent!'

More than a sport, a way of life: priests performing the annual Blessing of the Hounds at the opening meet of the Scarteen at Knocklong, in 1979. *Right* is Thady Ryan, Master since 1946 of these 'Black and Tan' hounds, owned and hunted by his family for ten generations.

Inevitably some of my most memorable Irish hunting has been with the **Scarteen**, the famous Black and Tans, hunted by the Ryan family for over three hundred years.

Thady Ryan, Master and formerly the huntsman since 1946, was hunting hounds during all my visits. He had a great gift for handling the famous Kerry Beagles, who always appear to me to be exceptionally independent. I recall one occasion when they were gathered round the huntsman while a dig for a fox was progressing several hundred yards away. Suddenly there was a holloa on a hill and in a trice the Black and Tans were away over the hills. 'I think we'd better go too,' said Thady with a huge smile, and we were suddenly engaged in a marvellous evening hunt. His natural charm, and his Irish golden tongue are among his many outstanding characteristics.

I recall an American visitor during a hunting day asking Thady how you blew a hunting horn. The Master stopped and gave a brief impromptu explanation and display; to my amazement he handed over the horn to the American to 'have a go'. I cannot imagine the same response in the hunting field from any English huntsman, amateur or professional. I recall Thady's wife going from one horse to another taking off sandwich boxes which first-time American visitors had strapped to their saddles. 'You won't be needing them, and you won't have the time' she said with a smile. After they had experienced their first ditches and slippery banks of the Scarteen country they fervently agreed.

At the end of the 2003–4 season the Black and Tans visited the Cottesmore country in Rutland, accompanied by about thirty mounted Irish followers who romped over the Shires fences with great exuberance.

At the meet Thady's son, Chris, who was maintaining family continuity by hunting hounds announced: 'We've got some lads here on young horses who need plenty of room. Best of all, the horses are all for sale – but I would advise making an offer right now!'

Before he moved off, rather later than the Cottesmore are used to, he declared: 'May the best team win.'

I soon learned to expect the unexpected when foxhunting in Ireland. Hunting with the **Meath**, over their wide and deep ditches in 1982 I had the luck to ride a superb chestnut gelding, provided by Mrs Ned Cash, wife of the renowned producer of top-class hunters. John Henry had been hunting hounds with distinction since 1962 and I saw his skills to great effect after the meet at Ratoath, only some fifteen miles from Dublin Airport, but deeply rural.

The best hunt of the day was in the afternoon when hounds found a fox at the Paddocks and flew from Wild Farm to Fairyhouse racecourse. To my delight the hunt continued right across the course.

We had an exciting ride as our horses were suddenly asked to elevate over the stiff stud rails around the course, a dramatic change from leaping open ditches all day. We galloped round part of the course, but did not jump the steeplechase fences, somewhat to my relief. We jumped over some formidable rails to exit the course over some gigantic ditches only to disappear into jungle-like bushes, and ran back over a good line of grass and more ditches to Wild Farm. It was a historic line because in the 1880s the Empress of Austria hunted with the Meath side-saddle, sewn into her glamorous habit, and on one occasion similarly enjoyed a run across Fairyhouse racecourse.

The Meath's Hon. Secretary, Capt. Jock Armstrong, had recently retired as chief pilot for Aer Lingus and after landing his jumbo jet at Dublin Airport was feted at a retirement ceremony when the Meath huntsman handed the captain a red hunting coat. He ceremonially donned it after taking off his pilot's uniform.

The most hunting days I experienced in Ireland were with the **County Limerick's** pack of English bred hounds, brought over from the Belvoir country just after the war by Lord Daresbury . We struck up a firm friendship and he was remarkably hospitable.

Toby Daresbury brought organisation and a deep purse to match his boundless energy and enthusiasm for the sport, and he engaged one of the finest professional huntsmen in Hugh Robards.

His Lordship mounted me extremely well on superb horses which made me feel I was far more competent over the Irish obstacles than was the case.

Some snapshot memories give a flavour of foxhunting I was fortunate and privileged to enjoy:

- During a fast hunt over the Limerick's walls country, hounds ran on to a railway line. I perceived to my horror that a passenger train stopped

One of the great personalities of twentieth century foxhunting, Lord (Toby) Daresbury, walking out his County Limerick hounds on a Sunday morning in 1976. Hounds are followed by Miss Meriel Atkinson, and the author.

Lord Daresbury in the hunting field in Ireland in 1974. Devoted to old English hounds, he was Master of the Belvoir (1934–47) and of the Limerick (1947–77).

Hugh Robards, brilliant huntsman of the Co. Limerick hounds (1972–97), and Joint Master and huntsman of the Rolling Rock Hunt in Pennsylvania, USA since 1998.

further up the line. The driver alighted from the train and stood by the track shouting in an incomprehensible brogue and waving his arms. 'We're in big trouble,' I said to an Irishman in the mounted field 'Not a bit,' he rejoined. 'The train driver's telling us he's seen the fox.'

- In another hunt in this country, hounds leaped a stone wall into a village school playground. Children were playing in the yard. They shouted with joy and cheered on the hounds. Hunt staff and several members of the field, including your correspondent, jumped into the playground in pursuit, and out the other side of the yard. The cheering from the children reached a crescendo. Hunting was certainly part of their local culture, and many children rode fearlessly over the banks. At one stage the Limerick held frequent special days for farmers' children. Adults could only come out if they were accompanying a child, and some people 'borrowed' children from friends for the day so that they could hunt too.

- The famous horseman and foxhunter P.P Hogan gave me a lead on one occasion over the biggest banks I have ever tackled. The horses leapt open ditches to land on near vertical slopes, somewhat scrabbling up to the top where they clambered through desperately thick thorns. Fortunately the amazing Hogan made a tunnel through and I escaped the worst of the briars, but on the far side his face was bleeding profusely from dozens of cuts, drenching his hunting tie and shirt with blood. He made absolutely no reference to his injuries, and finally soared down into a narrow lane where his horse subsided on its knees, giving him a very heavy fall. He simply re-mounted and galloped on; he was riding a 'four-year-old' but it was only January so the horse was nearer three.

- Meriel ('Merry') Atkinson, the diminutive house-keeper, companion, breeder and sustainer of hound puppies and foals at Toby Daresbury's estate, once had a nasty fall. She climbed on to a wall and shouted 'Pony, pony, pony!' Her horse, which she had bred and nurtured, was galloping into the distance. On hearing Merry he stopped, wheeled round and galloped back to her wall where she calmly re-mounted.

- In a sharp hunt one day we came to the banks of the River Deely, where to my horror hounds leaped in to swim across after their fox. Without hesitation P.P. Hogan and Hugh Robards jumped their horses about five feet down into the fast-running river. Their horses submerged and bobbed up, with each rider wet to the chin. They swam their horses down river, then steered them to a cattle watering slope on the far side, clambered out and galloped on after hounds without comment. As a mere hunting correspondent I knew exactly what to do: I turned my horse and galloped alongside the river bank for a quarter a mile until I came to a bridge which I crossed. I reflected afterwards that it would never have done to imperil the writing of my report by catching pneumonia!

- In the same hunt, hounds swept across the park at Alta Villa, Lord Daresbury's home. At that time Merry Atkinson was in a corner of the park feeding hound puppies she was walking. She was shrieking 'Puppy, puppy, puppy!' A section of the pack running in full cry checked immediately, and swung towards this tiny lady who had fed them when they were being walked. They were met by the redoubtable Merry growling sternly; 'Get back to him you naughty hounds!' Obediently they ran back to the line immediately and resumed their hunt.

These were but a few incidents which convinced me that when I visited the Limerick country I was in another world and another time. I always returned to England refreshed, and wreathed with smiles.

CHAPTER 10

IMAGE OF WAR

*'Unting is the sport of kings, the image of war without its
guilt, and only five-and-twenty per cent of its danger!'
– Mr Jorrocks*

FOXHUNTING, and the other hound sports, won their battles in a long war
to survive throughout the twentieth century. Once or twice, as the Duke
of Wellington admitted after Waterloo, it was 'the nearest run thing'.
The last decade of the century was the most crucial when a sustained attack

was launched in Parliament, aided substantially by Labour's electoral victories with inordinately large majorities.

The war against hound sports has continued in the twenty-first century, but as I write in 2004 there are encouraging signs that public opinion outside the House of Commons is far more sympathetic to the libertarian argument that it would be unjust to crush the life-style of a minority.

The Iraq war, and the subsequent world-wide concerns about terrorism have reminded even the most ardent anti-hunting politicians that it is ludicrously inappropriate to include banning foxhunting in their list of political priorities. However, in 2004 there were still ample reasons for serious concern about the future of hound sports, mainly because of continued large majorities in favour of abolition in the House of Commons whenever the subject came before MPs.

Throughout the twentieth century it was the dedicated work of small groups of field sportsmen and women which saved hunting from the political axe. Hunting was able to rally much greater support at times of crisis, in attendances at marches or rallies, but sustaining the defence in a long, wearing war was left to a minority. Most of the heroes fighting for hunting were unsung, but that is the way of most campaigning movements.

There had been sporadic expressions of opposition to hunting in the nineteenth century, although the Society for the Prevention of Cruelty to Animals when formed in 1824, confined its concerns to the plight of horses, domestic and farm animals. It became the RSPCA in 1840 with a warrant from Queen Victoria, and continued to avoid an anti-hunting policy, although there were small groups of Fabians within the Society who were keen on abolition of hound sports, and in 1891 formed the Humanitarian League which included a hunting ban in its aims. Their pacifism in the First World War turned public opinion against them, and the organisation subsided in 1919. They had attracted attention with essays against hunting by some leading intellectuals, including George Bernard Shaw.

The anti-hunting movement began tentative activities soon after the Great War, and in 1924 the League for the Prohibition of Cruel Sports was formed by several members of the RSPCA who were dissatisfied with its neutrality on hunting. Later it became simply the League Against Cruel Sports, a useful public relations title because it presumes the answer to the crucial question as to whether the activities it opposes are cruel. Pro-hunting organisations prefer simply to refer to it as LACS.

In 1929, and again in 1930, the League backed the tabling in the House of Commons of a Bill to abolish staghunting. It had absolutely no chance of succeeding as legislation, but some in the hunting world realised that positive action would have to be taken on a broad front to defend their sports. They took the right action in forming the BFSS because the war to save hunting was to become far more of a challenge than anyone could have foreseen in the 1920s.

The story is easier to understand in chronological terms:

1930 Formation of the British Field Sports Society

Backing for the formation of a pro-hunting society came from the Devon and Somerset Staghounds country in Devon and Somerset because its most fervently supported local hound sport was the first target of attack in the Commons. Fred Beadle, a staghunting farmer and businessman emerged as the leader of a group who had the vision to understand that their best defence weapon would be a national society representing all field sports.

He enlisted the aid of Lord Fortescue, a leading landowner, and Lord Bayford, an ex-Master of the D. and S. Staghounds (1895–1907). Formerly Robert Sanders, Bayford had been a Conservative MP and served as Tory Minister of Agriculture from 1922–24. Bayford's parliamentary experience made him an excellent choice as first Chairman of the British Field Sports Society which held its inaugural meeting in London on 4 December 1930. From the start it received warm support from the sporting press.

Master, the 10th Duke of Beaufort, accepted the post as President, and this helped considerably in encouraging foxhunters to join. Some understood that their sport would be the next target if there should be successful abolition of staghunting, although the threat was not taken very seriously in the 1930s. Shooters and anglers were warned that their sports would similarly be at risk if all the hound sports were abolished. Reminders of such threats were occasionally uttered by the more extreme members of the anti-hunting faction, and this helped BFSS recruitment. The Duke remained in office as BFSS President for fifty years, giving staunch leadership.

Efforts were made in the 1930s to counter letters and articles in the press attacking hunting, and the right to reply to broadcast propaganda from the antis was sought from the BBC. The Society was a long way from being able to launch major mass opinion campaigns, but the work in the 1930s was invaluable because an anti-hunting Bill would come before Parliament all too soon after the Second World War.

The most useful work achieved in the early years was the establishment of a national network of branches ensuring that most of its income came from annual subscriptions. Under the secretaryship of Toby Fitzwilliam (1931–53), BFSS membership rose from 3,450 in May 1931, to 8,549 in March 1932, stabilising at about 10,000 in 1938.

The RSPCA had abandoned its neutrality on the staghunting issue, supporting a ban, and it was accused of double standards by Lord Bayford in the House of Lords. He pointed out the RSPCA took membership subscriptions from many who hunted, and then campaigned against their sport.

Soon after the outbreak of war, the BFSS went into abeyance, but as early as 1940 it resumed on a limited scale to counter the propaganda still being churned out by the LACS's secretary, Mr Sharp. He wrote to newspapers complaining that hunting in wartime was unpatriotic, and attacked War Agricultural Committees for assisting the sport. Traditional anti-hunting sentiment within the Labour party, closely linked to the class war, was well known in the BFSS, and when Labour won the post-war General Election it was clear that a political battle was looming.

BFSS membership shot up from about 5,000 in 1946 to nearly 18,000 by 1948, and the following year there was a massive increase to an all time high of nearly 120,000 when the first post-war anti-hunting Bill was launched.

In 1932 there had been an almighty row within the LACS which led to a break-away organisation being formed, the National Society for the Abolition of Cruel Sports. Rows and schisms have featured in both camps in the hunting war, but the BFSS was far more successful at absorbing, or stifling, internal dissension. Its successor, the Countryside Alliance, received far more publicity for its internal rows.

There was a strong regimental flavour in the BFSS top echelon, where all the chief executives were senior ex-Army officers, which precluded public disloyalty, no matter how much argument occasionally erupted behind closed doors.

1948–49 Prohibition of Hunting and Coursing Bill

The National Society for the Abolition of Cruel Sports upstaged the LACS by persuading Seymour Cocks, Labour MP for Broxtowe, to present a Private Member's Bill drafted by the NSACS which would abolish staghunting and coursing.

The Bill was debated at the end of February 1949; if it achieved a Second Reading majority it was expected a second Bill to ban foxhunting would be presented to the House and passed. It was the first major crisis for the sport, and the highest peak of publicity so far attained for the attack on hunting. The Society's limited resources produced many articles, speeches, and distribution of leaflets.

The BFSS's tiny staff, and volunteer supporters, were magnificent, since the Society was operating on very little funding at a time of national austerity. Communication within the UK was far more difficult before the computer age, and relatively expensive. The Society launched a major publicity and fund raising campaign from mid-1948, collecting over 100,000 members and a superb achievement of 1.2 million signatures for a 'Countryman's and Sportsman's Pledge.'

While the Second Reading took place a group of West Midlands hunting men came to London in horse boxes, and rode their horses through the West End, blowing hunting horns. They gained considerable publicity, and that evening were welcomed at the *Horse & Hound* Ball taking place in Park Lane. The group became known as the Piccadilly Hunt and remained active in the hunting battle for the rest of the century. Their excursion into direct protest tactics was the first of many.

The Second Reading debate was impassioned, and at times bizarre. Seymour Cocks presented his Bill rhetorically as an instrument of civilising his fellow Britons, stating that civilisation was 'but a small island in the vast ocean of cruelty, selfishness and insanity inherited from millions of years of sub-human ancestry.'

The most important, and clinching, speech in the debate came from Labour's Minister of Agriculture, Tom Williams. He pointed out that farmers wanted foxes to be controlled by hunting, not by fox destruction societies. The sport was embedded in the farming community; in isolated areas it was the only winter recreation available to farm workers and shepherds.

He asserted that neither trapping, snaring nor even expert shooting could guarantee the minimum level of suffering achieved by hunting with hounds in carrying out a necessary cull. 'Shooting certainly produces a much higher rate of prolonged suffering than does the instantaneous kill of the Hunt,' said the Minister.

He declared: 'The prohibitions in this Bill have no economic foundation, and the humanitarian aspects are greatly exaggerated, if not wholly misconceived.

'Since this party has been given the power to govern the nation, I believe we have a record of achievement of which we ought to be proud, and I hope we are not going to forfeit the goodwill we have so rightly earned to go down in history as a party anxious to abolish the pleasure of others.'

These words should have reverberated through all Labour's later attempts to abolish hunting, but they were conveniently forgotten or ignored by most of its back-benchers at the end of the century. The Cocks Bill in 1949 was defeated by 214 votes to 101, and a Prohibition of Foxhunting Bill was withdrawn.

Scott Henderson Report

Labour in March, 1949, appointed Mr J. Scott Henderson KC as Chairman of a committee to investigate the issue of alleged cruelty to wild and hunting animals.

The Scott Henderson Report, published in 1951, posed the question as to whether hunting causes more suffering than other forms of control – and it acquitted hunting with hounds easily. It was not a white-wash of all aspects of hunting: Scott Henderson urged the Masters of Foxhounds Association to clarify and tighten up its rules on digging foxes, and it recommended abolishing the practice of bolting foxes which had run to earth to be hunted further by hounds.

Neither of these recommendations was acted upon radically, and with hind-sight the continuing lack of clarity on these issues was regrettable. Some thirty years later hasty amendments were made in response to individual cases which received damaging publicity.

Scott Henderson approved otter hunting with reservations, but the sport was to be abandoned voluntarily by otter hunters from an entirely correct sporting perspective: the quarry species was not sustainable; a cull was not appropriate.

Not due to hunting, but to man's toxic pollution of rivers, otters were becoming extinct in England and Wales in the 1960s. Urban pollution poisoned otters; rural use of rivers for chemical sheep dips in some cases made otters infertile. Led by Capt. Ronnie Wallace, one of the leading Masters of Otter Hounds (Hawkstone 1946–68) as well as of Foxhounds, the sport of otter hunting with hounds voluntarily closed down, or switched to mink hunting, well before otters were made a protected species in 1978.

1966–75 Parliamentary Attacks

Although not directly the target, it was equally important for foxhunting that after the return of a Labour government in 1964, the League Against Cruel Sports decided to launch a parliamentary attack on hare coursing.

With the support of Prime Minister Harold Wilson, a Bill prepared by the League was debated on second reading in February, 1967. Thanks to the efforts of pro-hunting MPs it was talked out, and this was to be the fate of thirteen attempts to ban hare coursing through Private Members' Bills between 1966 and 1975. An anti-coursing Bill in 1976 was sent to a Select committee which investigated the sport thoroughly and rejected the Bill.

The huge success of the BFSS in the parliamentary arena was mainly due to its chairman from 1964–81, Marcus Kimball, Conservative MP for Gainsborough, nowadays the life-peer Lord Kimball. He was a master of Parliamentary tactics, and brilliantly orchestrated the use of procedures to foil all the Labour attempts to ban coursing, including three government Bills. The 1966–7 Bill was lost ludicrously when its own supporters talked it out by mistake.

Labour government was in power only with tiny majorities, and it was beset with major domestic economic issues and internal political feuds.

Many in the field sports world interpreted the political situation as 'safe' for hunting and they neglected to support the BFSS. Its membership slumped desperately from 36,000 in 1950 to about 25,000 by 1975. The Society entered a downward spiral where it was unable to fund the recruitment campaigns it so badly needed, and its low profile did not bring it sufficiently to the attention of those who should have been its natural supporters. The aristocratic and military links had served it well in the past, but the BFSS was perceived as 'the Conservative party on a horse', and therefore its chances of converting opinion in the Labour party were negligible. A much wider base was badly needed for the hunting cause.

Allowing the BFSS to decline severely in membership strength was a major mistake on the part of the field sports community. A strong BFSS during those years could have created an effective mass persuasion campaign in the 1970s to ward off the huge pressure from the animal rights lobby which was soon to emerge. A major overhaul and update of rules and disciplinary procedures by the ruling bodies of the hound sports would have been highly beneficial well before 1980.

BFSS in the Wilderness

The Thatcher years, followed by the Major government, made the likelihood of an imminent parliamentary ban even less likely. Yet there were plenty of signs of growing strength by the animal rights lobby.

Anti-hunting propaganda, if luridly enough presented, brought new members, donations and above all huge legacy income to leading animal welfare organisations. Some anti-hunting organisations proved aggressively litigious, and it became even more important that the BFSS was run at a higher professional level, with plenty of financial backing.

After its membership drop in the 'seventies the BFSS was in a public relations wilderness, hard pressed to increase its funding in order to respond to increasing attacks. It badly needed sufficient economic strength to be far more pro-active, rather than constantly reacting to attacks in the media.

Matters were so serious that in 1975 the BFSS launched a Fighting Fund, on the advice of the late Robert Dean, an associate of Raymond Brooks-Ward, the TV showjumping commentator, who had been appointed public relations consultant to the BFSS in 1969.

Some £250,000 was raised, largely by the efforts of the campaign leader, Major Bob Hoare, the genial former Master and huntsman of the Cottesmore. This sum, worth millions in to-day's currency, underwrote much needed improvement in BFSS performance, but the Society dare not splurge the Fund in national advertising campaigns. Professional advice and expertise in public relations, broadcasting ability, and business management, were sorely needed.

Hunting with hounds was a PR or advertising account which would have tested even the best professional agencies. Advice was often available free, but carrying it out was another matter because a full staff network capable of operating on such a difficult project could not be afforded.

In 1975 Dick Tracey, an ex-BBC radio current affairs reporter, became the full time public relations manager, working with one of the best Directors the BFSS ever had, Major-General Robin Brockbank. A shrewd and tough ex-soldier, Robin engaged in pro-active intelligence gathering as well as defensive measures. Tracy was effective but later became Tory MP for Surbiton and was a Minister for Sport in Mrs Thatcher's second government.

Peter Atkinson, from the London *Evening Standard*, succeeded Tracy and brought journalistic professionalism to his task. He was also en route to the Commons, and is a great supporter of hunting as MP for Hexham.

The BFSS ran a 'Public Affairs Committee', for many years chaired by Capt. Ronnie Wallace who was vice-chairman of the Society while he was chairman of the MFHA. This enabled him to maintain a bridge between foxhunting and its defence. Although not trained in journalism or public relations, he took a great interest in both, and was careful to co-opt on to his committee an extraordinary array of talents.

They ranged from the unconventional John McCrirrick, famous as the TV betting pundit in bizarre clothing on Channel 4, to Dr Charles Goodson-Wickes who was being groomed as the next BFSS Chairman.

Ronnie was an excellent listener, and he encouraged everyone to 'sound off' at length on the current problems facing hunting. Unfortunately it was not the best forum for carrying out ideas; action projects were planned more discreetly between Ronnie and whoever he had designated for the latest ploy.

No Cooperation from the Co-op

The League Against Cruel Sports meanwhile was led by a new, lively Director, Richard Course who had a flair for capturing media attention. Since a parliamentary victory was impossible during Conservative administrations, Course devised enterprising attacks from new directions. Much later he was to perform an ideological somersault, but for now he was a sharp thorn in the side of field sports.

After speaking at a Co-operative Party meeting in Croydon in 1979, Richard Course persuaded a senior figure in that party, a Mr Mani, to take up the hunting issue. The Co-op, through the Co-operative Wholesale Society, owned about 50,000 acres of prime farmland. A group was formed called 'Co-operators against Bloodsports', and its pressures resulted in the CWS banning hunting on all its land from the beginning of the 1982–3 season.

The Fernie Hunt immediately lost one of its three fixtures each week because the Co-op farmed about 5,000 acres near its northern boundary with Leicester City. The VWH in Wiltshire lost some hunting territory too, and the Co-op ignored the wife of one its own farm managers in that area who spoke out bravely in defence of hunting as part of local recreation and conservation.

The Co-op continued to allow organised shooting on its land. The BFSS led a vigorous battle against the hunting ban decision. I attended a protest meeting in a Brighton seafront hall, held to lobby the annual conference of the Co-operative movement taking place in the town.

The Co-op would not listen to representations, nor would it receive a huge, signed petition from many country people, including some of its customers. It was an interesting lesson that a large organisation, with a Socialist background, could be completely implacable in exercising its will. Many letters of protest, and requests from the BFSS that it could send speakers to Co-op meetings were totally rejected, or more frequently ignored.

In the Midlands the pro-hunting protest was especially vocal, with many hunting people declaring they would in future boycott Co-op shops. Some Co-op milkmen appeared in the media in defence of hunting, stating that they followed hounds by car as their recreation.

Mr Mani, to his credit, accepted an invitation to appear at the BFSS protest meeting, and said with a smile it was against his beliefs to take life; he had never seen hunting, but he had viewed a film on the subject and that was good enough. He smiled politely, gave a little bow, and walked out.

The BFSS meeting was in the circumstances quite jolly, mainly due to the contribution of the comedian Jimmy Edwards, Joint Master of the Old Surrey and Burstow.

Afterwards Ronnie Wallace and I paddled in the sea and then sat on Brighton beach. We reflected ruefully in our unlikely protest venue, that any attempt to apply democratic pressures on the Co-op was unlikely to succeed: it was a bad omen for the future. Money linked with politics was a powerful enemy. Somehow the hunting world would have to raise its game in the art of mass persuasion.

Keeping the subject off the public agenda was no longer an option. Although largely fought on the staghunting issue, there was a running battle in the nineteen eighties and nineties within the National Trust to achieve a hunting ban on its land on Exmoor. Both sides tried 'entryism', seeking to get supporters elected on to the National Trust's ruling council.

In April 1997 Professor Patrick Bateson, professor of animal behaviour and

Provost of King's College, Cambridge, published a report alleging unacceptable levels of 'cruelty through stress' to deer during the chase.

National Trust Ban

The National Trust immediately banned deer hunting with hounds on its land on Exmoor and the Quantocks. The Bateson report has since been challenged fundamentally by other authoritative scientists, but the ban remains in place. A spate of reports on hunting began to appear: first was the Phelps Report, hailed as the first independent report on hunting since the Scott Henderson report forty-six years previously. Richard Phelps, a retired public administrator, headed the enquiry with extensive veterinary and academic assistance.

They proposed the formation of a new, independent body to regulate and supervise hunting with hounds, similar to the Press Complaints Commission. Such a proposal was not taken up until the end of the century when the Independent Supervisory Authority for Hunting was formed. It is highly doubtful that this strengthening of self-regulation would have warded off attempts to ban the sport, but it was another matter of regret that it took such a long time for the hunting world to achieve it. The inadequate self-regulatory machinery of the Masters of Foxhounds Association was a factor in such cases as the Quorn video debacle which proved so damaging to the sport's public image.

County Councils – A Ban Too Far

Apart from the Co-op, Richard Course's other main line of attack – through local authorities – was unsuccessful in stopping hunting, but yielded copious publicity for the anti-hunting cause, and it cost the hunting world a great deal of time and money in mounting a defence. Such lessons were absorbed the hard way.

County Councils throughout England and Wales owned many thousands of acres of farmland, much of it let to tenant farmers. The LACS had supported Labour with a £20,000 donation in the 1979 General Election which the party lost, but Course was assisted in increasing his contacts with local Labour parties, and he was adopted as Labour candidate for Southgate in 1987. He addressed Labour meetings on the hunting issue, and issued many anti-hunting letters. His reward was the support of some Labour controlled councils to abolish hunting on council-owned land.

In most cases this was impossible to achieve immediately because farm tenancy agreements would not permit it until a tenant farmer retired, and a new tenancy contract could be drawn up banning hunting. Although the BFSS gave advice and guidance, the impetus for local campaigns against the council bans was provided by Hunts. This tested hunting's local resolve, and on the whole the response was encouraging.

A ban in Leicestershire, synonymous with hunting, was a prize much sought-after by Mr Course and his friends. Brian Fanshawe, then Joint Master of the Cottesmore, in 1982 chaired a vigorous campaign by the Shires packs to counter an attempt for a ban on 8,000 acres of council owned land by the strong Labour faction within a 'hung' Leicestershire County Council.

After intensive lobbying, all the county's foxhound and foot packs paraded past Leicestershire County Council's offices, gaining huge local and national publicity. After debate the hunting ban was defeated – but only by one vote.

Eleven years later the anti-hunting faction was victorious with a vote of forty-two to thirty-three. Anti-hunting Labour members were this time aided by Liberal Democrats and one Tory. Politicians who cared a fig for libertarianism might well have pondered the fact that the tenant farmers of the County Council, none of whom hunted on horseback, continued to welcome the Quorn and other packs on their land. Not one acre of land was barred to hunting as a result of the Leicestershire vote.

During over a decade of local government campaigning there were futile political gestures such as the banning of hunting in Islington and Lambeth. There were anti-hunting victories in Labour county strongholds such as Derbyshire, Humberside and Mid-Glamorgan, but pro-hunting votes were achieved in Oxfordshire, Lincolnshire, Dorset and many other areas, mainly with strong Conservative majorities.

Hunting learned that it was at times no more than a political football to be kicked about by rival parties. It also learned that some of its opponents hated hunting people more than they hated hunting. They expressed opposition in harsh invective, and indulged in an orgy of personality bashing.

They were not open to argument or persuasion; they were locked in an emotional, long outdated battle where they saw hunting people as upper-class stereotypes, ignoring the reality of a late twentieth century hunting field widely representative of all sections of society. The issues concerning conservation of the fox, hare or deer, seemed entirely lost in anachronistic class war.

One member of the Leicestershire County Council Labour group expressed the class warrior's view with force and colour, bawling during the Council's hunting debate: 'The real vermin are the men in red coats . . . I am here to make political decisions.' Later in the 1990s the BFSS achieved a High Court judicial review which found that a hunting ban imposed by local authorities could not be legitimate whilst the sport continued to be sanctioned in law.

Millions of pounds of ratepayers' money had been expended in attempting bans which could not be enacted by local authorities. Throughout the last decade of the century the struggle would move to the House of Commons where millions more pounds of taxpayers' money would be squandered on attempting to abolish a rural pastime still beloved by a significant number of law abiding Britons.

1992 McNamara Bill

A Conservative government, led by John Major, was in power in 1992, but a vice-president of the League Against Cruel Sports, Kevin McNamara, Labour MP for Kingston upon Hull North, had drawn high enough in the Private Members' ballot to get a second reading for a Bill to ban hunting 'with dogs'. Labour MPs gleefully gave him every support.

The RSPCA in 1976 had declared itself opposed to hunting with hounds in all forms and joined in the fight alongside the LACS and the International Fund for Animal Welfare. The IFAW had received huge funding after campaigning internationally against the culling of Canadian seal pups, and it was able to spend thousands of pounds on eye-catching national advertising opposing hunting. McNamara's Wild Mammals (Protection) Bill stood virtually no chance of becoming law, but the resultant high levels of publicity were invaluable for the anti-hunting lobby.

The BFSS handed over much of the direction of the pro-hunting battle to a newly formed Campaign for Hunting Steering Committee. It was chaired and materially supported by Edmund Vestey, Master of the Thurlow, who was to succeed Ronnie Wallace as MFHA Chairman.

A key member was Bill Andrewes, Joint Master of the Ludlow (1986–96), with a high level business background in communications as an executive of the Granada group, who was to emerge as a backroom shaker and stirrer within the BFSS, ultimately creating the Countryside Alliance of which he is deputy chairman. The Campaign for Hunting was to become a permanent unit inside the Alliance.

As usual they were hampered by lack of funds to match the advertising campaigns of the antis, but volunteer support in the regions was readily available. High point of the pro-hunting campaign was a rally of Hunts, attended by about 16,000 people, and many hounds, at the National Agricultural Centre, Stoneleigh, Warwickshire.

BFSS Chairman Sir Stephen Hastings, former Conservative MP with a distinguished war record, and Joint Master of the Fitzwilliam, gave a rousing address, accusing Labour of being 'riddled with hypocrisy on the hunting issue'.

The Conservative government's Environment Secretary, Michael Heseltine, wrote a trenchant newspaper article pointing out: 'Britain is now a predominantly urban country, with most people isolated from the cycle of life and death that is so much a natural part of country life. For this reason, the shock effect of the often carefully selected images used by the opponents of hunting is much more telling.'

He went on to defend hunting as conservationist, directly and indirectly responsible for 33,000 jobs nationwide – 'the equivalent of twenty-four Ravenscraig steelworks' which had closed down – and a form of culling offering least suffering to the quarry. Most telling was an exclusive article in *Horse & Hound* by Richard Course who had fallen out with his LACS colleagues and was no longer its Director.

He recanted his view that hunting should be abolished, stating: 'When I became fully and objectively appraised of all facts, and conversant with all related arguments it was impossible to avoid the conclusion that the "prosecution" – or the anti-hunt case – would not advance "fox welfare" and consequently could not be justified.'

The LACS had secured lurid media attention in the autumn of 1991 when the McNamara Bill was launched, by releasing video footage of the Quorn hunt cubhunting incident which was widely shown on national and regional television. The Second Reading debate of the McNamara Bill in February, 1992, was eventually a victory for hunting, the Bill being rejected. The voting margin, however, was only twelve votes – 187 to 175.

Sir Nicholas Bonsor MP, who had succeeded Stephen Hastings as BFSS Chairman, candidly admitted to the press afterwards that the margin was 'horribly tight'.

He reflected: 'This is just a battle in a long war, and we really must see that our defences, and our means of attack, are much improved.'

The victory was numerically achieved by fourteen members of John Major's Cabinet breaking with tradition to vote against a Private Member's Bill. The Prime Minister did not attend, and had earlier in the week side-stepped an MP's demand to know whether or not he supported foxhunting.

In the debate Angela Rumbold, the Home Office Minister, expressed the government's 'neutrality'on the hunting issue, but stated they would not support this 'flawed Bill' because it would be highly expensive to implement, and an unjustifiable burden for farmers. The government believed hunting was a matter for 'individual conscience' said the Minister. The vote was not on strict party lines. Hunting people noted with concern that twenty-six Conservative MPs had voted for a ban.

1995 The McFall Bill

Parliamentary battle was resumed in March 1995 when the Commons debated a Private Member's Bill proposed by John McFall, Labour MP for Dumbarton, a non-hunting constituency by the Clyde.

He admitted in the House he had never seen foxhunting with hounds in his life, but he decided to take up the anti-hunting cause, having been heavily briefed by the lobby against the sport. The BFSS plunged again into an under-funded press and broadcasting campaign, as usual outgunned by the cash available to the leading anti organisations to spend on advertising propaganda. Some £2 million was spent by the anti-hunting lobby this time, and they sent hundreds of computer printed cards bearing anti-hunting material to MPs.

The BFSS had new leadership which proved among the most effective in the Society's history: the new chief executive, Robin Hanbury-Tenison, was of an entirely different mould to the military types who had served the cause devotedly in the past, but tended to lack charisma and had little idea how to deal with modern media.

Hanbury-Tenison brought to the Society a formidable reputation as an explorer, author and passionate advocate for conservation of environment and wildlife. He is an excellent speaker, and is far less conventional in appearance and expression than the pinstripe suited gentlemen who had ruled the BFSS hitherto.

The new chairman, Charles Goodson-Wickes, was yet another Conservative MP, but he brought considerable depth of experience and contacts to his new role. He is an ex-Cavalry Medical Officer, a distinguished physician, and has a law degree. Although lacking advertising back-up, the hunting issue expounded

Leaders of the pro-hunting battle in the mid-nineties: Lord Mancroft, and BFSS chief executive Robin Hanbury-Tenison, deputy chairman Bill Andrewes, and chairman, Charles Goodson-Wickes.

in a refreshingly new manner by Hanbury-Tenison, was beginning to receive a far better press.

He appointed as the BFSS press officer, a formidable Australian lady, Janet George. Instead of upper-middle class mellifluous tones expressing the hunting view, the public heard pithy and memorable sound bites in an Aussie twang. Janet was highly effective in the cut and thrust of debate on radio and TV, seizing the brief moments to make telling points for hunting and other country sports.

Formerly a regional public relations officer for the BFSS in Shropshire, Janet clearly relished the London limelight, and used it well, but her relationship with the BFSS was to explode publicly after Hanbury-Tenison relinquished his all too brief three years as her boss.

The libertarian argument was appearing more frequently in the press. Paul Johnson, writing in the *Daily Express* warned the urban majority that 'it is no use protecting the countryside while ignoring the wishes of the people who live there'. He lamented that the UK countryside could easily become 'an empty theme park', and predicted that 'we could wake up one day to find the people of the countryside and its spirit gone for ever.'

The thriller writer Frederick Forsyth asked in *The Times*: 'Are we now to abolish a three hundred-years-old practice that employs 35,000 people, not on the basis of profound study, but after a shrill and slanted campaign by a small group?'

The BFSS backed up the press campaign with regional rallies at six sites throughout Britain. These gained some media attention, but experience has since shown that a couple of foxhounds in Parliament Square and a few red coats easily attracts far more attention from our metropolitan minded national press than thousands of honest, sincere people parading in the regions to protect their long held freedom and their way of life.

The political handling of the Bill was fraught with difficulty because it was an ill conceived mess. Clause 1 sought to ban the 'kicking, beating or torture' of wild animals. The remainder of the Bill banned hunting with hounds.

No-one wished to oppose Clause 1, so it was decided by pro-hunting MPs that they would all abstain on the Second Reading vote. This resulted in the first ever Commons vote against hunting, and it was nominally by a huge majority – 253 votes to nil. The complication over Clause 1 was barely understood by many in the general public, and therefore the bald message from Parliament was that a Bill to ban hunting had been carried by a huge vote.

This added undeserved fuel to the anti-hunting cause, and made further Parliamentary assaults even more likely. There were some in the hunting lobby who felt it would have been better if the Bill had been defeated in the Commons, with pro-hunting MPs explaining the problem over Clause 1 in the debate which would have necessitated major re-framing of the Bill in committee.

In fact, McFall agreed to drop the clauses banning hunting, and the greatly reduced Bill cleared the Commons in mid-July and was on its way to the Lords, but ran out of time. Charles Goodson-Wickes at the BFSS annual meeting warned of fresh attempts at legislation to ban hunting, and promised that large-scale rallies in London would probably have to be mounted in future protest campaigns.

Tony Blair, the recently appointed Labour leader, opportunistically promised that if elected he would make Parliamentary time available for a free vote on the hunting issue, and if the vote approved a ban, Labour would introduce a government Bill to achieve abolition – although he promised that shooting and fishing would be immune from a Labour administration.

Unfortunately, some in the shooting lobby accepted this promise. Labour's abolition of target shooting, and the extremist attitude of many of its back-benchers has since shattered much of the complacency remaining among shooters. There is ample reason to believe that reared game shooting, increasingly criticised for its 'huge bags of nearly tame birds', would be banned simply by amending existing legislation.

1997 Hyde Park Rally

Tony Blair's landslide General Election victory on 1 May 1997, giving 'New Labour' an overall majority of 172, was the start of a vastly increased programme of what can justifiably be described as political persecution of hunting people. There were now only 165 Conservatives in the House, but the Liberal Democrats had increased to forty-six, and most were anti-hunting.

The continual return to the issue by Parliament resulting in constant calls for funds and action in defence, and the uncertainties about the future of their sport and its ancillary trades, would be deemed entirely unjust and unconstitutional if aimed at, for example, an ethnic minority instead of a sporting minority. Blair's

The British Field Sports Society's Hyde Park Rally on 1 May 1997, organised by Robin Hanbury-Tenison and his team, was notable for superb speeches, thoroughly appreciated by a crowd of about 120,000.

manifesto included the commitment: 'Labour has advocated a free vote on the subject of hunting with hounds.'

Threats were leaked even before Election day that if it gained power Labour would immediately ban hunting on the Forestry Commission's 2.8 million acres, and half a million acres of Ministry of Defence land. Some eighty Hunts used such land through licences, and although there was much dragging of feet the usual licences were eventually issued for the 1997–8 season.

Counter threats by some major private landowners of non-cooperation with the MoD over military manoeuvres may have concentrated minds in Westminster, but the legality of such bans was also doubtful.

The force of the Labour election victory was emphasised for the BFSS when Charles Goodson-Wickes lost his apparently unassailable seat at Wimbledon where he had a majority of nearly 15,000 since 1987, and the same fate befell former chairman Sir Nicholas Bonsor, who had been Conservative MP for Upminster since 1983, and the best known foxhunting MP, Nick Budgen, who had held for the Conservatives Enoch Powell's old seat, Wolverhampton SW, since 1974.

With great panache, since he had not then received official permission from the Royal Parks authority, Robin Hanbury-Tenison announced a major BFSS Rally in Hyde Park for 10 July. Final written permission arrived only on 9 July, but Robin in public showed not a tremor of anxiety. Thanks largely to his leadership and imagination, plus the devotion of the excellent team he had assembled, the Rally was a huge success – uplifting for the morale of country people, and a significant marker for politicians that the field sports world was utterly determined in a pro-active defence, and would take to the streets in very large numbers.

Groups of country people marched to gain useful publicity for several weeks from the West Country, Wales and Scotland to Hyde Park, but most of the crowd of 120,000 who assembled, were conveyed in 1,000 coaches and twelve special trains superbly organised by the hunting community.

There were twenty-eight speakers, most significantly with representation from the main political parties. William Hague, the new Conservative leader was not a platform speaker, but he attended, and said he warmly supported the Rally's aims. Baroness (Ann) Mallalieu QC, distinguished barrister and Labour peeress, spoke eloquently for the hunting cause from her own experience hunting with the Bicester in Buckinghamshire and on Exmoor. She has served as a superb President of the Countryside Alliance, not shrinking from tart public criticism of her party's handling of the hunting issue.

Hunting horns and community singing made it a morale boosting occasion for

Baroness (Ann) Mallalieu QC, a Labour peeress, speaking for hunting at the Hyde Park Rally, 1997. She has since served as President of the Countryside Alliance.

Huntsmen at the launch of the Union of Country Sports Workers, 1997, in Westminster: *l. to r.* Peter Jones, Pytchley; Micky Wills, Grafton; John Fretwell, Stowe Beagles, Chairman UCW; John Holliday, Ledbury; George Adams, Fitzwilliam.

hunting people, assembled in warm sunshine. The crowd astonished the national press by their dignified and peaceful protest – and most of all by picking up all their litter before leaving Hyde Park. Already some field sportsmen were muttering that peaceful protests were a waste of time. They predicted Labour would only take notice of militancy.

The BFSS adopted a policy continued by the Countryside Alliance, that the general public would soon lose all sympathy with people who used violent protest in favour of a sport or recreation. Blocking motorways, or otherwise inconveniencing the general uncommitted public, were firmly ruled out by the Alliance.

1997–8 The Foster Bill

Michael Foster, the new Labour MP for Worcester, drew first place in the Private Members' Bill ballot in the summer of 1997. The Labour government briefed journalists that it did not want an anti-hunting Bill so early in the new Parliament. It would consume much needed time for far more important Bills. Tony Blair, asked in a TV interview for his view on foxhunting, remarked: 'Most people think it is particularly vicious'. The Prime Minister's wife, Cherie Blair, was known to be firmly anti-hunting, and it is believed by many that Mrs Blair is a major influence in maintaining Labour's obsession with the subject. I find this hard to believe, since there is much evidence the Prime Minister has been keen to lob the issue into 'the long grass', and it was pressure from his back-benchers which has repeatedly brought the hunting to the fore.

All the evidence from Labour's back-benches in recent years is that no encouragement from Number 10 has been necessary in igniting a fierce desire by a group of MPs in the Parliamentary Labour Party to hunt the hunting people to an eventual 'kill' of their sport. Echoes of the old class-war resound in their fulminations against hunting people.

Michael Foster, a keen angler, apparently acceded to the blandishments of the animal rights lobby and went ahead with his Wild Mammals (Hunting with Dogs) Bill. He could see no connection between fishing and hunting in animal welfare terms he told the House of Commons.

It was never likely to become law because the Blair cabinet decided that it would not be given government time. Nevertheless, the tide was running strongly for the animal rights lobby. They believed Labour would have little option but to bring in government legislation later if the Foster Bill appealed to a sub-stantial majority of the House. Blair did not wish to embark on a lengthy tussle with the House of Lords so early in his administration.

The International Fund for Animal Welfare (IFAW) formed a coalition in support of the Bill with the RSPCA and LACS. IFAW before the General Election gave a donation of over £1 million through its charitable trust, the Political Animal Lobby, to the Labour Party, and £4,000 to the Conservative Party's Animal Welfare Group. The difference in donation levels speaks for itself. The lobbying operation in support of the Bill was estimated to have cost the anti-hunting organisations some £5 million.

The Shires Hunts staged a mass meet at Melton Mowbray on 27 November 1997, the day before the Foster Bill was to get its Second Reading debate. Mr Vini Faal, chairman of a terrier and lurcher club, was one of the speakers. He quoted a Welsh ex-miner who had said: 'The Tories took away my living; now the Labour Party wants to take away my life.'

Ann Mallalieu told the press she had 'never seen such anger and determination among country people as has been aroused by this Bill. Millions of people are saying they do not want to live in a country which is governed by majority dictation.' MPs spoke on the Bill for five hours in a debate which produced far more heat than light.

It was a gift for the sketch writers; one of them, Simon Hoggart, remarked: 'Foxhunting is a gut, emotional issue. You loathe it or you don't. It is not suscep-tible to rational argument. You can't debate it as if it were interest rates.' Hoggart's verdict on former accountant Michael Foster's speech was that it was a 'turkey' – 'unfortunately you can't address the Commons as if they were a group of promising trainee accountants.'

The speeches which made most impact were topsy-turvy politically – a superb plea for tolerance and understanding of hunting from the Labour benches, bravely delivered by Kate Hoey, Labour MP for urban Vauxhall; and an attack on hunting from the Tory side, thundered across the House by Ann Widdecombe, Conservative MP for the more rural Maidstone and the Weald.

Kate Hoey made many Tory MPs across the floor roar with approval when she defended hunting staunchly and declared: 'I cannot understand why a country that prides itself on its pluralism and tolerance . . . can be so prejudiced against its rural inhabitants.' Miss Hoey told MPs: 'If this Bill is passed we are going to make criminals of many law-abiding citizens. This is bad legislation. It is an intolerant Bill. It will do nothing to stop cruelty and it will ruin the countryside.'

Similar views to Miss Hoey's on the need to respect minorities, were expressed by Alan Beith for the Liberal Democrats, but most of his colleagues voted for a ban.

After a brief appointment on Labour's front bench as Minister of Sport, Miss Hoey was later consigned again to the back-benches, and has since continued to fight staunchly for the hunting cause despite the unpopularity of her views with most of her fellow Labour MPs.

Ann Widdecombe asked: 'Is hunting so wrong that we wish to abolish it? If it is, all else flows from that – we don't need to be concerned about liberties to do wrong . . . Prolongation of terror is wrong. Those who praise it, when there are alternatives which are already widely practised, do wrong.

'Yes, the scenes of a hunt are splendid – they are all over my dining room curtains – but they are powerful scenes of Old England, and in Old England, not modern Britain, they belong.'

Unpopular though Miss Widdecombe's speech was with the hunting fraternity, I have often thought that by putting the alleged cruelty issue at the top of her complaints against the sport she provided a warning that hunting people themselves should place their defence on the cruelty issue much higher up their agenda.

Loss of jobs, damage to the rural culture, and libertarianism feature in every public debate on the subject – but if the cruelty issue can be disposed of satisfactorily what other rational reason can any government summon up to justify abolition?

Michael Heseltine made one of the best speeches for hunting, pointing out forcefully that the move to make foxhunting a criminal offence should be seen as part of an agenda which would eventually move through shooting and fishing.

After five hours of debate, the Foster Bill received a massive 260 majority voting for the Bill – 411 MPs in favour of abolition, and 151 against.

The government said it would consider the hunting issue again in the light of the Foster vote. Few could doubt the subject would come before the House again, this time with government backing.

Countryside Alliance is Born

Early in 1998 the BFSS endeavoured to widen its power base by transforming itself into the Countryside Alliance, a far better title. A firm case for the new name was made by a new co-opted member of the BFSS Board, John Jackson, much supported by Bill Andrewes.

The new organisation continued to benefit from the zestful leadership of Robin Hanbury-Tenison. Bill Andrewes became its invaluable Deputy Chairman. Some of his radical views on the way to defend hunting caused consternation among some traditionalists, unfortunately including Ronnie Wallace.

I heard Bill inform a slightly aghast audience of hunting people in Melton Mowbray: 'A large percentage of the general public doesn't like you. It thinks you are a bunch of rich, privileged, arrogant people. That is an inaccurate stereo-type, and we have to change it – we have to show that hunting crosses many social and economic boundaries in the countryside.'

The Alliance was born early in 1998, merging the BFSS with the Countryside Movement and an organisation called the Countryside Business Group. Neither of the latter organisations, launched with much hope and financial backing as wider bases of support for many aspects of country life including field sports, had been successful as stand-alone bodies. This probably reflected the fragmented nature of rural interests, with so many existing bodies, such as the Council for the Preservation of Rural England, already representing aspects of the rural cause.

First Countryside March

Hanbury-Tenison could not summon up many millions of pounds, but he could rely on many thousands of people who would be willing to walk the streets of London to defend their way of life. The Alliance launched its first Countryside March on Sunday, 1 March 1998 – timed for the Report stages of the Foster Bill. Beacons were lit by hunting people on hill-tops across Britain.

Trains and busloads of people trekked to the capital in remarkably benign weather; Robin Hanbury-Tenison was not only a good general, he was the sort Napoleon preferred – a lucky one. The march was resoundingly successful: over 285,000 people came from the countryside to astonish the capital in an orderly, peaceful procession from the Embankment to Hyde Park.

General dissatisfaction with government policies on many rural issues were on view, but a huge majority of placards made it plain that hunting was the over-riding concern. *The Guardian*, anything but a traditional supporter of hunting, published an article by Matthew Engel whose verdict was: 'The Countryside March was a phenomenally successful piece of politics.

'The extent of it became clear only if you went back to the start, and realised that people were still arriving, if anything in bigger numbers than ever, four hours after the first walkers set off.'

Engel observed: 'For years the hunters have been the hunted, politically, but their unexpectedly clever campaign has enabled them to draw away from the jaws of baying MPs. Master of Foxhounds Blair must now be desperate to find ways of calling the dogs off.'

The government had attempted to explain the march by saying it had been 'hi-jacked' by Conservatives and the 'blood sports lobby'.

After the march this line was abandoned, and the Environment Minister Michael Meacher adopted a more conciliatory tone, with the full support of Downing Street. He promised that government would in future take more trouble to listen to the concerns of rural people, and accepted that hunting was the core issue of the marchers.

The success of the march was all the more necessary because fresh perils were about to erupt within and without the field sports world.

1998 Alliance in Crisis

To the immense loss of the Alliance, Robin Hanbury-Tenison resigned early in 1998 as he had planned, after three years as Chief Executive. Janet George applied for the job. The Alliance Board instead appointed Edward Duke, a wealthy Yorkshire businessman with a passion for hunting; he specialised as a 'company doctor' in rescuing loss-making firms.

The Alliance was reported to be paying him a £200,000 a year package, and this figure upset more than a few who had worked for the cause for many years for a pittance, or nothing. The appointment was to plunge the Alliance into crisis.

Janet George and some other heads of departments did not approve of Duke's management style nor methods, and after internal dissension Janet George was sacked as head of press and public relations, having declined to resign. She did not go quietly; the story broke widely in the national press, and caused some damaging divisions within the Alliance at a critical time.

After only twelve weeks in office, Edward Duke resigned, stating he had decided he was the wrong person for the job; the Alliance needed a campaigner, not a businessman to lead it – a job for which he was not qualified. *The Daily Telegraph* said Duke had been 'dignified in defeat', and there had been 'often untruthful whispering against him'.

The Foster Bill was allowed by the government to fall at the end of the spring session in 1998, but the threat was growing that the Labour government would be forced to take action to placate backbencher opinion. This was vociferously led by such arch abolitionists as Tony Banks, Labour MP for Newham and Gerald Kaufman, Labour MP for Manchester Gorton.

The task of restoring morale and leadership to the Countryside Alliance fell to two individuals of a more radical mould: as Chief Executive, Richard Burge, former Director of the Zoological Society, and a supporter of the Labour party; and as Chairman, John Jackson, a Fabian Society member in his seventies, Chairman of the West End solicitors Mishcon De Reya, Chairman of Ladbroke's the bookmakers and holding a diversity of non-executive directorships. Bill Andrewes had much to do with both appointments and thoroughly welcomed the change in emphasis at the top of the field sports world.

Jackson has always made it plain that his over-riding aim is to preserve a diverse British countryside and its wildlife. It was fervently hoped in hunting circles that these two men stood a better chance of building bridges with New Labour. Both were to learn that dealing with dissension and misunderstandings within their own ranks at times could be even more severe a challenge than fighting the external war against the anti-hunting lobby.

It is highly doubtful that their political views made any appreciable difference in dealing with government. Both were to deliver stinging public rebukes to the Labour government for its mishandling of the hunting issue.

John Jackson brought tough-minded resolution to the political battle, backed

Lord Kimball, former BFSS chairman and Richard Burge, charismatic
chief executive of the Countryside Alliance 1998–2003.

by intellectual force, invaluable legal experience, and a keen tactical sense. He
delivers detailed political analysis in measured tones and thoroughly enjoys the
political arena. As an unpaid, elected Chairman, he gives a huge amount of time
and commitment, but although he makes valiant efforts to attend meetings
outside London, these are sometimes restricted by his other commitments and
he suffers the complaint, however unfair, facing most of his predecessors that he
is too remote from the grass roots. Recently he has given regular nationwide
conference telephone calls to address this problem.

Jackson behind the scenes is a forceful chairman who adheres to his chosen
path of action, although he will listen to people he respects, notably the Alliance's
high powered committee of hunting, shooting and fishing barristers who give
their time and expertise to the cause.

Burge is at his best with a large audience; a charismatic performer who
summons passion as well as eloquence, and he travelled the length and breadth
of the United Kingdom. He was criticised by some for not running the Alliance
on a tight enough budget, but he claimed there had never been a more critical
time when millions needed to be spent in the defence of hunting.

Both leaders have suffered to some extent from endeavouring to justify to the
hard core hunting enthusiasts the need to engage in lengthy dialogue with a
government apparently hostile to hunting, and to avoid confrontational direct
action which might be law-breaking.

'The trouble with the strategy of playing a long game is that your own side gets
restive; you can't always give the troops enough to do,' Jackson has remarked.

Attempts to widen the focus of the Alliance to include agricultural and

European issues have also been misunderstood by some members at times, partly because satisfactory machinery for including the wider membership in policy making in these areas has been difficult to achieve.

The need constantly to ask members for funds in an apparently never ending war, to fill major deficits in the Alliance accounts, and has inevitably provoked irritation or worse among some members.

The hunting war hotted up after Tony Blair appeared on late night television on 8 July 1999, answering questions off the cuff. He promised legislation to ban hunting with hounds 'as soon as possible'. Downing Street announced that government would soon announce its plans on the hunting issue.

The Independent newspaper described Mr Blair's remarks as 'fundamentally illiberal' and 'hypocritical, motivated by political rather than animal welfare concerns.'

In September, 1999, the Alliance organised a demonstration in which 16,000 supporters marched to the Labour Party Conference in Bournemouth. It was extremely well organised by a keen hunting man, James Stanford, who farms in Dorset and has an impressive background in industry and charity, including seven years as Director General of the Leonard Cheshire organisation.

Over 100,000 country people attended regional Countryside Alliance rallies in October and November, 1999. It could not be said that the Alliance was operating at a low profile. The means of communicating with, and activating members, was hugely improved by the regular and emergency use of e-mail messages.

John Jackson wrote an article for *The Times* in September calling for a public inquiry into hunting. Apparently, the government was listening: on 11 November Jack Straw announced a Committee of Inquiry into 'Hunting with Dogs', chaired by the former Treasury Permanent Secretary, Lord (Terry) Burns.

1999–2000 The Burns Report

The Burns Inquiry was charged with reporting on the impact of hunting on the rural economy, agriculture and pest control, the social and cultural life of the countryside, management and conservation of wildlife, and animal welfare.

The hunting world noted gloomily that Burns was instructed to report on 'the consequences for these issues of any ban on hunting dogs, and how any ban might be implemented.' So was Burns simply the executioner's assistant, or would the Report be instrumental in saving hunting by presenting the unvarnished truth about its role in the countryside?

Some on the hunting side had little doubt that Labour was simply providing a justification of 'consultation' for the abolition course on which most of its MPs were hell-bent . Burns was not asked to recommend whether hunting should or should not be banned, nor to find a compromise solution. Blair was far too canny to have his hands tied by a firm recommendation that a ban would be inappropriate and unjust; he was well aware of the political need to placate the many backbenchers who would not be susceptible to any rational recommendation from Burns. It was a political issue, not one of animal welfare.

It was decided by the Alliance that whatever doubts existed about the

Machiavellian terms of reference, hunting would make strenuous efforts to provide Burns with every scrap of information needed. There was every good reason for keeping consultations going as long as possible. John Jackson was proving an astute tactician, and well knew the value of time as a delaying weapon against unwanted legislation. The inquiry only concerned England and Wales because a devolved Scotland could make its own decision on hunting – and was soon to do so with disastrous consequences.

The Alliance spent about £1 million in providing an expertly presented detailed case to Lord Burns and his colleagues, Dr Victoria Edwards, Professor Sir John Marsh, Lord Soulsby and Professor Michael Winter. They travelled widely, heard verbal evidence from packed seminars, visited Hunt establishments, and commissioned research papers. Even though they made no recommendation, the tone and content of the Burns Report, published in June 2000, could not possibly justify a ban to anyone prepared to read it with an open mind.

Crucially it pointed out that other forms of control of foxes, hares and deer also involved suffering and it could not be proved that hunting was the worst method on welfare terms. The Committee noted a 'lack of firm scientific evidence about the effect on the welfare of a fox of being closely pursued caught and killed above ground by hounds. We are satisfied, nevertheless, that this experience seriously compromises the welfare of the fox.' Burns made a similar comment on the effects of digging out and shooting a fox.

The anti-hunting lobby launched a campaign interpreting these findings as concluding cruelty, but when Lord Burns and Lord Soulsby were tackled on this point in a later debate in the House of Lords both denied their report meant that hunting was cruel, as there was insufficient verifiable data or evidence to decide the point.

The Report surmised that if there was a ban on hunting, 'many farmers and landowners would resort to a greater degree than at present to other methods to control the numbers of foxes. We cannot say if this would lead to more, or fewer foxes being killed than at present.'

The Report pointed out: 'None of the legal methods of fox control is without difficulty from an animal welfare perspective. Both snaring and shooting can have serious adverse welfare applications.'

A government contemplating a ban could get no substantial comfort from Burns on the likelihood of achieving a law which could be adequately and fairly implemented.

The Burns Report said there could be challenges under the European Convention of Human Rights, and warned 'implementing a ban might well pose some enforcement difficulties for the police'.

This point was later to be taken up by several chief constables who said they did not have adequate manpower to monitor and police illegal forms of hunting after a ban.

Burns said 'consideration should be given to whether any ban would be manifestly unjust, bearing in mind the activities caught and not caught by it.' They recommended against using banning laws only in certain regions. This would rule out proposals for allowing foot packs to hunt foxes only in upland sheep rearing areas.

Anyone who knows the countryside's hierarchy of unofficial hunters of wild life using snares, guns, illegal traps and poisons, and spades and terriers, is aware of the huge dangers of anarchy in culling foxes by other means, totally un-monitored, which would prevail after a selective ban on hunting with hounds.

Without hunting's rules and codes of conduct, a virtual extermination of foxes would all too easily prevail, with no curtailment of killing vixens and litters during the breeding season, and scarce chance of police effectively controlling freelance terrier and digging work. Currently all Hunt terrier men are licensed and strictly bound to MFHA rules. The influence of Hunts and hunting people in owning fox coverts has huge implications for the welfare of foxes during the breeding season.

2000 Watson Bill – A Ban in Scotland

On 1 March 2000, Lord Watson's Bill to ban 'hunting with dogs' in Scotland was introduced in the Labour dominated newly devolved Scottish Parliament – incredibly, amid the welter of domestic issues, the first Private Member's Bill to come before it.

Scotland had only ten packs of foxhounds, but they included some of the oldest and best supported Hunts in the United Kingdom. Ironically Lord ('Call me Mike') Watson of Invergowrie, was appointed Minister for Tourism, Culture and Sport.

There was scathing comment by numerous commentators in the Scottish press about the grotesque priorities of Scotland's new rulers. The Bill was widely described as a play-back of old Left wing class-war revenge politics, unworthy of a new Parliament pledged to represent the whole of Scotland.

Katie Grant, columnist in *Scotland on Sunday* demanded: 'How have we allowed a few lumpen ex-councillors from the discredited Labour politburos of the central belt to circumscribe our lives?

'The tyranny of the majority rules supreme. Scotland has been failed by her leaders. Had our MSPs done their duty, they would have expressed their dislike of hunting, and in the name of freedom and democracy voted for its continuance; the Scottish Parliament would have grown up.'

The Scottish Parliament's new systems entailed the Bill being considered by its Rural Development Committee. The verdict of that Committee was that the Bill was so badly drafted it should be scrapped.

In September 2001 the Scottish Parliament nevertheless voted by eighty-three to thirty-four to proceed with the Bill which curiously sought to ban 'mounted foxhunting, hare coursing and fox baiting'. Wryly, the hunting community noted that it was more politically correct to hunt a fox if you followed hounds on foot, but not on horseback.

Earnest zealots in the Scottish Parliament clearly were not aware that foot followers of hounds enjoy the day too – and there is no evidence the fox cares how the followers of the hunt are transported. Yet again, the quarry of the banning brigade was 'those men in red coats on their high horses'.

The Scottish Countryside Alliance, heavily backed by the English and Welsh

CA held a protest march through the heart of Edinburgh in December, 2001, attended by some 15,000 field sportsmen, and led by a brave skirl of bagpipes.

The CA called it the 'March on the Mound', and again accepted the services of James Stanford as Director. His blend of good cheer and steely organisation produced an exceptionally well organised protest. He managed to get the huge procession to march past a hospital in absolute silence to avoid disturbing patients. Once again hunting people showed they were not prepared to inconvenience the general public in making their plea for tolerance and understanding of their sport.

Ann Mallalieu gave a superb rallying address in support of 'your fight against bigotry in the face of facts, intolerance against a bully who targets a minority, and those who would use their power in office not to do good, but to force their own prejudice on others . . .'

Some of the placards carried in the march were less polite about Lord Watson. There were some humorous ones from England, such as 'Norfolk Peasants Christmas Outing', and 'Save a Cow – Eat a Vegetarian.' There were representatives from at least nine overseas hunting communities.

Edinburgh police commented on the 'extremely orderly' march, but earlier that week a group of people calling themselves 'Rural Rebels' had blockaded the city centre, the Forth Road Bridge and major roads in the Borders.

Some were showing they were tired of peaceful protest – and this was to be reflected south of the Border soon. The fringes of the field sports world were beginning to split in favour of direct action. The Countryside Alliance backed a legal attempt to overturn the banning Bill, but Scotland's Court of Session at the end of July, 2002, dismissed a call for a judicial review, and agreed with the Scottish Executive that compensation should not be paid to rural workers who lost their jobs.

So badly bungled was the drafting of the Scottish Bill that foxes have continued to be hunted by nine Scottish Hunts operating as gun packs. The Dumfriesshire decided to call it a day, and not to operate as a gun pack. The decision was largely that of Sir Rupert Buchanan-Jardine, senior Joint Master of the Dumfriesshire since 1950, and owner of their distinctive black and tan hounds which were created by his father, Jock Buchanan-Jardine as a breed through skilful selective breeding.

The Scottish Bill left a loophole that 'dogs' could be used to flush out a quarry if it was to be shot; this was to ensure that game shooting, involving pointers and retrievers, could continue in Scotland.

Under the new hunting system shooters, some using quad bikes, are positioned at the end of draws, and hounds followed by mounted hunt staff and followers, find foxes in covert, hunting them across country towards the guns.

Some Hunts have reported greatly increased tallies of foxes killed by this method, and there have also been complaints that it can involve greater suffering for foxes wounded but not killed by the guns, and hounds then have to be used to ensure a 'mercy kill'. Mike Rumbles, a Liberal Democrat MSP was reported as saying: 'The public perception was that Parliament was passing a Bill to stop foxhunting in its entirety. In practice it is a disaster. It is the worst piece of legislation the Parliament has passed, and it makes us look stupid.'

Others have predicted the Scottish attempt at abolishing foxhunting will keep lawyers in work for years. No matter how carefully drawn up, any banning Bill in England and Wales allowing the culling of foxes by other means would offer the same workload for the legal procession. Shooters use dogs too.

The Scottish Countryside Alliance engaged in protracted and hugely expensive legal appeals against the Protection of Wild Mammals (Scotland) Act. Judges at the Court of Session in Edinburgh on 3 June 2004, dismissed the appeal, stating: 'our own conclusion is that there was adequate factual information to entitle the Parliament to conclude that foxhunting inflicted pain upon the fox, and that there was an adequate and proper basis on which it could make the judgement that the infliction of such pain in such circumstances constituted cruelty.'

The Alliance in London commented that no parallels could be drawn between the situation in Scotland and that in England and Wales. There were major differences between the legislation in Scotland and the Westminster banning bill. The 'serious human rights implications of the Westminster bill' remained.

The Middle Way

An attempt at a constructive move within the House of Commons was the formation in May, 1998, of a ' Middle Way ' Group of MPs seeking compromise on the hunting issue. Kate Hoey, who had spoken so eloquently for hunting, represented Labour in the Group, joining forces with Lembit Opik, Liberal Democrat MP for Montgomeryshire, and Peter Luff, Conservative MP for Mid-Worcestershire.

Some Labour Ministers, including Jack Straw, then Home Secretary, were believed to be in favour of a compromise whereby hunting could continue under a licensing system run by an independent authority. The Middle Way Group opposed the Foster Bill as 'draconian', and entirely inappropriate. Michael Foster dismissed the Group as pro-hunters who merely wanted to endorse 'hunting for toffs', a tell-tale class reference.

Middle Way had its origins in 'Wildlife Network', a body seeking constructive compromise formed by another 'born again' former chief executive of the League Against Cruel Sports, James Barrington, who had rebelled against the policy of complete abolition on the hunting issue. He held talks with hunting bodies on compromise issues, and had departed the League as a result.

After publication of the Burns Report, the Middle Way Group published its own solution: hunting and coursing would be permitted only by licence, under strict approval and supervision of a new hunting authority appointed by the Home Secretary. Anyone caught hunting without permission would be subject to criminal charges and fines up to £5,000. Hunts breaching rules would face bans or suspensions.

The Middle Way Group expected the Commons to vote for an outright ban, and that the Lords would send the Middle Way option back to the Commons. The scheme found little or no favour with the Countryside Alliance and the hunting organisations. They felt it was impractical, and would enable a government to make hunting impossible in a sporting format, by imposing any severe conditions it wished.

The devil would be in the detail. It seemed to be a political rather than a practical 'solution' to an animal welfare problem they denied existed. Masters of Hounds believed their sport would be suffocated by the Middle Way proposals, instead of being axed by a total ban.

The Middle Way option had the approval of Home Secretary Jack Straw and several other senior Ministers in Blair's cabinet, including Robin Cook. The unofficial advice to the hunting community coming from certain civil servants in Whitehall was: 'Take this option – it's the best you will get under a Labour government.'

2001 Government's Optional Bill

In September 2000 the Countryside Alliance again organised protests at Labour's annual conference, this time at Brighton. Inside the conference hall Deputy Prime Minister John Prescott infamously condemned the protestors, referring contemptuously to their 'contorted faces'. This seemed glaringly inappropriate from a leader of a Socialist party believing itself to be democratic, and based on protest on social issues early in the twentieth century.

Jack Straw confirmed to the House in December 2000, that he would indeed support a compromise licensing solution for hunting. He said in the New Year MPs would have a free vote on three mutually exclusive options in a Government optional Bill. These offered:

- Self regulation by Hunts, supervised by an independent authority; an option drafted by the Countryside Alliance.
- The compromise Middle Way formula described above, where control was exercised by a government appointed authority.
- An outright ban.

There had been twenty-two attempts in Parliament to deal with hunting through Private Members' Bills. Now a government was directly involved. The darkest hours for the hunting world were signalled. Nevertheless, the Home Secretary's announcement caused fury among Labour backbenchers who believed they had government support for a total ban.

And while Straw made his announcement, field sportsmen gathered in Parliament Square to bay their disapproval. Tony Blair could hardly have imagined that any action on hunting was to be a vote winner.

Alun Michael MP, former Welsh Secretary, and MP for Cardiff South and Penarth, was the junior DEFRA Minister given the poisoned chalice of 'dealing with the hunting question'. He was well known to oppose hunting, having voted against it at every opportunity, but he promised to follow a policy based on ' principle and evidence'.

All the other DEFRA Ministers had anti-hunting voting records, and one of them, Elliot Morley, is a former vice-president of the League Against Cruel

Sports. Lord Donoughue, Minister of Food and Farming in Labour's former Ministry of Agriculture, strongly opposes a hunting ban, but he resigned before Blair's reshuffle in July 1999. Bernard Donoughue had forged many friendships and alliances in the horse and hunting communities.

Margaret Beckett, chief DEFRA Minister has distanced herself as much as possible from the heat of the hunting battle, but she is certainly an anti, and earned scorn when she remarked publicly that she 'could not see that hunting had anything to do with social life in the countryside'.

Alun Michael's hunting role was a crass mistake by Tony Blair and his advisers, probably born of ignorance and disinterest in rural affairs. At the same time that he was earning mountainous levels of rural unpopularity in the hunting battle, Mr Michael was endeavouring to carry through major changes for which he needed cooperation in rural areas. He could not attend rural functions without attendance by angry field sportsmen protesting on the hunting issue.

In his new, much needed role of 'Minister for the Horse' he was engaged in a worthwhile project to bring about essential development in the British horse industry. Equestrianism's close links with mounted hunting, poisoned the waters considerably for Mr Michael, and made trust and cooperation difficult for some. It was a pity because the Minister worked hard to help the horse industry.

On 18 January 2001, the well known arguments were aired yet again on the three options open to the House of Commons. Self-regulation was rejected by an emphatic 399 to 155 votes, a majority of 244; the Middle Way option was backed by 182 MPs, almost twice as many as had been predicted, although it was heavily defeated by a 200 majority; and the option of an outright ban was backed by 387 to 174, a majority of 213.

Tony Blair was assumed by some observers to be looking for an escape route to avoid imposing a ban on hunting, but the 'will of the House' remained strong for just such a course of action. Hunts across Britain held mass meets; the Countryside Alliance decided it was time to take to the streets again, and plans were announced for a second Countryside March on Sunday, 18 March.

On 22 February 2001, catastrophe hit the British countryside with the start of a nationwide outbreak of foot and mouth disease which was to rage for most of the year.

Hunting voluntarily ceased immediately, and very soon the Alliance made the inevitable decision that its Countryside March would have to be postponed. It was a highly expensive decision because thousands of pounds had already been spent to make it the biggest ever. Richard Burge delivered a 'calling card' in March to Parliament which showed that at least half a million people had indicated they would have joined the Alliance's Liberty and Livelihood March.

The Countryside Alliance mounted an intensive letter writing campaign to peers, and the pro-hunting lobby in the Lords worked immensely hard to ensure that the Hunting Bill would be frustrated in the upper House.

The Hunting Bill was debated in the Committee Stage in the House of Lords on 26 March 2001. The peers voted for the continuance of hunting by voluntary self-regulation with a majority of 141 (249 to 108); they rejected the Middle Way with a majority of 80 (122 to 202); and rejected an outright ban even more decisively with a majority of 249 (68 to 317).

The libertarian issue was clearly a decisive factor in the Lords, and it was a major triumph for the Alliance that its lobbying, its briefing of peers, and its influence of public opinion through the press on this issue had been so effective.

John Gardiner, who leads the Alliance's lobbying activities is a modest, like-able man with an air of sweet reasonableness. His political expertise is immense, and MPs and peers have paid warm tribute to the high standards of the briefings they receive from Gardiner's office. His appointment as a Joint Deputy Chief Executive under Simon Hart has strengthened the Alliance's top team.

Gardiner is anything but the traditional image of a blimpish hunting man, but he is passionate about his hunting and has made a great contribution as Chairman of the largest amalgamated Hunt, the Vale of Aylesbury with Garth and South Berks.

Great efforts were made to restrain Alliance members from disruptive demon-strations. The Alliance continued to insist it wished hunting people to be perceived as peaceful, law-abiding people striving to protect their rights only by legitimate means.

Tony Blair's partially 'reformed' House of Lords saw a substantial number of Labour peers among those who voted against a ban. There was agonising by some in the pro-hunting lobby that it would have been better if the Lords had plumped for the Middle Way option.

Lord (Bernard) Donoughue, who was senior policy advisor to Harold Wilson's 'kitchen cabinet' in the 1970s, was scathing about the Conservative peers' decision to vote against the Middle Way. Donoughue wrote in his auto-biography published in 2003 (*The Heat of the Kitchen*, Politico's): 'Even more inexplicably, the Countryside Alliance, established to preserve hunting, encouraged the Tories to vote against the Middle Way, resisting the common sense arguments of my Conservative friends William Astor and David Willoughby de Broke that they should take the only hope of preserving hunting in reality on offer.'

Donoughue recalled 'I could not believe my eyes when I saw senior Tories in the Chamber physically dissuading their fellow peers from moving to vote for the Middle Way.' Afterwards he pointed out to the Countryside Alliance leadership that they had 'no negotiating position' with government on hunting. He believed the only hope of protecting hunting from the zealots in the Commons was the Middle Way because Number 10 'just might be attracted to it as a way through in the coming election . . . I sensed that the hunting cause had suffered a serious and possibly fatal self-inflicted wound.'

Whether or not Donoughue's argument was valid, yet again a hunting Bill was to bite the dust as Labour ran out of time, on this occasion due to the disso-lution of Parliament for the delayed 2001 Election on 7 June, but the issue was to return to the Lords all too soon.

2002 Summer of Discontent

Tony Blair, his party returned to power with a majority of 166, again embarrass-ingly large, announced in the Queen's Speech 'a free vote to take place on the future of hunting with dogs'.

Political correspondents noted caustically that no other rural initiatives were contained in the Speech indicating a very low priority for the countryside's major problems after the foot and mouth crisis.

Plans to press ahead with hunting legislation in the autumn of 2001 were delayed by a rush of emergency laws to tackle terrorism after New York's 11 September World Trade Centre catastrophic air attack.

A world struggle against terrorism failed to put Labour's keen anti-hunters off the scent of another hunting Bill. They railed angrily against delays, and pressed Blair for action early in 2002.

On 18 March 2002, the House of Commons voted on the three options – again firmly supporting a complete hunting ban, this time by 386 to 175 (majority 211). They rejected the Middle way 371 to 169 (majority 202), and self-regulation 401 to 154 (347 majority).

Next day the House of Lords was in direct confrontation with the Commons by voting in favour of the Middle Way proposal by 366 to 59 (307 majority).

The changed stance of the Countryside Alliance was clear when its board member Lord Mancroft led Tory peers towards mass support for the Middle Way, arguing that it was 'the only way to find a peaceful solution to this inter-minable dispute.'

Mancroft admitted there were 'considerable risks' for the hunting community in going down the Middle Way path. He warned they would not throw away coursing and staghunting as a price, and they would not tolerate government ratchetting up regulations to put hunting with hounds out of business.

There were forty speakers in an eight hour debate. Lord Donoughue begged Conservative peers to abandon their 'previous mistake' in supporting the un-licensed status quo of voluntary self-regulation.

'It is not seriously on offer from the government,' he warned. 'You rejected the prospect of preserving legitimate hunting, so giving hope to those who seek a ban.'

Donoughue's warning perhaps came too late because the government was in no mind at this stage to adopt the Middle Way approach without a great deal more mind-numbing politics still to be endured.

He wrote afterwards that he was 'not actually pro-hunting, I am against a ban – and sometimes feel that the only fresh ban we need is a ban on bans.'

The ex-Labour Minister reflected sadly that the hunting issue had seen the Labour Party in the Commons 'reverting to its earlier instincts, based on class prejudice and deeply ingrained resentments . . . it is politically crazy that a Labour government with a massive future legislative programme of modernising Britain's social services, its law and order and its transport infrastructure, should waste valuable political energy on such a marginal and divisive issue.'

Hunting now seemed to have become part of the political game plan in Tony Blair's attempts to 'reform' the House of Lords, with an eventual aim of producing a Labour majority of peers largely chosen by himself.

Two days later this was rammed home when Alun Michael addressed the House of Commons, and promised that Government was ready to use the Parliament Act to over-rule the will of the House of Lords if it again blocked a decision by the Commons on the hunting issue.

The Minister promised there would be a Bill in the autumn, following six months of consultation. He said there had been 'no deals' and there would be no 'middle way'. The way forward for hunting would be judged on the issues of cruelty and utility, Mr Michael declared.

The government's unofficial spin briefings indicated that a licensing Bill would result which would effectively cease all hunting except that which could be proved to be strictly a form of pest control, probably limited to upland and moorland sheep rearing areas.

The Countryside Alliance promptly announced it would cooperate with the consultations, but it led a 'Summer of Discontent' and renewed plans for an autumn Liberty and Livelihood March. John Jackson roundly condemned any attempt to use the Parliament Act, declaring it would be totally unconstitutional, and warning that the Alliance would test in the courts any attempt to use it to achieve a hunting ban.

Discerning members of the pro-hunting lobby felt the Alliance had already achieved miracles in ensuring the survival so long during two Labour administrations. This was no time to rock the boat, but the frustrations and fears raised by Labour's latest tactics unsurprisingly produced splinter groups intent on more direct forms of protest action.

The Countryside Action Network was formed as an independent ginger group, with Janet George as one of its leaders. She ran her own website and used it sometimes to criticise fiercely the Countryside Alliance, accusing it of being far too compliant with Labour's machinations. John Jackson took a sanguine view of the CAN's activities, merely pointing out to government that it indicated the risks of anarchy in the countryside if the present avenues of negotiation were ignored by government.

With hindsight it is perfectly clear that the Alliance played a difficult, and at times perilous, strategy of carrying out delaying tactics which ensured for many months that every time a Hunting Bill neared completion the government would have to shelve it in favour of far greater priorities.

The crucial role of the Tory peers in the House of Lords was not only to block anti-hunting Bills, but to issue threats that other government legislation would be fatally delayed in reprisals if government persisted in using the Parliament Bill on hunting.

It was a process entirely inappropriate for a matter of conscience, pointed out those opposed to a hunting ban, not least Kate Hoey who said she 'could not believe' that Tony Blair would engage in such an unconstitutional action. The frustration of Labour's Hunting Bills in the Lords was only achieved because a majority of Labour peers voted against them, mainly on the grounds that the Bill was anti-libertarian and would not assist wild animal welfare.

The Alliance publicised its Summer of Discontent with increasingly imaginative protest actions. More than 20,000 people delivered letters to DEFRA's regional offices. In Nottingham a parade of hunting people through busy streets to DEFRA's office followed a meeting of over 4,000 at the Goose Fair site in the heart of the city. Excellent relationships had been achieved between DEFRA staffs and Hunts during the foot and mouth stoppage, and on each occasion the protest petitions were received politely and even cordially for onward transmission to London.

Tabloid photographers were thrilled when Millie Jackson, comely blonde daughter of the MFHA Director Alastair Jackson and his wife Tessa, performed a Lady Godiva routine, riding topless – albeit briefly – in Smith Square, Westminster, when a Countryside Alliance parade delivered a protest to DEFRA's head office. Millie brandished a placard saying 'DEFRA – No Cover Up!'

'If she doesn't put her clothes on she will be arrested,' warned a police officer, according to a *Sun* report. 'Put your coat on darling' said Alastair, and Millie willingly obliged. 'I'm glad it's over, but glad I made the protest,' she said.

From 15 May a round the clock vigil began in Parliament Square. Alliance members vowed to maintain it until the countryside felt it was being listened to. The slogan 'Listen to Us' became a potent element in the campaign.

Hunting farmer Geoff Brooks from the Quorn country and several friends organised a protest ride by over 1,000 hunting horses and ponies through Leicester . It was described as the biggest equine event since the Battle of Naseby

Millie Jackson captured huge attention from the tabloids when she performed a Lady Godiva act in support of a pro-hunting march to DEFRA's headquarters in Smith Square, Westminster.

in 1645. Leicester police manned the route in huge strength to 'keep apart warring factions'. They need hardly have bothered; the antis could only muster a dozen or so men and women shouting incoherent insults which were smilingly ignored. The ride was a model of calm, peaceful behaviour and this undoubtedly reduced its 'news impact' in the press. Over 1,000 working dogs were taken to the RSPCA's headquarters in Sussex to highlight the threat to hounds and other working dogs in the event of a hunting ban.

On 10 July 2002 the original Piccadilly Hunt of 1949 was recalled when over eighty hunting people on horseback set off from Hyde Park Corner, down Piccadilly and on to Parliament Square. This protest was organised by the Union of Country Sports Workers, 4,500 strong, including Hunt staff, gamekeepers and others whose livelihood depends on field sports.

Warnings from the National Equine Welfare Council that 15,000 horses and ponies would have to be put down within a year of a hunting ban, were met with indifference by the Bill's backers. A NEWC study showed that about 19,000 quality horses would immediately be released on to the market, causing a glut of 15,000 unwanted lower value animals needing disposal lower down the market. Many more ex-hunters would be at risk in succeeding years.

Nor have anti-hunting MPs expressed much interest in the fate of working hounds after a ban. Miles Cooper, the former LACS researcher and undercover operative, released a study showing that 20,000 hunting hounds, plus some 70,000 lurchers, and 100,000 working terriers would be at risk; far outside any possible re-homing and retraining plan promised by the RSPCA. The loss of redundant hounds would erase over two centuries of selective breeding.

DEFRA's consultation process, held at Portcullis House in Whitehall from 9 to 11 September 2002, set a precedent by being broadcast on TV. The government seemed determined to prove that its consultation was 'fair and open'. Would it make any difference to the Hunting Bill eventually produced?

Many in the hunting world doubted it, but the Countryside Alliance played a pragmatic political strategy engaging in consultation and all Parliamentary processes. Those within the hunting world who grumbled petulantly about the Alliance 'wasting time talking to the enemy' failed to understand the Byzantine delaying processes necessary in one of the world's oldest democracies to ensure that threatened legislation is averted or frustrated.

At the hunting hearings Alun Michael chaired a panel from the three interest groups: the Alliance's Campaign for Hunting, the Middle Way Group, and a consortium of anti-hunting organisations called the Campaign for the Hunted Animal. Michael said he wanted the hearings to define the principles that might be used in a Bill based on the issues of 'utility and cruelty'. There was the inevitable clash of opinions from various academic and scientific sources produced by the two sides in the hunting argument.

Professor Stephen Harris, professor of environmental sciences at Bristol University, a long-time outspoken opponent of hunting, put forward his well worn case that food supply and environment were the most influential factors on fox populations, and culling by hunting was unnecessary and irrelevant. This was rebutted by Dr Jonathan Reynolds, head of predation control studies at the Game Conservancy Trust, who referred to surveys showing that culling had a notable impact. There were similar debating points throughout the consultation which gained far less public interest than either side had hoped for.

Liberty and Livelihood March

On 22 September 2002, the Countryside Alliance held its second great March in London, and its third major protest gathering in the capital since the Rally. It was essential that the attendance far exceeded the 1998 March, and this was magnificently achieved with a total of marchers carefully counted by the Alliance at 407,791.

The pre-March press conference was the Alliance's 'finest hour', receiving massive press and broadcasting coverage. There was a remarkable display of unity from right across the rural spectrum. Most important was the solidarity expressed by the National Farmers' Union which was represented by its leader Ben Gill. He delivered trenchant criticism of the government's handling of rural matters, including its lack of action to save a declining farming industry.

Kate Hoey, wearing a Liberty and Livelihood shirt, warned Tony Blair that 'he should display some leadership on this, recognising he was elected to bring people together, not to create division.'

Iain Duncan-Smith, then the Tory leader, took part in the March, and there was plenty of other support from his side, but apart from Miss Hoey, official Labour presence was negligible.

The Countryside Alliance's Liberty and Livelihood March, on 22 September 2002, jammed central London streets in a massive protest against a hunting ban and condemnation of Labour's rule in the countryside.

The hunting message came over strongly in the Liberty and Livelihood March. Many children carried banners, such as this one at Horseguards, Whitehall.

Alun Michael watched it on TV and later infuriated those who had marched by commenting in weasel words that their message was 'a muddle', and had been 'hi-jacked' by the pro-hunting lobby. Some of those Marchers spoke as if they thought it was an attempt to intimidate Parliament. I think it would be wrong to be intimidated,' said Mr Michael. He doubted there would be mass protest against a hunting ban in rural areas.

Organiser of the great march, James Stanford, again taking on a huge load with sang froid, had begged hunting people not to blow hunting horns while they walked. His pleas were largely ignored; there were plenty of hunting horns reverberating through central London that day, but there was an even louder clamour of whistles sold by opportunistic street traders at the start of the march.

There was plenty of evidence that those taking part were far more representative of the rural community than just the hard core of foxhunters. Perhaps most significant were the many family groups in which infants were carried on fathers' backs throughout the weary trudge when the Marchers were often reduced to a stand-still or a very slow walk by the huge press of people in front.

To tempt the press, the Alliance had assembled an array of pro-hunting celebrities, ranging from the TV cook Clarissa Dickson-Wright to the actor and former footballer Vinnie Jones. Richard Burge asked: 'What has gone so wrong that ordinary, decent people with their families and kids have had to take to the streets to ensure their freedom and a way of life?'

The March started at two points, in the City and south of the Thames, then joined to march along the Embankment in a huge surge of people strolling calmly and chatting cheerfully, up to Whitehall, to finish in Parliament Square. The Prime Minister we understood was not at home to hear a special crescendo of roars from Marchers as they passed Downing Street before complete silence at the Cenotaph. Police stood along the route with nothing to do but watch. It was demonstrably a march by reasonable, responsible citizens who knew how to behave themselves. Several policemen were seen to applaud as Marchers passed them.

Would anger, smashing of barriers, and fights with police, have done hunting's

End of the March route was marked dramatically at the junction of Whitehall and Parliament Square with an automatic count. Altogether 407,791 attended – a record size civil rights march, and the most orderly ever seen in central London.

cause more good? It would have resulted in a different sort of publicity, but the Alliance was surely sound in its opinion that the wider public would react strongly against a group of people engaging in hooliganism in support of a minority sport which the urban population scarcely understood, and with which many were still unsympathetic.

Over one hundred organisations were represented, and there were visiting delegations from twenty-eight countries. I was among British hunting people who cheered rapturously when a small group of American MFHs joined us bearing the Stars and Stripes.

Despite the genial tone of the March, John Jackson was widely quoted when he predicted the countryside would 'erupt in fury' if the government did not listen to the Liberty and Livelihood March's concern about a possible ban on hunting.

'We will see public outrage at a level we have not seen for a very long time,' said Jackson.

Fleet Street saw the force of the argument and acknowledged the width of the protest. Some of the tabloids produced special 'March supplements', all in favour of the libertarian argument on hunting.

There were huge gains for the hunting issue in terms of publicity and enhanced support. Amazingly, the Alliance itself attracted few material gains. Some three-quarters of the Marchers did not join the Alliance, and its membership remained stubbornly around 100,000.

Leading US foxhunters flew to London to take part in the Liberty and Livelihood March. Expressing solidarity on Westminster Bridge were: Marty and Daphne Wood MFHs, Live Oak Hunt; Carol Anne Morley, Wentworth; Pennt Denegre MFH and Pat Rogers, Middleburg; and Brent Concilio, North Country.

Young Marchers gave an entirely new image to the pro-hunting campaign. Girls with painted faces carried a banner stating 'Hunting is Better than Sex'.

Nor was there successful fund raising from the Marchers; far from achieving a handsome surplus, the total sums raised in limited collecting attempts still left a heavy deficit to be filled by existing funds. Metropolitan police regulations about overtly collecting money on the streets were blamed for the disappointing cash result from the mammoth march.

By 2003 the Alliance was operating on substantial overdrafts, and a new initiative to 'fund the fight ' was launched among field sportsmen in 2004. Members were also asked for a one off voluntary levy of £15 each to enable the Alliance to clear its overdraft and change its status. It had been an unincorporated association since the start of the BFSS; now it was time to strengthen its status and seek incorporation as a limited company.

John Jackson had already told members at Alliance annual meetings that the organisation could not be run on 'business lines' for profit; everything had to be thrown into massive campaigns which were impossible to cost accurately, and he pointed out that the very fact that hunting still existed far into the second term of a Labour administration was in itself proof of the Alliance's success. Legal costs of challenging anti-hunting legislation in Scotland, and other areas of the campaign, were especially heavy.

2002–3 Second Government Hunting Bill

In the 2002 Queen's Speech Blair's government promised a Bill which it said vaguely 'will enable Parliament to reach a conclusion on the contentious issue of hunting with dogs in England and Wales'.

Convinced the Liberty and Livelihood March had been far too peaceful and unthreatening, small militant groups of field sportsmen in November 2002 at the start of a new hunting season gained some publicity by promising to step up the 'war' against government.

There were dark mutterings of threats to sabotage essential services, electricity, gas and food deliveries. There were reports of something called 'the Real CA', an unfortunate and ill-chosen echo of the 'Real IRA' title of the extremist group in Northern Ireland.

The Alliance leadership warned that public support and confidence which had been gained by the great marches could all too easily be lost if hunting people engaged in direct action, and were seen fighting policemen on TV. The public would have far less sympathy than they had shown towards the poll tax riots when Mrs Thatcher was in power.

Lord Donoughue introduced in the Lords in March 2003, for the second time, a Private Bill seeking to amend the 1996 Wild Mammals (Protection) Act to stop deliberate and avoidable cruelty to animals, and to eliminate the exemptions for 'hunting with dogs'. It completed all its stages in the Lords but ran out of time to secure a First Reading in the Commons.

The Countryside Alliance gave it a guarded welcome: '. . . any measure designed to promote higher standards of welfare, coupled with greater openness, is to be welcomed. Proper consideration of wildlife and bio-diversity, and how we can foster it in our all too diminishing countryside, should be the way forward.'

Donoughue re-introduced it in the Lords at the start of the 2003–4 session, and Lembit Opik introduced a similar Private Bill in the Commons, but it was too low down on the ballot to make progress.

They intended to produce a sensible alternative way out for the government, but it was nowhere near enough to satisfy Labour's back-bench zealots in the Commons.

New Hunting Bill

On 3 December 2002, Alun Michael announced a new Hunting Bill which would ban hare coursing and deer hunting, but which would allow foxhunting under licence. To gain a licence from a Government appointed Registrar, a Fox Hunt would have to pass a utility test involving 'what is necessary to prevent serious damage to livestock, crops and other property or biological diversity'.

And there was to be a 'cruelty test' which asked 'which effective method of achieving that purpose involved least suffering'. Activities which had 'no utility but involved cruelty' would not be allowed to continue, said Mr Michael. Appeals against the Registrar's decisions could be made to a tribunal set up by the Lord Chancellor. Hunts would come under the law on animal welfare for the first time, with breaches being subject to fines up to £5,000. No compensation would be available for jobs or incomes lost.

It was soon evident the government's new Bill was evoking huge anger on both sides. The Alliance was extremely unhappy and vowed to fight to save deer hunting and hare coursing. It brought no pleasure either to the anti-hunters. Gerald Kaufman, one of the most barbed tongued back-benchers, in the House described the Bill as a 'botched' attempt to run with the hares and hunt with the hounds, and said he would settle for nothing less than a complete ban.

Tory MP David Heathcoat-Amory said the proposals were filled with 'fatuous bureaucracy' and were 'truly the low point of Labour's Third Way'. Nicholas Soames, Conservative MP for Mid-Sussex, and grandson of Sir Winston Churchill, condemned the Bill as 'mischief' and warned 'hunting will fight this, and hunting will be right.'

Hunting people could see that the licensing system was designed to end 'recreational foxhunting'. It was expected that licences would go only to foot packs operating on moors and uplands where there was intensive sheep rearing.

Max Hastings, former Editor of *The Daily Telegraph* and *Evening Standard* dismissed the Bill as 'a silly fudge', and remarked: 'It is no more possible for a tribunal which includes opponents of hunting to have a rational debate about licencing one pack of foxhounds against another, than for a panel of vegetarians to arbitrate on whether lobsters or pheasants represent unacceptably cruel food.'

He referred to the 'obsessive malevolence of Labour back-benchers who would scarcely bother to turn up for a debate on, say, child abuse or the future of the transport system'.

The path of the Bill was to be rent with slapstick inside and outside the Commons. Countryside Alliance leaders were appalled when at last the patience of the hard core of the hunting community was exhausted, and the much feared spectacle of field sportsmen members grappling with police at the very walls of the House of Commons erupted on to TV screens.

This occurred on 16 December 2002, during the new Bill's Second Reading. Richard Burge addressed a smallish gathering of CA members at Hyde Park Corner, which I attended, and led us on a well mannered march through Victoria.

There was confusion among the marchers; some of us believed we were headed for Parliament Square, but the law forbids demonstrations in the precincts of Parliament while it is sitting, although this is liberally interpreted.

On this occasion the Metropolitan police on the Embankment barred the march's entrance to Parliament Square, and the main body of the CA march set off across Lambeth Bridge, turning along the Albert Embankment to demonstrate opposite Parliament. This infuriated many marchers who sought to return to the north side of the Thames despite police road blocks.

Some of the more militant field sports splinter groups had already managed to infiltrate into Parliament Square, and an element of the original CA march pushed its way past police blocks on Westminster Bridge to join a growing scrimmage in front of New Palace Yard, the main entrance to the House of Commons.

A few people threw fireworks and flares and a few chained themselves to Parliament's railings; skirmishes developed with the police. The protestors were notably unafraid of the horses when a group of mounted police arrived to strengthen police on foot, standing shoulder to shoulder. One protestor calmly undid the throat lash and removed the bridle of a police horse while giving the animal a pat on the neck.

About 1,500 people were protesting, but only a few hundred were engaged in confrontation with police at the gates of New Palace Yard. There were traffic hold-ups and Westminster Underground Station was temporarily closed.

An Alliance supporter climbed on to a bus in Westminster Square to urge protestors to cease and go home. Most of those present did so soon after this appeal. Police had arrested about six people, and four were charged, three under the Public Order Act, and one for being drunk and disorderly.

Noise of the demonstration could be heard in the Commons, and Alun Michael angrily said during the debate that 'nothing better illustrated the tribal nature' of the debate than the rowdy protest outside, and accused some Conservative MPs of supporting the protestors.

Later the Countryside Alliance officially expressed disappointment over the 'misbehaviour' but stated: 'We don't condemn the emotion, fear and anger of people whose livelihoods are threatened.'

The demonstration, although widely reported, did not result in lengthy condemnation by the press and media, but was interpreted as a spontaneous expression of frustration and anger. However, it caused misgivings among some of those who advocated an organised programme of militancy. Any more TV publicity of this sort would be disastrous.

An NOP poll commissioned by the Countryside Alliance, and published on Boxing Day 2002, showed that fifty-nine per cent believed that hunting should not be abolished by law. This was highly encouraging for the Alliance because past polls had shown a majority, sometimes as a high as about eighty per cent, in favour of a ban. The fifty-nine per cent figure was to be used in a vigorous pro-hunting poster campaign. Some eighteen per cent believed it should continue as at present, while forty-one per cent agreed with regulation.

Among Labour voters forty-two per cent supported a ban; fifty-six per cent wanted it to continue, with forty-four per cent backing regulation.

The Campaign to Protect Hunted Animals (CPHA) published the findings of a poll conducted by MORI which asked 1,000 adults which phrases applied most to hunting. It found eighty-two per cent describing it as 'cruel or inhumane' and only twenty-seven per cent describing it as 'enjoyable or humane'.

The Committee stage of the Hunting Bill reflected the ongoing struggle for hearts and minds on the issue. The Conservatives' shadow rural affairs minister was a keen foxhunter, James Gray, MP for North Wiltshire. He led a spirited defence of foxhunting in the Committee debates on the Bill, but anti-hunting MPs had a clear majority on the committee of thirty-two; about twenty were in favour of an outright ban, another ten supported the status quo or the Middle Way, and only two were thought to be keen supporters of the licencing Bill.

There was renewed anger among hunting people in January, 2003, when Alun Michael accepted an amendment from the anti-hunt MPs restricting hunting solely to pest control purposes. The pro-hunting lobby accused the Minister of reneging on his promise to base the Bill on evidence rather than politics. Later Mr Michael caused more fury when he declined to vote in favour of his own Bill while anti-hunt MPs succeeded in voting for an amendment to ban hare hunting completely.

James Gray commented: 'The whole Bill is now out of control. It has been taken over by back-benchers who are ripping it to pieces. As presented by Alun Michael it had some intellectual coherence. We didn't like it, but that has now been completely destroyed.' Simon Hart, Director of the Countryside Alliance's Campaign for Hunting declared it was 'outrageous' of the Minister not to vote for his own Bill.

Much worse was to come, but a crisis intervened yet again to push hunting back in the waiting list. As Harold Macmillan once said, governments are blown off course ' by events, dear boy'. The Iraq war erupted in April, 2003 and caused the postponement of the final Commons stages of the Bill.

It was felt 'inappropriate' in government circles to spend Parliamentary time on such a measure of low priority at a time when British servicemen were losing their lives in the Coalition force with American troops. Since the government was now embarked on a permanent war on world terrorism, foxhunting as a political priority became even more ludicrous.

But hordes of Labour back-benchers were assured the delay was only tempo-rary, and sure enough the Hunting Bill emerged on the floor of the Commons again for its Third Reading on 1 July. John Jackson for the Alliance condemned the government for giving way to back-bench pressure to bring the Bill back for them to 'savage in the Commons'. He asserted the Bill 'has very little to do with animal welfare and nothing to do with the management of wildlife as an im-portant national asset.'

He pointed out the 'whole situation is degenerating into farce', and in a searing attack on Alun Michael, Jackson asked: 'Can anyone respect a Minister who started out armed with principle and evidence, and ended up allowing his back-bench colleagues to cow him into abandoning both?'

Nevertheless, after its mauling in the Committee stages the Bill had some resemblance to that which Alun Michael had drafted to set up a regulatory framework, claiming he was trying to reconcile the principles of cruelty and utility. It now allowed only foxhunting, banning outright hare hunting and coursing and deer hunting.

The government Bill was still not what Labour back-benchers wanted. Alun Michael was reported to have written to the Deputy Prime Minister John Prescott the previous month saying that an attempt by Labour back-benchers to insert a complete ban into his Bill 'would be a wrecking amendment.'

Mr Michael and other DEFRA ministers had a bad summer in the country-side, frequently confronted on official visits by protesting field sportsmen and women. At the Royal Show a group of pro-hunting ladies threw bunches of knickers at Mr Michael. The Alliance used the power of the fair sex even more imaginatively in Parliament Square during the Hunting Bill debate.

A crowd of over 2,000 Alliance women members, called 'Families 4 Hunting', in a two day vigil hoisted a washing line of frilly knickers in Parliament Square, and a few went further to ensure that the national press gave them full attention. Two attractive, curvaceous hunting girls appeared topless in body paint depicting scarlet hunt coats, capturing acres of space in the tabloids and some broadsheets next day.

It was certainly an antidote to the 'toffs image' so often the target of snarling Labour MPs. At the same time the Alliance used an innovative advertising campaign showing the Worcestershire Hunt's pretty twenty-five-year-old hunting nurse Sarah Bell. She appeared in a picture in a hunting clothes and alongside in her NHS uniform. The slogans under each were 'Now you hate her; Now you don't.'

The strategy was to demonstrate that under the red or black coats of hunting people lurks a large cross-section of real people with worthwhile jobs in modern society, far removed from the pre-1939 stereotypes of the 'idle rich'.

The Alliance's Action Office, run by husband and wife team Charles and 'Chipps' Mann in Gloucestershire, was benefiting from professional public relations advice. It aimed to destroy as many of the old stereotype images of hunting people which added to the layers of prejudice against the sport.

In a 'National Action Weekend' Alliance members 'painted the countryside red and green', claiming it had distributed 200 mega banners, 17,000 corex boards, 10,000 vinyl posters, and 55,000 car stickers.

'Middle aged, middle-class men' were much less frequently called upon by the Alliance PR department to appear on TV to defend hunting. Professional huntsmen and young, preferably attractive hunting people were preferred. It was a fair tactic: foxhunting has always relied for its survival on an annual influx of fit young people.

What happened inside the House of Commons on 1 July was worse for the government than any ridicule outside. Much of the press described it as a 'humiliating setback' for the government when its own backbenchers forced it to abandon its regulatory Bill formed after months of vastly expensive consultation, and instead allow a Bill imposing a straight ban on all forms of hunting with hounds.

Quentin Letts in his *Daily Mail* political sketch reported: 'At the despatch box was Alun Michael, a failed former First Minister of Wales, who was made hunting minister presumably as part of some cruel practical joke.

'Mr Michael's eyes barely lifted above the horizontal. His shoulders were hunched. He looked like a spaniel that has been kicked. Gerald Kaufman (Labour, Gorton) was horrible to him, repeatedly – to the point, in fact, that it might have been kinder to have whipped out a small firearm and shot the dog.'

Under the leadership of Tony Banks 145 Labour rebels signed an amendment calling for a total ban. They were infuriated because the Blair government tried a procedural device which would have robbed them of a vote on a total ban.

An order laid before the Commons meant that MPs voted first on the government proposal to register Fox Hunts which, if carried, would have prevented MPs from then voting on the back-bench total ban amendment because they were legally incompatible.

The government put down an amendment to 'toughen up' the Bill by banning cub-hunting, making the period August to November a close season. All terrier work underground was to be banned. In practice this would cripple the sport completely: trying to start a hunting every season on 1 November with hounds that had not hunted that autumn would be virtually impossible in terms of entering young hounds, and culling fox populations.

There was not much left for the antis to oppose, but they could not resist going for the kill on the already maimed Bill. Tony Banks jeered: 'The government has snatched defeat from the jaws of victory' in an 'act of bad faith'. Kaufman said in his attacks on the government that Tony Blair had deliberately 'shoe-horned' the amendment 'in order to pre-empt a proper decision by the House.'

From the other side of the House Ann Widdecombe joined the hunt in pursuit of the DEFRA Minister, urging a vote on an outright ban. At the start of the five hour debate Alun Michael described his Bill as 'still tough but fair'. He said he had concluded 'that what we needed to target was cruelty rather than activity – to ban cruelty rather than what people undertake or what clothes they wear.' At the end of the tumultuous debate in which he had received a verbal pummelling from his own back benches, Alun Michael capitulated.

He announced the government withdrew its own amendment, and allowed a vote on the back-bench amendment converting the Bill to a complete ban. This was passed by an overwhelming majority of 208. Tony Blair stayed in Number 10 and did not vote, having approved the capitulation, but Alun Michael was supported by his boss, the senior DEFRA Minister Margaret Beckett and Hilary Armstrong, the Chief Whip.

Seven Cabinet Ministers, led by John Prescott, joined in voting for an outright ban. The more thoughtful members of the pro-hunting lobby reflected that hunting's best friend in politics had probably been the Prime Minister. He had been elected twice on a manifesto promising Parliament to decide on hunting. He had never really wanted to ban it, and had spent six years using every procedural device to delay a decision, while trying to give the impression he was in favour of a ban.

As usual after a hunting debate, tempers were frayed in the House. The sick joke was that Labour MPs had sunk the chance of the Bill becoming law because Parliamentary time was under great pressure from more important Bills near the end of the session. There was also the problem of opposition looming in the House of Lords, and the unwelcome prospect of having to apply the Parliament Act to overcome this. The Countryside Alliance encouraged members to send thousands of letters to peers. One peer said he had received the biggest and heaviest mailbag ever.

When the Bill came before the Lords for a Second Reading on 16 September, in the words of Quentin Letts: 'The Commons voted for a total ban on hunting. The Lords told them they were barking . . . The Hunting Bill as presented to their Lordships went down like a helium-filled submarine. A very small handful thought it all right. The rest simply, utterly, totally hated it. I have never known a Bill flayed quite so.'

Lord Bragg, the broadcaster and novelist Melvyn Bragg said: 'Banning that which harms no-one and brings much pleasure to parts of our society is a dangerous course of action. One aspect of our democracy is that we respect the rights of a majority. We must also defend the rights of a minority.' Lord Donoughue said the Bill 'restricts individual freedoms unacceptably. It will deprive thousands of hard working and law abiding countrymen of their livelihoods and many of their homes. I didn't join the Labour Party to create unemployment.'

Lord Whitty for the government said he hoped for a compromise, but warned that if there was a clash it would be up to the Commons to decide if the Parliament Act was used to force it into law.

The government allowed the Lords only two days to debate the Bill in committee. This was a stark contrast to the Commons which had considered it for twenty-seven sittings in Standing Committee, lasting over seventy-seven hours.

However, the Lords voted 261 to 49 in favour of a system of regulated hunting. Even without the votes of Conservative and hereditary peers, registered hunting was still supported by a majority of 100 peers. Labour's own members of the Lords would not provide sufficient support for the banning ambitions of the back-benchers in the Commons.

The Lords also overturned the Commons' outright ban on hare coursing, voting by 129 to 59 to allow it to be subject to tests of registration along with all other forms of hunting. Despite Lord Whitty's threats, and all the heat generated by Labour MPs, Tony Blair's government allowed the Bill to die through lack of time scheduled for it to complete its Committee Stage in the Lords.

Why was the Bill allowed to expire? It had cost a huge amount of public money and valuable Parliamentary time: the Alliance had prepared 170 briefing papers, and assisted with over 500 amendments.

The answer for the Bill's demise possibly resided in a report by the Parliamentary Joint Committee on Human Rights that the Bill, as introduced to the House of Lords, breached the Human Rights Act due to the absence of any compensation scheme to those who lost jobs and livelihoods. The Treasury was not at all inclined to meet a bill for billions of pounds.

In comparison to 120 hours debating the Hunting Bill, it was estimated Parliament had debated the Iraq issue before going to war for some eleven hours. No wonder the rest of the world is bemused by the obsession of so many British politicians with the issue of a fox being chased by a pack of hounds.

2004 – What of the Future?

There was no mention of hunting in the Queen's Speech on 26 November 2003. But in reply to the famously cantankerous Labour MP Denis Skinner, asking the Prime Minister to guarantee that hunting would be banned before the next General Election, the Prime Minister said: 'We have said that we will resolve the issue during this Parliament, and so we will resolve the issue during this Parliament.'

In Blair-speak, the word 'resolve' could mean a variety of 'solutions'. The hunting world was well aware that its fate was still threatened.

On 1 November 2003, over 60,000 hunting people attended twelve mass meets throughout England and Wales, and over 40,000 of them signed a 'Hunting Declaration' which promised that in the event of a ban they would be prepared to break the law and accept the legal consequences. Altogether some 55,000 had signed the Declaration by the spring of 2004, and the media had widely picked up the theme of 'Say No To Unjust Law'.

The Countryside Alliance stated it would support people at the time of their trial, provided they had specifically broken a hunting law, that if civil disobedience was involved they would submit to trial and punishment and not seek to avoid capture, and that there should be no inconvenience or upset to the general public. The late Duke of Devonshire, owner of the Chatsworth estate, stated he would break the law by allowing hunting on his land after a ban.

The foxhunting philosopher Roger Scruton favours breaking a banning law, and has warned: 'After hunting will come shooting, and fishing, steeplechasing and any other activity that offends the urban conscience. Indeed, anything that smacks of our past – the settled, rural, manly past of England – will be just disapproved of, and then forbidden by law.'

Various public relations stunts were held during 2003 to display the determination of the field sports lobby to fight any more attempted bans. They demonstrated at the Liberal Democrat and Labour Party conferences, using a 'Bikers for Hunting Rally' with dozens of motor-cycles at the latter.

In the spring of 2004 there were unofficial leaked reports that the government was planning to introduce yet another anti-Hunting Bill – but the prospect of a General Election in a year to eighteen months made yet another Parliamentary attempt to criminalise a substantial minority in the electorate seem a highly unwise tactic for a Prime Minister seeking a third term in office.

Richard Burge retired as Chief Executive of the Countryside Alliance in mid-2003. His legacy was that the Alliance was by now regarded in Westminster as the most effective of all non-political public persuasion movements on rural issues.

It manifestly had a far wider base of membership than when Burge took over, and it had so far succeeded in thwarting a Bill to ban hunting or any other field sport.

Burge was succeeded internally by Simon Hart, aged thirty-nine, already experienced and effective as Director of the CA's Campaign for Hunting for three years. A quietly convincing, no-nonsense, speaker, Simon is battle-hardened in constant radio and TV interviews. He never appears to get rattled, and makes the hunting case well.

These qualities are similar to those of his father, the late Anthony Hart, who was an MFH and amateur huntsman with the Cotswold Vale Farmers, the Albrighton, and the South and West Wilts, before becoming Secretary of the MFHA for twenty-two years (1975–97). Simon's mother, Judy Hart, still works in the MFHA office.

Simon was a chartered surveyor in land management for sixteen years before joining the Alliance, and he was Joint Master and huntsman of the South Pembrokeshire for a decade (1988–99). His background made him immediately acceptable to the hunting community as a leader, and he strives to ensure the backing of the angling and shooting fraternities. One of his priorities on taking over was to streamline the Alliance's administration, and cut costs.

As CA Chief Executive, Simon Hart sent a message to members in May 2004 warning 'We are now entering a critical phase in our campaigning. We do not know exactly what the government is planning, but we may well have a crucial battle just round the corner.'

The core of pro-hunting warriors believe that no blandishments, no arguments will alter the view of the extremist anti-hunters on Labour's back-benches. The best hope was that many would lose their seats in a General Election when Labour is seeking a third term. A House of Commons with Labour governing on a much smaller majority, or a Conservative victory by the party rejuvenated by Michael Howard would not be such a threat to foxhunting.

Far less back-bench pressure would be exerted on a future Labour prime minister with a much smaller majority. The issue could be allowed eventually subside to its proper negligible level of political priority. It can best be resolved in Parliament by the application of that quality which modern politicians constantly urge when dealing with other minorities within our borders – tolerance.

But it is up to foxhunting and the other hound sports to operate self-regulation and discipline of a high order, and to adapt where necessary to the pressures of our small over-crowded island, not least in re-drawing hunting country boundaries sensibly to avoid infringing suburban and urban areas.

In April 2004, the Alliance published the result of an NOP poll which found that ninety-nine per cent of Labour supporters 'think there are more important issues for the government to tackle than hunting.'

Simon Hart commented: 'The House of Commons seems to be the only place left where a ban is considered either important or desirable. The continuing obsession of some back-bench Labour MPs with this issue, will only add to the impression that politicians are out of touch with ordinary voters – and they risk making their government look completely ridiculous.'

End of the Phoney War

Throughout the summer of 2004 press reports sporadically predicted that Tony Blair would re-launch the Bill to ban hunting completely, and would use the Parliament Act to force it through if the House of Lords blocked it.

The first of such reports erupted in April and May, and the *Daily Mail,* in a perceptive leader on 23 May, pointed out that the postwar Iraq situation was going from bad to worse, public services were in crisis, and European policy in chaos.

So the Prime Minister's 'latest initiative' was to revive plans for a hunting ban.

The *Daily Mail* believed this owed 'little to moral conviction and everything to manipulating the levers of power to suit his short term ends.'

The leader predicted accurately: 'Those on either side of the argument will be dismayed to see this issue treated as a political convenience by Mr Blair.'

Countryside Alliance leaders, John Jackson and Simon Hart, maintained a calm response to predictions of doom. They insisted they did not know the government's intention, and Hart pointed out that bringing back the Bill before a General Election would be 'crazy politics' from Tony Blair.

Since I was receiving firm predictions the Bill was returning from journalistic and political friends on both sides of the House, I suspected that some in the Alliance were in something of a state of denial.

They simply could not believe that having fought their exhausting fight for seven years, the enemy was about to reappear yet again over the hill. This reflected the view of many hunting people, who either scoffed at 'doom-mongering', or were so confused they put the problem out of their mind.

They bred their hounds, exercised their horses, bought raffle tickets to keep their Hunts going, and prepared for the 2004-5 season exactly as normal.

Most were war weary,and distrusted "newspaper talk" about foxhunting's future.

Fortunately, despite its bland public stance amid the fog of imminent war, the Alliance's Action Office and Campaign for Hunting department were quietly making plans for the worst, led by Sam Butler and Charles and Chipps Mann. Tactically this proved an excellent policy because when the war started they were ready – and greatly surprised their opponents.

Outbreak of Real War

On Wednesday, 8 September, 2004, the day after Parliament resumed, Alun Michael revealed the government would reintroduce its hunting bill the following Wednesday. They planned to ban coursing by the end of February, well before the annual Waterloo Cup coursing event, and deer, mink, hare and foxhunting would receive a two year reprieve until November 2006.

This would give Hunts time to wind down, said the Minister, claiming with a nauseating show of concern this would give "even less reason" for hounds and horses to be shot.

The value of the Alliance's earlier public calm was now apparent, because the

279

sudden surge of action on the public relations and practical protest front was astounding.

Groups of activists were making their own plans too, mainly unknown to the Alliance. One, in particular, was to shock Parliament – to a historic extent none could have predicted.

No British political party could have summoned its supporters so effectively and swiftly, and received such prompt response, as that achieved by the Alliance after the Minister of Rural Affairs' statement. Peter Hain's announcement in the Commons next day could not have been calculated better to anger hunting people, and many others in rural communities.

In detestably patronising tones, he advised that the RSPCA was prepared to 're-home' or assist in the humane destruction of as many 'hunting dogs' as needed to be put down after a ban. He expected there would be alternative jobs, and most hunting horses could be absorbed, in what he believed to be a 'buoyant' horse industry!

Since the bottom had dropped out of the hunter market already in the previous two years this was one more example of the chasm of ignorance between the men in suits on Labour's front benches and the country sports people they now proposed to crush.

Hain, and later Alun Michael, blandly invited those who objected to a hunting ban to vote Conservative at the next General Election which was some clue to the political calculations of Number Ten that the Conservatives could suffer some electoral embarrassment by being the pro-hunting party in a General Election.

The government's proposed two year wait for enactment of the ban on all forms of hunting, excepting coursing, was condemned out of hand by press commentators, as well as the Alliance, as a cynical attempt to dilute the pro-hunting campaign during the General Election campaign expected in May, 2005.

'If someone says he is going to kill you, does it really matter whether he plans to do it this week or next?' asked Simon Hart on Radio 4.

Hain announced blandly that all stages of the Hunting Bill, and a separate motion to delay it, were to be completed in a one day hearing next Wednesday. The government believed there had had already been too many hours of debate on the subject, and the will of the House in favour of a ban had been expressed repeatedly.

Torrents of condemnation of the draconian procedure immediately poured from most of the national press, and echoed continuously on radio and TV channels.

The *Sun* condemned abolition, surely a matter for real concern to Tony Blair's normally acute sensitivity to mass opinion. Only the *Daily Mirror* warmly welcomed a ban, and this source could have been of little satisfaction at Number Ten since the *Mirror* was a bitter critic of Blair's Iraq war adventure.

Never before, even during the great London marches, had the Alliance's views been sought by the media so assiduously. Huntsmen, their wives and children, were photographed and interviewed endlessly about the impending loss of jobs and homes. Simon Hart and his team had the answers and arguments ready in a well conducted barrage of words, condemning and ridiculing Blair and his government for an illiberal and oppressive attack on the countryside.

The Alliance's plans swung into action with remarkable efficiency: halls had been booked for 21 'barnstorming meetings' on Saturday, 11 September.

I chaired the East Midlands meeting in a huge hangar at Sywell airfield, near Northampton. Over 400 people surged in, and heard David Lowes, former deputy chief executive of the Alliance, Andrew Rowbotham, Conservative MP for Blaby, Leicestershire,and Jim Barrington the former Director of the League Against Cruel Sports who changed his stance to support hunting, under regulation, and espouses the Middle Way.

I sensed far more steel in the mood that evening than I had observed in previous jolly London marches.

One man at the back sternly questioned: 'The meek do not inherit the earth. When are we going to block the M1?'

David Lowes and I told him that if we alienated the general public by punishing them we would lose most of the excellent press support we were receiving. Little did we know what was coming in four days' time.

David announced plans for a massive presence by hunting people in Parliament Square on Wednesday while the Bill was being debated. He urged us to go in huge numbers. We were to provide window dressing for the TV cameras to show just how many of us cared, and he urged us to behave ourselves. We nodded and went home swiftly to see the end of 'Last Night at the Proms' on the TV.

David Lowes sent us off with the news that pro-hunting protestors were that night blocking roads to Chequers to prevent guests attending the 50th birthday of the Prime Minister's wife, Cherie Blair. Police had to ferry some guests through road blocks from a Tesco car park, the press reported next day.

The hunters had already scored press coverage for protesting outside the Prime Minister's home in his Sedgefield constituency. He had invited a few in for a chat, advising them he was only carrying out 'the will of Parliament' before driving off amid jeers from others waiting outside.

But would Blair really go all the way with the ban? Charles Moore, in a perceptive article in the *Telegraph* pointed out that 'if Mr Blair is desperate to ban hunting, he has chosen a funny way of doing it,' referring to the tight timing at the end of the Parliamentary session when the matter could have been disposed of much earlier in seven years when Labour commanded huge majorities.

Moore commented: 'So the choice that confronts Mr Blair is between succumbing to backbenchers and activists, most of whom want him out anyway, provoking an enormous rural rebellion within a year of an election, or quietly playing for time once again.'

Drama Beyond Their Dreams

The prediction of a 'rural revolution' still seemed unreal when Wednesday, 15 September dawned into a delightful sunny autumn morning with a light breeze in central London.

I set off from a farmyard near Oakham, Rutland, with a nearly-full coach-load of hunting people. I had cancelled another coach after a very sluggish bookings response because most people said they preferred to 'make their own way' to Parliament Square.

Sitting in the coach were the Hunt chairman, genial head of a firm of Leicester based clothing retailers, the wife of a local barrister, but also farmers' wives, and a large group of young people comprising a youthful farrier, and male and female grooms from the area.

The Cottesmore's young whipper-in Michael Stokes, tall, lean, crop-haired, shy and with little to say, was sitting next to our youthful terrierman – both facing the probability of losing their jobs and homes at the Kennels very early in a career life-style they adored.

The young on the coach laughed, they puffed at the occasional cigarette, a few cans of lager were consumed. They neither moaned nor dramatised their lot; they made jokes about the day ahead. Were there some good pubs near Parliament Square?

Their youth and hope brought a lump to my throat; I who had enjoyed over half a century of hunting, and in my youth could take foxhunting for granted as a normal part of country life.

As soon as we left the coach at the Millbank Embankment and walked towards Parliament Square I sensed this was to be totally different from previous Alliance demos in London. There were police everywhere, and many did not smile; they eyed us suspiciously. Scores of country people walked in groups towards the Palace of Westminster, many men in corduroys, some carrying thumb sticks, many elderly women in sensible tweeds, and there were young people in jeans and sweaters, carrying Barbour jackets.

In a London threatened by terrorism, the police had hundreds of new riot vehicles parked in the back streets, with extra police waiting inside; many wore helmets with plastic visors, and padded riot gear.

I was surprised by a burst of sound when I entered the Square, coming from a huge platform equipped with massive public address systems, and run by the Alliance. Well done. This must have been well planned much earlier.

So the authorities had conceded a public meeting to us, right outside Parliament, despite the law that no demonstration is permitted in the precincts of the House while it is sitting.

Every few yards I met hunting friends from all over England and Wales on the increasingly crowded grass in the centre of the square . We had all dressed down, and we older ones greeted each other guardedly, almost shyly. This was a day we had long dreaded, but had never really come to terms with as a reality. What were we doing here? Were we doing any good? How could a British government treat us so? Were we really regarded by the government as a 'sub-species', as one press columnist had assured us?

My friends and I had enjoyed decades of hunting. We were now a little stiff to sit down on grass easily, but we did so.

We listened to a continous range of speakers organised by the Alliance. It was sometimes stirring, occasionally amusing, and it held our attention.

Johnny Scott and Clarissa Dickson Wright, the 'Fat Cook' of TV, were examples of light relief.

Johnny boomed on the loudspeaker: 'I have a message for the Prime Minister – Mr Blair, you are a f——— nuisance. Why don't you go away!'

We roared with the relief of laugher. It was not so funny when lurcher enthusiast Vini Faal looked at the hundreds of police in attendance and shouted: 'As a working class man I sense Fascism here!'

Overhead three or four police helicopters clattered continuously.

On the ground the police preserved a no-go corridor in front of the Parliament buildings. Hundreds of policemen in riot gear stood shoulder to shoulder behind barriers to ensure that the growing crowd, said to be over 20,000, did not surge towards the Palace of Westminster.

During the speeches we heard occasional firework bangs. Small clouds of orange smoke drifted over us. Heads turned as shouting and the sound of conflict came from the barriers nearer the House of Lords. The fringe protestors the Alliance could not control were busy. A few empty plastic bottles hurtled towards the police from somewhere in the crowd.

I walked over and peered from the back of the crowd at scuffles developing by the barrier between police and protestors. I saw new style police batons scything up and down, but I could not immediately see the effect. Several ambulances rushed to that end of the barriers. Then I saw several young men on the ground with blood streaming from the heads. A few were pinioned by policemen and taken away in police vans.

Part of the crowd of 20,000, mostly entirely peaceful, in the Parliament Square protest while the House of Commons was voting to ban hunting on 15 September 2004.

From the platform Countryside Alliance President Ann Mallalieu, after condemning her own party's Hunting Bill as 'madness', appealed to protestors not to fight with the police who were 'only doing their job'. There were other similar appeals from Alliance speakers for moderation. We were experiencing, as chairman John Jackson had predicted, the first signs of the countryside 'erupting in fury'.

The Countryside Action Network, the so-called Real Countryside Alliance, the Union of Countryside Workers and other small ginger groups had their own agendas, not calling for violence, but operating outside the Alliance umbrella.

At about 4 pm I wandered to a pub next to the old Methodist Central Hall where scores of country people were cramming the bar and drinking in the street outside. Suddenly there was a roar of approval as we saw on the television screen above the bar an extraordinary scene as a group of young men burst into the Commons chamber where they were wrestled to the floor by the 'men in tights,' tail-coated staff of the Serjeant-at-Arms.

'They're our people – and they've got in!' shouted someone. Cheers re-doubled as the Sky News bulletin re-played the scene continuously. A text message on the screen said the session had been temporarily suspended – and cheers echoed again.

A young man next to me at the bar was nursing his head; blood soaked down from his brow to his collar.

'The police hit me when I was doing nothing, absolutely nothing,' he said with a grin. 'I was at the front and I was just shoved forward a bit.'

In TV bulletins that evening, and next day in dozens of press pictures, pro-testors were depicted with head injuries after baton attacks. Sixteen people, including one policemen, were officially reported hurt in ugly clashes, but I suspect the figure was higher. Some of the injured protestors were women. Two hunting housewives from the Fitzwilliam country, with bloodied faces, told reporters they had been pushed to the ground by police 'when all we wanted to do is sit down and sing songs'.

Allegations of over-policing were denied by the Metropolitan force, but I was surprised by the fierce reaction of British policemen. As a war correspondent I have seen far more violent street clashes, with police responding by shooting, but in Blair's Britain the sudden escalation of violence from the police was still shocking.

The lurid colour photographs of bloodied protestors in next day's newspapers might well have persuaded the public that something unnecessarily ugly and menacing was being sparked off by the government's draconian implementation of a ban on a country practice regarded as a right for centuries.

The amazing invasion of the House of Commons in session was said to be the first since Cromwell and his troops dismissed the Barebones Parliament 351 years ago.

The modern intruders were: Otis Ferrry, 21-years-old son of the Rock star, Brian Ferry, and newly appointed Joint Master of the South Shropshire; John Holliday, 37-year-old professional huntsman of the Ledbury; Nick Wood, 41, formerly a Buckingham Palace chef; Robert Thame, 34, professional polo player; David Redvers, 34, bloodstock agent; Richard Wakeham, 34, loss adjuster and amateur jockey; Andrew Elliott, 42, horse auctioneer; and Luke Tomlinson, polo player.

After release from a night in police custody they were reported as saying they found entering the Commons chamber 'astonishingly easy' after they gained access disguised as electricians, then doffing their overalls to dash into the chamber in pro-hunting T shirts.

They interrupted Conservative rural spokesman James Gray who was attacking the Hunting Bill, and the young men were carried out after Otis Ferry put a hand on the mace, and said he shouted at the Labour front bench, where Alun Michael was sitting, 'something like "You are a disgrace!".'

The sitting was suspended for 18 minutes before James Gray resumed his speech. A huge Parliamentary row developed thereafter over security in the Palace of Westminster.

But the eight protestors were regarded by many in the hunting world as the first 'heroes of the revolution', and received warm welcomes and congratulations when they returned to the hunting field. Ferry and Holliday were hunting hounds again very soon after their release.

Impetuous youth had somehow captured the world's headlines, and so far there had not been a backlash in public opinion from the stunts achieved to attract attention to hunting's plight.

If anything the escapade had emphasised just how much hunting still meant to many in the younger generation. The involvement of a professional huntsman concerned about his job leavened the strong public school element in the protest, but some hunting opponents could not resist class war mud-slinging. *Independent* columnist Deborah Orr said their intrusion had confirmed 'the widespread belief hunting is the hobby of a privileged social elite with bugger all else to do except seek dangerous and expensive thrills.'

What a pity she did not come into Parliament Square to speak to thousands of 'ordinary' British citizens, many of whom follow hounds on moorlands and hillsides where there is no hectic jumping, simply a love of hounds, the art of venery and the countryside in which it takes place.

The inescapable fact was that the hunting ban Bill cleared the Commons with a massive majority vote of 190 (356 in favour to 166 against). After a deal with its anti-hunting back benchers, the government reduced the waiting period for the ban on foxhunting and other hound sports, except coursing, to 18 months, and this was passed by 327 votes (342 to 15). It meant the foxhunting ban would start on 31 July, 2006.

It still ensured the Bill could not take effect until after the latest date for the General Election – clearly a political move, rather than an easement for the Hunts.

Alun Michael repeated to the House the same unreal gibberish that the deferment would allow more time for the 'dispersal and re-homing of dogs used in hunting', and he repeated the RSPCA's offer to help.

The foolishness of offering domestic, or any other homes, to Foxhounds from packs is so manifest that the Minister's offer could only fall on the ears of any huntsman like the ravings of a madman.

Arbitrarily taking away precious animals for death, or life in an alien environment, is one of the most provocative acts one could inflict on any dog owner – and the Minister's words could only infuriate hunting people still further.

Mr Michael asserted there were not the same animal welfare concerns for dogs involved in coursing, and said he was concerned about problems of illegal hare coursing, so deferment was not appropriate here.

Despite an 18 minutes suspension of the House following the young protestors' dramatic arrival, James Gray made an effective attack on the Bill, within the indecent haste of the one-day procedure enforced by government, but it was entirely lost on the Labour benches. Only three Labour MPs voted against the Bill.

Mr Gray said the Conservatives would seek to repeal the Bill 'when we come to power', by a free vote. With the intervening General Election in mind, he said this would give a clear message to 'lovers of freedom and tolerance, and lovers of the countryside, of whatever political persuasion, a very clear message: if they want to save hunting, they can do that by using every ounce of muscle, straining every sinew and spending every pound that may be necessary to hound this illiberal and hated Labour government from office.'

He reminded the House that the Minister was seeking to rush through a Bill that he himself had earlier attacked scathingly, a Bill created by 'rebellious back benchers', neither a manifesto commitment, nor mentioned in the Queen's Speech, nor compliant with the Human Rights Act. He was referring to the lack of compensation element in the Bill.

'It is a Bill for which there is little real demand in the country, and its claimed animal welfare benefits are illusory to say the least. It is a legal mess, and will need huge amendment, which I hope the other place (the Lords) will give it,' said Mr Gray.

He described the threatened use of the Parliament Act as 'a constitutional scandal of the worst kind, which brings Parliament into disrepute and makes the Minister and his party look both desperate and a laughing stock in the eyes of the public.

'This is an intolerant, ignorant and prejudiced Bill. It is an affront to liberal democracy. It will stir the heart of every citizen who values liberty. The people of this country, and the countryside, will neither tolerate nor forget it.'

This summarised much of the opinion in the national press following the Commons second reading.

It was bluntly dismissed by a dedicated long-time opponent of hunting, Elliot Morley, Environment minister in DEFRA, when he wound up the debate. It was, he insisted, 'a moral issue' decided on a free vote. He believed it was 'not always rational to take into account minority views'.

He risked stoking the fires of future division in British society by declaring that 'a minority of people – I would not claim they speak for all hunt supporters – care little for animals, and little for people today.'

Those who suspected one of the real reasons for re-launching the hunting issue was to attack the House of Lords heard full confirmation when the Minister defended the proposed use of the Parliament Act by lashing the 'unrepresentative, unelected and unaccountable House of Lords' which he said was prepared to ignore the results of a Commons free vote.

'If there is an affront,' he said, 'it is an affront that it has taken until four years into the 21st century to end an activity that comes down to inflicting prolonged pain and stress on animals for no other reason than the entertainment of their tormentors.'

There spoke the traditional left wing voice of prejudice, and it was sad that in the 21st century it still came from the front bench spokesman of a Labour party in power.

Hunting with hounds had to go because of a dislike of the people who do it, not the ample 'evidence and principle' available in a dispassionate study of the cases for and against the sport.

So much for all the veterinary evidence that hunting causes least suffering, compared with other methods, in effecting a clean kill in the animal's natural environment.

But after the Black Wednesday of 15 September, there were still huge questions to be answered. What would the Lords do with the Bill? Would Tony Blair really use the Parliament Act? Just how significant was it that he had neither attended the debate, nor crossed the road from Downing street to vote? Some commentators described this as cynical; others said it was cowardly. Was Blair leaving himself room for a back track after the Lords had rejected the Bill?

John Jackson, chairman of the Alliance, received a letter from Alun Michael objecting to Jackson's public declaration that 'corrupt politics' were involved in the government's method of reintroducing the Bill.

Jackson replied robustly that 'no-one believes you, or Peter Hain, when you talk of the welfare of hounds. If you are that interested in animal welfare why permit hunting to continue at all if you think it is so wrong?

'It is an attempt to avoid "distractions" in the run up to the next General Election that you propose deferment. That is why I use the world "corrupt".'

On November 17, the House of Lords persisted in massive changes to the Hunting Act, restoring licensed hunting, and inserting a three year implementation process instead of the 18 months proposed by government.

Next day there was a farcical shuttling between the two Houses. Rural Affairs Minister Alun Michael angered his own back-benches by trying vainly to delay the ban until July 2007, seeking to 'go the extra mile' as a compromise. It was pointed out scornfully by pro-hunting MPs that the government was merely striving to stave off civil unrest in the run-up to the next General Election early in 2005.

The Minister's amendment was heavily defeated by 299 votes, but MPs then voted that it be delayed until July, 2006.

Amid confusion and chaos, the Bill was shuttled back to the Lords who promptly rejected the delay, thus preventing the Commons amendment.

'Democracy was lurching around like a drunk at closing time,' wrote Ann Treneman in the Time.

At 9 pm in the Commons the Speaker, Michael Martin, amid cries of 'Shame' announced the Hunting Bill had met all the provisions of the Parliament Act and would become law.

This meant it would be enacted after the normal three months period – and the Countryside Alliance announced it would be challenging the use of the Parliament Act in the High Court in London. There would also be a challenge to the EC Court of Human Rights.

A third avenue of hope could be the overthrow of the government at the impending General Election, the Conservatives having promised to repeal the ban if they gained power.

For hunting people it meant the crack of doom even before the end of the current season. Desperately difficult problems had to be solved over keeping hounds, horses and staff.

They declared war on Tony Blair's government, promising civil disobedience, protests and non-cooperation with government.

The future looked desperately bleak, but Simon Hart promised the Alliance would fight to ensure the repeal whether it took months or years.

I remembered the words of the hunting poet Will Ogilvie:

> *There's many a threat to our sport today*
> *But those who are threatened live long they say.*
> *Hunting will live 'til our sons have gone,*
> *Sons of our grandsons, riding keen*
> *To the flash of scarlet on England's green.*
>
> *. . . If you ride the earth in one hundred years*
> *And look at the land through a horse's ears*
> *You'll see the fields as you see them now –*
> *With foxhounds feathering over the plough.*

APPENDIX 1

Locations UK and Irish Hunts

England and Wales:

Aber Valley:	Snowdonia.
Albrighton:	Shropshire, Staffordshire.
Albrighton Woodland:	Shropshire, Staffordshire.
Ashford Valley:	Kent.
Atherstone:	Warwickshire, Leicestershire.
Avon Vale:	Wiltshire.
Axe Vale:	Devon.
Badsworth and Bramham Moor:	Yorkshire.
Banwen Miners:	West Glamorgan.
Barlow:	North East Derbyshire, Nottinghamshire, South Yorkshire.
Duke of Beaufort:	Gloucestershire, Wiltshire.
Bedale:	North Yorkshire.
Belvoir:	Leicestershire, Lincolnshire.
Berkeley:	Gloucestershire, Avon.
Old Berkshire:	Oxfordshire.
Bewcastle:	Scottish Borders, Northumberland, Cumberland.
Bicester with Whaddon Chase:	Oxfordshire, Buckinghamshire, Northamptonshire.
Bilsdale:	Thirsk, Stokesley.
Blackmore and Sparkford Vale:	Dorset, Somerset.
Blankney:	Lincolnshire, Nottinghamshire.
Blencathra:	Cumbria.
Border:	English/Scottish border.
Braes of Derwent:	Northumberland, Co Durham.

Brecon and Talybont:	Black Mountains, Brecon Beacons, Eppynt Hills.
Brocklesby:	Humber Estuary to Market Rasen.
Burton:	North Lincolnshire.
Caerphilly & District:	North Cardiff.
Cambridgeshire with Enfield Chace:	Cambridgeshire, Bedfordshire, Hertfordshire, Middlesex.
Camarthenshire:	Camarthenshire (Dyfed).
Cattistock:	Dorset, Somerset.
Cheshire:	Cheshire.
Cheshire Forest:	Cheshire.
Chiddingfold Leconfied & Cowdray:	Surrey, Sussex.
Cleveland:	Cleveland, North Yorkshire. Mr
Clifton-On-Teme:	Worcestershire, Herefordshire.
College Valley/North Northumberland:	North Northumberland.
Coniston:	Cumbria.
East Cornwall:	Cornwall.
North Cornwall:	Cornwall.
South Cornwall:	Cornwall.
Cotley:	Devon, Somerset, Dorset.
Cotswold:	Gloucestershire.
North Cotswold:	Gloucestershire, Worcestershire.
Cotswold Vale Farmers:	Gloucestershire.
Cottesmore:	Leicestershire, Rutland, Lincolnshire.
Crawley and Horsham:	Sussex.
Croome and West Warwickshire:	Worcestershire, Warwickshire, Gloucestershire.
Cumberland:	Cumberland.
Cumberland Farmers:	Cumberland.
Curre and Llangibby:	Monmouthshire.
Cury:	Cornwall.
Cwrty Y Cadno Farmers:	Camarthenshire.
Dartmoor:	South Devon.
David Davies:	Powys.
Derwent:	North Yorkshire.
East Devon:	Devon.

Mid Devon:	Devon.
South Devon:	Devon.
South Dorset:	Dorset.
Dulverton Farmers:	Devon, Somerset.
Dulverton (West):	North Devon, West Somerset.
South Durham:	County Durham.
Eggesford:	Devon.
Eryri (Cwn Hela Fryri):	Caernarvonshire, Anglesey.
Eskdale and Ennerdale:	West Cumbria.
Essex:	Essex.
East Essex:	Essex.
Essex Farmers and Union:	Essex.
Essex and Suffolk:	Essex, Suffolk.
Exmoor:	North Devon, Somerset.
Farndale:	North Yorkshire.
Fernie:	Leicestershire.
Fitzwilliam (Milton):	Lincolnshire, Cambridgeshire.
Flint and Denbigh:	Denbighshire.
Four Burrow:	Cornwall.
Gelligaer Farmers:	Mid Glamorgan, Gwent.
Glaisdale:	North Yorkshire.
Glamorgan:	South Glamorgan.
Goathland:	North Yorkshire.
Gogerddan:	Ceredigion.
Golden Valley:	Wye Valley, Welsh Borders.
Grafton:	Northamptonshire.
Grove and Rufford:	Nottingham, Yorkshire, Derbyshire.
Hampshire 'HH':	Hampshire.
Haydon:	Northumberland.
North Herefordshire:	Herefordshire.
South Herefordshire:	Herefordshire.
Heythrop:	Oxfordshire, Gloucestershire.
Holcombe:	Lancashire.
Holderness:	East Yorkshire.
Hursley Hambledon:	Wiltshire, Hampshire.
Hurworth:	North Yorkshire.
Isle of Wight:	Isle of Wight.

East Kent:	Kent.
Lamerton:	Devon, Cornwall.
Ledbury:	Herefordshire, Worcestershire, Gloucestershire.
North Ledbury:	Herefordshire, Worcestershire.
Llandeilo Farmers:	Carmarthenshire.
Llangeinor:	Mid Glamorgan.
Llanwnnen and District Farmers:	West Wales.
North Lonsdale:	Cumbria.
Ludlow:	Shropshire, Herefordshire, Worcestershire.
Lunesdale:	Cumbria.
Melbreak:	West Cumbria.
Mendip Farmers:	Somerset, Avon.
Meynell and South Staffordshire:	Derbyshire, Staffordshire.
Middleton:	North Yorkshire.
Monmouthshire:	Monmouthshire.
Morpeth:	Northumberland.
Nantcol Valley:	Gwynedd.
New Forest:	Hampshire.
West Norfolk:	Norfolk.
South Notts:	Nottinghamshire, Derbyshire.
Oakley:	Bedfordshire, Buckinghamshire, Northamptonshire, Cambridgeshire.
Pembrokeshire:	Pembrokeshire.
South Pembrokeshire:	Pembrokeshire.
Pendle Forest and Craven:	Lancashire. N. Yorkshire.
Pennine:	Pennine Ridge.
North Pennine:	Co Durham.
Pentyrch:	East Glamorgan.
Percy:	Northumberland.
West Percy:	Northumberland.
Portman:	Dorset.
Puckeridge:	Hertfordshire, Essex, Cambridgeshire.
Pytchley:	Northamptonshire, Leicestershire.
Woodland Pytchley:	Northamptonshire.
Quorn:	Leicestershire.
Radnorshire and West Herefordshire:	Radnorshire, Herefordshire.

Royal Artillery (Salisbury Plain):	Salisbury Plain.
Saltersgate Farmers:	North Yorkshire.
Seavington:	Dorset, Somerset.
Sennybridge Farmers:	Powys.
North Shropshire:	Shropshire.
South Shropshire:	Shropshire.
Silverton:	Devon.
Sinnington:	North Yorkshire.
West Somerset:	Somerset.
West Somerset Vale:	Somerset.
Southdown & Eridge:	Sussex.
South Wold:	Lincolnshire.
Spooner's and West Dartmoor:	Devon.
Staffordshire Moorland:	Staffordshire.
North Staffordshire:	Staffordshire.
Staintondale:	Yorkshire.
Stevenson:	North Devon.
Suffolk:	Suffolk.
Old Surrey, Burstow and West Kent:	Surrey, Sussex, Kent.
Surrey Union:	Surrey.
East Sussex and Romney Marsh:	East Sussex, Kent.
Tanatside:	Powys, Shropshire.
Taunton Vale:	Somerset.
Tedworth:	Wiltshire, Hampshire.
Teme Valley:	Radnorshire, Shropshire, Herefordshire.
Tetcott:	Cornwall.
South Tetcott:	West Devon, Cornwall.
Thurlow:	Suffolk, Cambridgeshire.
Tiverton:	Devon.
Tivyside:	Cardiganshire, Pembrokeshire.
Torrington Farmers:	Devon.
Towy and Cothi:	Carmarthenshire.
Tredegar Farmers Hunt Club:	Monmouthshire.
North Tyne:	Northumberland.
Tynedale:	Northumberland.
Ullswater:	Cumbria.

United:	Shropshire.
Vale of Aylesbury with Garth and South Berks:	Oxfordshire, Buckinghamshire, Bedfordshire.
Vale of Clettwr:	Carmarthenshire.
VWH:	Wiltshire, Gloucestershire.
Vine and Craven:	West Berkshire, North Hampshire, Wiltshire.
Warwickshire:	Warwickshire, Gloucestershire, Worcestershire, Oxfordshire.
Wensleydale:	Yorkshire.
Western:	Cornwall.
West Street Tickham:	Kent.
West of Yore:	Yorkshire.
Wheatland:	Shropshire.
Sir Watkin Williams-Wynn's:	Denbigh, Flint (Clwyd).
Wilton:	Wiltshire, Hampshire, Dorset.
South and West Wilts:	Dorset, Wiltshire, Somerset.
Worcestershire:	Worcestershire.
York and Ainsty (North):	North Yorkshire.
York and Ainsty (South):	Yorkshire.
Ystrad Taf Fechan:	Gwent.
Zetland:	County Durham, North Yorkshire.

Scotland:

Berwickshire:	Berwickshire.
Duke of Buccleuch's:	Roxburghshire, Selkirk, Berwickshire.
Dumfriesshire:	Dumfriesshire.
Eglinton:	Ayrshire.
Fife:	Fife.
Jed Forest:	Roxburghshire.
Kincardineshire:	Aberdeenshire.
Lanarkshire and Renfrewshire:	Renfrewshire.
Lauderdale	Berwickshire.
Liddesdale:	Roxburghshire.

Ireland:

Avondhu Hunt Club:	Co Cork, Tipperary, Waterford.
Ballymacad:	Meath, Cavan.

Bree:	Blackstairs Mountain, Kilkurin.
Carbery:	Co Cork.
West Carbery:	West Carbery Barony.
Carlow Farmers:	Co Carlow.
County Clare:	Ennis.
East Down:	Co Down.
North Down Harriers:	Co Down.
Duhallow:	Co Cork.
Dungannon:	Tyrone.
County Galway ('The Blazers'):	Co Galway.
East Galway:	Galway, Roscommon.
North Galway:	Galway, Co Mayo, Co Roscommon.
Golden Vale:	North Tipperary.
Island:	Wexford.
Kildare Hunt Club:	Co Kildare.
Kilkenny:	Co Kilkenny.
North Kilkenny:	Co Kilkenny.
Kilmoganny:	West Kilkenny.
Laois (Queen's County):	Queen's County.
County Limerick:	Co Limerick.
Louth:	Louth, Meath, Dublin, Cavan, Monaghan.
Macroom:	Co Cork.
Meath:	Meath.
Muskerry:	Co Cork.
Ormond:	Offaly, Co Tipperary.
Scarteen (The Black and Tans):	Tipperary, Limerick.
Shillelagh and District Limited:	Co Wicklow.
South Union:	Co. Cork.
Tipperary:	Co Tipperary.
North Tipperary:	Co Tipperary.
United Hunt Club:	Co Cork.
Waterford:	Co Waterford.
West Waterford:	Co Waterford.
Westmeath:	Co. Westmeath.
Wexford:	Co Wexford.
Wicklow:	Co Wicklow, Wexford.

Appendix 2

Location USA, Canada and Australia Fox Hunts

USA

Abington Hills Hunt:	Pennsylvania.
Aiken Hounds:	South Carolina.
Amwell Valley Hounds:	Pennsylvania.
Andrews Bridge Foxhounds:	Pennsylvania.
Annapolis Valley Hunt:	Nova Scotia.
Arapahoe Hunt:	Colorado.
Artillery Hunt:	Okalahoma.
Battle Creek Hunt:	Michigan.
Beaufort Hunt:	Pennsylvania.
Beaver Meadow Foxhounds:	Ontario.
Bedford County Hunt:	Virginia.
Beech Grove Hunt:	Tennessee.
Belle Meade Hunt:	Georgia.
Bethany Hills-Frontenac Hunt:	Ontario.
Bijou Springs Hunt:	Colorado.
Blue Ridge Hunt:	Virginia.
Brandywine Hounds:	Pennsylvania. .
Brazos Valley Hunt:	Texas.
Bridlespur Hunt:	Missouri.
Bull Run Hunt:	Virginia.
Camargo Hunt:	Ohio.
Camden Hunt:	South Carolina.
Caroline Hunt:	Virginia.
Casanova Hunt:	Virginia.
Caza Ladron:	New Mexico.

Chagrin Valley Hunt:	Ohio.
Chula Homa Hunt:	Missouri, Louisiana.
Cloudline Hounds:	Texas.
Colonial Fox Hounds:	Virginia.
Commonwealth Fox Hounds:	Virginia.
Cornwall Hounds:	Illinois.
De La Brooke Foxhounds W:	Maryland.
Deep Run Hunt:	Virginia.
Edisto-Mount Vintage Hounds:	South Carolina.
Eglinton and Caledon Hunt:	Ontario.
Elkridge-Harford Hunt:	Maryland.
Essex Fox Hounds:	New Jersey.
Fairfax Hunt:	Virginia.
Fairfield County Hounds:	Connecticut.
Farmington Hunt:	Virginia.
Ferndale hunt:	Arkansas.
Flat Branch Hounds:	North Carolina.
Fort Leavenworth Hunt:	Kansas.
Fort Valley Hunt:	Virginia.
Four Winds:	Florida.
Fourth Bluff Hounds:	Tennessee.
Fox River Valley Hunt:	Illinois.
Fraser Valley Hunt:	British Columbia.
Full Cry Hounds:	Alabama.
Gamble Hill Hounds:	Indiana.
Glenmore Hunt:	Virginia.
Golden Bridge Hounds:	New York.
Goshen Hunt:	Maryland.
Grand River Hunt:	Ohio.
Green Creek Hounds:	North Carolina.
Green Spring Valley Hounds:	Maryland.
Greenville County Hounds:	North Carolina. .
Guilford Hounds:	Vermont.
Gully Ridge Hounds:	Ohio.
Hamilton Hunt:	Ontario.
Hard Away Hounds:	Alabama.
Harvard Fox Hounds:	Oklahoma.

Hickory Creek Hunt:	Texas.
High Country Hounds:	Arizona.
Hillsboro Hounds:	Tennessee.
Hopper Hills Hunt:	New York.
Howard County-Iron Bridge Hounds:	Maryland.
Huntingdon Valley Hunt:	Pennsylvania.
Iroquois Hunt:	Kentucky.
Juan Thomas Hounds:	New Mexico.
Kenada Fox Hounds:	Texas.
Keswick Hunt:	Virginia.
Lake of Two Mountains Hunt:	Ontario.
Limestone Creek Hunt:	New York.
Live Oak Hounds:	Florida.
London Hunt:	Ontario.
Lonesome Palm Hounds:	Florida.
Long Lake Hounds:	Minnesota.
Long Run Hounds:	Kentucky.
Longacre Hunt:	Texas.
Los Altos Hounds:	California.
Loudoun Hunt:	Virginia.
Loudoun West Hunt:	Virginia.
Marlborough Hunt:	Maryland.
Mecklenburg Hounds:	North Carolina. .
Mells Fox Hounds:	Tennessee.
Metamora Hunt:	Michigan.
Miami Valley Hunt:	Ohio.
Middlebrook Hounds:	Virginia.
Middleburg Hunt:	Virginia.
Middleton Place Hounds:	South Carolina.
Midland Fox Hounds:	Georgia. .
Mill Creek Hunt:	Illinois.
Millbrook Hunt:	New York.
Mission Valley Hunt:	Kansas.
Misty Morning Hounds:	Florida.
Misty River Hounds:	Arizona.
Moingona Hunt:	Iowa.

Monmouth County Hunt:	New Jersey.
Montreal Hunt:	Quebec.
Moore County Hounds:	North Carolina.
Mooreland Hunt:	Alabama.
Mr Jeffords' Hounds:	Colorado.
Mr Stewart's Cheshire Foxhounds:	Pennsylvania.
Myopia Hunt:	Massachusetts.
Nashoba Valley Hunt:	Massachusetts.
New Britton Hunt:	Illinois.
New Market-Middletown Valley Hounds:	Virginia.
Nodaway River Hounds:	Iowa.
Norfolk Hunt:	Massachusetts.
North Country Hounds:	Vermont.
North Hills Hunt:	Nebraska.
Oak Grove Hunt:	Tennessee, Mississippi.
Oak Ridge Fox Hunt:	Virginia.
Old Chatham Hunt:	New York.
Old Dominion Hunt:	Virginia.
Old North Bridge Hounds:	Massachusetts.
Orange County Hunt:	Virginia.
Ottawa Valley Hunt.	Ottawa.
Palm Beach Hounds:	Florida.
Pickering Hunt:	Pennsylvania.
Piedmont Fox Hounds:	Virginia.
Plum Run Hunt:	Pennsylvania.
Potomac Hunt:	Maryland.
Princess Anne Hunt:	Virginia.
Radnor Hunt:	Pennsylvania.
Rappahannock Hunt:	Virginia.
Red Mountain Foxhounds:	North Carolina.
Red Oak Hounds:	North Carolina.
Red Rock Hounds:	Nevada.
Reedy Creek Hounds:	Virginia.
River to River Hounds:	Illinois.
Roaring Fork Hounds:	Colorado.
Rockbridge Hunt:	Virginia.

Rocky Fort Headley Hunt:	Ohio.
Rolling Rock Hunt:	Pennsylvania. .
Rombout Hunt:	New York.
Rose Tree Foxhunting Club:	Pennsylvania.
Santa Fe Hunt:	California.
Santa Ynez Valley Hunt:	California.
Sedgefield Hunt:	North Carolina.
Sewickley Hunt:	Pennsylvania.
Shakerag Hounds:	Georgia.
Shamrock Hounds:	Georgia.
Shawnee Hounds:	Illinois.
Smith Mountain Hounds:	Virginia.
Smithtown Hunt:	New York.
South Creek Foxhounds:	Florida.
Spring Valley Hounds:	New Jersey.
Stonewall Foxhounds:	Virginia.
Tanheath Hunt:	Connecticut.
Tennessee Valley Hunt:	Tennessee.
Toronto and North York Hunt:	Ontario.
Traders Point Hunt:	Indiana.
Triangle Hunt:	North Carolina.
Tryon Hounds:	South Carolina.
Wabash Hounds:	Nebraska.
Warrenton Hunt:	Virginia.
Waterloo Hunt:	Michigan.
Wayne-Dupage Hunt:	Illinois.
Wellington Waterloo Hunt:	Ontario.
Wentowrth Hunt:	New Hampshire.
West Hills Hunt:	Califonia.
Whiskey Road Fox Hounds:	South Carolina.
Whitwirth Hunt:	Mississippi.
Why Worry Hounds:	South Carolina.
Wicomico Hunt:	Maryland.
Wildlife Manor Hounds:	Tennessee.
Windy Hollow Hunt:	New Jersey.
Wolf Creek Hunt:	Illinois.
Woodbrook Hunt:	Nebraska.

300

Woodford Hounds:	Kentucky.
Yadkin Valley Hounds:	North Carolina.

CANADA (French)

Equipage Du Raille-Kebec:	Quebec.

AUSTRALIA

Adelaide Hunt Club Inc:	South Australia.
Barwon Hunt:	Victoria.
Boggy Creek Hunt Club:	Victoria.
Brook Hunt:	Western Australia.
Casterton-Coleraine Hunt Club:	Victoria.
Ellerslie Camperdown:	Victoria.
Findon	
Hume Hunt Inc:	Victoria.
Hunter Valley Hunt:	New South Wales.
Mansfield Hunt Club:	Victoria.
Melbourne Hunt Inc:	Victoria.
Midland Hunt Club Inc:	Tasmania.
Murray Valley Hunt Club:	Victoria.
Northern Hunt Club:	Tasmania.
Oaklands Hunt Club:	Victoria.
Perth Hunt Club:	Western Australia.
The Riverina Hunt:	Victoria.
Southern Tablelands Hunt:	New South Wales.
Sydney Hunt Club:	New South Wales.
Tocumwal Hunt Club:	Victoria.
The West Australian Hunt Club :	Western Australia.
Yarra Glen & Lilydale Hunt Club :	Victoria. .

Appendix 3

Glossary of terms

ALL ON   the expression used by the whipper-in to tell the huntsman that every hound in the pack is present

ACCOUNT FOR   to kill or run the fox to ground

AT FAULT   means that the hounds have stopped during a hunt because they have lost the scent

AUTUMN HUNTING   *see* cubhunting for explanation

BABBLER   a hound that gives tongue (or bays) when it has not picked up the scent of a fox, thus misleading the huntsman and the rest of the pack

BAG FOX   a fox loosed from a bag for hounds to hunt; a deplorable practice forbidden by the Master of Foxhounds Association and *not* undertaken in modern foxhunting

BILLETT   a fox's droppings

BINDER   the top strand of a cut-and-laid fence; you may hear of a horse falling after 'catching its leg in a binder'

BLIND   a 'blind' ditch is one covered with grass or weeds; the country generally is blind and 'hairy' in early autumn

BLOWING AWAY   the huntsman's series of quick notes on his horn when hounds leave a covert on the line of a fox; a most stirring sound

BLOWING OUT   a slightly less exuberant note on the horn which the huntsman blows to bring hounds out of a covert which is blank, or empty of foxes

BOB-TAILED   a fox with little or no brush

BOLT   to drive a fox from an earth or a drain, usually by putting a terrier down

BOTTOM   a deep gulley or steep ravine which cannot be jumped and must be skirted on horseback; to say that a covert has plenty of 'bottom' means that it has much thick undergrowth

BREAK   a fox breaks covert when it runs from it

BREAK-UP   when hounds kill the fox and eat its carcase, an extremely quick process

BRUSH   the fox's tail. Sometimes a guest is presented with the brush at the end of a good run; or it goes to a member of the field who has done well to stay with hounds during the hunt

BYE-DAY   an additional day's hunting to those normally hunted by a pack

BULLFINCH   often a formidable jump, it is a high hedge with a spreading, thin top; you have to jump boldly through the upper part

CAP   as well as being the headgear of the huntsman, the Master, farmers and children, it is the term used for the sum paid by a visitor for one day's hunting; or the smaller amount, paid by regular subscribers each time they come out hunting, usually in aid of the fund to take down wire nowadays

CARRY   the horn to be a huntsman

CARRIES A SCENT   ground surface 'carries a scent' if it is good scenting country, such as clean pasture land

CARRY   plough, or some other sticky surface, 'carries' when it sticks to the feet of a fox or a hound, usually after a frost

CAST   the hounds' efforts to recover a lost scent; a huntsman casts hounds when he tries to help their efforts

CHALLENGE   the hound which first gives tongue on striking the scent of a fox can be said to 'challenge' or 'open'

CHECK   to lose the scent either temporarily or permanently; after hounds have checked they have to cast (see above)

CHOP   to kill a fox before it has had time to run from covert

CLEAN GROUND   land which is free of distracting scents such as sheep or cattle stains, or the foil of horses

COLD LINE   an old scent

COLD SCENTING COUNTRY   a country which does not carry scent readily

COUPLE   hounds are always counted in pairs; thus a pack may be 15½ couple, or 31 hounds; the traditional way to put hounds on a leash is to couple two hounds together with links of chain joining two collars

COURSE   when hounds pursue a fox which is in view

COVERT   (pronounced 'cover') any stretch of growth where a fox resides; usually a coppice, a stretch of gorse, or a wood; in addition foxes are found in a 'woodland', which in foxhunting terms is usually a big area of trees

CRY   the noise made by hounds when they are hunting

CUB   a young fox

CUBHUNTING   the preliminary period of hunting, mainly September and October, before the season proper starts on 1 November, now referred to as Autumn Hunting

DOUBLE   the short term for a fence with a ditch on both sides; a double bank is a big, wide bank with a ditch on both sides. The huntsman 'doubles' his horn when he blows a succession of short notes on it

DRAFT   hounds which are sent out of the pack are 'drafted', to be given to another pack

DRAG   the scent line left by a fox when it returns to its bed after a night's hunting on its own account

DRAG LINE   an artificial line used by trailing some suitable substance across country for a pack of hounds to follow; hence the title 'Drag Hunt' for packs which habitually follow artificial lines to provide guaranteed runs for the mounted followers

DRAW   the process of sending hounds through a covert to look for a fox; 'the draw' is the area of country where the huntsman intends to search for foxes during a particular day's hunting. To 'draw' a hound from a pack is the practice of hunt staff in calling an individual hound's name and making it come forward from the other hounds

EARTH   a fox's underground home

ENTER   to initiate young hounds in the skill of hunting a fox by taking them cubhunting for the first time

FEATHER   a hound feathers when it is uncertain of the line it is following; usually it waves its stern and keeps its head down, but it does not give tongue under these circumstances

FIELD   the mounted followers of the hunt – not including the Master and Hunt servants

FIELD MASTER   either the Master himself, or someone he appoints, to be in charge of the mounted field; he tells followers when to stop and when to gallop on, and he keeps them off cultivated land, etc.

FLY FENCES   those which can be cleared from a gallop, preferably a collected gallop

FOIL   any odour which tends to obliterate that of the hunted fox; if a fox doubles back on its tracks he is said to be 'running his foil'

FRESH FIND   to rouse the hunted fox anew after losing him

GOOD HEAD   'carry a good head' hounds running well together and not strung out

GUARANTEE   the sum of money which a Master receives from the Hunt Committee towards his costs in hunting a country

HACKLES   the hairs along the ridge of a hound's neck and spine

HAIRY   an overgrown straggly hedge which can be a tricky jump

HARK FORWARD   (pronounced on the lines of 'Harrk For-or-orrard') the huntsman's shout to the hounds indicating that one or several hounds further on have spoken on finding the line of the fox, or it could indicate that the fox has been seen further on

HEAD   to head a fox is to turn it from the direction it is running; cars on roads are very likely to do this

HEADS UP   (getting their heads up) hounds lifting their heads from the scent

HEEL   (to run the heel way, or to hunt the heel-line) to follow the scent in the opposite direction to which the fox is travelling - something the huntsman must always be careful to prevent

HIT THE LINE   what a hound does when it finds the scent

HOLD UP   to surround a covert with horsemen and prevent foxes leaving it; usually done during the cubhunting season

HOUND JOG   the half-trot pace of a horse which is accompanying hounds along a roadway

HOLLOA   (or 'View Holloa', pronounced 'Holler') the shout or screech given by someone who has just seen the fox; the intention is to inform the huntsman and hounds of the fact

HUIC HOLLOA   (pronounced 'Hike Holler' - 'Huic' means 'Hark') a shout or screech to draw hounds' (and perhaps the huntsmen's) attention to a holloa further away. Thus a whipper-in might hear a good holloa two fields from a covert where hounds are drawing. The whipper-in might canter up a ride inside the covert shouting to the huntsman and hounds: 'Huic Holloa! Huic Holloa! Huic Holloa!'

KENNEL-HUNTSMAN   a professional Hunt servant who looks after the management of the kennels where hounds are kept. This applies only to a pack where hounds are hunted by an amateur. A professional huntsman is his own kennel-huntsman

LAY ON   to start hounds on a scent

LARK   to lark in the hunting field is to jump fences when hounds are not running; or to do it on your way home unnecessarily; usually frowned upon unless you have no other way of going from one field to the next

LIFT   what a huntsman does when he calls his hounds to him, and takes them to a point where he thinks the fox has gone, and where they can hit the scent again without having to try to find the scent over the ground in between. He may take them some distance if he is sure that he knows the route the fox has taken. To lift hounds and then disappoint them is bad practice

LINE   the scent trail of the hunted fox

MAKING THE PACK   counting it

MARKING   when hounds give tongue at the mouth of an earth or a drain after the fox has entered it

MASK   a fox's head

MIXED PACK   a pack comprising both bitches and dog- hounds

MOB   to mob a fox is when hounds surround a fox in covert and kill it without giving it any chance to escape; this could happen when a covert is held up during cubhunting

MUSIC   a commonly used term for the cry of hounds, e.g. a 'crash of hound music'

MUTE   hounds often run mute, without giving tongue, when they are running hard on a good scent; when a hound habitually runs mute and never speaks to the line it is a serious fault

NOSE   to breed hounds 'for nose' is to breed them for their scenting qualities

OPEN   to give tongue on hitting the line

OPENING MEET   the first meet of the season proper, usually on or soon after 1 November

OVER-RIDE   to over-ride hounds is to ride in among them; a hunting misdemeanour

OWN THE LINE   to speak to the line, e.g. 'a bitch named Rambler owned the line first'

OXER   an ox fence: a thorn fence with a rail on the side of it; a double-oxer has a rail on each side

PAD   a fox's foot; this is sometimes presented to followers for the same reasons as a brush (see above)

POINT   the distance in a straight line between the start of a run and its end, e.g. 'Blankshire Hunt score 6-mile point . . .'; hounds, and the followers, will usually run much further than 6 miles in achieving a six-mile point

QUICK THING   a very fast run; a popular phrase in the galloping grass countries where some huntsmen have been renowned for providing 'a quick thing'

RASPER   a splendidly evocative name for a formidable fence

RATE   to rate a hound is to tell it off; a function strictly reserved for Hunt staff

RINGING   running in circles; applied to a fox which will not run straight

RIOT   a foxhound riots when it hunts any animal other than a fox; it is strictly trained not to do so as a young hound; but the temptation to hunt, say, a hare or a deer is often very strong for a foxhound

SCENT   the smell given off by the hunted animal

SKIRT   a hound which cuts corners instead of following the exact line of the fox it is hunting is said to skirt, or to be a skirter

SPEAK   to give tongue, or bay

STAIN   a sheep-stained field is one which is foiled by sheep for scenting purposes

STALE LINE   an old line of scent left long after a fox has gone

STERN   a hound's tail

STOPPING   blocking earths at night so that the fox which is out foraging cannot get below ground when he returns. One system of earth stopping was to stop the earths within the area of the day's draw, and to put to others adjacent. Thus the foxes it is hoped to hunt will be above ground and cannot run to ground nearby; nor can hounds change during a run to a fresh fox nearby

STUD-BRED   foxes bred above ground rather than in an earth

TAIL HOUNDS   hounds behind the main body of the pack when they are running

TALLY-HO   same as 'View Holloa'. 'Tally-Ho back' is a shout which means that the fox has been viewed coming out of a covert, but he has headed back into the covert

THROW THEIR TONGUES   when hounds are in full cry tongue when hounds 'give tongue' they are baying

TRENCHER-FED   the old system whereby each hound was kept by an individual farmer at home and then brought to the meet to form a pack with other hounds on a hunting day, i.e. 'a trencher-fed pack'

UNENTERED   a hound which has not finished his first cubhunting season

VIEW   to sight the hunted fox vixen a female fox

WALK   to walk a foxhound puppy is to rear it at your own home

WHELPS   unweaned puppies

WHIPPERS-IN   (first and second) the huntsman's assistants in the field

Bibliography

Books I have consulted include the following:

A Leicestershire Sketch Book, Lionel Edwards (Haggerston Press, 1935 and 1991)

Baily's Hunting Companion (Baily's, 1994)

British Hunts and Huntsmen, J.N.P. Watson, Vols I, II and III, (Batsford, 1982 1986)

English Foxhunting, Raymond Carr (Weidenfeld and Nicolson, 1976)

Famous Foxhunters, Daphne Moore (Saiga Publishing, 1978)

Fields Elysian, Simon Blow (J.M. Dent, 1983)

Foxhunting in North America, Alexander Mackay-Smith (American Foxhound Club, 1985)

Foxhunting in the Twentieth Century, William Scarth Dixon (Hurst and Blackett, 1925)

Foxhunting, 10th Duke of Beaufort (David and Charles 1980)

Foxhunting, J.N.P. Watson (Batsford, 1977)

Foxhunting, A. Henry Higginson (Collins 1948)

Foxiana, Isaac Bell (Country Life, 1929)

Here Lies My Story, C.N. de Courcy Parry (Grayling Books, 1981)

History of the Althorpe and Pytchley Hunt, Guy Paget (1937)

History of the Puckeridge, Michael Berry (Country Life, 1950)

Hounds of France, George Johnston and Maria Ericson (Saiga Publishing, 1979)

Hounds of the World, Sir John Buchanan-Jardine (Grayling Books, 1937)

Hunting in Hard Times, G. Bowers (Methuen, re-print 1986)

Huntsmen of our Time, Kenneth Ligertwood (Pelham Books, 1968)

Huntsman's Log Book, Isaac Bell (Eyre and Spottiswoode, 1947)

John Leech and the Victorian Scene, Simon Houfe (Antique Collectors Club, 1984)

Jorrocks's England, Anthony Steel (Methuen, 1932)

Ladies of the Chase, Meriel Buxton, The Sportsman's Press, 1987

Leicestershire and the Quorn Hunt, Colin D.B. Ellis (Edgar Backus, 1951)

Magic of the Quorn, Ulrica Murray Smith (J.A. Allen, 1980)

Master of One, Dorian Williams (J.M.Dent, 1978)

Memoirs, The Duke of Beaufort, (Country Life, 1981)

Peculiar Privilege, David C. Itzkowtiz (The Harvester Press, 1977)
Peter Beckford, A. Henry Higginson (Collins, 1937)

Ronnie Wallace, A Manual of Foxhunting, R.E. Wallace, edited Michael Clayton (Swan Hill Press, 2003)

Ronnie Wallace, the Authorised Version, Robin Rhoderick-Jones (Quiller Press, 1992)

Rycroft on Hounds, Hunting and Country, Sir Newton Rycroft, edited James F. Scharnberg (2001, The Derrydale Press)

The Book of the Foxhound, Daphne Moore (J.A. Allen, 1964)

The Foxhunter's Bedside Book, compiled by Lady Apsley (Eyre and Spottiswoode, 1949)

The Green Collars, Tarporley Hunt Club and Cheshire Hunt, Gordon Fergusson (Quiller Press, 1993)

The Harboro' Country, Charles Simpson (Bodley Head, 1927)

The Heat of the Kitchen, Lord Donoughue (Politico's 2003)

The History of Foxhunting, Roger Longrigg (Macmillan, 1975)

The History of Hunting, Patrick Chalmers (Seely Service, 1936)

The Hunting Diaries of Stanley Barker, Stuart Newsham (Standfast Press, 1981)

The Politics of Hunting, Richard H. Thomas (Gower, 1983)

The Yellow Earl, Douglas Sutherland (The Molendinar Press, 1980)

Tom Firr of the Quorn, Roy Heron (Nimrod Book Services, 1984)

Thoughts on Hunting, Peter Beckford (1781, re-published J.A. Allen 1981)

INDEX